LIBERATING
EVERYDAY
GENIUS

LIBERATING EVERYDAY GENIUS

A Revolutionary Guide for Identifying
and Mastering Your Exceptional Gifts

MARY-ELAINE JACOBSEN, PSY.D.

Clair –
Soar high,
fly free –
leave room for
other flyers!
Mary

Ballantine Books • New York

A Ballantine Book
Published by The Ballantine Publishing Group

http://www.randomhouse.com/BB/

Library of Congress Cataloging-in-Publication Data
Jacobsen, Mary-Elaine.
Liberating everyday genius : a revolutionary guide for identifying and
mastering your exceptional gifts / Mary-Elaine Jacobsen. — 1st ed.
    p.   cm.
ISBN 0-345-42771-8 (alk. paper)
1. Gifted persons.   I. Title.
BF412.J25   1999
153.9′8—DC21   99-30112
CIP

Manufactured in the United States of America

First Edition: November 1999

10 9 8 7 6 5 4 3 2 1

To Todd, Chrissie, and Ross, the greatest gifts of my life.

And with immeasurable gratitude to Arlette, my spirit-filled mother,
and Alma, my courageous and loving grandmother,
who gave me sturdy shoes for solid footing, a driving enthusiasm for each new day,
laughter to throw in the face of adversity, and wings of faith to soar high and fly free.
You left far too soon, yet have never been gone.

CONTENTS

LIBERATING
EVERYDAY
GENIUS

PART ONE

IDENTIFYING EVERYDAY GENIUS

1

BEYOND GIFTEDNESS:
EVERYDAY GENIUS DEFINED

No bird soars too high, if he soars with his own wings.
—Friedrich Nietzsche

To look at her, you would never suspect that Ann was in the midst of a crisis. She sat in my office, composed and resplendent in a black Tahari suit. The only sign of any agitation was her habit of coiling and uncoiling her index finger around her strand of pearls. She looked much younger than forty-three. As my client now for nearly four months, she, at first, had been at a loss to explain rationally what brought her to me.

"No one ever expects a midlife crisis, Dr. Jacobsen. I certainly didn't," were the first words that Ann spoke to me.

At one point in her legal career, Ann had been a dynamo, working on a team that won a major case involving suspected violations of interstate commerce laws in the dairy industry. The lead attorney acknowledged that it was her dogged efforts that helped dismantle the government's case. Ann seemed destined to make partner before she was thirty-five and was guaranteed the pick of the firm's highest-profile and potentially most lucrative cases.

Success hadn't come without a price. Those who were passed over for promotion in favor of Ann attributed her meteoric rise to favoritism and not her razor-sharp analytical skills, her amazing intuition, and her twenty-six-hour workdays. Once lauded as the consummate most valuable player, Ann was eventually plagued by not-so-quiet whispers about her chameleonlike ability to transform herself into whomever each partner wanted her to be. Suddenly the qualities that had once been her most valuable assets felt like her greatest liabilities.

Always someone who took every criticism to heart, Ann stopped trusting her intuition and her allies. Rather than ranging far and wide to offer colleagues help, anticipating their problems before they even identified them, she kept to a carefully circumscribed territory in order to restore her coworkers' regard for her. Her boundless interest and enthusiasm, previously characterized by being the first to volunteer to tackle the thorniest problem, now slid precipitously. She became aloof and distant.

"After all the problems I created by being a standout, I decided that the best way to get along was to go along and just joylessly grind my way through the day like everyone else. It seemed to be the only way that I could make working there bearable. Everyone else seemed pleased about my so-called change, but I was miserable."

A few months before Ann first came to see me, I'd walked into my office one afternoon and was startled to find a man standing at the window tugging at one of the slats in the miniblinds and peering out at the street. He turned around and saw me. Then he took a couple of steps toward me, muttered, "How ya doing, Doc?" and stalked to the bookcase lining one wall. He pulled a book off the shelf and started leafing through it.

"You must be John," I said as evenly as I could. "My clients usually wait in the reception area."

"Well, I saw that other woman come out, so I came on in. You don't mind, do you." There was little to suggest that John was asking a question.

John soon put back the book and took down a few others, smiling ruefully and shaking his head after examining a couple of their titles. Eventually I came to understand that John was very nearly incapable of keeping still for longer than a few minutes at a time. In this instance, the classic stereotype of the patient lying on the couch was laughable. John was the epitome of the restless peripatetic at home and at the office.

Early on, John described how he perceived others. "It's like the rest of the world is moving along at twenty-four frames per second, normal film speed, but to me that's slow motion. Even when somebody's talking during a meeting, I swear I look at their mouths and it's like I'm advancing the tape frame by frame on my VCR. So, okay, film and videotape are two very different things, so maybe that's not the best example, but maybe it's more like the world's a blender on stir and I'm on liquefy."

John's self-editing and criticism aside, his description is apt. To someone like John, the rest of the world does seem as if it's lagging behind. From people walking too slowly on sidewalks and those counting out exact change in a supermarket checkout line to others arriving at a solution that seemed obvious to John minutes, days, or sometimes weeks before, everyone else always seemed to be moving at a glacial pace. A true multitasker, John used to upset everyone at meetings because he could monitor the flow of the conversation, read a report, scan the agenda for the next item of discussion, then jump ahead or interject at seemingly inappropriate moments.

"I'm sick of being told to slow down. If I'm on an express train and they're on a local, why don't they switch trains and get onto mine? It's time for them to be responsible for catching up to me."

Unfortunately for John, what others perceived as his uncooperative attitude eventually caught up with him. While he hadn't been fired from his job as a creative director at an advertising agency, he'd been essentially stripped of all authority. He'd been asked to stay on in a consulting capacity but was given little real work to do. John clearly sensed what was about to happen to him, but that only made him dig in his heels more deeply on some issues and veer recklessly from one more outlandish idea to the next, wielding his considerable wit like a saber. He'd gone from being a visionary Renaissance man of the company to persona non grata in a matter of months.

"It wouldn't bother me so much, but before I came along most of them thought that HTML was what you saw when some of the letters burned out in a neon hotel or motel sign. I got us a jump start into Web advertising, and now everyone is reaping the benefits and claiming they were the masterminds behind the whole thing. It's like working with a bunch of Al Gores claiming they were the ones who helped develop the World Wide Web. Of course, everybody knows that Dan Quayle was the one who invented the spell checker."

GIFTEDNESS DENIED

While John and Ann couldn't have been more different in certain respects, they do have much in common. They are both gifted adults standing poised at a crossroads. And they both initially recoiled at my suggestion that they were gifted.

Like John and Ann, when many of us hear the word *gifted* we almost always think two things: (1) "Only schoolchildren are gifted" and (2) "Since I'm not a child, I can't be gifted." These automatic responses are understandable given what most of us have been told about bright people. But most of what we have been told is radically incorrect and enormously incomplete.

Most of us think we know what giftedness is, but we're unable to describe it or define it accurately. Part of the reason for that is that we live in a culture that emphasizes products over process. We can see what gifted people produce, but we can't see the internal systems and operations that produced those products. In the previous sentence, even I had to resort to using words more suited to something manufactured mechanically than to how the brain really functions. While most people in society would accept the definition that giftedness is as giftedness does, it is not adequate for the purposes of this book.

Most definitions of giftedness include these components:

- Initially having and using natural abilities without benefit of formal training
- Rapid learning
- Creative and productive thinking
- High academic achievement
- Superior proficiency in one or more domains (e.g., mathematics, performing arts, leadership)

As you can see, the emphasis is on the cognitive components of giftedness. While the cognitive components are certainly important to consider in discussing giftedness, too often there is a piece missing. Giftedness is not merely as giftedness does or as giftedness thinks. Instead, giftedness is as it thinks as well as feels, senses, perceives, and does.

Liberating Everyday Genius explores the psychology and personality of gifted adults—the most underidentified group of potential achievers in our society. Regrettably, too often in our society those who would most readily be identified as "smart" are most at odds with making their intelligence work for them. Quite often it works against gifted adults, preventing them from producing the kind of products that traditionally are the markers of giftedness. One possible explanation for this discrepancy is that we place a great deal of emphasis on educating gifted children. We understand that gifted children operate differently from those in the mainstream. As a result, we try to accommodate these differences among children by providing them with special programs and enrichment activities. However, even in the best school districts these programs are often inadequate and make the fundamental mistake of using only standard measures such as IQ as a basis for admission.

Programs for the talented and gifted are a relatively recent phenomenon. As a mother of three very different gifted children, as a former educator and advocate for gifted education, I can attest to the benefits and deficits of these programs. However, despite the varying quality of such programs and their methods of identifying students, they stand head and shoulders above earlier efforts to educate gifted children, since specialized programs simply did not exist. From firsthand experience, I know that many gifted "programs" consisted primarily of removing the "smart" kids from the classroom and giving them busywork or enlisting their aid as tutors for the "slow" kids.

If we accept the notion that some children are gifted, then we have to account for what happens to these children when they grow up. After all, it's not as though these former children slough off their giftedness like discarded skin at the age of sixteen or eighteen or twenty-one. Gifted children do grow up, and they become gifted adults. It seems like an obvious comment to make, yet little is written about giftedness and how it applies to adults. So instead of asking if gifted adults exist, we might be better served by asking questions like the following: How many gifted adults are there? What are they doing with their lives? What do we know about how they function in society? What do they have to do to be successful and fully use their abilities? These are all important questions, and it is this initial line of inquiry that led me to more fully investigate the concept of giftedness as it applies to adults.

Interestingly enough, my answer to the first question about the number of gifted adults in this country demands that we radically revise our thinking about the very nature of giftedness. Today there are at least twenty million Americans who would be classified as gifted adults. That number dwarfs the estimated three million gifted children in our schools. So where do these gifted adults come from? They can be found in every age bracket, culture, gender, and socioeconomic stratum across the nation. "They" are many of "us." Given these statistics, quite a number of people you know are gifted adults, and perhaps even you are a member of this not-so-exclusive group. Despite our John- and Ann-like claims to the contrary, it is not the proverbial others who are truly gifted. We who are what I term the Everyday Geniuses in our society comprise a group that together would be equal to the size of the entire population of New York State!

So-called baby boomers comprise the largest portion of the unidentified gifted adult population. The baby boom was a sharp rise in the birth rate that began after World War II and lasted for nearly twenty years. Using the crudest of statistical analyses, it is clear that with more children being born, the greater the number of potentially gifted children there would be in that boom. Since there were no programs to accommodate their needs, many of these youngsters spent their formative years adrift, a great number of them choosing to swim against the tide of societal expectation. Furthermore, when you consider that the bulk of the baby boomer generation is presently moving into, or has already moved into, midlife, the time at which many of these identity issues resurface, you can understand why I felt so compelled to write this book. Since 1991, when I began specializing in counseling gifted adults, I have become increasingly aware that a kind of cascade effect has been created by this group's collective discontent. While we are no longer taking over administration buildings or taking to the streets in protest, we are experiencing a similar kind of discomfort with maintaining our individual and collective status quo. For many of us, life has become a kind of dance to avoid the vaguely déjà vu–like feelings from early adulthood that kept tangling our feet and sent us tripping along widely varied paths.

THE GIFTED ADULT

Like Ann and John, the individuals who come into my office have a vague awareness that the root of their problems is far deeper than surface symptoms. They realize they are intense, complex, and driven, but they have been taught that their strong personalities are perceived as excessive, too different from the norm, and consequently wrong. In a culture that often equates different with wrong, it's inevitable that gifted adults point a critical finger toward themselves as the source of their discontent: Why can't I just be like everybody else? Shouldn't I have outgrown this kind of identity crisis by now? Why can't I shake this nagging sense of urgency? Will I ever feel satisfied? What's wrong with me? When I hear my clients say these things to me, what immediately becomes obvious is that they are in dire need of accurate information about themselves. Frequently, the very traits that make an adult gifted are the same traits that society demands they suppress. This is a book about normalizing giftedness. My purpose is to show gifted adults how they can bring their gifts to fruition by fully expressing the very qualities that are the foundation of their personality.

THE SOURCE OF GIFTEDNESS

Not surprisingly, in order to more fully understand adult giftedness, we need to turn our attention back to children. One fundamental reason why many researchers use children as their subjects in studies of giftedness is that children have not been exposed to as many environmental factors as adolescents or adults. Consequently, researchers can see the nature side of the nature/nurture debate in a more pristine state. What studies have shown is that gifted children perceive the world in fundamentally different ways than other children. It is as if their sensory apparatus is more finely tuned to detect input that others either filter out or ignore. This heightened receptivity is present from the earliest stages of development and later gives rise to the urge to perfect.

Because gifted children perceive in ways that are different in kind and degree than others, their heightened receptivity makes them "hot receptors"—capable of automatically detecting even the slightest change in their external environment. They also possess an innate sense of how things should be and not just how they are. In other words, they have an innate urge to perfect. We often see these two traits displayed in children who aren't satisfied with things until they are just so.

I call these two underlying components of giftedness, heightened receptivity and the urge to perfect, "First Nature" traits. We often talk about how things become "second nature" to us over a period of time. In this case, the gifted don't experience any real adjustment period. They are hardwired from the very start with these two traits. For that reason, First Nature is a convenient shorthand to describe them.

It is the First Nature traits that give rise to the Intensity, Complexity, and Drive that are the more visible characteristics of giftedness. The only way to manifest what is the norm for someone with such a highly sensitive sensory apparatus and vision of how things ought to be in a world that seems radically out of sync (think of John's colleagues' slow-motion mouths) is to be intense, complex, and driven. As Abraham Maslow pointed out, we are all driven by the urge to meet our needs. What if one of our most fundamental needs is to have things be just so? What do we do if our precise sense of proportion sets off an alarm in our heads when the figures we've drawn are slightly skewed? We stop, assess, and start over, again and again, until we get it right. And we don't do this so much by choice but because of a mandate from somewhere both inside and outside of ourselves.

Unless you've experienced this urge to perfect and are a hot receptor yourself, it is difficult to make clear how fundamentally a part of a gifted person's core personality these First Nature traits are and how much they affect their overall development. One way to think about First Nature traits is to compare them to hand preference. Unless we've suffered some accident that has rendered our dominant hand useless, we don't think much about the subject. Yet, like the First Nature of the gifted, our handedness has a major influence on how we negotiate our way in the world. And like those well-intentioned teachers and family members who once forced left-handers to abandon the use of the naturally dominant hand, gifted adults often experience the same kind of treatment.

Most gifted people are not able to articulate that it is their First Nature that makes them extraordinarily aware, compels them to make things "just so" or makes them so dissatisfied when things are not that way. Consequently, when these underlying formative personality traits express themselves, other people not only usually misinterpret the message but may sometimes fantasize about getting rid of the messenger as well. Like so many aspects of human misbehavior, we have to separate the act from the actor. In John's and Ann's cases, they weren't acting badly; they were enacting a fundamental aspect of their personality. I hope to provide a bridge between this society's expectations of how we ought to behave and the gifted personality, so that we can understand that it is the desire of the gifted person to live authentically and not suppress the First Nature traits that produce what some consider aberrant behavior.

In fact, I would agree that Ann's and John's behaviors were somewhat aberrant. However, it is more important for us to understand that they were behaving aberrantly in terms of their own First Nature rather than acknowledge their supposed transgressions against society's norms. In the course of working with gifted adults over the years I've discovered that they've learned that they can't express their First Nature traits without censure. As a result, they modify their behavior in one of two ways—by either collapsing it or exaggerating it. Let's take a closer look at John and Ann to see how they are the perfect examples of this forced accommodation that gifted adults make and the ways in which Intensity, Complexity, and Drive function.

On one hand, Ann's experiences and reactions typify the collapsed response when one's Intensity, Complexity, and Drive are challenged. She lowered her standards to conform and began to distrust herself and her intuition. Over the years, she developed the habit of being too trusting and was too easily wounded as a result. She had always been consumed by the projects she undertook, and when she wasn't rewarded in proportion to her efforts, she became indifferent, adopting a fatalistic view of her mistakes.

On the other hand, John is the perfect example of exaggerated Intensity, Complexity, and Drive. His high energy posed a threat to others when he dominated conversations, used words as weapons, and posed potentially embarrassing questions. John was as raw and overstimulated as they come, a provocateur who openly defied authority and ducked responsibility for his choices.

In addition to the umbrella traits of Intensity, Complexity, and Drive, Ann, John, and other gifted adults have a penchant for what I call Complex Thinking as well as sensory and emotional sensitivity, deep empathy, excitability, perceptivity, and goal-oriented motivation.

THE CONCEPT OF
GIFTEDNESS EXPANDED

Since I have worked with a wide range of gifted individuals in a variety of settings, I've dared to take the risk of offering this new platform for the discussion of adult giftedness. After counseling hundreds of gifted people, I was increasingly alarmed to see how confused they are by their unexplained inner conflicts, which only grow stronger over the years. Although most of them appear to be navigating life with considerable success, the inner story is one of lost identity. Repeatedly, I have been struck by their lack of freedom to express themselves and to fulfill their potential. And on a much larger scale I am dismayed by the precious commodity our society loses when our most creative people are overwrought with self-doubt and self-sabotage.

More important, no one has offered a suitable road map for how gifted adults may live out the promise of their high potential, fit in and have successful relationships, and manage themselves so that their traits are truly assets instead of liabilities. This means that how we conceptualize giftedness has to be expanded to include two concepts—Everyday Genius and Evolutionary Intelligence. These two concepts fundamentally alter our conception of giftedness and offer a new paradigm, which is a risky venture. I owe a debt of gratitude to others in the field upon whose work I have built, such as Lee Anne Bell, Mihaly Csikszentmihalyi, Kazimierz Dabrowski, Howard Gardner, Leta Hollingworth, Carl Gustav Jung, Lawerence Kohlberg, Dierdre Lovecky, Alice Miller, Michael Piechowski, Jane Piirto, Joseph Renzulli, Mary Rocamora, Annemarie Roeper, Martin Seligman, Linda Kreger Silverman, Robert Sternberg, and James T. Webb. I hope that what I present in this book will serve as a catalyst to others so that we can be certain that one of our most valuable resources—the Everyday Geniuses in our midst—are free to fully contribute to our collective advancement.

For the past twenty years, Howard Gardner has been doing groundbreaking research into intelligence. His work at Harvard University on Project Zero has fundamentally changed the way in which many approach the study of intelligence. His theory of multiple intelligences suggests that rather than being a single discrete entity, intelligence is composed of various domains. The eight areas, or types, of intelligence that he identifies are linguistic, logical-mathematical, spatial, musical, kinesthetic, interpersonal, intrapersonal, and naturalist. His work has led us away from seeking answers to the question of how smart someone is and toward a consideration of the ways in which someone is smart.

Everyone possesses each of the eight components of multiple intelligence to some degree; however, as we know, not everyone is as intense, complex, and driven as the gifted adult. Although everyone exhibits multiple intelligences, fewer people also have the First Nature traits and the array of gifted characteristics that exist under the umbrella of Intensity, Complexity, and Drive (ICD). Those people who possess this combination of multiple intelligence and gifted characteristics are traditionally described as gifted.

I believe that another group of eminently gifted people exists in our society. I call them Everyday Geniuses. What separates the Everyday Genius from the gifted adult is that Everyday Geniuses possess an additional set of tools, the potential for Advanced Development. Advanced Development consists of a Humanistic Vision, a Mandated Mission, and Revolutionary Action. The gifted adults that I work with generally have made some progress in their Advanced Development. Whatever the reason, their progress has been sporadic. Whether it's the push/pull of wanting to fit in or the exaggerated or collapsed expression of one part of the First Nature, they've been proceeding haphazardly. Their movement has been tentative mostly because they have yet to recognize and accept that they are gifted adults. It is only when that first step is complete that they can then take the subsequent steps toward Advanced Development.

Still, fewer people have been able to liberate and integrate their gifts to perform revolutionary acts that, in large or small ways, change the world. I call this group of people Evolutionaries because not only do they possess the complex of gifted traits that the Everyday Genius possesses (including their hardwired First Nature, their multiple intelligences, and their ICD), but they have embraced the call of Advanced Development that results in Evolutionary Intelligence (EvI). These individuals have learned to employ their multiple intelligences and gifted traits, catalyzed by their Advanced Development traits, to actualize their gifts in service of their Mandated Mission in the real world. By actualizing these gifts in the service of self and others, these Evolutionaries are destined to push progress forward.

The diagram below graphically illustrates this point:

Multiple Intelligence

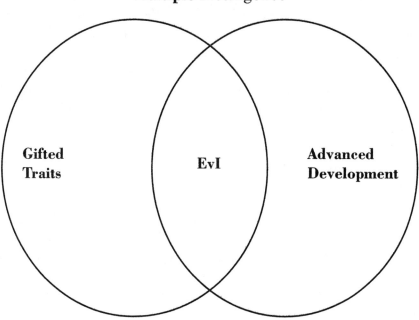

Gifted Traits   **EvI**   **Advanced Development**

Multiple Intelligence

My main goal then, is to expand the area of overlap, ideally to the point where we have concentric circles—where everyone with multiple intelligences, who also has gifted traits, can manage his or her Intensity, Complexity, and Drive and employ them in service of his or her Humanistic Vision and Mandated Mission through Revolutionary Action. It's an ambitious goal, but can we expect any less of ourselves when our urge to perfect helps define our existence?

The first step toward expanding this group of people who possess Evolutionary Intelligence is identifying those who have gifted traits.

One of my prime motivations for writing this book is the fact that there are so many Everyday Geniuses in the world who are undervalued and underutilized. These people are a vital national resource, as potentially powerful and existence-altering as any new energy source, medical discovery, or microchip. Not to tap this vital resource and put it to its best use is unproductive and unhealthy for the individual and the society.

To demystify giftedness we have to deconstruct it. We have to break it down into its component parts and then examine how each of these parts, assembled in different combinations in every individual, forms a personality that is capable, when truly liberated, of transforming the world. Beyond that, I've created a model for looking at the core personality traits of the gifted adult that gives us a way to understand and manage these traits in the real world. It is both theoretical and practical.

For too long the most ardent desire of many of my patients has been to find out what's wrong with them and fix it. The guiding philosophy of my practice and the theme of this book is that every individual should find out what's *right* with him or her and manage it.

Imagine, if you will, that reading had come very naturally to you as a young child and no one ever had to teach you how to read. Neither you nor anyone else could explain how this happened, but it did. Later, over a period of years, both at school and at home, others intervened and mistaught you that the "correct" way to read was to hold the book or other text upside down when reading. Not only did you have to read from right to left instead of left to right, but recognizing individual letters became a tedious and frustrating exercise. To add to your frustration, everyone else around you in school seemed to manage just fine. Since you were having reading difficulties, your grades suffered and your self-image plummeted. You heard a nearly constant chorus of "What's wrong with you?" Whenever you tried to explain that there was a better or easier way to do it, you received that slow, sad wag of the head that told you that you were indeed the sorriest of cases. You started to wonder, "What's wrong with me?" and "Why can't I get this right?"

In a very real sense, this example illustrates what many of my gifted clients experience. And without fail my response to their self-criticism is: "What if what's 'wrong' with you is actually what's right?"

One purpose of this book is to turn upside-down—or better yet, to re-turn to right side up—many of the conceptions that gifted adults hold about themselves. Very often, reading ourselves is the most crucial read-ing we will ever do.

To feel like an outsider, to constantly pressure yourself to hold back your gifts in order to fit in or avoid disapproval, to erroneously believe that you are overly sensitive, compulsively perfectionistic, and blindly driven, to live without knowing the basic truths about the core of your being—too often this is the life of Everyday Geniuses who have been kept in the dark about who they are and misinformed about their differ-ences. No one ever took them aside and explained: "Of course you're dif-ferent. You're intense, complex, and driven because you're gifted." No one told them they cannot escape the fact that they will always be *quanti-tatively, qualitatively*, and *motivationally* different from most other peo-ple. Nor do they know that these very same things that are the basis of criticism are fundamental building blocks of excellence and Advanced Development.

Is it any wonder, then, that when faced with a choice of whether or not to accept that they are gifted, many of them initially reject the label or demand tangible proof of their giftedness?

Because so many of my clients demand concrete evidence and prefer numbers over an intuitive sense that an idea feels right, I've devised the Evolutionary Intelligence Profile as a means to identify the potential for Evolutionary Intelligence in each of us. This 240-item questionnaire is the first practical tool for measuring Evolutionary Intelligence. It iden-tifies the dynamic and complex interaction between the urge to perfect and heightened receptivity, by measuring multiple intelligences, Gifted Traits (Intensity, Complexity, and Drive), and Advanced Development. This in-depth personality-type profile is reminiscent of the Myers-Briggs Type Indicator and the Enneagram and allows you to rate your level of Evolutionary Intelligence.

The Evolutionary Intelligence Profile was the first tool that I used to really make a difference in Ann's and John's lives. Once I had concrete evidence to support my contention that they were indeed gifted, we could move on to the next stages in their personal evolution. Whether you or someone close to you may be an unidentified gifted adult, you have gifted children, or you work with gifted people, nothing will work very well for you until you know the truth and what to do with it. What you will learn in this book is based on the Five Facets of Freedom—the five essential steps to the liberation of Everyday Genius. Like Ann and John, all unidentified gifted adults are diamonds in the rough and merely need a nudge to send them on their way to mastering and applying their exceptional gifts. Each facet of freedom is a critical phase in the refinement of the gifted adult, and none can be overlooked if the desired outcome is self-actualization— the brilliant multifaceted diamond of human potential.

THE FIVE FACETS OF FREEDOM

- Identify thyself
- Understand thyself
- Reveal and heal thyself
- Manage thyself
- Liberate thyself

Identify thyself, the first facet of freedom, is the most important because it takes us out of the dark about the gifted personality so we can clearly see who and what we are and are not—that like the ugly duckling, we were born swans, not ducks. A giftedness checklist offers a quick way to identify basic Everyday Genius characteristics that are widely misunderstood. This allows us a new way of thinking about our traits. We get a glimpse of how the psychology and personality of Everyday Genius is far more important than creative products or history as a prodigy. The individual and collective importance of this factor is explained, as well as how the swan of Everyday Genius gets lost in the duck yard and the high price of remaining lost over the years.

Understand thyself, the second facet of freedom, allows us to move beyond outdated IQ and other misleading notions about intelligence that keep our abilities under wraps. We see ourselves in the faces of the Everyday Geniuses next door. As we separate the truth from indoctrinated untruths we begin to learn how "different" becomes "wrong" in our society, and discover ways to normalize our experience so that we no longer feel odd, like a minority of one.

At this point we are ready to take an essential leap that links intelligence with evolution. You will learn detailed information about your Multiple Abilities, Gifted Traits, and Advanced Development by rating yourself on the EvI Profile. The EvI Profile measures Evolutionary Intelligence and offers a new, more comprehensive look at how intelligence fits the Everyday Genius's purpose and design. Within the inventory you will begin to see how Gardner's Multiple Intelligences and Gifted Traits, combined with the markers of Advanced Development, complement your unique First Nature and can liberate your Everyday Genius into fully realized Evolutionary Intelligence.

Reveal and heal thyself, the third facet of freedom, looks at liberation's real enemy, fitting in. By looking back at the EvI Profile, we see more clearly how our gifted personality traits and behaviors come under the influence of our Intensity, Complexity, and Drive. What we have learned compels us to redefine our differences, recognizing them no longer as liabilities but as true assets and the foundation of creative excellence.

We also explore how our self-image has been distorted by the Ten Criticisms—the ten most common complaints that others have leveled against us. By deconstructing and confronting these criticisms, we can learn to see through these distortions and start to respond with new insight and self-confidence.

We begin to reveal our true selves by meeting the "false self" who often dominated our personalities during our developmental years to protect us from disapproval and rejection. We begin to realize that the false self has outlived its usefulness and is now an obstacle with a destructive agenda. With the help of guided reflection, we learn how being misinterpreted wounded us and how we in turn punished ourselves for our differences. We learn to face and heal old wounds in order to move forward. Recognizing the difference between the false self and the true self prepares us for a reckoning.

Seeing and acknowledging how gifted assets can get out of control and become liabilities is possibly the most significant step in the quest to complete healing. Consequently we must deal with the shadow side of giftedness—our false-self reactions to people and situations when our primary wounds are reopened—or when our unmanaged assets turn against us in the form of disorderly conduct.

The fourth facet of freedom—*manage thyself*—starts with learning to regulate the flow of Everyday Genius energy, especially Intensity, Complexity, and Drive. As we embrace our ICD differences we gain strength from knowing what it means to be quantitatively, qualitatively, and motivationally different. We learn how to redirect self-defeating misuses of energy and avoid unintentional abuse of our gifts. By developing new coping strategies to replace outmoded defenses and by establishing balance plans, we make great strides to take charge of ourselves and our lives—which means we can be less reactive and more prudently responsive. By learning to manage our ICD in our relationships, we can discover new ways of interacting that allow us to be both individually free and intimately connected.

The fifth and final facet of freedom—*liberate thyself*—is the end of the beginning, the place where Everyday Genius traits and skills and vision are finally integrated. This is when we revisit our Evolutionary Intelligence and formulate a plan for the constructive enactment of Advanced Development. The full potential of the liberated Everyday Genius gift is delivered for the betterment of the world in the form of fully realized Evolutionary Intelligence. Here is where we finally accept that there has always been a fundamental reason for our particular way of thinking, perceiving, and feeling. We recognize from where our power and insight actually originate and how to cooperate with our soul's destiny in support of our collective evolution.

Passion, wisdom, and motivation are consciously mastered and regulated so that the full force of high potential can be put to good use. Self-liberation is more than simply getting comfortable with being different, and more than developing expertise or even becoming successful. By understanding the Evolutionary Moment—the life-altering or subtle turning points that aim us toward our life purpose—we learn to accept the real-life process of self-actualization, and even find comfort in the dark nights of the soul that are necessary turning points in our lives.

Many gifted adults active in my workshops say: "Being gifted would have been great, but it's too late for all that now. I didn't start soon enough or in the right direction." Yet it is never as late as we think.

Excellence emerges only over time because Advanced Development is rooted in the process of integration. The path to fulfillment is one of pressures and Evolutionary Moments that disturb and shape us.

None of us knows exactly when our abilities and life experience and opportunities will jell. Giftedness is like an ember: It may turn cold and dim on the outside, but its radiance is always there, awaiting the spark of renewal. Everyday Geniuses spend the first part of their lives trying to be who they are and meeting with disapproval. The second part is spent pretending to be someone they are not in order to fit in. And, if they're determined and lucky, they can spend the third part chipping away at the rock of that created false self and moving closer to being the authentic individuals they were uniquely destined to be.

At this time in our evolution, when human beings are the major agent of change on our planet, we cannot afford to repress those who have the capacity to create a better world. The problems we face today cannot be resolved using yesterday's ways of thinking. Those in every corner of the globe who possess the wisdom and the integrity to take revolutionary action are already too few in number. This is the challenge for the Everyday Genius, who bears, along with the gift of exceptional ability, the responsibility to create a better tomorrow. It is my hope that this work will offer the next step in personal evolution for gifted adults—and for those who know, love, and work with them—and guide them toward the liberation of their destinies. In a society that often favors individuality over the collective good, Everyday Geniuses have labored far too long under the false assumption that they must go it alone. This book is meant to reassure and challenge. Everyday Geniuses are not alone and they *must* move forward to undertake their great task and earn its many rewards.

2

GIFTED? NOT ME

Improvement makes straight roads; but the crooked roads without
improvement are the roads of genius. —William Blake

The world in which we live is indeed an extraordinary place. Out of every generation and culture, remarkable people with exceptional gifts emerge to truly make a difference in our lives. In my practice I see some of these outstanding individuals in a setting where they are allowed to be completely candid. Though they would never use the word *genius* to describe themselves, peeling away the layers of the definition of genius reveals a nugget of truth that is crucial to their self-understanding. They may feel bad about being different, guilty for not having lived up to their own high standards, or like frauds who are not nearly as smart as other people think. Nonetheless, their keenness of mind shines through their veneer of denial, and their genius, once liberated, exerts a strong influence on all of us.

Like a diamond, genius is extremely valuable and often hidden under the rough edges of an outer layer of stone. For genius to be truly valuable and useful, it must be expertly mined and precisely shaped to reveal its many sparkling facets. Genius is as tough as it is fragile. Genius is rare enough to be sought after and revered, though it is not as rare as we think. History is filled with high achievers. They serve a useful purpose. They give us something to look up to that is awe-inspiring. They demonstrate just how high the bar of human accomplishment can be raised. Evidence of the effects of genius is all around us, yet throughout history society has maintained a strange love-hate relationship with it.

WE LOVE YOUR UNIQUE PRODUCTS.
JUST STOP BEING SO DIFFERENT!

We are enamored with the *idea* of genius and admire those who stand out, who create new things to make our lives richer and easier. We love their creativity and their contributions to society, yet all too often we do not love their unique and intense natures. They're *too* different! Society would rather explain them away as eccentrics or separate these creators from their creations.

"Cherish the product, chastise the person" is the general rule. The more impertinent and bold the person, the steeper the climb, the harder the fall if things go badly, and the heartier the collective laugh. With few exceptions we feel better about ourselves when we stereotype and pigeonhole the brightest and the best. Consequently, what we don't always see is that nearly all of them are multiply talented and amazingly diverse, often succeeding at several distinct careers over the course of a lifetime.

From a distance, we can set the notion of genius upon a pedestal that is out of reach. Once genius is recognized, there's scant room for shortcomings. We simultaneously set impossibly high standards for what constitutes genius and then view it as commonplace. When accredited geniuses create something startlingly new or superb, we think nothing of it because we have come to expect such feats from them. "After all," we explain to ourselves, "if I had the same talent, the same brains, and the right connections, I'd be able to do the same thing myself."

There's something about human nature that has always been inclined toward pushing geniuses off the pedestals upon which we ourselves place them. We love these exemplars for filling in the blanks of ordinary life with excitement, curiosity, and passion. Yet we hate them when we feel inferior in the tall shadow of their success. It stands to reason that anyone of exceptional ability must by nature be equipped to deliver the goods without much effort, does it not? Likewise, we assume that being who they are and doing what they do must be easy for them.

Is it fair to make such assumptions? How much do we really know about genius and geniuses, particularly those who exist far outside the limelight? Is there more to these individuals than meets the eye? Who are the real people behind these outstanding deeds, and what is their world like?

Strangely enough, the life of the Everyday Genius is a paradox. The inner landscapes and personality traits that make them what they are have long been kept under wraps. What do we know about their psyches and inner experience? Research tells us there is a great deal more to giftedness and intelligence than we can immediately observe. Until someone moves into the range of the public eye, for most of us they don't exist; who they were before and what they did prior to attaining recognition is, for the most part, a mystery. It's as if geniuses spring up out of nowhere.

Even though most gifted people have to grow into their genius, it is present as a seed from the beginning. Something in them cannot be ignored. Frequently behind their workaday smiles and greetings lies a question that rarely comes up in their conversations: "Who am I, and what am I doing here?" Most gifted adults were socialized in a way that encouraged them to dismiss such deep inquiry. Finding answers to their most profound existential speculations is a task that requires immeasurable courage and fortitude.

It is little wonder a shiver runs up their spines whenever their minds dare to wander into such deep woods. There is little support for basic inquiries into our beingness. Yet these are the very questions that clients present when they enter my office.

Though they truly long for peace of mind and heart, and crave the creative lives they imagine for themselves, at the same time they want their growth to be smooth so that everyone around them will continue to like them. They ask themselves: "Why is any of this necessary? Even if I wanted to know my true self and my life purpose, where and how would I begin?"

It seems to me the "why" question must precede the "where and how." In my years of experience as a psychologist I have found that the "why" presents itself initially to my clients in the form of pain. It is the cry heard in the secret hour, that makes its way from the recesses of the inner world into daylight, where the conscious mind can grapple with it.

Regrettably, we live in a society that has become habituated to the quick-fix solutions that are implied in pathologizing labels such as "depression," "anxiety," "bad marriage," "bad job." At times, of course, these classifications are useful, at least for diagnostic purposes. However, for certain people such simplistic identification tags not only miss the point, but carry a heavy price. For when categorical thinking is ruled by surface assumptions, the essential design and character of the personality and soul are disregarded, depersonalized, and neglected.

Such labels and surface assumptions can frequently cause irreversible damage when applied to the millions of individuals whose identity centers on high potential, special talents, and gifts of intellect. In many cases, the final result is that there is something crucial missing from the "Who am I?" puzzle. Their real identities continue to appear on the missing-persons list because of a perceptual gap in their self-image. Instead of knowing who they are and what they're supposed to be doing with their lives, they are stuck with socialized stampings, catalogued and ranked by faulty criteria. They fail to see their perception of reality reflected in the world around them.

The one critical puzzle piece they must find in order to ascertain their rightful place in the universe is this: *The promise of high potential and creative intelligence is accompanied by a specific set of personality traits and inner processes—not simply more of some attribute, but an altogether different quality of thinking and experiencing.* When put into place, that piece has the power to change everything. For years we've labored under the false assumption that genius is a difference in degree and not a difference in kind, that genius simply meant more. That's not the case. Genius is more and it is different.

The vast majority of gifted adults were given poor information about their essential selves. Indicators of giftedness are subtle and complex. Says Stephanie Tolan, an award-winning author of children's books who also speaks and writes about the challenges unidentified gifted adults face:

> "Who am I?" is a question they may need to ask themselves all over again because the answers devised in childhood and adolescence were inaccurate or incomplete. . . . The gifted frequently take their own capacities for granted, believing that it is people with different abilities who are the really bright ones. Not understanding the source of their frustration or ways to alleviate it, they may . . . simply hunker down and live their lives in survival mode.[1]

Indeed, the term *gifted* leaves most adults shaking their heads in denial: "Not me. I'm no genius. I couldn't possibly be gifted!"

GIFTED? NOT ME:
UNIDENTIFIED EVERYDAY GENIUS

Gifted adults are not, as you may have thought, a tiny group of profoundly brilliant Einsteins. Rather, they are everyday people of unusual vision who are more appropriately called Everyday Geniuses because of one dominant trait—their ability to give progress a push forward.

Nevertheless, as gifted and talented adults, what they have been taught about their idiosyncratic nature and atypical characteristics is often either incorrect or insulting. In a society addicted to final products, we have been brainwashed with the obsolete notion that giftedness is exclusively defined by academic achievement, fame, and fortune. Even former straight-A students and people who are obvious success stories resist the idea of acknowledging that their abilities are bona fide.

Perhaps the greatest obstacle to claiming one's gifted identity comes from the modern Western world's insistence that fairness is bound to sameness, that the concept of giftedness is elitist. By extension, then, more of us believe that people with special abilities can make it on their own and need nothing from society to fulfill their potential. As a result, some people shy away from their giftedness because they have been taught to believe that such a claim would be arrogant. Given the fact that in their experience being smart sometimes meant being left out, what other conclusion could they draw?

TELLTALE SIGNS OF EVERYDAY GENIUS

Everyday Geniuses are everywhere in the world. They are the ones who can and will look beyond what is obvious to design the better cart, attach the wheels in new places, and pull hard to get things moving. Many times they do so against all odds, and often alone. In the most basic terms, gifted adults are obviously different to the untrained eye in fundamental ways.

Some Everyday Geniuses have talents that are highly specialized, or single-tracked. Others possess broad-ranging potentialities, able to draw from a pool of abilities to excel in all sorts of things. A handful become millionaire entertainers, eminent physicians, Pulitzer and Nobel prize winners. Many more are firefighters, librarians, kindergarten teachers, chefs, and secretaries. Some are conventional, some eccentric; some shy, some outgoing; some honorable, some not.

Everyday Geniuses have regular jobs, families, and friends. They love a good baseball game, like other people. Most often they are quietly gifted. They come from every culture and exhibit every type of outward appearance. Yet they share several distinct traits that compel them to be intense seekers of self-actualization who are lured forward by their unshakable First Nature traits—heightened receptivity and the urge to perfect. Ironically, these are the same traits that become the focus of others' disapproval.

To varying degrees, Everyday Geniuses possess the following characteristics:

- Capacity for keen observation
- Exceptional ability to predict and foresee problems and trends
- Special problem-solving resources; extraordinary tolerance for ambiguity; fascination with dichotomous puzzles
- Preference for original thinking and creative solutions
- Excitability, enthusiasm, expressiveness, and renewable energy
- Heightened sensitivity, intense emotion, and compassion
- Playful attitude and childlike sense of wonder throughout life
- Extra perceptivity, powerful intuition, persistent curiosity, potential for deep insight, early spiritual experiences
- Ability to learn rapidly, concentrate for long periods of time, comprehend readily, and retain what is learned; development of more than one area of expertise
- Exceptional verbal ability; love of subtleties of written and spoken words, new information, theory, and discussion
- Tendency to set own standards and evaluate own efforts
- Unusual sense of humor, not always understood by others
- Experience of feeling inherently different or odd
- History of being misunderstood and undersupported
- Deep concerns about universal issues and nature, and reverence for the interconnectedness of all things
- Powerful sense of justice and intolerance for unfairness
- Strong sense of independence and willingness to challenge authority
- Awareness of an inner force that "pulls" for meaning, fulfillment, and excellence

- Feelings of urgency about personal destiny and a yearning at a spiritual level for answers to existential puzzles

Identifying gifted adults is not easy because the issue has been confounded and obstructed by the following:

- Nearly all gifted adults were never formally or informally assessed for exceptional potentiality.
- Giftedness is not a simple either/or matter; just as any other feature of human ability, it includes gradations within a range (for example, musical talent, agility, developmental delay).
- Giftedness occurs in various forms and intensities as well, and may be viewed in terms of mild, moderate, extraordinary, and profound levels, or broad-ranging and single-tracked types.
- The term *gifted* means different things to people who approach the construct of human potential from varying viewpoints; some of these viewpoints are positive, and others are negatively founded on stereotypes.
- Gifted individuals who have been unrecognized and unsupported and whose gifts have been underutilized may find their potentialities are dismissed by unknowing observers, and so they may consider themselves to be "nothing special."
- Gifted people with cultural differences, physical limitations, or learning disabilities are predisposed to developmental neglect that keeps the seed of their abilities buried.
- Many people emphasize childhood-education-oriented views of giftedness as it relates to academic achievement, often to the exclusion of both the personality components that are attendant to giftedness and the inner processes and needs of the gifted adult over the life span. Conventional methods of determining ability appear to seriously underestimate potential and fail to measure specialized aspects of intelligence and aptitude.
- Once the gifted person goes beyond traditional schooling into the more complex roles of adulthood and work, he or she blends into society. Moreover, in the adult world the definition of giftedness tends to be revised and translated into high-profile "success" with accompanying wealth, fame, or influential position, thus effectively eliminating untold numbers of bona fide gifted individuals from the recognized ranks.

FACING THE TRUTH ABOUT OURSELVES

Why does any of this really matter? some may ask. After all, many educators and scholars still hold fast to the notion that the gifted will do just fine on their own. While theories and untested philosophy suffice for academic dialogue, real-life self-actualization calls for the willingness to question our most basic assumptions.

It wasn't so long ago that I was struggling with many of the same false assumptions. Making the transition from teacher to therapist was difficult. I struggled to find a topic for my thesis and found one in the complexity of my life.

For a while, investigating the effects of adoption on adoptees fascinated me, since I had been adopted, and I had always attributed my sense of displacement and incompleteness to that fact. However, upon further reflection I found that that didn't feel like the right direction to pursue.

Several other topics intrigued my boundless curiosity. I focused on interpersonal relationships between bright, strong-willed adults—knowing how difficult it can be to share a life without sacrificing one's true nature. That held my interest temporarily, but ultimately I returned to my roots and decided to investigate perfectionism. While growing up I was labeled "Little Miss Perfect," because I stubbornly believed that perfectionism and excellence were inseparable. As I reflected back on this experience I felt certain that this was the ideal topic—one that would benefit me and others.

For several weeks, I dutifully researched the subject, convincing myself that my anxiety about this topic was typical and would diminish over time. By "chance" a few days later I met my adviser, who was moving to a new office. I helped her carry some boxes as I explained my dilemma. She set down a box, leaned over to look through it, and handed me a stack of professional journal articles. "Here," she said, "I was just going to pitch these, but then I thought of you. I suspect you can put them to good use."

Thumbing through them, I noticed that each of the articles concerned the personality traits and life experiences of gifted adults. Feeling my pulse beating in my temples and my mind racing, I scanned them for content and suddenly tears welled up in my eyes. I looked up at my adviser, somewhat embarrassed by my inappropriate response. She stood there placidly, and then her face registered compassionate bemusement. I heard my voice asking her why she saved the articles for me.

My adviser began speaking in a near whisper. "Mary, I know a bit about adoption, and while that subject is important to you, it's not essential to your search. Perfectionism seems an attractive option, though I suspect that it may not take you as far as your need to go. You're getting closer, but you're not quite there yet. Based on your reaction a moment ago, I think your subject has already chosen you. You're going to investigate advanced development and the psychology of gifted adults, aren't you?"

I was startled by the word "gifted." However, I managed to say, "That sounds promising, since I've raised three very different gifted children. Also, I used to teach gifted children and now I counsel the gifted and talented. I know that there's not a lot of research available. I've always considered myself an advocate for the gifted because of society's distorted perceptions of them."

"So you'd like to"—she paused and I could see her fighting a smile—"challenge those perceptions?"

"Yes," I said as I turned to go. " Thanks." My dissertation decision had been made.

"Just a second, Mary," my adviser said. "You've solved half the puzzle. You know the what, but I don't think you fully understand the why. This will not be just an intellectual exercise for you. Of course you're drawn to the questions of inner life and the challenges of gifted people, because you are one."

This time I was more than stunned. For once in my life I was speechless, as an avalanche of emotion rushed through me. I was struck by the strange sensation of soaring liberation mingled with pangs of fear and apprehension.

However, my adviser was not finished. She pointed to the articles. "The complete answer is not in these pages, but there's enough to get you started, Mary. You're bright, sensitive, intense, and driven. That's who you are, and there are lots of others out there like you. A topic like this will present you with plenty of questions, and you will find some of the answers right away. The rest will elude you for some time, but you will solve most of them in the course of your work. I'm around when you need to talk."

That night I stayed up until my eyes were blurred from exhaustion reading articles about gifted adults. For the first time in my life my unorthodox nature could no longer be reduced to being the odd duck in the pond. There were others out there like me. This revelation was the sum and substance of who I was and why. It was about selfhood and purpose and my place in the world.

Over time I understood that not only was my experience of lost identity not unusual—it was, in fact, the norm.

WHY MUST I KNOW THIS ABOUT MYSELF?

The question "Why must I know this about myself?" lies at the heart of this book. It is the central issue for the gifted person, even more closely linked to well-being than physical health, financial condition, or circumstance. Gifted adults need to *know* who they are and cannot escape the pull toward self-actualization, the unyielding inner pressure to make their lives count. For them, health, or well-being, is more than getting by, existing, or making do. Knowing thyself means puzzling out how identity and fulfillment, meaning and destiny, are inextricably linked.

In this culture, though it may seem otherwise, to achieve beyond the norm is much harder than people imagine. Excellence is about authenticity, and living authentically is always a process that is fraught with risk, setbacks, and self-doubt. Nevertheless, Everyday Geniuses are specially equipped to defy the limits of the ordinary and break the mold. All of them—from the person who invented the electric drill (whose name we may not know) to Madame Curie and Albert Einstein—share one overarching trait: the ability and the drive to push progress forward.

HOW CAN I KNOW THIS ABOUT MYSELF?

Until now, Everyday Geniuses have had no guidebook to assist them in identifying themselves, accepting their traits and abilities, nurturing their creative spirits, and navigating the real world. Liberating Everyday Genius is intended to be that guidebook, a source of essential realities that will bring the concept of giftedness out of the dark ages and liberate the twenty million Everyday Geniuses among us.

Most important, you need new information about who you are and who you are not. To have a fighting chance of living up to your potential, you must correct early messages you received that led you to make vital errors of self-perception. Only after that will you be ready to confidently embrace the full realization of your gifts.

The pages that follow are the culmination of years of life experience and research. The goal is liberation founded on authenticity—creating a new way to live out the promise of high potential through the power of truth. For the Everyday Genius to take his or her rightful place in unfolding human progress, to courageously stand up and be counted in a society that equates worthiness with being a winner, the Everyday Genius must detach from self-negating habits and thoughts. For Everyday Geniuses, claiming their true identity is the only stronghold.

MISCONCEPTIONS ABOUT GIFTEDNESS

If we hope to support in any meaningful way those who have the potential to contribute so much, a handful of harmful misconceptions need to be discarded:

- Gifted people know they're gifted
- Giftedness solves all of its own problems
- Giftedness has nothing to do with personality
- Early underachievement is a sure sign that one is *not* gifted
- The truly gifted never suffer from self-doubt or feel like impostors
- A gifted person automatically grasps and aims for his or her best career direction
- The gifted always do great things early in life

Because of widespread stereotyping and misinformation, Everyday Geniuses are susceptible to trouble in jobs, in relationships, and especially in their own inner world. Because we don't often see the whole picture, both those who observe and those who possess Everyday Genius will continue to misinterpret its signals and disparage its expression. As is true of any aspect of personality, not fully accepting it and living unacquainted with one's whole self can be very costly. It is all too easy to stay lost. Unless we understand how it really works and find a a way to express it, giftedness can become a heavy burden.

Clearing the way for any abundant life, the adventure of the possible self, replete with setbacks and triumphs—is the heart of being and becoming authentic. Along with accepting the responsibility of giftedness comes the duty to identify oneself accurately and fully.

As gifted adults we are duty-bound to find ourselves. Once we know who we are and who we are not, we can begin to see ourselves as the swans we are intended to become. Only then can we determine how to express our gifts fully. It is critical that we resist society's attempts to excise or cure what instead should be honored and cultivated. Humanity as a whole cannot afford to forfeit what the Everyday Geniuses have to offer.

3

THE EVERYDAY GENIUS:
LOST AND FOUND

From a hundred cultures, [there is] one culture which does what no culture has ever done before—gives a place to every human gift.

—Margaret Mead

THE UGLY DUCKLING

It was a lovely summer day in the country. The oats were still green and the wheat stood golden and tall. Down in the meadow the hay was piled into sturdy stacks. In the bright rays of the sunshine an old manor house with a deep moat surrounding it stood with burdock growing from its heavy walls all the way down to the edge of the water. Under the dense green cover of the thicket a duck had built her nest. She felt somewhat sorry for herself as she sat on the eggs. The hatching was taking so long.

Finally one egg began to crack, then another. "Cheep! Cheep!" the young chicks said as they came to life and stuck out their curious heads. "Quack! Quack! Look around," said their mother. The newborns peered out at the green world around them.

"Well, you're almost all here now, aren't you?" the mother said as she turned around to look at her nest. "The biggest egg hasn't hatched yet, and I'm so tired of sitting here! I wonder how long it will take?"

Soon one old duck waddled over for a visit, and the mother duck complained to her about the unhatched egg. "I am quite certain it's a turkey egg!" insisted the old duck. "I was fooled like that once myself. I had my sorrows and troubles, to be sure, for turkeys are afraid of the water. You just let it lie there and teach the others how to swim, that's my advice."

"Oh, I've been sitting on it for so long that I might just as well wait a little longer," replied the mother duck.

The old duck bristled. "Suit yourself!" she huffed, waddling on her way.

At last the big egg cracked open and the last-born tumbled out, an ugly gray one. "He's awfully big for his age," said the mother. "None of the others look like that! Could he be a turkey chick after all? Well, we shall soon see."

The mother duck led her brood down to the moat. "Into the water we will go!" *Splash!* She jumped into the water. "Quack! Quack!" she ordered, and one after another the little ducklings obeyed. Their heads disappeared, then quickly popped up again, and they floated about like corks. They knew just what to do, and even the misfit gray one swam splendidly.

"He is no turkey!" proclaimed the mother, who set off to present her brood to everyone. "See how beautifully he uses his legs and how straight he holds his neck. That's my own child. When you look closely you can see he's quite handsome."

"Very pretty children, except that gray one; he didn't turn out right," said the grand dowager of the duck yard. "I do wish you could make him over again."

"That's not possible, Your Grace," replied the mother duck. "Perhaps he will grow to be better-proportioned over time. He may not be handsome, but he is of good character and swims as well as the others. Yes, I might venture to say he swims a bit better."

However, time passed and the poor gray duckling was bitten, shoved, and ridiculed by the other ducks and even the hens. He grieved over his ugliness. Each day was worse than the one before. Even his mother said, "I wish you were far away."

Before long the gray duckling was so miserable he flew over the hedge. When the little birds in the bushes flew up in fright, he shut his eyes and confessed: "It's because I'm so ugly!" He kept on running until he came to a great marsh where the wild ducks lived.

In the morning the wild ducks gawked at him, asking, "What kind of bird are you?" The duckling bowed to greet them as best he could. "How ugly you are!" ridiculed the wild ducks. "Don't marry into our family!"

Toward evening he came to a little house in the woods. An old woman lived in the house with a hen that laid good eggs and a cat that could arch his back and give off sparks if you rubbed his fur the wrong way.

"What's that?" said the old woman, who noticed the intruder at the first light of dawn. She couldn't see very well. When she first spied the duckling she thought it was a fat, full-grown duck. "Now we shall have duck eggs," she exclaimed, and the duckling was accepted.

The duckling sat quietly in the corner. He began to think of the fresh air, the sunshine, and how much he wanted to float on the water. At last he couldn't help himself; he had to tell the hen of his longing.

"What's wrong with you? You're just putting on airs. Lay eggs and you'll feel better." But when the duckling went on and on about the water, the hen said scornfully, "You must be quite mad!"

"You don't understand me," the duckling protested.

"Well," said the hen, "if we don't understand you, who would? Believe you me, when I tell you harsh truths, it's for your own good. See to it that you start laying eggs."

"I might go out into the wide world instead!" the duckling dared to reply.

"You just do that!" the hen sneered.

True to his word, the duckling found a lake where he floated alone on the water and dived to the bottom. In autumn the leaves of the forest turned golden and scarlet. One evening, just as the sun was setting in all its splendor, a great flock of beautiful birds rose out of the bushes. They uttered a loud, strange cry as they spread their powerful, glistening wings, craning their long, supple necks to survey the terrain around them. They were flying away from the cold meadow to a warm climate where the lakes did not freeze in the winter. As they soared into the sky the duckling was struck with a strange urge. He spun around in the water like a wheel, stretched his neck toward the sky, and sounded a cry so shrill that he frightened even himself.

He didn't know what those birds were called or where they were flying, but he longed to go with them. The winter turned bitterly cold. It was so cold that the duckling kept swimming in an unfrozen part of the lake to stay alive. But each night the hole became smaller and smaller. The duckling tried hard to keep his feet moving so the hole wouldn't close, but when he grew tired and couldn't swim anymore the ice froze him fast in place.

The next morning a farmer came along. He saw the duckling and freed it by breaking the ice with his wooden shoe. He carried the duckling back to his wife, who nursed him back to health. But the duckling couldn't remain in the house because the children chased and teased him. The bird spilled the milk pail and flapped his wings into the butter and flour. After this he was to suffer through the rest of the long winter alone.

Months passed and the sun began to shine warmly again. The larks sang—spring had arrived! All at once the ugly duckling raised his wings, which beat more strongly now. Before he knew it, he was flying over a beautiful garden. Suddenly out of the thicket came three beautiful swans, who ruffled their feathers and glided ever so lightly on the water.

He recognized the magnificent birds at once and was overcome with a strange sadness. "I will fly straight to those royal birds, though they will surely peck me to death because I am such an ugly duckling. It doesn't matter," he decided. And he flew out into the water and swam over to the swans.

As the poor creature landed, he bent his head humbly. But what was that in the water? It was his own reflection. He was no longer an awkward, ugly gray bird. He was a swan himself!

The newfound swan felt so shy that he hid his head beneath his wing. He was very happy, but not too proud, for he remembered how he had been ridiculed and persecuted. The big swans made a circle around him and caressed him gently with their bills. "Being born in a duck yard does not matter if one has lain in a swan's egg!" the swans affirmed. Now everyone agreed the new swan was the most beautiful of them all. The lilacs bowed their branches right down to the water for him, and the sun shone warm and bright. He ruffled his feathers, lifted his slender, graceful neck, and from the depths of his heart cried out in joy: "I never dreamed of so much happiness when I was the ugly duckling."[1]

WHEN A DUCK IS NOT A DUCK

It's hard to imagine that the poor swan in the story was so badly mistreated because he didn't look like, sound like, and act like the others. No matter what the ugly duckling did, he couldn't fit in. It's also hard to imagine twenty million "ugly ducklings," the millions of unidentified gifted adults or Everyday Geniuses within American society. Like the ill-informed gray duckling, nearly all of them have no idea who they truly are. So they suffer needlessly with low confidence, self-criticism, career dissatisfaction, and relationship problems of unknown origin. These are accompanied by a set of recurring problems that defy all efforts to be figured out.

Likewise, these unidentified geniuses wrestle with self-doubt despite their confident and accomplished facade. They feel detoured and scattered, often jumping from one thing to another, not finding a fulfilling role. They are aware of unshakable inner pressures and a vague sense that they are accountable to someone or something. Against a cultural backdrop of success worship, they struggle with postponed and abandoned dreams.

They have always known they are bright and talented, with something valuable to offer. In spite of that, tension is their steady companion, because often the counterpart to high potential is feeling trapped and unsure while not knowing why. At the center of their frustrated attempts to find meaning and serenity in their lives is their often unspoken quest to find themselves. This search is so fundamental that it must be completed before they can achieve their duck-to-swan transformation.

SEEING THE SWAN OF EVERYDAY GENIUS

Who are the Everyday Geniuses, the multitude of swans domesticated for a duck's life? They wear no ID tags, so we can't spot them by appearance or even by asking. Few of them know the markers of their core identity. Even so, they are all around us. Everyday Geniuses are the visionaries who make things happen, those who willingly and enthusiastically pursue answers to life's "unanswerable" questions. They are the problem solvers on whom society relies, the original thinkers and innovators who can creatively merge information, experience, and intuition. They are the builders who bridge the gaps that befuddle others, the ones we turn to to make things work. Yet untold numbers of them are lost within the fabric of a society that seems to have issued an edict against knowing oneself, being oneself, and expressing oneself in full.

How, then, do we begin to see who we really are when we are surrounded by others who see us as "odd ducks"? Assuredly, others do not have the answers. Furthermore, in the case of the Everyday Genius the problem is compounded by the fact that nearly all the other "swans" who might otherwise be useful resources think they're abnormal ducks, too.

The good news is this: *Creative intelligence and high potential are accompanied by specific personality traits and identifiable inner processes.* Frequently Everyday Geniuses were told they were "special," "really smart," "gifted," or "talented," and that if they just put their mind to it, they could be or do anything. For them success became a given as well as an obligation. But no one ever told them how it all works. No one ever explained the high cost of exceptional ability. In fact, the psychology and inner life of the noneminent gifted person have been virtually ignored.

Luckily, research has provided us with ways to identify giftedness that are more useful and accurate than our outdated stereotyped ideas of smart people. This is information that is more about how they tick than what they are capable of producing. So at the edge of the identity pond we first look for five characteristics that fall under the umbrella traits of Intensity, Complexity, and Drive (ICD):

INTENSITY

Energy: Exhibited by the high-energy enthusiasm of a person with many interests who is easily engrossed and easily hurt, who quickly switches gears when bored, is emotionally reactive and dares to "tell the truth," even when it backfires

Sensitivity: Exemplified by someone with princess-and-the-pea sensitivity, who's seen as overly responsible; one who can read the subtle tone of a situation and decipher others' feelings; someone who sees the ideal and values harmony, whose well of compassion is deep and seemingly never empty

COMPLEXITY

Complex Thinking: Manifests as a learn-fast, think-fast, talk-fast, independent idea activator who is relentlessly curious, prefers creative solutions and complexity, and is willing to rock the boat to get things done in a better way; someone who tends to "spin off" relationships because of frequent changes

Perceptivity: Marked by the keen observations and characterized as a strong intuition of someone who can see all sides of an issue; a quick "problem finder" who is sometimes blunt and judgmental; one who understands and likes metaphor and symbolism, who is a champion of values and a seeker of ultimate truths; a naturally perceptive person with a feeling for the transcendent

DRIVE

Demonstrated by the goal orientation of a self-starter who pushes toward perfection; one who feels an inner sense of urgency and can feel shattered when an important dream seems to fall apart; one who looks for security in systems, rules, and order; one who struggles with self-doubt and high standards; a big-picture trail-blazer who is driven by a sense of personal mission

THE EVERYDAY GENIUS
BROUGHT TO LIGHT

The abilities of the Everyday Genius fall somewhere within the above-average range of intelligence, talent, and achievement, from mild to moderate to profound. Some of their lives are high-profile, though most are not. Their special gifts can be broad-ranging or narrow. For example, one might be an unschooled math whiz with mediocre abilities in other unrelated areas, like the main character in the film *Good Will Hunting*.

Everyday Geniuses sometimes develop early, and a child prodigy results. Picasso, son of a Spanish painter of mediocre ability, drew continuously as a very young child, essentially using drawing as his primary mode of communication. His drawings made before age ten already demonstrated extraordinary composition and expression of emotion that went beyond the capacities of his teachers. His gifts spanned a broad range of abilities, especially his remarkable grasp of the visual, spatial, and perceptual aspects of symbols and the human body, and he could combine and employ his resources in ingenious ways. In his artwork he was unafraid of the darker moods and realities of life, and was able to express them with facility and power. Paradoxically, though not unusually, the deep sensitivities that plagued Picasso into adulthood with disturbing memories of childhood traumas and his love-hate relationship with his father were pivotal to his eventual artistic success. Though Picasso stands as an exemplar of gifted precocity, he was a very poor student, hated school, and struggled to learn to read and write.

Early gifted development and discernible accomplishment, as with Picasso or Mozart, is rare indeed. Nevertheless, we erroneously believe this is the sole definition of genius. Indeed, if this were true, the life and psychology of those with high potential would be of little more use to most of us than a study of the scarcest tsetse fly of ancient Africa. Rarifying genius to a tiny group of renowned figures of unquestionable influence and historical preeminence is incorrect, exclusionary, and a pointless misinterpretation of intelligence.

We can imagine what it must be like for the cause-committed Everyday Genius who has no expectation of fame or even endorsement. Consider Susan B. Anthony, who brought such courage and tenacity of spirit to the cause of women's suffrage. Classified a "dour spinster," she received a letter from her disapproving brother that said: "Although you are now fifty years old and have worked like a slave all your life, you have not a dollar to show for it. This is not right. Do make a change."[2] She responded to his objections by following her sense of justice with another thirty-six years of legendary commitment to and leadership of the women's movement.

How else do Everyday Geniuses appear in our midst? Innumerable ones go by unseen within the varied terrain of society, often serving as promoters or facilitators of others' talents. Sometimes an astute and unselfish parent paves the way, or a sibling mercilessly challenges and competes with a brother or sister for supremacy, thus "forcing" the more gifted one to outdo the other time and again. Occasionally there is a teacher who can see and instill belief in what might be, or a predecessor who graciously steps out of the limelight at the opportune moment for the protégé to step forward.

Once in a while unknowing Everyday Geniuses find each other, and a mentorship develops. In Andrew Carroll's *Letters of a Nation,* we glimpse the unusual pen-pal relationship between Nathaniel Hawthorne and a fifteen-year-younger Herman Melville, who, while laboring tirelessly on what he called his "Whale book," "found a soulmate and favorable audience" in Hawthorne. "Melville wrote lengthy, almost stream-of-consciousness and immodest letters. . . . But within his sometimes rambling paragraphs there are flashes of profound thoughtfulness and humanity."

Pittsfield, Monday afternoon [November, 1851]
My Dear Hawthorne—
. . . I say your appreciation is my glorious gratuity . . .
[T]he atmospheric skepticisms steal into me now, and make me doubtful of my sanity in writing you thus. . . . But with you for a passenger, I am content and can be happy.[3]

THE UGLY DUCKLING SYNDROME

The duckling in our story didn't know he was not a duck at all, much less that he was meant to grow into a remarkable swan, an aquatic virtuoso of great distinction. Yet only over time did the true beauty of the swan become visible. He repeatedly fought an inner battle as he struggled to fit it, eventually withdrawing from the hostile world around him and daring to live as he must.

By the same token, the life story of the Everyday Genius begins with a distorted image. The only hope the "odd one" has of fitting in seems to depend upon continuous self-monitoring and keeping one's peculiarities in check. To be sure, holding back the natural intensity and rapid-fire ideas of the gifted personality in order to avoid criticism misdirects tremendous amounts of creative energy. Being too obvious about one's differences can be costly. As one of my highly insightful clients put it, "I know what being a gifted adult means; it means being punished if you dare to be yourself"—a sad commentary on the current state of affairs for those among us to whom we must look for innovations and solutions.

Exceptional people should not have to go through life suffering from misidentification, curbing the development of our potential because others fail to see who we really are. More important is that with no accurate point of reference, like the ugly duckling, we too will learn to devalue our unique "honk" expressions when everyone around us quacks instead. Since all people draw their self-portrait from social cues, often Everyday Geniuses cannot see the value in being different.

Each Everyday Genius is unique, though in one respect we are all the same: Until we seek our personal truths in updated, individualized ways, we are apt to remain lost in a culture that has no way to understand us, much less support and value us. Even more harmful, we are in danger of going through life lost unto ourselves, our true nature obscured because our "Who am I?" questions have been incorrectly answered again and again.

Most of us were born into environments that demanded, desired, and rewarded "duckhood." In other words, we may have been born smart, but we weren't considered beautiful the way we were. Sure, everybody loved our precocious antics and early displays of talent. But did they hold dear the rest of our "odd duck" nature? Like the ugly duckling, we grew up believing much of how we were just "too smart for our own good." We grew used to restraining ourselves in order to fit in. Short on the facts as adults, our genuine identities were covered over by others' definitions of who we were.

For a while, settling into the daily grind in our usual adaptive, stalwart way seems a suitable and satisfying arrangement: wake to a predictable day, shower, dress, race to work, have meetings that don't get things done, make small talk about the weather and the latest big game, drive home at a snail's pace, eat dinner, get the kids to do their homework, and so on.

Routine is okay, but one way or another, the swan in the Everyday Genius presses to be heard. Deeply unsettling questions of who, what, and why regularly knock us off center in the midst of our routines. Getting caught up in them is a frustrating matter of fate. Yet trying to block or ignore them can be disastrous.

What are the fears that hold back individuals who have such potential, such potency, such possibilities for contribution? First and foremost, giftedness can be frightening. In many respects daring to actualize one's potential to its fullest is a damned-if-you-do, damned-if-you-don't proposition. We fear being overwhelmed as much as we fear being constrained. We fear being undersupported as much as we fear being controlled. We fear success as much as we fear failure, for after all, once we achieve that first success, expectations and risk rise.

We are afraid to be vulnerable and open to others, yet we are terrified of being alone and misunderstood in our relationships. We can become bewildered and distrust our perceptions and ideas while at the same time be fervently attached to them because we know we are right. We have learned to suppress our differences for fear of rejection or exploitation despite needing to be recognized. Because our own standards of "good enough" are sky high, we get cold feet when we imagine the even higher expectations others have of us.

And yet the subconscious mind of the Everyday Genius is imprinted with a summons, an insistent call that something vital is yet to be discovered. An intractable sense of urgency and accountability tugs on one arm, while a desire to have peace of mind and to belong yanks on the other. Though we long to be actualized, we don't know why or how, since we have never been told how the gifted mind and personality work.

Jane: Lost in Her Own Life

No one ever expects a midlife crisis. Jane certainly didn't. She had always been an adapter whose versatility and optimism could carry her through difficult transitions. But in hindsight there had been a crisis, and now it was crystal clear to Jane that she and the world in which she lived had been transformed.

In a very real sense, Jane was a "seer." Everyone knew her as the "idea person" who could turn the lights on in the darkness of confusion.

Long before Jane had been promoted to vice president of new markets at the software company, she recognized that people always complimented her on her unusual insight, though she never thought much of it herself. It seemed she had a gift of perception that allowed her to size up any situation quickly, to read between the lines and untangle the knots of human interaction. She could sniff out hidden agendas and hypocrisy like a bloodhound, and draw out the best in others who were yet unaware of their potential. In the face of complexity and ambiguity Jane's abilities shone. Like a veteran sailor, she could anticipate the most subtle shift in the winds.

Over the years Jane had developed a love-hate relationship with her sensitivity and skilled insight; on one hand it was a help, on the other a hazard. Though her extraordinary perceptivity could solve a variety of complex challenges, it could also create land mines that betrayed her socially. Not everyone liked being so easily "known." More than once Jane had looked to the sky pleading to be less aware, especially after unsuccessfully butting heads with a teacher or supervisor, or exposing the "obvious truth" in a situation that demanded that she know less than she knew.

Five years back, Jane's unexplainable way of knowing things had saved her life. One day out of the blue her attention had been drawn to an area of her body just above her left knee. At first glance she noticed nothing out of the ordinary, just the usual assortment of skin spots—light and dark, large and small—that were the expected by-products of an Irish heritage. She tried to dismiss the vague pulsing sensations that sounded her inner alarm, but to no avail. Something was happening, and she knew it was important. Unwilling to articulate what she felt, she ignored her intuition. Nevertheless, Jane's anxiety rose as she berated herself for all the beach-loving days as a sun worshiper when, like her young friends, she had felt invincible.

Two days later Jane reluctantly ventured into the dermatologist's office, almost as if some invisible force had driven her there. She was noticeably agitated and even a bit angry. She attempted to make herself out as a rather unintelligent worrywart, partly because of the many times before in her life that others had discounted what she knew for lack of "hard evidence," and partly because she hoped her suspicions were unfounded. After all, she tried to convince herself, the dot she pointed out to the doctor was no larger than the head of a small pin, so how could something so tiny mean trouble? But even before the doctor spoke, Jane had her answer; she sensed it, and she was sure. It was cancer.

After surgery to excise enough tissue around the malignant melanoma to prevent its taking a lethal foothold in her bloodstream, Jane's specialist told her the university pathologists were absolutely baffled. Hers was the tiniest diagnosable melanoma ever detected by a patient. What had led her to seek her doctor's opinion? they wondered. Even to the medically trained eye, Jane's skin cancer looked at first to be just another freckle, one that might easily have been disregarded until it was too late.

To the doctors' collective incredulity, Jane answered their query by simply stating: "I can't explain it. I had sensations there, a tingling of a sort, I suppose. I just knew. It's always been that way for me. That's all I can tell you. Believe me, if I could put it into a formula that could be shared with everyone, I'd do it in a heartbeat. But I think it's just a gift I was given, and I really don't know how it works myself."

As it does with so many survivors, the diagnosis of cancer had brought Jane to her knees. Her uncanny self-rescue had opened a new channel of awareness. At some level Jane knew that others had inaccurately defined her despite her apparent willingness to accept their labeling pretty much without question. Suddenly Jane felt obliged to come to terms with the very characteristics and abilities that had long been a source of inner tension and confusion. She was quite right to take this commanding new perception seriously.

Jane sensed she was on the verge of a personal truth of great magnitude as she began to discard her mistaken identity. She was able to interpret her traits in a radically different way as she began to redefine the frequent complaints that had all begun with the word *too*.

Certainly Jane would still live in a culture that had trouble understanding and accepting her particular style of intelligence, a culture that mocked its claimed reverence for individuality with intolerance while rewarding those who maintained the status quo. But her spirit soared as she finally understood that she had been given "a gauntlet with a gift in it."

Jane's ability to see deep and far, her sensitive and empathic nature, and indeed her perfectionistic yearning for the ideal were all parts of a puzzle that when rightly fitted together revealed a gifted adult whose extraordinary talents could be fully realized and freely given. It was a picture of an Everyday Genius with her face on it.

KNOW THYSELF OR LOSE THYSELF

Like Jane, day after day, throngs of Everyday Geniuses gaze into the waters of the identity pond only to see an ugly duckling, whose creative ideas and products are all that is praiseworthy, staring back up at them. They see that they are not valued in whole, but only in part for their ability to deliver the goods society deems desirable. For them, the ugly duckling story is all too real.

The distinguishing marks of exceptional intelligence appear undesirable and excessive when one views oneself in only one pond, society's norm-pool. As with the unexpected swan in Hans Christian Andersen's story, when traits of high potential are mislabeled as deformity, the image of the beautiful swan is sometimes lost forever in the muck of misidentification.

Yet confusion, self-doubt, and alienation are not where the story ends. A second reading reveals another tale, a reflection that ultimately uncovers the master key of liberation. For it is not until the ugly-duckling-turned-swan has an epiphany that he reveals the truth of character to himself and reclaims his missing identity. It is in this visionary instant, when the upside-down "facts" of the past are turned right side up, that the very soul and destiny of the swan are set free.

Like the swan, Everyday Geniuses must search out the truth of who they are before they can take their intended place in the universe. For the multitude of individuals whose future is blueprinted with high potential, gifts of intellect, and creative achievement, three prime pieces of information are nearly always missing—three facts that when left uncorrected warp individuality and keep accomplishment tied to a short leash. However, a revised identity picture has the power to change everything—to turn pipe dreams into reality, and mediocrity into excellence.

Liberation is possible only when we accept these three things:

1. Everyday Genius is accompanied by a specific set of personality traits and inner processes. High potential and intelligence are not just about being "more" of something, but rather about an altogether different manner of thinking and experiencing.
2. The mislabeled "excesses" of Everyday Genius are actually *assets*—the very cornerstones of excellence, leadership, and revolutionary contributions to the universal good.
3. To fulfill the promise of high potential, the Everyday Genius must

learn to master the delicate balance between "could" and "must" with strategies to avoid physical and mental burnout and spiritual bankruptcy.

In the bigger picture, each Everyday Genius must confront the forces of conformity. Society has always had its own agenda for those who exhibit the idiosyncrasies that come with swan potential, and that is to shape them into ducks. Because this is so, the identified Everyday Genius is the only one who can reveal the qualities and gifts of the swan. The quest begins by taking a second look into an undistorted pond and reevaluating what we see there.

Everyday Geniuses look like birds of a different feather, as indeed they are. But like the swan, they have the right to know the truth of their identity—that their characteristics are not destructive liabilities but powerful assets—and how to manage their lives to dodge the pitfalls that often accompany high potential, so that their talents may finally be realized.

The right to know is imperative.

HOW DID THE SWAN GET LOST?

How did our metaphorical swan's identity get lost in a duck yard in the first place? One of the most common ways to get lost is to become entangled in the IQ game. Confusion about what's smart and what's not overshadows the entire domain of intelligence. In fact, of all the truly gifted people who have entered my office, *not one* has easily embraced the idea of being gifted or distinctively intelligent. They have been so programmed to disavow their own abilities that it usually takes several sessions before they dare accept the possibility of a swan's life.

It's always the proverbial "others" who are truly gifted, of this they are certain. Because giftedness always entails vulnerability, to submit to obsolete beliefs is to bargain for little more than a life filled with frustration. Without being exposed to the truths of who they are and why they are just the way they are, the swan will never fly free.

4

LOST IN THE IQ GAME

Now intelligence seemed quantifiable. You could measure someone's
actual or potential height, and now, it seemed, you could also measure
someone's actual or potential intelligence. We had one dimension of
mental ability along which we could array everyone. . . . The whole
concept has to be challenged; in fact, it has to be replaced.

—Howard Gardner

Certain abbreviations, such as FBI and IRS, have the power to make
the hair on the back of our neck stand on end. Another abbreviation
that sets the knees to shaking and furrows the brow with instant
self-doubt is IQ. Getting caught up in the entanglements of the IQ game
is one sure way to stifle the early promises of Everyday Genius. Perhaps as nothing else, IQ, a number *presumed* to sum up and rank the
limits of individual intelligence, strikes fear in the heart of all but the
superconfident—not surprising, considering that we live in a society that
reveres IQ, along with grade point averages, achievement awards, athletic prowess, wealth, and physical beauty.

In general, we have come to think of a global IQ of 100 as average,
and anything above 125 as indicating superior to very superior intellectual ability. But the sweeping generalizations drawn by the average person can be far from helpful, even when the scores are high. In an issue of
Harvard Magazine, Denison Andrews wrote about his internal reaction to
learning from his former elementary school principal that his IQ had
measured "only 125":

Keep cool . . . Control wobbly knees . . . 125. Not brilliant . . . Every-day bright like everyone else . . . No brighter than my stockbroker . . . No brighter than my insurance agent . . . Totally discredited . . . No one takes it seriously . . . I test badly . . . Maybe I was depressed . . . A bad night's sleep . . .[1]

WHAT'S SMART AND WHAT'S NOT?

Despite widespread misunderstandings about IQ, overemphasis on test scores persists. I have long been puzzled by the power of IQ beliefs. Hardly anyone I know, gifted or not, was ever formally evaluated for special abilities. Most people confuse achievement with inborn aptitude. We tend to mistake scores on group tests that measure school learning, such as the Iowa Test of Basic Skills, for a comprehensive readout of individual potential.

Regardless, most of us carry around a hazy yet fixed idea of where we stand in terms of IQ. Each of us bears a private sense of our mental ability that governs our self-concept. One way or another we have made a decision about our intelligence that awards us a gleaming badge of honor that fills us with pride, or a satchel of regret that bogs us down with shame and self-doubt.

As time passes, assumptions about our intelligence become embedded in our psyches and we script our lives accordingly. Whatever our conclusions about intelligence, they tend to function as an internal holy writ, sacrosanct and undisturbed for a lifetime. Rarely do we question our trust in IQ as a sound basis for making important life decisions. It is the invisible gauge we use to determine how to establish standards and how high to set the bar. In fact, we can go so far as to equate IQ with our very self-worth. Then we mix into the "How smart am I?" formula a personal history of external evaluations: how well we did in school, how we were judged by authority figures, how closely we fit the desired mold of acceptability, and what was expected of us as determined by our gender, race, and class.

The original agenda of the intelligence measurement movement was not to create a hierarchy of social value. It was far from that. In the mid-1800s English scientist Sir Francis Galton (Charles Darwin's cousin) attempted to quantify such qualities as "even-temperedness," female beauty, reaction time, and intellectual "strength."

Later, French psychologist Alfred Binet and his colleague Théodore Simon were commissioned by their government to develop tests that would reduce bias in the evaluation of schoolchildren's potential for learning. Together they identified test items that could predict how some children would perform in school. Yet Binet firmly declared his test was not to be taken as a measure of inborn ability. Rather, it was intended only to identify and help students in need of special educational attention.

How, then, did we arrive at today's powerful, though limited, concept of intelligence? IQ as we have now come to understand it had its origins in the U.S. military. Prior to World War I, a Stanford University professor, Lewis Terman, revised Binet's test, producing the Stanford-Binet, in an effort to measure children's abilities for "vocational fitness." For these tests, a German psychologist coined the term "intelligence quotient," which was simply a person's test-derived "mental age" divided by his or her chronological age. Though intelligence "quotient" is now a misnomer, IQ has come to mean "intelligence test scores" in common parlance.

Terman went on to assist the U.S. government in developing new tests to evaluate the two million new recruits that overwhelmed the army at the onset of the First World War. Since the military needed a fast, low-cost method, individual testing was out of the question. Inductees were given the Army Alpha test in groups, the first paper-and-pencil intelligence test designed to assess aptitude for specific military skills.

Binet was later horrified to discover that a handful of unethical psychologists were using skewed adaptations of his tests with immigrants to support claims of "inferiority" and ethnicity-based "feeblemindedness." His efforts to measure intelligence, once grounded in humanistic service, had been repackaged to be used as an agent of oppression.

WHAT IS IQ, REALLY?

Fortunately, great strides have been made since then in both the ethics and efficacy of intelligence tests to guard against their misuse. At present a battery of tests or at least a valid and reliable standardized measure— such as the Wechsler Intelligence Scales—is required to establish a credible IQ. Tests are given one-on-one and interpreted individually by a qualified professional psychologist. According to Alan S. Kaufman, a highly respected expert in intelligence measurement, the emotionally laden concept of IQ rests on certain assumptions frequently overlooked:

- "The focus of any assessment is the PERSON being assessed, not the test. . . . The content of the responses and the person's style of responding to various types of tasks can be more important as a determiner of developmental level and intellectual maturity than the scores assigned."
- The goal of any examiner is to be "a shrewd detective to uncover test interpretations that are truly individual."
- The IQ test, like the SAT, assesses past learning or "developed abilities" like an achievement test. It is not a simple test of aptitude.
- The overall IQ score "does not equal a person's total capacity for intellectual accomplishment."
- "Intelligence tests are best used to generate hypotheses of potential HELP to the person . . . not to label or categorize."[2]

Everyday Geniuses often do not display the stereotypical model of intelligence. They are not always top-of-the-class conventional types who are verbally savvy, self-assured, and teacher-endorsed. They may fail to supply "evidence" of high potential. Thus they may not be recommended for special programs, if indeed there are any. The undeveloped potential of those with learning disabilities, physical impairments, and cultural disadvantage has little to no chance of being recognized or guided.

Sometimes testing can be a more objective identification method than teacher or parent recommendations. Nevertheless, when probing for "giftedness" with intelligence tests, caution remains the byword. Most professionals agree that because intelligence tests measure a single aspect of giftedness—academic giftedness—they misrepresent the dynamic and intricate fundamentals of exceptional ability. And all test scores, even those from the most reliable and valid instruments, are never free from measurement error.

People must always make decisions about test results; test scores must never be allowed to speak for themselves. Fundamentally, intelligence tests should never be used as the sole criterion for determining giftedness. Specialized tests designed to measure creativity and higher-level thinking can be more useful than traditional IQ tests, though they are rarely given. Yet in every case, test results are intended to be analyzed to form strategies to meet educational, career, psychological, and relationship needs. In brief, IQ tests measure *learned* ability, not *potential* ability. At best, they are keys that open particular doors of understanding, and must never be used to lock the door of possibility.

Unfortunately, in our current educational system, individual IQ tests are rarely given. Current tests largely ignore any measure of creative thinking and avoid any comprehensive measure of intelligence. Group achievement testing is commonly used while individual assessment of ability is rare. The types of tests generally given are for purposes of determining subject-matter mastery versus aptitude. Perhaps this is why skewed concepts about intelligence such as those offered in Herrnstein and Murray's *The Bell Curve* can lead people astray by pandering to our ignorance and our prejudices.

BEYOND OUTDATED IQ

The intention behind most measures of intelligence is essentially honorable. Conventional intelligence tests can be occasionally helpful for some people in that they provide a snapshot of information about a limited aspect of human cognition: the linguistic and logical aspects of intelligence. Psychometric testing has indeed provided us with a great deal of information that can be useful as part of a selection process in situations that call for an assessment of specific skills and abilities, such as entrance to medical or law school. However, it is always unwise and unfair to overinterpret test results and label individuals. Luckily, several new and more comprehensive theories of intelligence have emerged in recent years.

In 1983 American psychologist Howard Gardner proposed a theory of "multiple intelligences," asserting there is no such thing as singular intelligence. Gardner argues that earlier measures of intelligence disregarded vital faculties that greatly impact everyday life. He suggests intelligence is many-sided and has identified eight "domains" of intelligence.

> *Linguistic intelligence:* A proficient and easy use of words and sensitivity to phrasing and the rhythm of language in poetry, song lyrics, and persuasive speaking, as with poet Walt Whitman, Nobel laureate Toni Morrison, musical wordsmith Bob Dylan, evangelist Billy Graham, and congressional orator Barbara Jordan
>
> *Musical intelligence:* A special sensitivity to tempo, pitch, timbre, and tone, and an ability to create and express musical arrange-

ments that correspond to emotional experience, as in great composers, singers, and musicians such as conductor Arturo Toscanini, violinist Jascha Heifetz, legendary jazz composer Duke Ellington, and operatic diva Maria Callas

Logical-mathematical intelligence: Powers of inductive and deductive reasoning in handling abstract relationship and predictions based on numbers and equations, so obvious in eminent economist John Kenneth Galbraith, the Harvard professor who administered the system of price controls during World War II; physicist Robert Goddard, father of modern space rocketry; statistician George Gallup, whose polls quantified public opinion; Arno Penzias, the Nobel laureate who confirmed the fabled big-bang theory of creation and pioneered new computer logic; and Lise Meitner, who coined the term "atomic fission" and solved extraordinary mathematical puzzles in her 1930s experiments with barium emission

Spatial intelligence: The ability to visualize objects in the mind and transfer the information to something concrete, such as designing an airplane or laying out a movie set, as visible in phenoms such as Walt Disney; William Mulholland, the self-taught engineer whose photographic memory and "ditchdigger" genius developed the Los Angeles aqueduct system in the early 1900s; Howard Roark, the architect character in Ayn Rand's *The Fountainhead;* and painter and sculptor Pablo Picasso

Bodily (kinesthetic) intelligence: Exceptional body control and refined motion that permits skillful expression of ideas and feelings through movement, as with Martha Graham's poignant choreography and dance, Michael Jordan's superstar athleticism, and the classic slapstick antics of Charlie Chaplin

Interpersonal intelligence: Advanced understanding of human relations and management of feelings, as in the revolutionary insights of Carl Jung, Clara Barton, Eleanor Roosevelt, Nobel laureate Martin Luther King Jr., and Mourning Dove, who possessed the spirit to chronicle her people's honored traditions both as a folklorist and novelist

Intrapersonal intelligence: A sharp understanding of one's inner landscape, motivations, emotions, needs, and goals, as with Herman Hesse, Sigmund Freud, Mahatma Gandhi, Thomas Merton, and Ingmar Bergman

Naturalist intelligence: A special ability to grasp the intricate work-
ings and relationships within nature; an instinctive reverence for
a connection with animals, plants, minerals, ocean, sky, desert,
and mountain, as in Henry David Thoreau; John Muir, founder of
the Sierra Club, who at age sixty-eight began a campaign to preserve the Yosemite Valley; and Isak Dinesen, whose years as a
farmer on an East African highlands coffee plantation inspired
her to write her celebrated memoir *Out of Africa*

From this standpoint, hip-hop kids might be perceived as masters of
musical, linguistic, and kinesthetic intelligences. The effective TV interviewer could be said to excel in linguistic and interpersonal intelligences.
Members of Greenpeace who successfully activate their conscience and
persuade the powers that be to pay attention to environmental problems
by allocating funds and changing laws probably have unusual strengths in
naturalist, interpersonal, and linguistic intelligence. The Everyday Genius
may wear several hats at once and, for example, envision, obtain financial backing for, and direct an outdoor community dance theater by com-
bining all eight intelligences.

Gardner's concept promotes the identification and development of
domains of potential excellence and high performance. Though he is
mindful of test misuses, ethnocentricity, and cultural bias, and so is not a
proponent of testing and labeling, he aims for universality. We can benefit from identifying abilities according to Gardner's domains, but not by
labeling, ranking, and tussling about who has what and which domain is
more or less valuable. What we need to do is mindfully consider and
build upon given talents, cultivate skills that are necessary but in which
we are deficient, track our progress, and unveil avenues of growth that
may bolster satisfaction and achievement.

Harvard professor Daniel Goleman finds our traditional view of
human intelligence incomplete, especially because in his estimation,
"IQ is only one of many abilities that determine success or failure in our
private or emotional lives." Moreover, he asserts, "IQ offers little to explain the different destinies of people." Goleman offers a persuasive ra-
tionale for the concept of emotional intelligence, an ability to manage five
domains of emotion in ways that enhance intellectual ability and contribute to both mental and emotional acuity.

Goleman zeroes in on essential factors that lead to being, in his
words, "more fully human," claiming emotionally intelligent people have

a "life that is rich, but appropriate; they are comfortable with themselves, others, and the social universe they live in." This, he proposes, is the result of an artful blending of self-awareness, sensitivity, and people skills with basic cognitive ability.

In *Successful Intelligence,* Robert Sternberg of Yale University writes about the "kind of intelligence used to achieve important goals." He too thought conventional ideas of intelligence were too narrow, but Sternberg argues Gardner's multiple domains really amount to distinct "talents" rather than forms of intelligence. Sternberg's concept of intelligence contains three interdependent components of experience: internal (core thought), external (application of thought in the everyday world), and a mediating combination of the two (coping successfully with new situations). His theory suggests a highly intelligent person is one who capitalizes on personal strengths and compensates for weaknesses, eventually finding a niche in which to perform optimally.

THE UNEXPECTED GIFTED ADULT

The quest to quantify or categorize intelligence has come a long way. Yet even the best measures of ability barely scratch the surface of what it means to be an Everyday Genius. The typical gifted person has never been accurately tested, has no factual information about the nature of giftedness over the life span, and has determined what's right and wrong about her or his personality from behind a smoke screen. Because of sweeping stereotypes, such people are faced with a socially inherited reluctance to acknowledge and invest in their special gifts.

Faulty images of the gifted have been around for centuries, culturally defined as truths. This makes it nearly impossible for us to value and honor our own characteristics without also signing up for a set of very negative associated traits. Those who have never been given insider information on what it means to be gifted are also harmed by society's judgments. Even if such individuals never acknowledge their membership in the gifted ranks, they are at risk because at an unconscious level they know the criticisms are aimed at them.

Gifted children do grow up—they just don't see themselves as gifted. Unidentified gifted adults enter my office like other first-time psychotherapy clients: a bit wary, not quite sure they want to be there, yet in need of understanding and a new perspective of themselves. Little by little their problems come to the surface, laid bare against a backdrop of individual quirks, dreams, regrets, fears, and wounds. But at no point does the new client use the word *gifted*.

MISTAKEN IDENTITIES
BY THE MILLIONS

As we have seen, we have been indoctrinated with the notion that a single IQ number, such as 109, 123, or 145, is a true indicator of ability from which we can determine the limits of our potential, including giftedness. However, we now know that a single IQ rating (1) does not validly describe the intelligence of many individuals, (2) is a finite measure of performance that can change over time, (3) cannot claim to measure the multifaceted factors of ability proposed by current research on intelligence, (4) all but ignores creativity and other specialized aspects of human potential. Giftedness is far more complex than just more intellectual capacity, which means we must look anew for the Everyday Genius in our daily lives and unexpectedly in ourselves.

Contrary to popular opinion, gifted adults are many in number. And because this is so, the most crucial aspects of such individuals' character, their intellectual and emotional intensities, are mistaken for something else; hence there are mistaken identities by the millions. Instead of being viewed as exceptionally aware, insightful, and responsive, gifted people naturally exhibit traits that are considered excessive. It is no wonder that gifted adults are ignored or misinterpreted when we have not met the needs of society's gifted children.

Perhaps it will help to look at early observable traits that distinguish the bright child from the gifted child:

Bright Child	*Gifted Child*
Knows the answers	Asks the questions
Interested	Extremely curious
Pays attention	Gets involved physically and mentally
Works hard	Plays around, still gets good test scores
Answers questions	Questions the answers
Enjoys same-age peers	Prefers adults or older children
Good at memorization	Good at guessing
Learns easily	Bored. Already knew the answers
Listens well	Shows strong feelings and opinions
Self-satisfied	Highly critical of self (perfectionistic)[3]

The Council for Exceptional Children makes a good point regarding the elusive nature of giftedness and inaccurate perceptions about how it relates to IQ: "We recommend that you do not become bogged down in probing into the concept of intelligence. Its intricacies and mysteries are fascinating, but it must not become a convenient synonym for giftedness." In two recent articles in the *Monitor,* an official publication of the American Psychological Association, entitled "Searching for Intelligence Beyond *g*" and "'Gifted' Label Stretches, It's More than High IQ," staff writer Beth Azar reports:

> Doogie Howser and Little Man Tate are modern-day media images of "gifted" children: super-smart kids who enter accelerated programs and go to college before their peers can form complex sentences. . . . Academic achievement remains the primary yardstick for determining which children are gifted, but the definition is beginning to expand.[4] . . .
>
> For hundreds of years, cultures have distinguished between smart and not-so-smart people, judging their success and failures, general knowledge and abilities to interact socially. In the last 100 years, psychologists have tried to make the concept of intelligence more objective. Their efforts spawned the theory of general intelligence—or "g"—and the design of tests, such as IQ measures, to quantify g.
>
> Many intelligence researchers consider g to be the cornerstone of intelligence. . . But a growing number of researchers reject the view that intelligence revolves around g. Although they agree that IQ represents an aspect of intelligence, they disagree that it's the tell-all of intellectual capacity. Basing an evaluation of intelligence on IQ alone will greatly underestimate a person's potential.[5]

Even by narrowly focused IQ-type measurement standards, *more than 5 percent of the adult population in this country would be termed "gifted."* When we broaden the definition of giftedness and intelligence to include specialized exceptional traits (for example, spatial or linguistic ability, mathematical reasoning, memory), as current research recommends, it seems obvious that there are many more gifted adults than previously believed. According to the director of the National Research Center for the Gifted at the University of Connecticut, Joseph Renzulli, those who fall into the category of "superior ability" are more likely twice that number: "As a general estimate it is safe to assume that 10 percent of the adult population, by any set of psychometric criteria, can be considered gifted."

This means that the total number of unidentified gifted adults in the United States amounts to approximately twenty million individuals. Furthermore, it can reasonably be assumed the greater portion of them have never been identified as gifted and have no idea how deeply that lack of information affects their lives and well-being.

THE EVERYDAY GENIUS NEXT DOOR

Everyday Geniuses are the people you and I know, but don't really know in total. They are the ones we have always known as bright and inventive, or have viewed as "odd ducks." They are like Amelia, Ethan, and Susan, unidentified Everyday Geniuses compelled by an inner force to search for their true identity.

Amelia

The very first label Amelia acquired was "Little Miss Perfect." By the time Amelia was eight she had been named "Miss Oh-So-Special" and "The Great A.R." (short for "anal retentive"). Despite the criticism, she took great pride in rearranging her dolls, games, stuffed animals, and furniture to make her blue and white room "just so." She did this repeatedly whenever the mood struck her. One day when she was quite bored she noticed the books on her shelf; they clearly had "too many different colors" on their spines to fit in with her decor. So she set about the business of covering each of them in white and blue construction paper.

Over the years, Amelia often heard friends say things like, "Well, Amelia, I can see where some people might not like to be around you. You're just so nice, smart, accomplished, and enthusiastic. It's really kind of sickening, you know?" Amelia often thought intelligence should come with a built-in suit of emotional armor.

Twenty years later Amelia had successfully completed medical school and was packing to relocate for her surgery training. Sorting through her many books, she thought back to her childhood room of blue and white. She good-naturedly laughed at herself when she told her fiancé about the construction paper incident: "What a little nitpicker I was. No wonder everybody made fun of me. It's a wonder I turned out okay at all!" Amelia had no inkling that her early exactitude, which seemed so silly, was in fact prophetic: She was destined to become a surgeon of exceptional skill and uncompromising standards. And what patient would have wanted it any other way?

Ethan

Ethan rarely became noticeably angry. For the most part, he was a man who had grown gracefully into his mid-fifties. In truth, he was generally a happy sort of guy. However, when he came to grips with his gifted self, he was finally able to express outwardly his inner frustration:

"Nobody has any idea just how much I hold back! It's there, just under the surface; the irritation. Oh, I'm skilled enough to keep it in check. But that doesn't mean it's gone. People who know me would be floored if they knew what was going on in my head all the time. I guess I've needed to say this to someone for a long time. I have no intention of ever telling this to anyone outside these four walls.

"It's just this: When others gripe at me to slow down, I want to say: 'Why don't you speed it up?' In meetings when we keep covering the same ground repeatedly, like we're in a fixed orbit, I want to stand up and shout, 'Doesn't anyone in this room have anything new to say? Can't we look at this from a different direction?' I get tired of being the person to conjure up the larger vision, lay it all out for everyone. When I suggest a new set of objectives to make the vision concrete, all I hear is a lot of hesitation from the doubting Thomases who fight any forward progress. Worse yet, inevitably one of them introduces the same idea six months later as if it were brand-new."

Susan

When Susan was seven her mother reluctantly agreed to have her tested by a school psychologist because she was thought to be gifted. As it turned out, Susan's basic IQ was very high, showing great promise, especially in the areas of math and science. She loved to experiment with everything from kitchen chemicals to bird feathers to measuring the wind. However, Susan was raised during a time when math and science were the domain of boys, not nice girls like her.

Like many girls, Susan was taught to demonstrate impenetrable ignorance. She was told to never be dramatic, never appear "*too* smart." Though at the time she didn't understand precisely what that meant, the young woman saw it modeled by her parents, who firmly believed unassertive conformity was the best route for a girl. Because of this, her mother told her nothing about her test results because she didn't want Susan to develop a "big head."

Susan, at thirty-seven, struggled with what might be called the "little-head syndrome," the overcompliant and self-deprecating attitudes that often appear in gifted women. She was so afraid of stepping on any-one's toes that she hardly spoke above a whisper, her sentences often trailing off.

While reflecting on her indecisiveness, Susan discovered her counterfeit self: "At eleven I dreamed of becoming a research scientist, finding a cure for breast cancer or diabetes. But that's not what I did. And you know why? Because at thirteen I said to hell with science and math and my IQ! I decided not being cute and popular were life-threatening is-sues. In the wink of an eye I would have sold the devil thirty IQ points just to be the most well-liked, sought-after girl in school. Can you believe it?" I hear stories like these over and over in my office. The details may change, but the theme remains the same: individuals struggling within the confinement of societal expectation, imprisoned by self-doubt, and shackled by their misidentification.

If gifted adults are so great in number, what must be done to liberate them? What must we learn about the personality and the psyche of gift-edness so that we may unleash the fertile mind and translate gifts into real-life achievements? To look and decide for ourselves is our way, and so we must embark upon the discovery trail, to seek the truth even when we are weighed down with doubt and fear.

5

STANDING WHAT YOU "KNOW"
ON ITS HEAD

Until you are willing to be confused about what you already know,
what you know will never grow bigger, better, or more useful.
— Milton Erickson

Revised concepts of intelligence such as those of Gardner, Goleman, and Sternberg take an important step forward by redefining what aptitude means in today's world. Their innovative perspectives help us debunk stereotypical ideas about individual ability that have traditionally been as oppressive as they are incomplete. These stereotypes don't adequately reflect the full spectrum of giftedness, nor do they offer insight into the personality, inner experience, or coping strategies essential to the gifted adult.

THE EVERYDAY GENIUS MIND:
THE SAME *AND* DIFFERENT

Since early childhood, we are trained to categorize and label. In preschool we memorize basic opposites: on/off, up/down, in/out, over/under, good/bad. This process teaches us how to compare and contrast by using all-or-nothing methods of evaluation. Something either is or isn't. It is a mental process that has its uses, to be sure. By thinking in terms of opposites we can determine the boundaries of a range, such as "here" versus "there." We can quickly sum up and make decisions by sifting through learned classifications in nanoseconds.

Classification is the way human beings order their thinking to efficiently assimilate sensory input from the external world. Our minds have a resident librarian that allows us to look, hear, and store data, then offers relevant categories from previously learned information. We need this quick-sort ability to evaluate and choose what things in our environment to attend to and what to ignore.

For instance, when driving by a metal box on a stick near the curb it would be absurd to do anything more than to see it, note it, classify it as a mailbox, and forget it. If we paid any greater attention to such trivialities, our mental files would quickly become overburdened. To avoid stimulation overload, the human brain generally requires seven or more repetitions to store away something new in long-term memory. Like a seasoned trout fisherman, this "catch and release" selection process permits our minds to focus on important matters without endless distractions.

The mind of the Everyday Genius is the same as everyone else's— *and* it is different. Interestingly, a critical distinction occurs in the genius mind when complex thinking becomes more than simply tagging an observation and discarding it once a label has been assigned. The minds of advanced thinkers normally resist too much conscious control over ideas, which is why highly creative thinkers seem changeable or inconsistent. These advanced thinkers are unwilling to hold to any rigid perspective because the genius mind must seek new combinations. In a sense, their mental librarian knows that there are multiple ways to classify a piece of data. This pursuit of innovation means that such individuals not only tolerate ambiguities, but even prefer double meanings and puzzling complexity over predictability. Nearly all Everyday Geniuses love to confront the maze of life's labyrinths, weblike predicaments, and brain-twisting riddles.

Geniuses intuitively know that there is an interconnectedness in all things, frequently concluding that what is pleasantly puzzling now is almost always relevant at a later date. They use more of the vast areas of the human brain that are uncommitted to survival and repetitive thought process, seeking new connections between things they have learned before. The process that bridges the gap between two seemingly foreign points, which to all ordinary appearances is a waste of time, works like a mental spark for them. The genius mind knows it is the "empty space" between two endpoints where the spark of innovative energy is ignited.

Everyday Geniuses often force connections. In his efforts to produce the telegraph, Samuel Morse struggled to find a way to make the signal powerful enough to transmit over long distances. He needed some way to link the signals in a consistent manner. When Morse spotted a pair of horses being changed at a relay station, he imaginatively created a connection between the horses and his signal. By forcing the two relationships like a square-peg-round-hole puzzle, Morse came up with the idea to periodically boost the power to his traveling signal, conquering the last major obstacle to completing his invention.[1]

Dedication to connectivity is central to advanced thinking. Innovation is made possible by a suspension of judgment, a willingness to forgo easy classification, and an ability to let ideas exist as they please, for the most original ideas possess an autonomy all their own. At "rest," the mind is free to explore ideas both consciously and subconsciously. Geniuses cherish the merging of idea fragments and the challenge of uncovering surprising junction points between apparent opposites.

Michael Michalko, author of *Cracking Creativity: The Secrets of Creative Geniuses,* explains the genius' ability to "subvert habituation by actively seeking alternative ways to look at things and alternative ways to think about them" As Michalko describes:

> Physicist Niels Bohr believed that if you held opposites together, then you suspend your thought and your mind moves to a new level. The suspension of thought allows an intelligence beyond thought to act and create a new form. The swirling of opposites creates the conditions for a new point of view to bubble freely from your mind. Bohr's ability to imagine light as both a particle and a wave led to his conception of the principle of complementarity. Thomas Edison's invention of a practical system of lighting involved combining wiring in parallel circuits with high resistance filaments in his bulbs—two things that were not considered possible by conventional thinkers.[2]

The genius mind does not simply replicate solutions to problems, but instead looks for the most promising ways of viewing them from new angles, reconceptualizing the problem itself in many ways. It is prone to depart from the known in favor of variation, for variation is fundamental to evolutionary progress. Without it adaptation and creativity would ultimately flounder, because at the heart of Everyday Genius is a devotion to fresh ideas and a commitment to resourcefulness. In fact, they are a hand-in-glove operation. To think in terms of words, numbers, spatial relationships, *and* visual images is more productive than relying on any one faculty to the exclusion of others. The genius mind works by looking, researching, looking some more, pulling up stored material from experience, and then doodling, drawing, charting, or diagramming. Words and equations alone are fine for textbooks that reiterate the tried and true but are insufficient for the creative genius.

Famed film and theater costume designer Ann Roth is guided in her work by a commitment to realism, insisting on historical accuracy. She is reported to have become upset when she noticed the use of shoulder pads in the costumes of *Gone With the Wind* since it emphasized Hollywood taste over period correctness. Roth has successfully combined fastidiousness with a creatively visual technique over her illustrious career, which has spanned nearly forty years.

> When Roth takes on a costuming job, the first thing she does is to spend up to several weeks researching the period and milieu. A first stop is often at what might be called her creative home, the Costume Depot, in New York City, which she shares with six other designers. . . . It is packed with everything from vintage Chanel pumps to men's suits, and also includes a sizable library of books on modern and period clothing. Roth also checks out photo and historical archives when necessary. For a contemporary piece, her most important research is done on the street. Roth and her assistant of many years, Gary Jones, made several trips on the Staten Island ferry to come up with the looks seen on Melanie Griffith and Joan Cusack in "Working Girl." . . . When she feels she has done enough research, Roth begins to develop a vision of the look and feel of the project as a whole. She starts making sketches for characters and entire scenes. This is a crucial part of the process for Roth. . . . Although she has several more-than-capable assistants, she always does the fittings herself. Roth's persistence and high standards have paid off. She knows that when she finds the perfect clothes, a character really jumps off the screen. . . . It is such dedication to quality that has made Roth one of the most sought-after costume designers in Hollywood. While she can almost have her pick of films, she announced in 1994 that she would be willing to reduce her fee for projects that challenged her creativity.[3]

The prudent genius befriends chance. "Accidents" and "failures" are often the predecessors of insight and discovery. For instance, Jerry Yang and David Filo shared an office during the early 1990s at Stanford University, where they spent countless hours playing on the Web, which was then in its infancy. Frustrated by the inability to recall Web site addresses, the pair decided it would be useful to put together a listing of their favorites. In 1994 they posted their list online as "David and Jerry's

Guide to the World Wide Web" so others could also access "cool" sites. Their chance relationship, mutual interest, and disillusionment with the status quo led to the birth of Yahoo!, an online search engine now valued at more than $500 million.[4]

Perhaps the most important characteristic of genius is the distinction between being *creative* and becoming a *creative producer*. Everyday Geniuses work at the things they love with results. They write, choreograph, build, test, and draft many more creative products than their less driven contemporaries. They do so because they must! It's as if every inventive product is like an uncontrollable sneeze; it cannot be denied its moment. For the titans of science and music and art, such as Edison, Mozart, and Leonardo da Vinci, it was standard procedure to generate thousands of creative works. Even for the paragons of genius, many fits and starts are required for something consequential to make its way into the world. Though the end product may make it seem otherwise, excellence never comes easily.

It's not enough to be academically proficient. It's not enough to be artistic or skillful. And it's not enough to be intelligent. Michael Michalko cautions us to reconsider our ideas of genius:

> For years, scholars and researchers tried to study genius by analyzing statistics, as if piles of data somehow illuminate genius. In his 1904 study of genius, Havelock Ellis noted that most geniuses are fathered by men older than 30, had mothers younger than 25, and usually were sickly as children. Other scholars reported that many were celibate (Descartes), others were fatherless (Dickens) or motherless (Darwin). In the end, the piles of data illuminated nothing.
>
> Academics also tried to measure the links between intelligence and genius. But intelligence is not enough. Run-of-the-mill physicists have IQs much higher than Nobel Prize–winner Richard Feynman, widely acclaimed for his extraordinary genius, whose IQ was a merely respectable 122.
>
> Genius is not about scoring 1600 on the Scholastic Aptitude Test, mastering 14 languages at the age of seven, finishing Mensa exercises in record time, having an extraordinarily high IQ, or even being smart. . . . Too many people fail to answer opportunity's knock at the door because they have to finish some preconceived plan. Creative geniuses do not wait for the gifts of chance; instead they actively seek the accidental discovery.[5]

HOW "DIFFERENT" BECOMES "WRONG"

As humanity heats up its love affair with speed and information, turning technojargon into sound-bite speech, our categorical thinking is easily sidetracked from open-minded genius reasoning into faulty labeling. Fast judgments can all too easily act as springboards for irrational fault-finding, intolerance, sexism, and racism. Hasty categorizing is simplistic, and ironically it is often the Everyday Genius who takes the hit. The idio-syncrasies of giftedness are rarely seen as "different = interesting," but instead are deemed "different = wrong."

In many ways, commonplace ratings such as "normal/abnormal" and "acceptable/unacceptable" hamper the gifted person who requires not either/or dichotomies but an accepting, both/and type of environment in order to thrive. Everyday Geniuses are, and need to be, different *and* common, proficient *and* imperfect, seasoned experts *and* novice learners, autonomous *and* dependent, self-sufficient *and* needy. Yet an atmosphere that accommodates the gifted both/and personality is very difficult to attain.

Nearly every gifted person bears some scar of ridicule from having introduced a new idea, being considered weird or rebellious, or simply being ignored because of their striking differences. In fact, gifted people are more vulnerable than their contemporaries because they frequently work and live in isolation from their own kind, experiencing everyday life outside the bounds of their true peer group.

Today the most common problem for the gifted child continues to be rooted in ineffective labeling. Like many controversial topics, in today's culture talk of giftedness always brings on a rash of heated debates: "Does advanced ability deserve the same investment of time, money, and attention as disability?" "Does someone with different ways of thinking and quick understanding require special attention and support?"

If we dare to look underneath worn-out ideas about higher intelli-gence, we may find something hidden under the rug that exposes why the debates are so fierce. Would we find jealousy, envy, or rivalrous ill will? Might we uncover ignorance, confusion, narrow-mindedness, or bigotry? Can we reach a new degree of honesty by admitting that everyone tends to feel better when no one stands out as being too different?

Are we dealing with a contradiction in society's thinking, attempting to strike a balance by making everyone the same because we falsely equate *sameness* with *democracy?* What, then, happens to the rights and liberties of those who fall outside the "normal curve," those who cannot redesign themselves as "average" no matter how hard they may try?

GIFTED NEEDS

Whether or not we can accept the fact that gifted individuals have real needs, the narrow classification niche for gifted children offered by traditional education is just as off the mark as it is for children who are developmentally delayed. How, then, could it be reasonable to offer identical programs and learning methods for everyone? Above all, doesn't every child deserve the opportunity to fulfill her or his potential to its utmost?

The controversies over opportunities for the gifted are still debated passionately. They continue because as a society we refuse to acknowledge that for the gifted, giftedness is the core of their identity, the axis around which well-being, achievement, career, and relationships must be built.

Errors of omission and curricular foot-dragging are justified by a shortsighted misconception that nourishing individuals' talents and abilities with specially designed opportunities is tantamount to favoritism. Limited thinking of this kind sustains itself by cries of unfairness. After all, if the gifted are unrecognized or determined to have no special needs, no money need be spent on their account and no curriculum changes need be implemented to safeguard their development.

Only a tiny percentage of America's school systems have established formal procedures to identify gifted children and adolescents, with many of those relying on faulty and/or narrow assessment methods. Of a total U.S. enrollment in grades K–12 in 1996 (41,621,000), only 6.4 percent were actually assigned to special programs for the gifted and talented. According to Rodney Pelton, former Gifted Coordinator for the National Council for Exceptional Children: "The real number of gifted youngsters may be half again as large because of inadequate identification procedures and the great number of school districts lacking any type of services for the gifted."

Of the academic institutions with protocols in place to identify gifted students, only a few translate their findings into beneficial programming. Fully developed curricula for the gifted that are comprehensive, well-planned, and effective are a rare commodity. More widespread is the practice of throwing the gifted a bone in the form of "pull-out" hours, when students leave the regular classroom to go down the hall to an enrichment activity such as a discussion or to work on "advanced" projects, usually of the teacher's choosing. What this amounts to is mostly fits and starts of advanced busywork. This means gifted students everywhere are chomping at the bit with untapped energy.

Far too many of the existing programs for gifted children cater only to high achievers who fit the conventional model of education. Those with high potential who cannot redesign themselves to walk the fine line of the traditional educational system's requirements are at a loss. As one might imagine, an ill-conceived education can easily destroy self-esteem and motivation in any student, gifted or otherwise, though the gifted person most often blames him- or herself to a greater degree for a perceived failure to measure up. In every case of lack of attention and resources, the budding Everyday Genius is left holding the bag, a bag full of holes that drains away the likelihood of self-fulfillment and success.

THE DESTINY QUESTION:
DISOWN OR DELIVER?

The common assumption that high achievers are gifted while underachievers are not is a real obstacle not only for gifted students, but for gifted adults as well. Given the lack of advancement in identification, acceptance, and education of the gifted, it is no wonder exceptional adults almost always cringe at the mention of the word *gifted*. When I first broach the subject of unidentified giftedness with my clients, many react with a heated disclaimer often based on past unexceptional school performance.

It is startling to see how the negative effects of school experience and disapproving parents linger throughout one's lifetime and influence our self-image. Twenty or thirty years later images of authority figures resurface as pedagogical apparitions waving report cards with a piercing look of disapproval. Even with a history of stellar achievement, adults shun the idea of being gifted. Nancy Alvarado, a past editor of the *Mensa Bulletin*, contends:

> [M]any gifted adults have no idea that they are more intelligent than
> the norm. This means they must face problems related to high intelli-
> gence without realizing the source of these problems. Having missed
> the routine screening that is identifying today's gifted children, highly

intelligent adults may know they are different from average, yet not realize why. . . .

[T]alented adults almost routinely disclaim extraordinary intelligence or ability, settling for "brightness" even when such a claim is patently absurd. Perhaps, because gifted individuals set high internal standards for themselves rather than comparing themselves to others, as most people do, they are more harsh in their self-judgments and are less likely to consider themselves exceptional.

As a recurring theme in various parts of the country, members of Mensa report that they consider most other members of the group to be smarter than they are, even when little evidence indicates that this should be so. Many members say they were admitted to the group only on a fluke and fear they would never pass another admittance test. . . . The Mensa "retest" is a running joke in the organization, and I believe that it reflects the uneasiness of group members with considering themselves highly intelligent.[6]

Adults denying their giftedness is understandable when people confuse ability and talent with past school performance or early super-success. We have a difficult time accepting the fact that underachievement in school is quite common for the gifted person. This was true for Leonard, who adamantly resisted the idea that his characteristics were indicative of someone even marginally gifted. As the months of therapy went by, he rejected stereotypical images of intelligence and began to have a change of heart:

> Remember when I said to you that my older brother and sister might be what you'd consider gifted, but not me? And that I was always left bobbing in their wake of glorious achievements? When you suggested I might be gifted, too, I was hit with guilt and fear at the same time. I suppose I reacted that way because I knew it was probably true.
>
> And then, just as I was getting close to something really important and promising about myself, my internal critic started in with sarcastic remarks about having been a mediocre student, chiding me for how I could have gone to Harvard or Stanford if I'd put forth any kind of effort at all. I didn't try a lot of things because I had always maintained that I needed a sparkling list of credentials to be a person deserving of opportunity. I realized that when I felt guilty, as though I disappointed the collective "everybody," I was really ashamed because I'd cheated myself more than anyone else.

That belief turned into a twisted rope that has kept me tied up and stalled in uncertainty for years. Now, as I've started to reacquaint myself with my smart and creative parts, I don't feel so lost anymore. Amazingly, the more I face the old fears and recognize that I was educated in a setting that was all wrong for me, I can appreciate the way I responded, even though I still regret it. But anger and regret are a lot easier to channel into productive energy than shame.

And you know what? Last week I played a game with myself about all this. For two days I pretended in my head that I had graduated from Harvard—magna cum laude, even. It was an experiment to see how seeing myself this way would affect my behavior and attitude. I didn't act cocky or obnoxious, just confident and knowledgeable. It felt great!

Now I can see that giftedness doesn't have to be a burden. Now that I understand what makes me tick, I feel sturdier and more energetic. It's as if the most important aspect of my personality was lost and now it's finally been returned to its rightful place.

Like Leonard, most of us experience some kind of wake-up call in adulthood that rattles us to the core. Suddenly we feel uncomfortable living somebody else's life. Giftedness appears to have an agenda of its own. Gradually the true self makes a conscious appearance as memories, regrets, and shelved dreams reveal themselves in a unified urge to claim our true identity.

Accounts of the life experiences of the gifted can offer us some insight into the role giftedness plays. However, even then their inner experience is rarely revealed. There is scant information about the emotional and spiritual development of the gifted and less still about how they may live as well-adjusted individuals who lead meaningful lives with solid relationships and considerable satisfaction in their accomplishments. My investigation of scientific research, case studies, biographies, and autobiographies of gifted people clearly indicates that the gifted are more than people with above-average intelligence; they approach the world and problems differently, react in uncommon ways, learn atypically, and are concerned about things others are not.

ARE THERE OTHERS LIKE ME?
AND ARE THEY NORMAL?

Cut-and-paste histories of the Everyday Genius leave out the invaluable day-to-day reality and focus solely on great feats, altruistic deeds, or scandalous secrets. "Success stories" entice us to wrongly assume that truly gifted people are sure of their talents from the outset, that they wisely choose to invest their time and effort to perfect their strongest talent, and subsequently climb an unfettered ladder to recognition and influence with scarcely a flicker in their confidence.

Media heroics, stories of feats of genius that sift out all uncertainty and hardship, are among the most damaging images for the developing gifted adult who compares himself or herself as "too little" or "too late." One account of an emerging gifted adult that offers some insight and is worth reading is Eleanor Roosevelt's autobiography, *This Is My Story*. Phyllis Rose, editor of *The Norton Book of Women's Lives*, an anthology of excerpts of twentieth-century women's literature, agrees. She sought role models who were not merely women married to famous men, but individuals of substance and vitality. Rose wrote of her delight in Roosevelt's self-revelations, admitting that she read it with

> almost sinful excitement because for me then (as now) an autobiography held out the promise of dark truths that only friends confess to one another but are the knowledge you need to live. Some of this I found in Eleanor Roosevelt's book. She, too, was shy! She, too, had weak ankles! She, too, was a physical coward! She, too, was nuts about her father! This was the knowledge I needed to live![7]

I couldn't help but react in much the same way to a segment on the *Today* show featuring Tony Cothren, a visually impaired Alabama judge. What grabbed my attention was Judge Cothren's honesty about his early years as a gifted child. Rather than concentrating on his visual problems, he underscored instead his enduring sense of mandated mission in the face of societal obstacles.

Judge Cothren's giftedness was not identified early, and his childhood school years were far from exemplary. He admits, "I was a very rambunctious child. I know at least in second or third grade, I spent more time in the corner than I did in my seat. I mean, if there was a little girl sitting in front of me, she just needed a haircut, you know, with those scissors I had. I could complete my work real fast, and I just would get bored."

Cothren didn't find his way into his current career until he was in his forties, but he had always been driven to move forward and to excel. When asked about his ambition, he replied, "I just never wanted to be that blind kid who's just getting by, you know? . . . I want to leave here as I want to leave life—and have people say, 'He made a difference. He didn't just maintain the status quo; he actually made some changes for the good.' And that's all the heritage I want."

However, even accounts such as these leave us starving for more real-life information about the Everyday Genius, disclosures that might bring about a normalizing "Me too!" reaction. "Where," we wonder, "are the others like me?" Since we cannot be identified by gender, race, thumbprint, age, or any other obvious means, we push on in the dark. We unintentionally uphold a code of silence that makes us more inclined to hide our dreams and enact our objectives in isolation. Alone and without recourse, we are woefully bewildered by a baffling sense of urgency and unspoken anguish that comes from feeling disconnected. Despite ingrained self-concepts, Everyday Geniuses must ultimately seek their authentic natures, and they must do so steadfastly, for no confidence can arise from unanswered questions about one's core being.

REBEL, NERD, OR MARVEL?

When high potential becomes obvious, it becomes fair game for false assumptions and blind criticism. As writer Shana Alexander observes: "The sad truth is that excellence makes people nervous." Gifted people are repeatedly dubbed rebels or nerds, or portrayed as social dunces who stumble around in linty old sweaters covered with chalk dust, appearing preoccupied and out of touch.

The words *gifted* and *talented* often bring to mind images of the temperamental artist who throws tantrums at the least provocation, or a pathetic isolate whose abilities are lost in self-destructive behavior. The polar opposite is the glittering megasuccess, the stellar individual whose inventions and masterpieces rock the world, whose notoriety and influence are enormous. This perception gives rise to all kinds of responses that range from envy to veneration.

We wonder, "If I'm smarter than most, am I destined to become a social misfit? Must I have thick glasses and dress poorly to salve the jealousies of others? Is there no way to be exceptionally innovative, a charismatic leader, or a visionary futurist and still be attractive, athletic, and popular?" Or is it that we only like geniuses in certain ways: when they're already dead, when they don't outshine our efforts, or when we can bask in the glow of their talents for our own benefit?

Is this too harsh a view? Ask the Everyday Genius whose gifts have been blocked, unrecognized, and underutilized. Giftedness cannot be excised or traded in for something else, though I have had many a client who has complained at some point, "Why can't I just be like everybody else?" Yet somewhere deep inside they feel the responsibility to construct something wonderful and valuable—to make a difference.

Although we may not know any other gifted person, once we see our traits for what they truly are, for the first time we feel a part of a larger, universal group. This is a point of view from which we can see ourselves as able instead of aberrant. If we resign ourselves to fit another's life, we become the truth of Samuel Beckett's aphorism: "I say *me*, knowing all the while it's not me."[8]

REFRAMING GENIUS

For the Everyday Genius, personal "genius" must be reframed or reinterpreted in conjunction with the original meaning of the word. *Genius* was derived from a word used by the ancient Romans, who considered genius a guiding inborn spirit who protects, reassures, and coaches throughout life. The benefits of one's genius are, however, available only when the powers of intellect and creative passion are considered real and accessible. In this sense, inner genius is the gatekeeper of natural talent and is itself the vigor necessary for high achievement. A Roman paid homage to his or her personal guardian spirit, or genius, by giving it gifts on his or her own birthday, as to a loved one. The present-day Everyday Genius intuitively appreciates this inner-outer relationship and must come to cooperate with it in modern ways. Today, paying tribute to one's genius means listening deeply to it, fostering its growth, and using its power of influence honorably.

Terms connoting aliveness are used to refer to the gifted individual, words such as *quick, clever,* and *spirited.* When we examine terms such as *prodigy, special, exceptional,* and *superior intellect,* elitism taints the concept of uncommon ability. Yet the idea that giftedness is equivalent to preferential treatment is relatively new—and utterly untrue, since most Everyday Geniuses rarely receive special courtesies or educational services. But the belief lingers like a bad smell in the air, turning everyone away by misjudging worthy gifted traits as character flaws.

If we look logically at our characteristics without getting bogged down with worries about being too self-congratulatory or fearful of overshooting the mark, then we can relax into who and what we are. A part of this quest toward self-acceptance comes in a change in our self-concept and understanding the depth and breadth of our abilities.

In recent years, noted humanistic psychologist Abraham Maslow theorized about the human need for meaningful endeavor at the higher levels of human evolution. His famous "hierarchy of needs" suggests that well-being begins with aspects of survival (for example, food, shelter, water, procreation) and progresses through a system of needs that includes such things as a sense of belonging to a group. Up the scale we find a drive for the fulfillment of the individual, or self-actualization, and further experiences in the transpersonal realms.

The focus of the gifted person fortunate enough to have satisfied the basic necessities of life emphasizes what Maslow called "metamotives," development of the individual identity in response to something "higher," perhaps truth, beauty, justice, social service, innovation, or wisdom. From his lifetime study of self-actualizing people, Maslow developed a theory of metamotivation:

> I have called the basic needs instinctoid or biologically necessary for many reasons, but primarily because the person needs the basic gratifications in order to avoid illness, to avoid diminution of humanness, and positively stated, in order to move forward and upward toward self-actualization or full humanness. It is my strong impression that something very similar holds true for the metamotivations of self-actualizing people. . . . They are per se, in their own right, not dependent upon human vagaries for their existence. They are perceived, not invented. They are transhuman and transindividual. They exist beyond the life of the individual. They can be conceived to be a kind of perfection.[9]

Need is the salient point here, because aimlessness or misguided direction will never satisfy the gifted person. Self-realization and actualization of abilities is a force, a basic instinct. Everyday Geniuses cannot escape the pull of self-actualization and the farther reaches of life's frontiers. For most this means they must eventually enter the domain of higher consciousness, spirituality, and ethics. Well-being implies more than simply getting by and making do, for they are not the type who can comfortably exist without the meaningful growth and hard work that continually tests their high potential.

The scripted life most of us were prepared for may simply have us cast in the wrong role within the wrong plot—though no script will suit us until we know ourselves well and respect our very nature. The incentive for taking our gifts seriously is the rewriting of our life script in our own words, and playing the authentic part we are called to enact. For the future of the world, the repercussion is this: *Everyday Geniuses are an invaluable natural resource because of their differences—because they have inspired vision, the capacity to turn their dreams into reality, and the audacity to chase after them.*

For the Everyday Genius, being fully alive entails two distinct but inseparable missions: first, being free to be oneself, and second, being dedicated to the betterment of others' lives. There is more to being smart than knowing a great deal or doing something creative. Everyday Geniuses must take the next step, so that their giftedness can serve as the foundation of a more advanced future of intelligence. Once they unexpectedly experience their self-realization, they must recognize that their gift is also an obligation. Their self-realization links them with service, their Humanistic Vision with progress, and their giftedness with evolution. Lofty though this may sound, having a pinhole vision about high potential leads to costly mistakes.

No Everyday Genius can afford to squander entrusted gifts in order to avoid fear. Being fully alive and liberated means embracing this twofold life in earnest, accepting that the actualization journey is simultaneously freedom and obligation, threatening and electrifying, harassing and tranquil, crystal clear and totally confusing. There is no other way, no third door marked "safe and predictable" that will make the journey effortless and comfortable. And yet our innate both/and nature has already equipped us to walk this road with courage by accepting both ourselves and our entrusted purpose.

PART TWO

EVOLUTIONARY INTELLIGENCE

6

EVOLUTIONARY INTELLIGENCE: THE NEXT STEP

We are at a crossroads in human history. Never before has there been a moment so simultaneously perilous and promising. We are the first species to have taken our evolution into our own hands. —Carl Sagan

Even in today's information-hungry age, the predominant concepts about intelligence are far from intelligent. In fact, they are downright regressive. Whenever I speak about this to a roomful of people I ask for a show of hands by those who "know" their IQ. Nearly all raise a hand. Then I ask those who were ever formally, individually tested to keep their hands up. The number usually shrivels to a meager few. What we think we know is in dire need of a second look.

A long time ago American teacher, philosopher, and reformer John Dewey had a nagging suspicion that IQ might get out of hand: "The intelligence-testing business reminds me of the way they used to weigh hogs in Texas. They would get a long plank, put it over a cross-bar, and somehow tie the hog on one end of the plank. They'd search all around till they found a stone that would balance the weight of the hog and they'd put that on the other end of the plank. Then they'd guess the weight of the stone." This witticism is a good place to begin to retest the waters of intelligence and question what we think we know to be true.

RETESTING THE
WATERS OF INTELLIGENCE

Research has provided us with several ways to identify gifted characteristics in schoolchildren who might be considered for accelerated programs. Yet, as it now stands, there are no accurate measurement tests that target gifted traits. Our testing focus has centered on quantifying thinking power and ranking abilities instead of accenting the psychological characteristics and needs of the gifted adults from whom society expects so much. Few adults need to be formally tested with standard intelligence measures. The goal of testing at the adult level is different from the usual educational concerns. When adult testing is appropriate, it is used as a gauge for personal awareness and growth rather than to rank or label. Though general research on gifted adults examines personality traits, and though case studies offer us a glimpse into real-life experiences, we continue to be without a standard identification tool.

Most of the newer concepts of intelligence also lack measurement inventories. As we have seen, Gardner believes people have multiple intelligences that vary in proportion, and that the individual's idiosyncratic mix determines how he or she learns, achieves, and succeeds. Knowing which critical-thinking skills, talents, and abilities comprise our intellect allows us to measure our personal growth at various stages in our lives. Our talents are usually not developed one after the other in orderly fashion. Therefore, we need a broad-spectrum understanding of advanced human development that encompasses the broad scope of intelligence. This is why ordinary measures of intelligence fall short. In an effort to define and categorize, they limit and thereby eliminate the full range of human potential.

Critics fault Gardner for failing to index and measure his theorized multiple intelligences. Nevertheless, Gardner contends that a battery of tests would be incompatible with his theory, and, as we have seen, he is sensitive to the biases and limitations of intelligence tests:

> In the course of their careers in the American schools of today, most
> students take hundreds, if not thousands, of tests. They develop skill to
> a highly calibrated degree in an exercise that will essentially become
> useless immediately after their last day in school.[1]

Gardner's effort to humanize, clarify, and expand the meaning of intelligence is to be applauded. But to conclude that intelligence assessment is without merit, especially if such assessment tools are designed with the individual truly in mind, is shortsighted. Gifted adults have had no frame of reference to tell them the facts about their intellectual structure or their personal process. Without graphic evidence, they are unable to clear the murky waters of misinformation to see what's really there and what isn't. Lacking an organized framework against which to reevaluate their traits, Everyday Geniuses continue to be an easy target for social misidentification.

In the broader view, isn't the person of high ability "tested" covertly all the time? Everyday Geniuses have learned to judge themselves by means of existing societal standards of what is "normal." This counterfeit appraisal method is inescapable because it is at first externally imposed and then internally reinforced. It is a de facto process that adds up to their being involuntarily tested and graded repeatedly. Would we benefit from the creation of a research-based personality-type profile of unconventional intelligence that could be used as a corrective tool?

All of us believe the way we think, perceive, feel, and react is not so different from anyone else's, certainly not different or special enough to require a wholly new method of classification. Putting the inner life and behavioral traits of the gifted into words permits us to say, "Hey! That's just like me!" which in turn raises the odds of winning at the happiness and success game instead of settling for mindless conformity.

When individual evaluation is done for the purposes of truth and liberation, the ends really do justify the means. Testing does not need to be about labeling or done for the purpose of comparing and establishing a pecking order. The objective here is simpler, more helpful, and aimed at the liberation of individual promise. A procedure that could free up the powers of high potential must begin somewhere. It's a bird-in-the-hand issue, for a research-based assessment tool that exists *now* can enhance the lives of the misinformed gifted who have already waited far too long to understand and accept themselves.

The emancipation of individual gifts is the driving force behind the assessment instrument presented in this book. It is a tool that aims to provide the reader with a quick and concise method of reassessing characteristics and special abilities. It begins with a version of educator Kristen Nicholson-Nelson's adaptation of Gardner's theory of multiple intelligences.[2]

This is followed by a detailed road map of gifted traits based on scientific research. These are the inner secrets of the gifted personality and mind. They are far more revealing and useful criteria for any individual of high potential than conventional test items. Each of the categories represents a distinct and undeniable component of giftedness, and is directly linked to personal experience and thought patterns. As a general rule, Everyday Geniuses have always known they were smart, probably smarter than average. That is not the problem. The problem is believing it's true, understanding the *real* nature of giftedness, and adopting specific strategies to withstand the pressures and obstacles that usually accompany achievement and excellence. No ordinary test score or intelligence profile can provide this kind of insight.

Another step in evaluating Everyday Genius is required, one that takes intelligence beyond simply being exceptionally able and introduces a dimension decidedly different from any found in either traditional assessments or the magazine surveys that focus on gratification of self rather than living a meaningful life. Gifted people cannot escape a sense of calling, a mandate to put their abilities to the test of time and constructive purpose. This is the true legacy of giftedness, the sense of responsibility to leave something valuable behind.

We may have an understanding of how our particular combination of Multiple Intelligences and Gifted Traits functions, but with just those two elements, we still have an unstable foundation on which to build. Talent and high intellect are only two of the three building blocks that form the cornerstone for a new model of human intelligence. The next step in the evolution of human intelligence relies on our Advanced Development, the third element that acts as a keystone to lock together the foundational elements on which Evolutionary Intelligence lies. Advanced Development's signature characteristics of Humanistic Vision, Mandated Mission, and Revolutionary Action work in concert with our Multiple Intelligences and Gifted Traits as the cornerstone of this unconventional breakthrough intelligence.

By adding the evolutionary aspect to current concepts of intelligence, we further define a new horizon for the Everyday Geniuses who are especially equipped to respond to the call of a twenty-first-century renaissance. When the spiral of evolution is added to the ability formula, people of high potential are able to stand away from feelings of guilt, selfishness, grandiosity, and inhibition. They learn to support themselves—and what they believe about what they can accomplish gradually shifts from "possibly" to "probably," and later to "naturally"—as they learn that special gifts are not about being superior. Rather, they are charged with a duty to develop their talents in ways that contribute to collective evolution.

Evolutionary Intelligence fuses extraordinary abilities with three elements of Advanced Development: Humanistic Vision, Mandated Mission, and Revolutionary Action, which reenvisions what it means to be bright and capable. Intelligence cannot loiter about in me-myself-and-I ventures or be set aside as the responsibility of others. The Everyday Genius' gifts of intellect and talent are never given purely for ease and self-gratification. They are given with both a price tag and a prize.

Rather than worry so much about the *quantity* of our intelligence, might it not be more practical in our discussion of ability if we concern ourselves with the quality and dynamism of certain combinations of high potential? What if we were able to identify a human potential that combines traditional intelligence measures such as verbal or mathematical adeptness with a conceptual leap into the realm of destiny?

This new interpretation of intelligence would not limit the individual or antagonize others. Within this comprehensive understanding of human gifts and potential resides an atmosphere of boundless creative possibility. This kind of intelligence has an innate respect and desire for diversity that prevents the suppression of ability in response to the pressure to conform. Achievement at the expense of others would recede in favor of larger humanistic effort. Self-realization would accompany making a valuable difference.

For many an Everyday Genius, recognizing this comprehensive form of intelligence would mean no more selling out, no requisite isolation, no overwhelming loneliness, and no more self-loathing. Evolutionary Intelligence (EvI) as an integrative form of intelligence is brimming with possibilities for the full expression of individuality. It is a vastly potent and exciting concept because within its framework exceptional ability is united with universal principles, destiny, and the cycle of evolution itself. EvI takes human potential to new heights because it is inclusive and committed to real-life application. EvI does not underscore mathematical prowess at the expense of artistic expression, or become fixated on comparative degrees of ability. Rather, it weds natural abilities with contribution by providing a concept that can be used to greatly expand the power of the individual within society.

WHAT'S EVOLUTION
GOT TO DO WITH IT?

Those of us who are not neuroscientists or professors of anthropology may challenge: "What does evolution have to do with intelligence?" *Evolution* often brings forth images of a strange half-fish, half-animal poking its nose through the murky green of the primordial swamp as it dares to take that first step into an airy life. We envision our genetic predecessors who climbed down from the trees, stood partially erect, and grew bigger brains while their knuckles stopped scraping the ground.

Evolutionary theory derives from the belief that common ancestral forms of life have transformed over time, a branching-out process called *speciation* that resulted in the millions of organisms that inhabit today's world. Such evolutionary changes rarely occur swiftly, most take place over millennia, progressing at a slow but consistent rate.

Natural selection, the result of competition for resources and adaptation to environmental conditions, is believed to be the major cause of such changes. It has to do with competition for resources and adaptation to environmental conditions. Scientists believe the best-adapted survive to pass their genes down to future generations. Thus the process has been called "survival of the fittest." Another reason for species change is *mutation*, which is a chance or random variation in certain individuals. These mutations could be considered *xenogenic* offspring, markedly different from either of their parents. Everyday Geniuses live a xenogenic life. Without these odd ducks the gene pool would grow stagnant and progress would eventually cease, perhaps even threatening human survival.

Natural selection reacts to mutation. It either promotes it or eliminates it to support continued growth of the population. Mutations occur regularly, though sporadically, producing both favorable characteristics (a plant developing long roots in an arid climate) or disadvantageous ones (human hemophilia).

While studying the evening primrose, Dutch botanist Hugo de Vries discovered that variations caused by mutation can appear abruptly and become inheritable. Individuals of any species displaying the effect of genetic mutation may be poised to take advantage of changes in the environment.

From this vantage point one could argue that leaps of progress are nothing more than practical "accidents"—mutations that just happen to have a good outcome in a given environment. Correspondingly, exceptional human ability would be judged as equally coincidental. People with unusual capacities—those who are ahead of their time—are mutants in some sense of the word. Following this logic, marvels of human effort and invention would be chalked up to nothing more than chance.

But mutants have the capacity to affect the evolution of those with whom they interact, and to set off chain reactions of change. Unlike spontaneous mutation, genetic recombination is a process by which "better-fit" mutation occurs; the idea is that even a tiny change can cause a profound adaptation.

This is the fundamental precept of a relatively new model of evolution that theorizes population changes are caused by mutation spurts that lead to an "avalanche" of behavioral alterations after long periods of equilibrium. Such intermittent flare-ups of evolutionary activity are natural and necessary for progress, as opposed to insignificant errors or cataclysmic disturbances.

From a philosophical point of view, each entity strives toward some essential goal, including human intelligence. The eminent University of Chicago psychologist Mihaly Csikszentmihalyi argues that complexity is necessary for the enrichment and continuation of human evolution. In a *Psychology Today* interview he explains his views, which seem to be in agreement with my theory of Evolutionary Intelligence:

> [A]t this point we are one of the major—if not the major—selective mechanisms on the planet. Whether we like it or not, what we do is going to make a huge difference in the quality of the atmosphere, the quality of water, plant life, animal life, human life. Before, evolution could make all kinds of mistakes, and natural selection could have obliterated all types of life forms from the Earth. Slowly, over thousands of years, millions of years, some forms that were obviously more complex had a slight advantage and survived. And the effect has been that we have had more and more complex forms with time. . .
>
> I think that people should realize how important what they do can be in changing both their lives and history. We are unaware, really, of the powers we have. . . . We need to realize that in many ways life, or at least conscious life, begins only after you realize what you are supposed to do in terms of genetic and social instructions. It's only when you free yourself from the basic conditioning that we are born with do you start living. At the same time you realize that you are free to do it or not to do it. . . . Evolution will proceed some other way, somewhere else.[3]

Generally speaking, nature has identifiable patterns, some of which are static while others are dynamic. In the animal world, for example, certain creatures, such as the crocodile, have changed little over the centuries, while the modern horse, the descendant of numerous ancestors, has experienced a significant number of mutations beginning with the prehistoric "dawn horse" fifty million years ago, a greyhoundlike animal about twenty inches tall with an arched back and a snoutlike nose.

In nature, some static patterns exist because under prevailing conditions they are able to thrive. This becomes a problem when environmental factors take a significant turn in a new direction. When a responsive shift becomes necessary, not just any old change will suffice. For humankind, the key to successful adaptation is a dual process, one that encompasses both static and dynamic patterns. Both standard intelligence and EvI process and manipulate information efficiently. They both function optimally in a static environment.

What separates EvI from standard intelligence is its ability to thrive in dynamic environments while expanding the collective knowledge base. Evolutionaries—the bearers of Evolutionary Intelligence—achieve on a larger scale because their brains can adapt to both dynamic and static environments. Therefore, as things constantly change, they possess the basic tools to swiftly detect and define problems and envision and enact creative solutions. They are outfitted to lead us from the mechanical age to the electronic age to the digital age as information processing accelerates. They are the "mutants" who will help us survive.

Currently, such evolutionaries are experiencing enormous dissonance as they walk the tightrope between old and new. Their experience is akin to the earliest birds whose feathers first evolved from reptilian scales for thermal protection. We can imagine the first time this transitional creature ran along the same old ground only to find itself lifted up off its feet into the heavens.

The process of evolution is collective and visionary by nature, the scope of its agenda far-reaching. It is unnecessary to force an exclusionary relationship between high potential and evolution (that is, science versus God). Whatever the source, Evolutionary Intelligence has the advantage of seeing the big picture in an all-inclusive manner, and thus is equipped to stretch the limits of human progress. It is at once outwardly focused and inwardly inspired, both visionary and pragmatic.

Intelligence and evolution complement each other because they share many characteristics. Evolution and Evolutionary Intelligence are like an improvised dance, the performer not always sure of what to do next, but moving all the while. The pleasure derived from this process comes from the "guessing," the surprises of meaningful creation. Unlike other species, we can dream and conceptualize and distinguish between varying degrees of quality. Darwin's notion of the "survival of the fittest" is a shortsighted theory of the intent of evolution. Evolutionary Intelligence is not something that one can limit, for its scope and power are boundless.

THE EvI FORMULA

Many people define *intelligence* as "being smart, clever, quick-witted, or shrewd." And *evolve* means "to unfold, amplify, integrate, or blossom." However, when the two definitions are paired, it suggests a startling possibility. This combination of vision plus action as a permanent intellectual capacity introduces the new form of intelligence termed Evolutionary Intelligence.

It may help to think of Evolutionary Intelligence, or EvI, as a mathematical equation:

$$\boxed{EvI = MI + GT + AD}$$

MI (Multiple Intelligences). Multiple Intelligences (MI) are indicated by the presence of certain exceptional talents: musical, verbal, visual/spatial, bodily/kinesthetic, mathematical/logical, interpersonal (insightful about others), intrapersonal (insightful about self), and naturalist abilities.

GT (Gifted Traits) are present in the Intensity, Complexity, and Drive that include original thinking, sensory and emotional sensitivities and deep empathy, excitability, perceptive strengths (insight plus intuition), and goal-oriented motivation.

AD (Advanced Development) encompasses Humanistic Vision, Mandated Mission, and Revolutionary Action. These higher-level attributes enable those who develop them to both see the world and have a commitment to the collective good, rooted in spiritual values and the recognition of the oneness of all life. As an overarching, principled philosophy, this factor promotes benevolence and transpersonal methods of problem solving. Underlying HV is an intrinsic mental picture of what could be if humanity could join forces and overcome the ravages of war, poverty, disease, and destruction.

MM (Mandated Mission) can be defined as a resolute, inner-directed, uncompromising goal orientation that strives in concert with one's life purpose. It is most recognizable in the form of steadfast individual perseverance. The person who perseveres against all odds to fulfill an obligation or dream often seems foolhardy to less optimistic individuals. Michael Blake, who wrote the novel *Dances with Wolves*, revised and resubmitted manuscripts over a twenty-five-year period in spite of repeatedly being urged by everyone he knew to give up what clearly seemed to be a losing battle. Nevertheless, he pressed on. MM is grounded in unwavering work that is driven by an internal sense of direction and purpose. There is a duty-bound character to its relentless goal seeking. Even in the fog of uncertainty, long before basic questions can be answered with confidence, MM's purpose is to aim individual gifts toward a defined set of goals.

Combined, these two components—HV and MM—are catalyzed by *RA, Revolutionary Action.* Revolutionary Action is the conceptual leap, or leap of faith—the ability to take action beyond accepted norms. It is the active ingredient of Evolutionary Intelligence, through which we see a real-world manifestation of high potential. It is the dream made real, the word made flesh. In the material world we attribute such activities to the realm of the inventor, whose newfangled ideas are daring and radical and often transform life as we know it, such as Bell's telephone. Noted scientists such as Chien-hsiung Wu, whose experiments revolutionized one of the basic laws of particle physics, are obvious evolutionaries. Everyday Geniuses who strive day and night to find remedies for AIDS and Alzheimer's disease are evolutionaries despite the fact that their efforts have yet to afford them public recognition.

Quiet Revolutionary Actions can be just as momentous as the award-winning ones, often creating unexpected ripple effects, such as Edith Spurlock Sampson's pioneering efforts as the first African-American judge in America. Her appearance at a high-school career day ignited a love for the law in a young Barbara Jordan, who became a congresswoman from Texas and gained prominence during the Watergate hearings. Frequently RAs are a series of uncompromising efforts that go by all but unnoticed, ever so slightly pointing the compass of progress in a new direction. These unpretentious RAs proceed without fanfare until they quietly move the mountain and foster the breakthroughs that make a more noticeable difference.

How many of us know the names of the individuals whose Revolutionary Actions gave us the battery, who painstakingly translated the Bible into multiple languages, developed hybrid crops to better feed the multitudes, or designed and redesigned the microchip that we now take for granted? Helen Keller's promotion of opportunities for the "differently abled" was not motivated by expectations of fame and glory. She did what she did out of need, and she found meaning in turning her disabilities into special abilities that paved the way for others.

There is no standing ovation for the astute teacher who asks the provocative question of the right student at exactly the right moment, though the end result can light the fire of undeveloped genius. We tend to discount the maverick business manager who enlists much-needed raw talent in the company and then guides it through the tangles of office politics until the former protégé has altered the face of the industry. Nor do we televise award ceremonies for all the behind-the-scenes caregivers and advocates of the underprivileged and marginalized members of society. They're out there, all around us, these evolutionaries, quietly performing their Revolutionary Actions. For all Everyday Geniuses, from the high-profile luminary to the backstage mobilizer, EvI offers something far greater than the sum of its parts because it blends the best of human virtues with the abundant resources and drive of giftedness and the creative spirit.

And, as in any formula, the values of each of the factors may vary, and a zero in any one of them can cancel out the entire effect. Multiple Intelligences (MI) alone could conceivably produce nothing more than underachievement, a reservoir of untapped resources of an inherently rich mind. Humanistic Vision (HV) by itself is honorable, yet likely to be unproductive if resigned to idealism or wishful thinking. Ruinous effects can surface when powerful Gifted Traits (GT) are processed through Revolutionary Actions (RA) without the regulating influence of Advanced Development (AD).

No single profile distinguishes an individual as someone with Evolutionary Intelligence. Like most everything about human beings, there is an enormous spectrum of possibility. But in every case, the effect of EvI is a quantum leap toward the realization of human potential because it merges the properties of capability into the most dynamic and fluid form.

It is important to bear in mind that giftedness is never a simple matter. It is fraught with misunderstanding, especially about gradations. Just as musical ability can range from tone deafness to being able to sing on key to Yo-Yo Ma–like virtuosity, intelligence presents itself in many guises, all the way from profound mental disability to skillful thinkers to the Einsteins of the world, who stand out among even the brightest. Furthermore, the reason we recognize so few of the Everyday Geniuses around us is the tendency in the adult world to equate giftedness with high-profile "success," meaning obvious wealth, fame, or position of influence. Lamentably, this eliminates untold numbers of legitimately gifted individuals from the recognized ranks of potentiality and thereby hinders their development and reduces their resources to marginalia.

We must remember that Everyday Geniuses are all around us, in every corner of society. They are not a tiny group of rocket scientists or profoundly brilliant sensations. Nor are they all former straight-A students, award-winning debaters, charismatic rabble-rousers, or virtuoso musicians. Rather, they are the everyday people of unusual vision who give progress a forward push. When the owners of these special gifts allow themselves to shut out the world and listen to a place deep inside, they hear the voice of their inner agenda. And when they grow to trust it, they begin to hear the call of evolution itself.

When combined constructively, the EvI variables pay off with someone such as Mother Teresa, whose very high HV and MM were synthesized in her unique form of RA to apply Evolutionary Intelligence to the suffering of the ailing unwanted and the destitute. In a different configuration, Bill Gates' form of EvI is strongest in GT and MM, which when expressed in his particular RA style entirely overhauled the computer industry and made him a youthful billionaire. English prime minister Tony Blair's consolidated MI, GT, and HV manifested in Revolutionary Actions that in large part were responsible for a negotiated peace with Ireland, a feat nearly everyone had given up as a hopeless cause.

EvI and liberated Everyday Genius are really one and the same—a result not of boardroom shrewdness or science laboratory inspiration but of a twenty-four-hour-a-day, seven-day-a-week need to be free to stretch the mind farther, to crystallize knowledge, to apply creative energy without restraint, to use and at length use up the gifts one was given to develop. Many would agree that in contemporary American culture the seeds of Evolutionary Intelligence were born again in the post–World War II baby boomers. They grew up being infused with a level of idealism that has since been minimized by cynicism. President Kennedy's cabinet was a prime example of a merger of Everyday Genius strengths, translated into a Mandated Mission and Revolutionary Action.

It is my firm belief that Evolutionary Intelligence is the next step. It is more robust than simply being smart, more rewarding than being successful, and more electric than waiting for satisfaction on the installment plan. Moreover, it finally explains why gifted people are designed to have in their hardwiring extra sensitivity, drive, intensity, and creative vision. EvI makes sense of the fact that they intuit discoveries and innovations before they have the skills to make them real, and that throughout their lives they are relentlessly pursued by images of the ideal.

7

THE EVOLUTIONARY
INTELLIGENCE PROFILE

$$\boxed{EvI = MI + GT + AD}$$

ABOUT THE EvI PROFILE

The Evolutionary Intelligence Profile—the EvI Profile—is intended to provide you with a systematic way to identify your traits and behaviors and determine your potential for Evolutionary Intelligence. It is a tool that will help you discover vital information about the very essence of who you are, and provide you with a clearer understanding of your own unique strengths. The EvI Profile may be used for self-discovery and self-guidance, or, in situations where trust is high, coworkers, supervisors, teachers, or friends may complete it to offer feedback about how *they see you.* In team settings, sharing results can add valuable information to determine who is best suited for which parts of a project, to see whose strengths might be combined or used to compensate for other limitations, and to remove significant barriers to achievement that arise when individual differences in approach are misunderstood or disallowed.

The EvI Profile is a self-rated questionnaire of 240 items that will take you through a systematic exploration of the various components of Evolutionary Intelligence. Following descriptions of the types of questions in the profile, you will find more specific instructions on how to take and score the questionnaire.

Section One: (MI + GT)

Section One is divided into two parts that will evaluate the elements of your special abilities that have remained relatively stable over your lifetime. By rating your Multiple Intelligences (MI) and Gifted Traits (GT), you will be able to form a clearer picture of to what extent and in what form you possess the special abilities that are a part of what make you a gifted adult.

- *Multiple Intelligences (MI)*—In this part you will identify the range of your skills and talents based on Howard Gardner's model of multiple intelligences.
- *Gifted Traits (GT)*—This section helps you evaluate your gifted characteristics under the umbrella traits of Intensity, Complexity, and Drive. This will help you determine if you are among the millions of unidentified gifted adults, and which of the traits of giftedness have the greatest influence on your personality.

Section Two: Advanced Development (HV, MM, RA)

This section is divided into three parts, each of which rates a particular aspect of your Advanced Development. Profiles in this section will allow you to extend what you know about your abilities by determining your level of development in three specific areas: Humanistic Vision (HV), Mandated Mission (MM), and Revolutionary Action (RA).

Unlike the traits evaluated in Section One, your expression of Advanced Development changes over time, because these areas of development must be mastered through continuous learning and life experience. When you utilize your particular Special Abilities in concert with Humanistic Vision and Mandated Mission, your baseline Everyday Genius advances to potential Evolutionary Intelligence. When your potential EvIQ is released through Revolutionary Action, your Everyday Genius is liberated to achieve unconventional breakthrough intelligence— Evolutionary Intelligence.

- *Humanistic Vision (HV)*—Rates your current ability to make a meaningful and selfless contribution to society that is in sync with your unique gifts.
- *Mandated Mission (MM)*—Rates your capacity for seeking out your entrusted life purpose and direction, committing to a course

of action, overcoming obstacles, and negotiating the process of
self-actualization.
- *Revolutionary Action (RA)*—Rates the degree to which you are
  willing to defy conventions and withstand criticism and opposition
  in order to forge new paths and effect your mission.

TAKING THE EvI PROFILE

Allow yourself thirty to sixty minutes to complete the profile. Rate yourself (0, 1, 2, 3) on each item by circling the appropriate number that corresponds to how well the statement describes you: 0 = not at all like me,
1 = slightly like me, 2 = moderately like me, 3 = very much like me. Be
as honest with yourself as possible. Remember, there are no right or
wrong answers. Consequently, your responses should reflect how *you are*
and not how you would like to be. However, also bear in mind that as a result of socialization, the adult you may no longer express some of these
traits to the same degree you did at earlier stages in your life. For these
items, base your score on your past general aptitudes and behaviors.

No one else needs to see your results, but you may find it helpful to
discuss items about which you are uncertain with someone who knows
you well. It is important, however, not to overanalyze the statements.
After you have calculated your results, you will then be ready to consider your aptitude in view of the EvI equation. By using the charts to
plot your scores, you will have a graphic representation of *your type* of
Evolutionary Intelligence and your strengths and weaknesses. Your score
is a numerical representation of your Evolutionary Intelligence Quotient,
or EvIQ.

The items in this profile are based on solid scientific research. Currently, there are no
formal standardized measurement tools for gifted adults, and certainly no psychometric
instruments for measuring Everyday Genius or Evolutionary Intelligence. Statistical
standardization can take many years, and this instrument is not proposed as a decision-
making tool for school entrance or job placement. Remember, the EvIQ Profile is a proto-
type inventory intended to provide a systematic way to identify and rate your traits and
habits in terms of potential for Evolutionary Intelligence.

SECTION ONE:
SPECIAL ABILITIES (MI + GT)

PART 1: MULTIPLE INTELLIGENCES (MI)

Indicate how well each statement fits you.	Not at all	Slightly	Moderately	Very much
I instinctively use my body to express ideas.	0	1	2	3
I'm good at making things with my hands.	0	1	2	3
I can convey ideas and feelings via movement.	0	1	2	3
I tend to understand things through my body.	0	1	2	3
I have above-average mind/body coordination.	0	1	2	3
I rely on my body's dexterity in highly skilled ways.	0	1	2	3
I prefer hands-on methods of learning.	0	1	2	3
I often touch things to better understand them.	0	1	2	3
Ideas come to me best when I am in motion.	0	1	2	3
I regularly participate in sports or physical activities.	0	1	2	3

Body-smart SUBTOTAL = _____ a.

ENTER THIS SCORE ON THE SECTION ONE SCORE SHEET, PAGE 106, LINE A.

Indicate how well each statement fits you.	Not at all	Slightly	Moderately	Very much
I'm highly verbal and an easy talker.	0	1	2	3
My ears are "tuned in" to the rhythms, subtleties, patterns, and nuances of speech.	0	1	2	3
I can use dialogue to fluently express my ideas and feelings.	0	1	2	3
I tend to think out loud and use others as sounding boards for my ideas and concerns.	0	1	2	3
I make sense of things through words.	0	1	2	3
I rely on my communication skills to succeed.	0	1	2	3
Books are an important part of my life.	0	1	2	3
I can entertain myself with meaningful and nonsensical combinations of words.	0	1	2	3
Names, rhymes, and words run through my head all the time.	0	1	2	3
In school I found English and history classes were easier than science and math.	0	1	2	3

Word-smart SUBTOTAL = _____ b.

ENTER THIS SCORE ON THE SECTION ONE SCORE SHEET, PAGE 106, LINE B.

Indicate how well each statement fits you.	Not at all	Slightly	Moderately	Very much
I can turn mental images into something concrete.	0	1	2	3
I can re-create visual material from memory.	0	1	2	3
I have a reliable mental mapping system.	0	1	2	3
I can visualize things from various angles.	0	1	2	3
I notice details of arrangement in my surroundings.	0	1	2	3
I rely on graphs, charts, outlines, and diagrams.	0	1	2	3
I like puzzles, mazes, and visual brain teasers.	0	1	2	3
I liked geometry more than algebra.	0	1	2	3
I like to read things that have many illustrations.	0	1	2	3
I regularly doodle or sketch out my ideas.	0	1	2	3

Spatial-smart SUBTOTAL = _____ c.

ENTER THIS SCORE ON THE SECTION ONE SCORE SHEET, PAGE 106, LINE C.

Indicate how well each statement fits you.	Not at all	Slightly	Moderately	Very much
I'm sensitive to the pitch, tone, and rhythm of sounds.	0	1	2	3
I respond to the emotional impact of music.	0	1	2	3
For me, sound and music are linked to important symbolic meanings.	0	1	2	3
I can express ideas and feelings with music.	0	1	2	3
I can play at least one musical instrument.	0	1	2	3
I experience music as a powerful mood maker.	0	1	2	3
I am a better-than-average singer.	0	1	2	3
I often find myself tapping out an interesting beat.	0	1	2	3
Songs and jingles regularly run through my head.	0	1	2	3
It bothers me when music is off-key.	0	1	2	3

Music-smart SUBTOTAL = _____ d.

ENTER THIS SCORE ON THE SECTION ONE SCORE SHEET, PAGE 106, LINE D.

Indicate how well each statement fits you.	Not at all	Slightly	Moderately	Very much
I look at problems as "if __, then __" questions.	0	1	2	3
I often solve problems *before* I'm able to articulate the solution.	0	1	2	3
I value lists, timelines, numbers, and equations.	0	1	2	3

	Not at all	Slightly	Moderately	Very much
I like to develop and evaluate theories.	0	1	2	3
I tend to be a rational, scientific thinker.	0	1	2	3
I rely on my objective observation skills.	0	1	2	3
I am most comfortable with things that can be measured or analyzed with numbers.	0	1	2	3
In school I preferred math and science classes.	0	1	2	3
I enjoy reading about science and inventions.	0	1	2	3
I tend to look for holes in people's thinking.	0	1	2	3

Logic-smart SUBTOTAL = _____ e.

ENTER THIS SCORE ON THE SECTION ONE SCORE SHEET, PAGE 106, LINE E.

Indicate how well each statement fits you.	Not at all	Slightly	Moderately	Very much
I sensitively respond to others' needs and feelings.	0	1	2	3
I'm keenly aware of mood, temperament, intention.	0	1	2	3
I have a sophisticated way of "reading" situations.	0	1	2	3
I value social prowess and meaningful relationships.	0	1	2	3
I rely on my ability to listen perceptively.	0	1	2	3
I'm skilled at picking up and interpreting the subtleties of body language and intonation.	0	1	2	3
People tend to come to me for advice and support.	0	1	2	3
It's easy for me to make and keep friends.	0	1	2	3
I enjoy social events and group participation.	0	1	2	3
I seem to be a natural leader.	0	1	2	3

Relationship-smart SUBTOTAL = _____ f.

ENTER THIS SCORE ON THE SECTION ONE SCORE SHEET, PAGE 106, LINE F.

Indicate how well each statement fits you.	Not at all	Slightly	Moderately	Very much
I regularly notice and categorize plants/animals.	0	1	2	3
I'm fascinated by the patterns and ways of nature.	0	1	2	3
I am environmentally sensitive and attuned.	0	1	2	3
I can match my "frequency" with natural settings.	0	1	2	3
I have an affinity for agriculture/biology/ science.	0	1	2	3

Indicate how well each statement fits you.	Not at all	Slightly	Moderately	Very much
I find the world of nature comforting and exciting.	0	1	2	3
In school I enjoyed outdoor activities/field trips.	0	1	2	3
It bothers me when I am not outdoors very much.	0	1	2	3
I have often thought I get along with animals better than people.	0	1	2	3
I feel directed toward the protection of nature.	0	1	2	3

Nature-smart SUBTOTAL = _____ g.

ENTER THIS SCORE ON THE SECTION ONE SCORE SHEET, PAGE 106, LINE G.

Indicate how well each statement fits you.	Not at all	Slightly	Moderately	Very much
I comprehend my own emotions and goals.	0	1	2	3
I consider self-knowledge a source of guidance.	0	1	2	3
I have a good "working model" of my identity.	0	1	2	3
I can extract deep meaning from bits of daily life.	0	1	2	3
I have a private "observer-evaluator" at work within.	0	1	2	3
I enrich my life by reliving poignant memories.	0	1	2	3
I find personal-growth classes and counseling enlightening and helpful.	0	1	2	3
I regularly review my life goals.	0	1	2	3
I need time for contemplation and reflection.	0	1	2	3
I have an entrepreneurial nature.	0	1	2	3

Self-smart SUBTOTAL = _____ h.

ENTER THIS SCORE ON THE SECTION ONE SCORE SHEET, PAGE 106, LINE H.

PART 2: GIFTED TRAITS (GT) = INTENSITY, COMPLEXITY, DRIVE

A. INTENSITY (EXCITABILITY AND SENSITIVITY)

Indicate how well each statement fits you.	Not at all	Slightly	Moderately	Very much
My energy is a vital resource, not hyperactivity.	0	1	2	3
When I'm on task I can be so engrossed I neglect important relationships or responsibilities.	0	1	2	3
I am known for my enthusiasm and exuberance.	0	1	2	3
I have a wide array of interests	0	1	2	3
I have been prone to power struggles.	0	1	2	3
At times I have been too open and honest.	0	1	2	3

I dislike mundane or routine activities.	0	1	2	3
Staying calm and steady can be difficult for me.	0	1	2	3
I can be demanding and insist on instant answers.	0	1	2	3
At times I struggle with intense feelings of insecurity.	0	1	2	3
I'm often perturbed about not having enough time.	0	1	2	3
I can rouse enthusiasm in others.	0	1	2	3
My intensity can wear others out.	0	1	2	3
I am usually unafraid to share feelings with others.	0	1	2	3
I have flirted with dangerous forms of excitement.	0	1	2	3
I struggle with recurring job dissatisfaction.	0	1	2	3
As a child I was frustrated when I didn't yet have skills to produce what I envisioned.	0	1	2	3
I am easily bored and tend to "switch gears" often.	0	1	2	3
I often suffer from stimulation overload.	0	1	2	3
I find life both exciting and stressful.	0	1	2	3

Excitability SUBTOTAL = _____ i.

ENTER THIS SCORE ON THE SECTION ONE SCORE SHEET, PAGE 106, LINE I.

Indicate how well each statement fits you.	*Not at all*	*Slightly*	*Moderately*	*Very much*
I am sensitive to the slightest noise, aroma, bright light, or irritant like a scratchy shirt label.	0	1	2	3
Sometimes I feel *for* instead of *along with* others.	0	1	2	3
I feel awful when I think I hurt someone's feelings.	0	1	2	3
I am attuned to the emotional tone of situations.	0	1	2	3
Other people think I'm touchy or too sensitive.	0	1	2	3
When I feel an emotion, I *really* feel it.	0	1	2	3
I hear complaints that I am too easily bothered.	0	1	2	3
My concern for others can take over my life.	0	1	2	3
As a child I was troubled by problems of right and wrong.	0	1	2	3
It can be difficult to limit my dedication to a cause.	0	1	2	3

Indicate how well each statement fits you.	Not at all	Slightly	Moderately	Very much
I have struggled to set limits with others or to distance myself when I need time to myself.	0	1	2	3
Too often I want to "save the world," feeling like a one-person Salvation Army.	0	1	2	3
I have longed to feel understood and accepted.	0	1	2	3
I rely on my feelings as a valuable source of information.	0	1	2	3
I can easily be worn out by overresponsibility.	0	1	2	3
I empathize with the plight of the oppressed.	0	1	2	3
At times I am overcome with worry.	0	1	2	3
Sometimes I am overly attached to ideals.	0	1	2	3
It is easier to deal with others' feelings than my own.	0	1	2	3
It can be hard to separate my identity from the identities of those close to me.	0	1	2	3

Sensitivity SUBTOTAL = _____ j.

ENTER THIS SCORE ON THE SECTION ONE SCORE SHEET, PAGE 106, LINE J.

B. COMPLEXITY (COMPLEX THINKING AND PERCEPTION)

Indicate how well each statement fits you.	Not at all	Slightly	Moderately	Very much
I have an insatiable curiosity.	0	1	2	3
I prefer creative responses to problems.	0	1	2	3
I like puzzles, mysteries, and "can't-be-done" challenges.	0	1	2	3
I learn rapidly and apply what I learn.	0	1	2	3
I am energized by intense discussion.	0	1	2	3
I think on multiple levels at the same time.	0	1	2	3
I have always been a vivid fantasizer.	0	1	2	3
I tend to be an independent thinker.	0	1	2	3
Given the choice, I would prefer to work in a think-tank atmosphere.	0	1	2	3
Sometimes group effort feels like too much conformity, and I become resistant.	0	1	2	3
At times I have done poorly in situations requiring political correctness.	0	1	2	3
I tend to "rock the boat" of the status quo.	0	1	2	3
My thinking allows me to easily bridge concepts.	0	1	2	3
As a child, I was considered relatively advanced.	0	1	2	3

Frequently I find the processes of others to be insufferably slow.	0	1	2	3
I can readily discern cause-effect relationships.	0	1	2	3
I find humor in the absurdities of life.	0	1	2	3
I am considered versatile and adaptable.	0	1	2	3
I rely on my exceptional memory.	0	1	2	3
My preference for the complex can fool me into underestimating the simple answer.	0	1	2	3

Complex Thinking SUBTOTAL = _____ k.

ENTER THIS SCORE ON THE SECTION ONE SCORE SHEET, PAGE 106, LINE K.

Indicate how well each statement fits you.	*Not at all*	*Slightly*	*Moderately*	*Very much*
I seem to notice and take in everything.	0	1	2	3
I have learned to rely on my intuitive resources.	0	1	2	3
I can see many sides of an issue.	0	1	2	3
I grasp multiple facets of others' personalities.	0	1	2	3
I can "sniff out" falsehood and hidden agendas.	0	1	2	3
I am intolerant of insincerity and deceit and grapple with my urge to confront it.	0	1	2	3
At times I have had difficulty trusting others.	0	1	2	3
I seem to see, hear, and feel things others do not.	0	1	2	3
I can quickly zero in on the heart of the matter.	0	1	2	3
I am a proficient problem finder.	0	1	2	3
Transcendent moments are very important to me.	0	1	1	3
When others don't share my insights, I am prone to doubt my perceptions.	0	1	2	3
I understand and value metaphor and symbolism.	0	1	2	3
I monitor myself and try to objectively evaluate my intentions and behaviors.	0	1	2	3
My in-depth understanding of another can be threatening or off-putting.	0	1	2	3
Honesty, integrity, and ethics are important to me.	0	1	2	3
I don't understand others when they seem less determined than I to find the truth or a better way of doing things.	0	1	2	3
I can help others understand themselves better.	0	1	2	3
I am a seeker and champion of ultimate truths.	0	1	2	3
Now and again I get trapped by my own values.	0	1	2	3

Perception SUBTOTAL = _____ l.

ENTER THIS SCORE ON THE SECTION ONE SCORE SHEET, PAGE 106, LINE L.

C. DRIVE

Indicate how well each statement fits you.	*Not at all*	*Slightly*	*Moderately*	*Very much*
I push myself to work at things until I get it right.	0	1	2	3
I set high standards for myself and others.	0	1	2	3
I persistently evaluate my performance.	0	1	2	3
I tend to seek security in systems, rules, and order.	0	1	2	3
I can work hard and concentrate for long periods.	0	1	2	3
I endure and regroup in the face of setbacks.	0	1	2	3
Many consider me driven.	0	1	2	3
I need to feel positive to be my most creative self.	0	1	2	3
I force myself to wait to be happy until I reach the current goal. ("I'll be happy when . . .")	0	1	2	3
I can and do work myself to exhaustion.	0	1	2	3
I expect a great deal of myself.	0	1	2	3
I enjoy organizing, but can organize far too long.	0	1	2	3
Even when successful, I struggle with self-doubts.	0	1	2	3
I wrestle with perfectionism.	0	1	2	3
I can be too self-sufficient, and resist others' input.	0	1	2	3
I tend to be competitive in many areas of my life.	0	1	2	3
I can be my own worst critic.	0	1	2	3
It's hard to let go of interesting ideas if the timing is wrong or they're not meant for me to develop.	0	1	2	3
I seem to stick with things longer than others.	0	1	2	3
Lack of self-confidence is more inhibiting to my goals than nearly anything else.	0	1	2	3

Drive SUBTOTAL = _____ m.

ENTER THIS SCORE ON THE SECTION ONE SCORE SHEET, PAGE 106, LINE M.

SECTION TWO:
ADVANCED DEVELOPMENT (AD) =
Humanistic Vision (HV) + Mandated Mission (MM) +
Revolutionary Action (RA)

A. HUMANISTIC VISION (HV)

Indicate how well each statement fits you.	Not at all	Slightly	Moderately	Very much
I have maintained my childlike sense of wonder.	0	1	2	3
I am capable of deep concern and compassion.	0	1	2	3
I had an early awareness of the power of the spiritual.	0	1	2	3
I tend to have a philosophical nature.	0	1	2	3
Since childhood I have been easily upset by both large and small injustices.	0	1	2	3
I fare best when I employ my spiritual resources.	0	1	2	3
I have always carried a sense of the ideal.	0	1	2	3
I see life as a journey toward transcendent wisdom.	0	1	2	3
I am appreciative of the interconnectedness of everything.	0	1	2	3
I maintain a "seven-generation" view of life.	0	1	2	3
Humanitarian issues are of great concern to me.	0	1	2	3
I am drawn to the goals of ecumenicism.	0	1	2	3
I am intent on searching out universal truths.	0	1	2	3
My life is greatly enriched by divine dialogue.	0	1	2	3
My peak experiences have an otherworldly quality.	0	1	2	3
Integrity, honor, and character mean a lot to me.	0	1	2	3
I am intensely lured by the possibility of betterment.	0	1	2	3
I am deeply disturbed by inequity, exploitation, corruption, and needless human suffering.	0	1	2	3
I examine my actions against a backdrop of service.	0	1	2	3
I increasingly feel like an instrument or vessel of abilities for a purpose higher than my own.	0	1	2	3

Humanistic Vision (HV) TOTAL = _____

ENTER THIS SCORE ON THE SECTION TWO SCORE SHEET, PAGE 107.

B. MANDATED MISSION (MM)

Indicate how well each statement fits you.	Not at all	Slightly	Moderately	Very much
I passionately seek out new challenges and opportunities.	0	1	2	3
For me, self-actualization is a *need*, not an option.	0	1	2	3
I want to clarify and respond to my overarching sense of personal destiny.	0	1	2	3
I struggle with an inner sense of urgency.	0	1	2	3
I can feel shattered when a dream falls apart.	0	1	2	3
I have always felt a pull toward wisdom.	0	1	2	3
I battle with feelings of inner pressure, possible failure, or a fear of being "too late."	0	1	2	3
Authenticity is very important to me.	0	1	2	3
I am committed to the advancing the collective good.	0	1	2	3
I have questioned my true identity many times.	0	1	2	3
It is important for me to do something that really makes a difference.	0	1	2	3
I feel a duty to develop and share my gifts.	0	1	2	3
I envision the ideal and strive to reach it.	0	1	2	3
I am motivated and guided from within.	0	1	2	3
Crises and transcendent moments have helped shape my life's direction.	0	1	2	3
The integration of mind, body, and spirit is essential to fulfilling my potential.	0	1	2	3
Calculated risks are leaps of faith toward fulfilling my destiny, not simply taking chances.	0	1	2	3
Being "successful" is not the same as fulfilling one's inner call.	0	1	2	3
I derive happiness by living up to my expectations.	0	1	2	3
My life is as much an inner journey as outer action.	0	1	2	3
I feel compelled to match my abilities and actions with my soul's intention.	0	1	2	3

Mandated Mission (MM) TOTAL = _____

ENTER THIS SCORE ON THE SECTION TWO SCORE SHEET, PAGE 107.

C. REVOLUTIONARY ACTION (RA)

Indicate how well each statement fits you.	Not at all	Slightly	Moderately	Very much
I feel compelled to find ways to reduce suffering and preserve nature.	0	1	2	3
I have always been interested in social reform.	0	1	2	3
My efforts are founded on a sense of universal responsibility.	0	1	2	3
I empathetically identify with many others.	0	1	2	3
I value and will defend diversity.	0	1	2	3
I am willing to engage in acts of constructive dissent.	0	1	2	3
I am energized by teaching and drawing out the abilities of others.	0	1	2	3
I have frequently found myself in leadership roles whether I sought them or not.	0	1	2	3
I seem to be able to inspire others to action.	0	1	2	3
I have a strong need to make a difference.	0	1	2	3
I have a penchant for risk taking.	0	1	2	3
I can bring enthusiastic energy to a group.	0	1	2	3
I have an earnest need/desire to take charge.	0	1	2	3
I am good at rallying the support of others.	0	1	2	3
I can create order and direction in muddled or chaotic situations.	0	1	2	3
I'm good in an emergency.	0	1	2	3
I can foresee and predict trends/problems.	0	1	2	3
I can and do ignore my own needs for the sake of others.	0	1	2	3
I am willing to tolerate the loneliness of being a pioneer or frontrunner.	0	1	2	3
I'm not the type to wait for others to act.	0	1	2	3

Revolutionary Action (RA) TOTAL = _____

ENTER THIS SCORE ON THE SECTION TWO SCORE SHEET, PAGE 107.

SECTION ONE SCORE SHEET
DETERMINING YOUR SPECIAL ABILITIES

MULTIPLE INTELLIGENCES (MI) SCORES

1. Transfer each of your eight Multiple Intelligences subscores to the corresponding blanks below.

    a. Body-Smart   = _____   e. Logic-Smart   = _____

    b. Word-Smart   = _____   f. Relationship-Smart   = _____

    c. Spatial-Smart = _____   g. Nature-Smart   = _____

    d. Music-Smart   = _____   h. Self-Smart   = _____

2. Add each of these numbers together to determine your Multiple Intelligences raw score. To correctly interpret your results, divide this raw score by 4. Record this number below. *Round up or down to the nearest whole number.*

    MI raw score _____ ÷ 4 = _____ 1. MI

GIFTED TRAITS (GT) SCORES

1. Transfer each of your five Gifted Traits subscores to the corresponding blanks below.

    INTENSITY: COMPLEXITY:

    i. Excitability   = _____   k. Complex Thinking = _____

    j. Sensitivity   = _____   l. Perception   = _____

    DRIVE:

    m. = _____

2. Add each of these five Gifted Traits subscores to determine your Gifted Traits raw score. To correctly interpret your results, divide this raw score by 5. Record this number below. *Round up or down to the nearest whole number.*

    GT raw score _____ ÷ 5 = _____ 2. GT

SECTION TWO SCORE SHEET

HV = _____ (from total, page 103)

MM = _____ (from total, page 104)

RA = _____ (from total, page 105)

AD = _____ + _____ + _____

          HV   MM   RA

To correctly interpret your results, divide this raw score by 3. Record this number below. *Round up or down to the nearest whole number.*

_____ **3. AD**

DETERMINING YOUR EvIQ

Multiple Intelligences (MI) = _____ (from page 106)

Gifted Traits (GT) = _____ (from page 106)

Advanced Development (AD) = _____ (from above)

EvIQ = _____ + _____ + _____

          MI   GT   AD

EvIQ = _____

Plot your scores as instructed on the EvIQ Profile on page 108.

EvI PROFILE

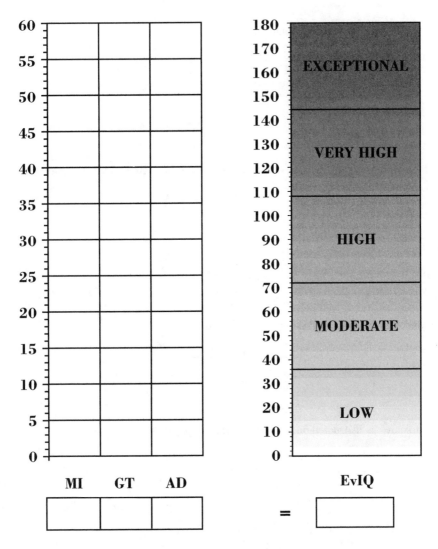

Place your Multiple Intelligences (MI), Gifted Traits (GT), and Advanced Development (AD) scores from pages 106 and 107 in the corresponding boxes above. Then place a mark on each bar that corresponds to your numerical score for MI, GT, and AD. Connect each of these points to create a line graph that profiles the factors of your Evolutionary Intelligence. Place your EvIQ score in the corresponding box and mark the place on the bar that corresponds to your numerical EvIQ score to indicate your current level of Evolutionary Intelligence.

WHAT THE EvIQ SCORE TELLS YOU

Begin by reviewing your high and low scores on each section of the inventory. On the Multiple Intelligences (MI) section, your highest scores identify your prominent skill and talent areas. Think about how you have or have not developed these skills and talents as a part of your work or personal life. Consider also how these high-scoring areas might be combined to your advantage to create a new pattern of success. Think of these strengths in terms of personal *needs* more than possibilities. For instance, if you score high on Music-Smart and Body-Smart, you may be able to significantly enhance your well-being through regular involvement in dance or therapeutic massage. If you score high on Word-Smart, Nature-Smart, and Relationship-Smart, think of how you might benefit from organizing a nature-book discussion group, becoming an urban environmental watchdog, or volunteering to lead tours at a nature center.

When reviewing your Gifted Traits (GT) profile, start by reminding yourself that each of these Intensity, Complexity, and Drive characteristics is a valuable basic asset that underlies excellence and self-actualization. You can take a giant step toward liberating your own brand of Everyday Genius by remembering that every one of these attributes can be a building block of excellence. Also, in evaluating your scores, you may be able to see that certain of these traits are out of balance. Depending on your career, personal situation, and basic personality type (for example, introverted or extroverted), you can consider how to work with, not around, your traits and habits in order to avoid setting obstacles in your own path. Take some time to reflect on how MI and GT can combine to work for you. This will give you a more detailed portrait of your Special Abilities (SA), which will trigger additional ideas about areas that are best fits for your time and energy.

Remember that the factors of Advanced Development (AD) in Section Two change and grow over time. The HV inventory is a kind of snapshot showing where you stand in terms of Humanistic Vision. Think about the items and how you rated your service, meaningful contribution, and sense of personal destiny. Make note of any regrets that come to mind, or dreams that were shelved for one reason or another. Give yourself an opportunity to reflect on your life from a future perspective by utilizing a kind of "rocking-chair mentality." Visualize yourself rocking leisurely on your front porch toward the end of your life, reviewing what you have contributed to the world. What acts give you the greatest sense of satisfaction? What regrets might you have if nothing changes in your life, and what might you do to avoid those regrets?

As you review your current level of understanding and implementation of your Mandated Mission, remember that the process of self-actualization can be likened to an endurance sport. The victory isn't always to the swiftest, but to the one who most consistently maintains the effort over the long haul. How does your sense of personal mission affect your confidence, motivation, and perseverance? Reflect on the ways (and the circumstances) in which you have doubted, sidetracked, or derailed yourself. What it would take to recover your lost dreams or passion? Think of ways to redirect your energies by recombining your strengths to develop new expertise.

Revolutionary Action (RA) is a special dimension of Evolutionary Intelligence. It is the catalyst that activates Special Abilities into EvI to attain new heights. It launches exceptional gifts into the realm of gifted leadership. As you consider your scores in this subsection, visualize Revolutionary Action as a pebble you toss into life's waters that causes a series of ripple effects that expand in many directions. Have you made your vision a reality, or have you been satisfied to think, "Wouldn't it be nice if . . . ?"

Any increase or decrease in one of the EvIQ factors can profoundly affect your EvIQ score. For example, even with an extraordinarily high MI and GT score, a low RA number can substantially reduce your EvIQ. Such a profile would suggest that tremendous abilities have not been fully activated. Likewise, an extremely high MM or RA score and low MI or GT could indicate a valuable outpouring of effort, though it might be low in the EvIQ range because of limited ability (MI or GT) or low Advanced Development (HV, MM, RA). Consider into what EvIQ ranges people you admire would fall and why. Think about what you would have to do to change your EvIQ range.

Following the EvI Profile you will find the Exploring Your EvIQ pages. Make note of ideas and questions about yourself that surfaced as you reflected on your scores. Add ongoing ideas, questions, and insights to these pages as you continue reading the book.

EXPLORING YOUR EvIQ SCORE

SECTION ONE: SPECIAL ABILITIES

Multiple Intelligences (MI): _____

_____

_____

_____

_____

_____

Gifted Traits (GT)

INTENSITY: _____

_____

_____

_____

COMPLEXITY: _____

_____

_____

_____

DRIVE: _____

_____

_____

SECTION TWO: ADVANCED DEVELOPMENT (HV, MM, RA)

Humanistic Vision (HV): _____

_____

_____

_____

Mandated Mission (MM) _____

_____

_____

_____

Revolutionary Action (RA) _____

_____

_____

_____

Current EvIQ: _____

_____

_____

_____

_____

_____

_____

Further Development of EvIQ: _____

_____

_____

_____

_____

_____

_____

_____

Other Ideas, Questions, and Insights: _____

_____

_____

EVOLUTIONARY INTELLIGENCE IN REAL LIFE

Having now taken the Evolutionary Intelligence Profile, you are familiar with the factors involved, and are more aware of the emerging pattern of your special traits. To make the EvI equation more tangible, let us take a look at a few individuals who serve as good illustrations of the various forms EvI can take, while being mindful of some of the key telltale markers of each of the primary factors.

Special Abilities (MI + GT)

Jordan—truly a man for all seasons—was known by his friends and coworkers as someone who was an expert in just about everything. He was indeed an exemplar of Multiple Intelligences. He was Body-Smart in that he could pick up nearly any sport and excel at it within just a few weeks. Since he could adroitly handle scissors and fashion intricate paper snowflakes before he was five years old, his extraordinary eye-hand coordination had been obvious. Over the years it became even more clear that Jordan's dexterity, strength, stamina, finesse, and easy efficiency of movement were beyond ordinary. Indeed, his coaches marveled at his deerlike fleetness of foot and catlike cunning on the playing field.

To everyone's surprise but his, Jordan had a tough time deciding what to do about his desire to become an environmental scientist when just before college he had several offers from big-league baseball and football teams vying for his outstanding pitching and quarterbacking abilities. He agonized over his choice, eventually sticking with his plans to become a scientist because his Self-Smart early wisdom told him his true path lay in that domain. No one but his sister agreed with his choice. She had always understood Jordan's affinity for nature. Indeed, it was his Nature-Smart ability to match his "frequency" with animals and plants that made his heart sing. He loved the intricate patterns of nature and seemed to grasp at almost a cellular level how the environment worked and how to protect and sustain its wonders.

And so Jordan continued to play ball in college, thoroughly enjoying the experience despite the fact that he was sorrowfully letting go of a highly coveted dream. Jordan had always been required to make difficult choices like this. Had he honestly answered standard "What do you want to be when you grow up?" questions he might have said: "Everything I have time for." When his high-school guidance counselor tried to help him with career choices, Jordan, like others with Multiple Intelligences, found little use in the usual recommendations, such as "Do what you love" (because he could dive into nearly any topic with real enthusiasm) or "Do what you're good at" (because he was better than most kids at nearly everything he tried).

Like most Everyday Geniuses, Jordan never thought of himself as exceptional. He knew he had special talents and learned things quickly, but he was used to that and so was everyone he knew. He was a sought-after friend and a trusted confidant of many. More often than not, Jordan was the enthusiastic one in the group, the person who seemed to bring a bit of magic to social gatherings. Because he was Word-Smart, Jordan was an easy talker who made good use of his verbal abilities. He relied on his Relationship-Smart abilities to shrewdly read situations and detect the needs and feelings of others, which kept him from abusing his powers of persuasion.

Jordan was a true specimen of the Gifted Traits of Complex Thinking and Perception. From childhood he had never ceased to be an endlessly curious person whose keen observations were amplified by a second sight for what would probably happen next. He was independent and self-motivated, and, like a dog after a bone, he was able to pursue something that caught his interest. As a scientist, he put these traits to excellent use. He could be energized by problems that seemed to defy resolution—problems that made others throw their hands up in defeat. When he was on the trail of something important, his Gifted Trait of Intensity allowed him to concentrate for long periods of time, making him highly productive. Unlike many of his colleagues, in the face of a deadline or crisis Jordan's capacity and imagination seemed to double, and somehow his energy appeared to be self-renewable.

For years it had been difficult for Jordan to balance his highly independent style with the needs of his work team. Yet by pooling his exceptional resources, he had discovered balance was not equivalent to settling for mediocrity. He had always been fascinated with the concept of a think tank, and came to understand think-tank methods as his natural way of working. When Jordan finally realized that neither the "meet until there's consensus" nor the "do it all yourself" approach offered the right solution, he brought an "in-and-out" procedure to his team. Each member would retain ownership, credit, and accountability for his or her element of the research, while all were committed to the same goal and underlying principle: Save the venerable oaks of the Midwest's Big Woods from extinction by oak wilt and urban sprawl.

Even though at first the others were skeptical, thinking Jordan's time- and ego-saving approach was too simple to be effective, they eventually found tremendous value in it. In large part this was because, just as in sports, Jordan had learned that timing was everything. Earlier in his career his sagacity had backfired because others distrusted and dismissed his ideas either when he revealed them too early in the process or if they required too great a leap of faith. Now he was more artistic in curbing his enthusiasm when necessary to better navigate the rapids of meaningful change.

Lately Jordan had been thinking a lot about the past, his days on the pitcher's mound and in the huddle in the last minutes of the big game. He smiled a knowing smile as he realized how it all fit together, even the intricate snowflakes he had made as a preschooler. The outdoors, challenge, teamwork, autonomy, complexity, the interconnectedness of all things, an artistic balance of thought and action, communicating effectively, winning a seemingly losing battle—there it all was. No real loss, and no bad choices, but rather, an adventurous life founded on a liberating amalgamation of traits and abilities, a growing synthesis that cleared the way for Jordan to enjoy each and every day while he advanced in his field more fleet-footed, self-assured, and directly aimed at his heart's true agenda and his distinct place in evolution.

Jordan illustrates the complexity and necessity of integrating Multiple Intelligences with Gifted Traits. The key ingredients in his pattern are:

- Excellent mind-body coordination and skillful movement
- Masterful, constructive use of the power of words
- Sophisticated ability to read situations and respect others' needs
- Insatiable curiosity, self-directed investigation, and creative energy
- Autonomy coupled with collaboration for unparalleled success

Humanistic Vision (HV)

Brenda was a benevolent and imaginative woman who had never been able to separate the notion of a good idea from the notion of something that was good for all. This ability allowed her to see possibilities differently than others. Since early childhood she had had an appreciation for the interconnectedness and value of all things.

Brenda was a bridge builder, someone naturally equipped to detect links between divided agendas, links that unearthed win-win resolutions that rarely occurred to others. Everyone thought of her as an advocate, a person who validated and upheld individuality in ways that, ironically, brought people together. Yet at times she struggled with her own individuality, finding it hard to square her own wants and needs with the needs of others. In midlife she was better at sticking up for herself than when she was young, though her ability to see all sides of an argument and to feel the feelings of others could turn empathy into exhaustion.

Brenda was unmistakably someone who loathed conflict, avoiding disagreements as much as possible. But her high-level ethics and standards meant she was intolerant of injustice and falsehood. More than once she had felt duty-bound to take a stand against injustice, especially for someone other than herself. To those around her these temporary changes of demeanor looked to be uncalled-for flare-ups of drama. What they failed to realize was that in all things Brenda's image of a future as humanely civilized as it is technologically advanced was the backbone of her thinking. Unfairness had always been a battle cry to which she responded by either creatively circumventing destructive rules and procedures or, if necessary, locking horns with authority figures. Whatever her disposition, Brenda always had one eye on the future and the promotion of a better world.

These days Brenda endeavored to choose her battles wisely, avoiding broken bridges with little possibility of being rebuilt, or letting go of tempting skirmishes that might better be righted by someone else. This was not as easy as it may sound. Because Brenda could skillfully track a problem and wrestle it to the ground before others left the starting gate, she had learned to feel answerable to her insight, as if seeing that something was wrong obligated her to fix it. Getting there first, in Brenda's case, was not always a triumph. It seemed she was often too early to summon the interest of others less aware, too charitable for many people's taste, or too blunt a truth teller to allow accountability to be overlooked. It was a predicament, because if something important was wrong and she knew it without doing anything to change it, her feelings of guilt could be crushing.

Brenda is a prime example of Humanistic Vision (HV) because she exemplifies:

- Benevolent compassion, deep concern, and pursuit of wisdom
- High ethical standards and dedication to universal ideals
- Ability to facilitate win-win resolutions that bring people together
- Powerful desire to create a better world and make a difference
- Intolerance for injustice, oppression, and suffering

Drive and Mandated Mission
Randall was a striver whose actions seemed to be pulled by an invisible tractor beam—he didn't seem to know the meaning of the phrase "give up." In many ways he was a modern-day marvel of stick-to-it-iveness who seemed to need no prodding from others to get going and stay with it. Some people thought of him as foolish, while others considered him overly serious and stubborn. Yet Randall had always thrived on challenge. In fact, he felt lost and deenergized without a formidable task in front of him.

Although it may have seemed that Randall was an oppositional child, he was not. He simply liked to master new ways, innovative ways, of doing things. Whether it was throwing out the directions for a model airplane so that he could do it his way or drawing up plans for a water-saving showerhead before conservation became popular, Randall was drawn to doing whatever was necessary to improve things.

Everyone knew that no grass would grow under Randall's feet. What they didn't know was why. Some had called him hyperactive, while others interpreted his zeal as self-focused, overly ambitious, or insatiable. None of these was an accurate assessment of Randall. Indeed, he found satisfaction in many things and was eager to share nearly everything he learned and owned. Yet he also intrinsically knew that real goal attainment often takes years of step-by-step effort interrupted by detours and mistakes. On the side, after his fifty-plus hours a week as a CPA for a Fortune 500 company, Randall diligently learned everything he could about filmmaking. During the first few years of his interest, he had confided in a few friends that he had a dream of one day producing a documentary on aging in America, an exposé of what he considered the "throwing away of American wisdom." Later he learned to keep his intentions to himself to avoid the negative comments of others who had no idea what it took to pull off such a venture.

Even Randall's wife began to take exception to his night-owl efforts. She worried that his hopes would be dashed and that all his hard work might be for naught. Randall knew that she had trouble understanding his zeal. He also knew that this was a labor of love and as much a need for him as eating and sleeping. No matter what the outcome, not trying was not an option. Randall was not undone by the long hours or the lack of ready-made success. His motivation came from the inside *and* outside worlds. Once he had figured out where his passion lay, he derived tremendous happiness from the endeavor, the process of attempting to live up to his own expectations, which were in turn fueled by what he truly believed to be an important issue.

Randall had always known his exceptional drive could get out of hand and become more of a liability than an asset. Having outgrown a hindering need for a lot of external approval, he could move forward with unprecedented confidence as his dream began to take shape. Getting rid of excessive approval needs was the first step to allowing his ideas to spring forth with a voice of authority. Next, even though he had often wished he didn't need to sleep or take breaks, Randall needed to learn to manage himself according to real-world criteria because his goal-oriented striving hadn't always worked out so well in relationships, or even in terms of his bodily health.

Once he saw how critical it was to counterbalance his driven effort with equalizing shifts from serious thinking to lighthearted play, from sitting to moving, from being alone to being together, from the abstract to the realities of daily life, he discovered that sometimes more was just more, not better. As he became accustomed to consciously and systematically centering himself each day, Randall was able to manage his life like a seasoned spider, venturing out farther than most on a broader web of experience. Now more could be better.

Randall's judicious self-management plan—knowing himself and managing his strengths—was the key to the realization of his dreams. The road upon which he felt duty-bound to travel was a path that called for his utmost courage, effort, and creativity of spirit. This was a path that could never fully succeed by reason of self-gratification alone; of that he was certain. And he also understood that it would be reasonable to tie his dreams to a star only when he could push forward on the zigzag route of self-actualization without burning himself or his relationships out, or sacrificing the value of living in the moment for the envisioned moment of getting to the desired end.

Randall's striving style is a model of the quality of Drive because he carried:

- A passion for innovation and new information
- A driving inner need to become all he could be
- Tolerance and appreciation for the painstaking efforts of excellence
- An ability to be energized by challenge
- Inner-directedness, self-starter zeal, and a dynamic sense of obligation

Humanistic Vision (HV) and Revolutionary Action (RA)

Mitch went to Vietnam as an infantryman in the army in 1969 when he was eighteen. He had grown up in the suburbs of Milwaukee, a typical middle-class life. Though he'd been in a few scrapes as a teenager, his upbringing was fairly safe and uneventful. Before he was shipped off to the Mekong Delta, the only deaths he had personally encountered were those of his pet turtle and of his ninety-year-old grandfather.

Like so many veterans of the Vietnam War, Mitch's callow psyche was forever altered by his experience. Seeing his buddies blown apart by land mines and helping to gather their dog tags and put them in body bags took a tremendous toll on his deep-seated idealism. Mitch had always been considered to be brighter than most—well liked, fair-minded, fun-loving, and a young man of his word.

Mitch came back from Vietnam embittered and hateful. Mostly he hated the Vietnamese. Even though he had spent time in their villages and held some of their smiling children in his arms, he had come to despise and blame them for all the atrocities of war. Perhaps by hating them he could justify killing them, children and all. When he returned to Milwaukee he decided to put all that behind him, as if it were simply a hideous nightmare. He closed the door to that part of his life.

Mitch was determined to take up where he had left off. Without delay he pursued his childhood dream of becoming a firefighter. Eight years later he found himself embroiled in a situation he had never expected. The inner city of Milwaukee had changed immensely over the years, now housing a large population of Southeast Asians—Vietnamese, Laotian, and Cambodian immigrants. That same year Mitch was promoted to captain and reassigned to a unit in the middle of the Asian neighborhood. At first he thought nothing of it—that is, until he came into direct contact with one of the families during a kitchen fire.

Though the fire was quickly extinguished, the drama of the screaming families together with the smoke and flames threw Mitch into a shocking reliving of his wartime feelings. Only his tremendous concentration and emergency training kept his mind on the task at hand.

In the apartment building he saw the faces of the very people he had hated so bitterly—here in his hometown. They were real people, scared, shivering in the winter cold, tears falling from their eyes as they surrounded the firefighters with animated gratitude.

Unsure at first of exactly why, Mitch returned to that same neighborhood again and again over the following weeks. Strangely, he felt something that he could describe only as a sentimental attraction. Mitch's Humanistic Vision was taking on a real form. In the weeks ahead he noticed groups of Asian teenagers hanging out on the street corners. When Mitch first approached them, they were wary and unresponsive. In their former homeland, anyone in uniform was menacing. Then they began to talk—the kind of conversation that happens in most neighborhoods when people aren't afraid. He found out many of them were having trouble in school, in terms of both fitting in and understanding the assignments because of their language and cultural differences. Having grown up as the gifted different kid in his own neighborhood, Mitch had always held a soft spot in his heart for anyone who felt alienated.

This was the beginning of a life-changing journey for Mitch that also radically changed the lives of Asian teens in Milwaukee. He organized the street kids into a group, found out what they liked to do, and garnered the support of local youth ministers and community service organizations to start a club for them. Part of the group spun off to develop a crime-watchers patrol with the help of one of Mitch's friends in the police department.

Within a few months the parents and grandparents of the members were coming to the club when the kids were in school. Mitch listened as they recounted their needs for transportation to and from work and their struggles with health care, legal assistance, tax forms, and the like. From them he learned about their customs and religious practices, and he was invited to their homes for dinner. He realized that they too had suffered, that they also experienced the horrors of warfare, that they had a chance to heal the old wounds with each other right there in Milwaukee. They had all been through hell. And even though a part of each of them would be lost forever, now, with Mitch's help, together they were gradually finding their way back from hell into a new life beyond the malignance of hatred.

Though people like Mitch never appear on magazine covers or in *Who's Who*, his benevolent efforts healed, liberated, and constructively altered his own life and the lives of many more than he would ever know, which made his courageously creative action far-reaching and in the final analysis revolutionary.

IT ONLY LOOKS REVOLUTIONARY
AFTER THE FACT

To our collective disadvantage, few bright and talented people who rise to public acclaim tell the details of their beginnings. If they did, it might be a great deal easier to imagine ourselves doing extraordinary things. But as it is, we rarely get a glimpse of the self-doubting, happenstance-abiding, lonely, persevering nature of developing excellence. Perhaps we elevate high achievers because we are in need of heroes, or perhaps by elevating them we justify not putting our own abilities on the line because we decide we must be out of the running. Yet rather than weigh ourselves down with qualms of "Not me," we would do better to ask ourselves, "Why not me?"

EvI offers something far greater than the sum of its parts when it intermixes virtues that embody the best of what is valuable about the human species with the abundant resources of giftedness and creative spirit.

In a different configuration, Bill Gates' form of EvI might be said to represent someone with indisputable Special Abilities (Multiple Intelligences + Gifted Traits), boundless Drive, and a Mandated Mission that is focused on catapulting technology to new heights to the advantage of humankind. His irrefutable Revolutionary Actions changed the face of the computer industry nearly overnight. We might also conclude, as is so often the case for entrepreneurs, that his Humanistic Vision is growing and gaining momentum over time.

Bill Gates is a controversial figure, an amalgam of talents and personality traits that have earned him many labels. Thus far in his illustrious career he seems to have gone from Geek Boy to Wonder Boy, from a sometimes admired, sometimes loathed wealthy man of power to a national corporate leader revered for his vision and daring. By his early forties he had amassed a fortune in the billions through a company that provided him a profit of about $30 million a day.

The enigmatic Gates was dubbed by one of his schoolteachers "a nerd before the term was invented" and by his college roommate "the smartest guy I've ever met." Gates is reported to have a cutthroat attitude, to have a temper that is barely in check, to be elusive, and to be fiercely competitive in everything he undertakes, which gets his "juices flowing." In a 1997 *Time* cover story, Walter Isaacson sought out "the real Bill Gates":

> In the 21 years since he dropped out of Harvard to start Microsoft, William Henry Gates, III, 41, has thrashed competitors in the world of desktop operating systems and application software. Now he is attempting the audacious feat of expanding Microsoft from a software company into a media and content company. . . .
>
> His success stems from his personality: an awesome and at times frightening blend of brilliance, drive, competitiveness and personal intensity. . . . [H]e has incredible processing power and unlimited bandwidth, an agility at parallel processing and multitasking. . . .
>
> [Gates' father recalls that when Bill was a child] "Trey" was more into the individual sports, such as water skiing, than the team ones. . . .
> We became concerned about him when he was ready for junior high.

He was so small and shy, in need of protection, and his interests were so very different from the typical sixth grader's. His intellectual drive and curiosity would not be satisfied in a big public school. . . ."

By 10th grade he was teaching computers and writing a program that handled class scheduling, which had a secret function that placed him in classes with the right girls. . . . He and his friends had started a profitable company to analyze and graph traffic data for the city. His confidence increased, and his sense of humor increased. He became a great storyteller, who could mimic the voices of each person. . . . [Reflecting on his Microsoft partnership with long-time friend Paul Allen, Gates said,] "We like to talk about how the fantasies we had as kids actually came true."

[On the human mind and the future, Gates maintains,] "Evolution is many orders of magnitude ahead of mankind today in creating a complex system. I don't think it's irreconcilable to say we will understand the human mind someday and explain it in software-like terms, and also to say it is a creation that shouldn't be compared to software. Religion has come around to the view that even things that can be explained scientifically can have an underlying purpose that goes beyond the science. Even though I am not religious, the amazement and wonder I have about the human mind is closer to religious awe than dispassionate analysis."[1]

One by one all the factors in the formula can and must be put together by each Everyday Genius in order to move high potential into the realm of Evolutionary Intelligence, where it can release its full power. To become all we might be—to do all we were intended to do, as creatively and responsibly as possible—is not an undertaking for the faint of heart. Yet at length what is most prized in our lives is invariably what is also an arduous ascent of a mountain. Each step matters and each is valuable, though for all intents and purposes the first step is most important because it is foundational. It is the initial step to know thyself that is prerequisite to Advanced Development and the eventual fulfillment of latent possibility.

PART THREE

WHEN WHAT'S "WRONG" WITH YOU IS WHAT'S RIGHT WITH YOU

REVEALING AND HEALING EVERYDAY GENIUS

8

GIFTED OR CURSED?

Quite often I have been faced with people who were praised and admired for their talents and their achievements. . . . According to prevailing attitudes, these people—the pride and joy of their parents— should have had a strong and stable sense of self-assurance. But the case is exactly the opposite. . . . [W]henever they suddenly get the feeling they have failed to live up to some ideal image or have not measured up to some standard, then they are plagued by anxiety or deep feelings of guilt and shame. What are the reasons for such disturbances in these competent, accomplished people?
—Alice Miller

No gifted person I know was ever approached as a child and told, "You have gifts that may make you very special. They may also make you very vulnerable." Consequently, developing our gifts is always a compensatory process, charged with aliveness and adventure while at the same time fraught with obstacles and moments of profound loneliness. With work, the effect of others' preconceived ideas about us and the unwanted indoctrination we experience that develops a false self falters under the weight of life's deeper truths and emerging self-knowledge. Over time we can grow to trust that our gifts came with an inner guidance system that can help us reclaim and fulfill the promise of our high potential.

Ironically, we also discover that much of our most potent creative energy arises from the flames of past injustices and inhibited creative efforts. Clarissa Pinkola Estés, Ph.D., author of *Women Who Run With the*

Wolves, Jungian analyst, poet, and *contadora*, or a keeper of a culture's traditional stories, illuminates creativity's natural cycles in *The Creative Fire*. She describes the creative process, which is analogous to the fulfillment of potential, as a "loss and restoration" pattern of slowing down, descent, underground gathering, quickening, and a burst of intensity. This ebb and flow is the reality of the creative life and that we must expect and accept.

Nonetheless, we must also understand the unnatural forces that impede the creative process and keep the resources of the true self out of reach. Although creative energy can never be extinguished entirely, sometimes, as Estés explains, due to such things as internalized complexes or fear to commit, the creative incubation period is interrupted or prolonged. Destructive complexes are often permitted to grow to a size where they can attack the soul and hold it hostage. These complexes are often the result of being denigrated and devalued.

Estés wrote *Ways to Silence a Woman* at a time when, as she notes, "over 85% of the books that were published were written by men, and over 90% of the awards in literature were given to men." She assures us, however, that her words apply to creative men as well as women. Here are a few excerpts from this provocative poem:

Say: "We're saying the same thing, don't you see?"
Say: "Don't defy my authority. If you want to pass, do it the way I tell you." . . .
Say: "Your ideas are dangerous." . . .
Say: "You're overreacting." . . .
Say: "I can't understand you when you're upset." . . .
Say: "You've missed the point." . . .
Say: "That's a wild idea." And then talk about your own work. . . .
Say: "Who do you think you are?"[1]

CORRECTING THE "TOO-TOO" MISDIAGNOSIS

The chief complaint directed toward the gifted is that they think, do, say, imagine, or emote "too much." They are simply "too-too" in comparison to the norm. Oddly, it remains a nearly unknown fact that the development of high potential and the advancement of excellence depend upon a reversal of society's defamation of the gifted character. As individual

Everyday Geniuses, our task is to contribute to this reversal by understanding that the Ten Criticisms comprise the very foundation of excellence and Evolutionary Intelligence. What we have been taught to think of as personal liabilities are, in fact, our greatest assets.

What on the surface may appear to others as a set of behaviors and attributes that are overblown, over-the-top exaggeration, or simply immaturity may not be that at all. In fact, many of the intense characteristics and expressions of gifted people are key factors in the process of developing insight, expertise, and ultimately the kind of integration of knowledge, experience, and personality that comprises wisdom. The problem is these foundations of exceptional achievement and Advanced Development have been given a bad rap. Because they tend to stand out a bit, these authentic assets are misdiagnosed as something wrong, something unacceptable. Yet something at the subconscious level of the Everyday Genius insists these traits are not wrong even though others may find them unacceptable. To reclaim lost gifts and damaged self-belief we must be clear about the inseparable nature of these traits and excellence. We must remind ourselves and others as often as necessary that what may at first look out of place will eventually be the very set of personal assets that helps us find our place in the larger scheme of things.

Too-Too "Liabilities"	Foundations of These
Skipping from one interest to another (*too scattered*)	Adaptability essential to creativity; multiple areas of expertise; ability to simultaneously grasp concepts on diverse levels
Deep concern for others; champion of ultimate truths; intolerance of injustice (*too crusading*)	Humanitarian benevolence; transpersonal problem solving and moral leadership
Rapid-fire thought and speech (*too glib*)	Advanced original thinking; constructive influence; creative productivity
High energy and single-minded, zealous effort (*too intense*)	Unorthodox innovation; breakthrough or trendsetting ideas; perseverance and endurance in the face of adversity

Too-Too "Liabilities"	Foundations of These
Extrasensitivity and excitability (*too sensitive and dramatic*)	Empathy, compassion, and responsiveness; arousing motivation and cooperation
Perfectionism (*too "anal" and demanding*)	Systems orientation; commitment; restructuring and synthesizing; excellence and eminence
Relentless pursuit of goals; impassioned concentration (*too driven*)	Advanced depth of knowledge; ability to delve into life's largest questions; outstanding achievement and self-actualization
Radical or unconventional ideas (*too different*)	Creative change, autonomy and courageous revolutionary acts; able to alter talent domain
Passion for intellectual scrutiny, abstract, cause-effect relationships, and paradox (*too complex*)	Visionary research and discovery; bridge-building effects on progress
Contemplative, open to spiritual and otherworldly experiences (*too intuitive*)	Transcendent insights; strong inner resources; integrity; richness of life; dynamic wisdom

As Everyday Geniuses, we are an intensely curious group of seekers, determined to become more than what we were yesterday, seeking the most complete answers to the universal questions. Nevertheless, a first-order question of our personal universe bedevils us: the "why" of our very nature. A *need to know* drives us like nothing else. As was the case with the early explorers, the world will remain flat for us until we dispel antiquated notions, which can be summed up in the Ten Criticisms of gifted people, which we will explore in detail later in the chapter.

We acquire the benefits of liberation by rolling up our sleeves and getting our hands right into the mess of what has hurt us and hindered us. This is the only way to steal our critics' thunder; to move from silent to shielded to strong. The process of discovering that what we've been told is wrong with us is precisely what's right and intelligent about us must begin with choosing to confront disapproval, something most of us have tried tirelessly to avoid.

This is work we must do against the odds, since there is no designated haven for the gifted adult. Since forced "normalcy" leaves us feeling robbed, we must never lose sight of two facts: Self-neglect and acceptance of the false self kill the potential of Everyday Genius, and knowing the true meaning of giftedness is the only way to open new avenues. If Everyday Genius is to be a blessing rather than a curse, we must get serious about which of the two we intend to support, remembering that resisting our gifts is a choice to ignore the true power of our abilities.

DÉJÀ VU

Several years ago I observed and relived the dilemma of the gifted child in the classroom. My gifted older son's encounters with early education tripped an internal switch in me that evoked old feelings. His kindergarten class had been learning about community helpers. One of the assignments was to choose an occupation and don the related hat or costume for a song and parade around the room. There were miniature firefighters, nurses, librarians, chefs, and even a mayor, each child seeming to enjoy the experience.

This was the type of event the school considered suitable for parental participation, a sort of show-and-tell of creative education. Indeed, the children were adorable and appeared by their words and actions to have learned something of value. However, as the parents beamed from their squeezed-in positions in the tiny chairs, I noticed that my son was not among them.

As I scanned the squirming crowd of five-year-olds, the teacher walked over to address my puzzled expression. An unusually astute and sensitive teacher, she inconspicuously pointed to the space behind the piano, where my son was encamped. Matter-of-factly she informed me that my son had announced that marching around the piano in hats was "stupid," and that he wanted to continue his work on a model of the solar system instead.

She thought that was just fine, and so did I. Regrettably, the other children and their parents reacted quite differently to his independence and assertion. Most responded with irritation, punishing questions, and eventually polite dismissal. The everyday bittersweet experience of being a gifted child was repeating itself right before my eyes.

I walked over to my son and delighted in his creation of his own universe. "So, are you going to help your community by being an astronomer or an astronaut?" I questioned. He smiled and pointed at the planet he'd surrounded with rings. "I'm going to have a house on Saturn. Will you come and visit me there?"

His response pleased me greatly, for his acceptance of his uniqueness was completely natural. He seemed unaffected by the opinions and assumptions of others. His experience stood in stark contrast to my own childhood when I dutifully followed the rules, submitted to the expectations of others, and nearly lost my true self.

GIFTED OR CURSED?
MY OWN BEGINNINGS

The same world that occasionally flung erroneous complaints at me also told me I could do anything I wanted, because I was "special." While I was glad for my ability to do well in school, it was confusing when I was chided for being "too curious," "too inquisitive," and "too concerned for such a little girl." But then, I was just a kid, so what did I know?

What I learned was to faithfully follow the rules, to be a good girl, to make people smile to gain approval, and to keep my unusual ideas to myself. When I dared to be authentic, the cost was often high. I blushed easily and often. At times I naively placed my trust in the wrong hands and suffered the hurtful consequence of betrayal.

One of the first such experiences occurred in the fifth grade when to my horror my teacher shredded a poem I had written in praise of the Divine for the wonder of animals. She insisted that I had copied it from a book, humiliating me in front of the class by bellowing: "No one your age could have written such a thing! Shame on you!" I learned that expressing myself was a dangerous thing to do. Becoming a person of few words was difficult for an enthusiastic extrovert such as myself.

Granted, my poems, drawings, pointed questions, and occasional challenges to authority were not always badly received. Yet when they were, I found that my spirit withered quickly. "Who do you think you are?" still rings in my ears, words that made me feel small, pressuring me to try even harder to keep quiet. I conformed and played the part I was given.

I didn't understand that the withering feeling I experienced didn't come from my own fragility or instability. It was the side effect of a culture that insists on pigeonholing and limiting the creative spirit and uncommon intelligence. Though I was taught that uniqueness and individuality were the American way, this proved to be more myth than reality. So I stayed on the approved track and played my prescribed part quite successfully. I put away my watercolors and poems and lived a conventional adult life that by most people's estimation should have been "good enough."

For a long time I made believe that I was content, because that was true on many fronts. Yet in my quiet times I was bothered by a profound feeling of emptiness, as though I had lost something vital. I couldn't figure out the source of my discomfort. Years later, in midlife, this memory came to the forefront when I hit the identity wall, suddenly unable to recognize myself. Worse still, I noticed that instead of becoming more clearminded as the years went on, I felt increasingly uneasy and scattered.

I started to think that the possibilities of life I had always imagined were destined to be nothing more than faded childhood fantasies. After all, I concluded, I had "lost so many years" being unclear about the direction I wanted my life to take. I'd had the bad luck of being an early orphan, and had studied the wrong subjects in school. This anxiety began to mount into an increasing fear that I had made my bed and must now be content to lie in it.

I reexamined my special fondness for counseling gifted and talented adolescents and adults, noting a special kinship with them. This was the beginning of a fascinating and revealing self-exploration. Since I had never been formally identified as a gifted child, I never expected to see myself in the books and scientific studies I was researching.

I enthusiastically shared my interest in gifted adults with a valued professor. Her revealing remark both shocked and relieved me: "Of course you're interested in gifted people," she insisted, "because you are one!" I was stunned, and wondered, "Could she be right? Am I a gifted person?"

It was as if a switch had been tripped, turning on a series of floodlights that illuminated areas of my experience that had been bathed in darkness. Insights and memories flooded my consciousness. I was finally able to find pieces of my personal puzzle that I thought had been lost. Suddenly I understood with uncharacteristic certainty that my gifted nature had nothing to do with arrogance or eccentricity. Rather, it had everything to do with finally making sense of my life, especially those unanswered questions of who I truly was and was not. It was a bombshell that blasted me into a personal cycle of newfound energy, possibility, and confidence that has not slackened to this day.

In retrospect, I am utterly convinced that a corrected self-image was the only thing powerful enough to release me from the dominance of my false self. Liberation of any kind is a blessed deliverance. For me it unleashed a rush of wild enthusiasm and ideas, a renewed vitality that ignited an episode of intense reading and relentless efforts to survey my inner landscape. I was determined to recollect my true self from the inside out. I rejected my old self-doubts and fielded fewer instances of false-self pretending. Over time I developed a new assertive attitude stemming from giving myself permission to take risks. The overall effect was a clarity and firmness of mind lost to me since early childhood.

At the age of five I already knew how and what to hold back. My child's view of the world informed me I needed to be on guard to protect myself. Of course, I told no one that I talked to the birds outside my window every morning or that I had an imaginary mouse named Moutie who was my confidant and best friend. No one knew I wrote poems just for the fun of it, or asked questions about God and death and heaven and hell that made my Sunday-school teachers cringe. Surely, I decided, I must keep secret the fact that I sometimes sat alone in my room at night trying to send my thoughts to other kids across town and even to England and Russia.

I discovered it was not always safe to let others hear me sing my own songs. Soon I learned to downplay the fact that I could earn A's without much effort, figure out the end of the story before the teacher read it, and throw a pretty mean fastball. Gradually, whenever a leader was called for, I didn't step forward the way I had before. I developed a management system that I now call "selective stupidity." In order not to outdo others, especially boys, whom I had been told had "fragile egos," I feigned ignorance or at least pretended to be slow on the uptake.

Nevertheless, because of my talents, hard work, and laserlike focus on things I deemed important, people seemed to think I could do just about anything. They were convinced that was how I felt, too, that I was as strong on the inside as I appeared on the outside. In contrast, in my private world I felt far from exceptional. After all, there were so many things I could imagine doing but couldn't actually do. For example, I was completely unable to paint the three-dimensional pictures I contrived in my mind's eye, or write down the musical arrangements I composed so easily in my dreams. And I was totally unable to do anything to help the poor boy down the street everyone made fun of because he had one leg shorter than the other. I had no bag of magic tricks that really mattered.

There were so many accomplished others who were already recognized. I fretted, "What could I possibly offer that hasn't already been done better?" I had them all fooled, I decided. If they only knew the whole story, they would see that I was not special after all.

Eventually I agreed with those who said I was "too sensitive." I think that stemmed from the time when my realization that some people in the world went to bed hungry kept my stomach in knots for days. The slaughter of turkeys for Thanksgiving made me cry, but I was the only one who did. "Why does God let these things happen, and why aren't the adults doing something about it?" I worried.

Very early on I was sometimes a strident stickler for fairness who was profoundly upset by acts of cruelty or neglect. I felt responsible for each and every hurt that crossed my awareness. Everything in my world had feelings: the house, the furniture, the frogs in the pond, and even the moon. Once in a terrible storm I remember rushing outside to brace a newly planted tree so it wouldn't break in the wind, and even to comfort it so it wouldn't be scared. Anthropomorphism seemed perfectly reasonable to me—that is, until the neighborhood kids found out and I became a laughingstock.

I was also an odd duck in that I loved school. To me, school was a world of ideas and new information. My teachers said I was a "nice girl" and a good student, and that made me feel as though I fit in. I quickly learned that too many questions were bad and that my frequent "smart remarks" were "not funny at all." I was also chastised for not knowing when to "leave well enough alone." Clearly the unimpeded me was too much for everyone else's taste; if I wanted to keep my good standing, I needed to learn to keep a lid on it.

It wasn't long before I discovered the first (and at the time the only available) key to personal liberation: mastery. Whether making a papier-mâché penguin out of a milk carton, categorizing rocks from the beach, memorizing lines for the school play, or scoring big in kickball, I was intent on proficiency. Outstanding achievement did two things: It brought on smiles of approval, and it fit well with the fact that I found nearly everything an exciting challenge.

There were things I simply *had* to know and which I needed to understand in great detail; I had to create and revise (and revise, and revise), and to be active, exuberant, and playful. I needed to discuss and then discuss some more and again some more after I had thought about it awhile. When all of these factors came together—wonder, investigate, understand, create, and activate—I felt as though I could fly. That scared me, too, because what would happen if I did? Where would I go? What would become of me? Creative bursts had a way of setting off alarms of secondary worry and guilt.

In one respect I was fortunate. There was one pair of eyes that consistently looked upon me with understanding and approval: my mother's. She too found nearly everything in the world to be something of spectacular wonder. Together she and I took in the richness of nature, the joy of imagination, and relished in the joy of the common moment. She was truly a descended angel in my life, who made it possible for me to grow up with my sense of wonder and playful spirit intact. Yet she died early, leaving me with no one to help me figure out the difficulties of life as a gifted adult.

No one was there to support my efforts to grow up and into my abilities. No one told me my personality and needs were inextricably tied to traits of the gifted self. Never did anyone mention that my numerous career changes were common among gifted people, that people like me thrived on change and challenge and either shifted fields altogether or moved from one thing to another within a professional arena. Most important, no one ever suggested that my "odd duck" differences, my perfectionistic and excitable ways, or my obvious sensitivity and drive could be what was most right about me instead of what was most wrong. Inevitably, this experience set the stage for my Mandated Mission: to identify and comprehend the complexities of the gifted personality and to share my discoveries with the world.

FIVE BASIC TRUTHS
ABOUT GIFTEDNESS

- Being gifted means being unavoidably different in certain ways; these differences are not liabilities, but are actually assets and the building blocks of excellence.
- Occasionally others will misunderstand you and attempt to hinder your visionary efforts. You must acquire special "street smarts" to deal with this opposition effectively.
- Although gifted adults are smart and creative, to discover and fulfill one's life mission is a painstaking task that may take many years to complete. Be prepared to be patient.

- The cultivation of high potential is markedly enhanced by finding a gifted mentor and a few true peers whose support is unfettered by jealousy or self-serving agendas.
- You will benefit greatly from discovering your spiritual center. It can serve as a primary resource for guidance, affirmation, and inspiration.

A BITTERSWEET EXPERIENCE

Long before the word *gifted* was ever coined, people admired and respected individuals of special vision and pragmatic intuition. Many were acknowledged as seers, healers, inventors, business leaders, artists, and exemplars of all that is good about humankind. They were the children with exceptional intellectual abilities. They asked unusual questions, learned rapidly, and demonstrated an extraordinary interest in justice, ethics, and cause-effect relationships.

Nevertheless, the typical Everyday Genius has been preprogrammed with misinformation and left to cope without adequate resources in a world that sees him or her through foreign eyes. Most gifted adults find their life experience bittersweet. Yet much of the bitter is not necessary. In nearly every case gifted adults are ill-trained to understand themselves, much less to deal with the lifelong challenges they face, particularly because of others' tendency to stereotype them.

Because Everyday Geniuses are driven by the spirit of human progress, we possess a tendency to stir things up. Whether we intend to or not, we often make waves. Together with an awareness system that allows us to "see" things others may not, our sense of responsibility makes it hard for us to brush off our ideas and concerns. As might be expected, we are constantly faced with the dilemma of making a splash with our expanded perspectives or swimming silent laps in the norm pool.

This paradoxical "inability" to blend in while standing out must be acknowledged. We are incapable of always successfully approximating "normal." Just as it is for anyone who is obviously different, we are apt to become targets for discrimination.

Peter Bucky, author of *The Private Albert Einstein*, addressed this question of difference in his conversations with Einstein. In response to Bucky's inquiry about how the great scientist managed "judgments of the outside world," Einstein answered:

Well, I have considered myself to be very fortunate in that I have been able to do mostly only that which my inner self told me to do. . . . I am also aware that I do receive much criticism from the outside world for what I do and some people actually get angry at me. But this does not really touch me because I feel that these people do not live in the same world as do I.[2]

To his credit, Einstein, whose name had become nearly synonymous with science, resisted the label *gifted* because the term had historically implied superiority and advantage. Nonetheless, the great physicist, thinker, poet, musician, and theorist was quite aware that he was different:

I am not more gifted than the average human being. If you know anything about history, you would know this is so—what hard times I had in studying and the fact that I do not have a memory like some other people do. . . . I am just more curious than the average person and I will not give up on a problem until I have found the proper solution. This is one of my greatest satisfactions in life—solving problems—and the harder they are, the more satisfaction do I get out of them. Maybe you could consider me a bit more patient in continuing with my problems than is the average human being. Now, if you understand what I have just told you, you see that it is not a matter of being more gifted but a matter of being more curious and maybe more patient until you solve a problem.[3]

Einstein also recognized, as do we whose gifts are far less profound, that even if one is revered and well liked, it is not the same as being understood. Bucky goes on to tell us that in 1949 a German playwright sent Einstein some verses he had written to honor him on his seventieth birthday. Part of his poetic reply reflects his gratitude for the collegial words of a kindred spirit who also believed himself to be "not really gifted":

> *Non-comprehenders are often distressed.*
> *Not you, though—because with good humor you're blessed.*
> *After all, your thought went like this, I dare say:*
> *It was none but the Lord who made us that way.*[4]

THE ESSENTIALS OF SELF-DISCOVERY

Our life experience as evolutionaries is unavoidably set along a hazardous route, somewhere between self-denial and high-risk individuality. We may reasonably wonder, "Where is the road that leads Everyday Geniuses to fulfillment without dead-ending in loneliness?" The answer is often found in self-understanding.

Those of us who take the time to discover who we are can make peace with our nature and gain a decided advantage in our attempt to aim ourselves in the right direction. As a result, we can come to love our adventurous lives as travelers who are open to new opportunities that match our gifts, the delivery of which makes us feel extraordinarily alive. It is in these momentary reunions with the soul's Self that we remember how to fly free.

An excerpt from C. Day Lewis' "O Dreams, O Destinations" artfully expresses it:

> To travel like a bird, lightly to view
> Deserts where stone gods founder in the sand,
> Ocean embraced in a white sleep with land;
> To escape time, always to start anew . . .
> Hooded by a dark sense of destination . . .
> Travellers, we're fabric of the road we go;
> We settle, but like feathers on time's flow.[5]

As we come to know ourselves more completely, we may find it necessary to make changes in the application of our creative energies. If we have been typecast in unfulfilling roles, whether as a front-line manager under the thumb of a boss with narrow vision, a midlife mother in a dead-end job, or a bored retiree who finds conventional senior gatherings a disappointment, we may discover we have been going in the wrong direction.

In his writing on psychotherapy as theater, Sheldon Kopp observes:

Too often, as children, we are encouraged to try to be something other than ourselves. It is demanded that we assume a character not our own, live out a life-story written by another. The plot-line is given. Improvisations are unacceptable, and the direction is an oppressive form of close-quarter tyranny.[6]

As you shed the hindering aspects of misidentification you will begin to heal old wounds and to shift from acting the scripted role of performer to starring in your own authentic life. Keep in mind that self-discovery is a process and not an event because internalized criticisms take time and conscious effort to remove. Reclaiming your full-scale Everyday Genius is never the result of a simple salvational wish.

Yet it will help to know you are not a lone climber on the mountain. As you begin to recognize other gifted adults in your midst you will increasingly hear your true voice and trust in it. As you liberate your soul's frequency you will invariably discover other members of your evolutionary community who march to the same rhythm of life.

It is essential to remember to work with, not around, your own uniqueness. The most precious gifts you own, the ones that are yours to cherish, nourish, and deliver, are not to be found in such a combination in any other individual. While the collective task of Everyday Geniuses is the advancement of civilization, your individual challenge is to become the most complete self possible in this lifetime, which is, of course, your Everyday Genius made real.

Picasso's mother held great ambitions for him when he was a child. She instructed him: "If you become a soldier, you'll be a general. If you become a monk, you'll end up as Pope." "Instead," Picasso quipped, "I became a painter and became a Picasso."

THE REAL ENEMY—FITTING IN

Gifted children do have the inclination to adapt to the group, but at what price? If one works very hard at fitting in with others, especially when one feels very different from others, self-alienation can result. In their desperation to belong, many "well-adjusted" gifted youth and adults have given up or lost touch with vital parts of themselves.[7]

Fitting in is a high price to pay when it means selling out. It's an endless tightrope walk for Everyday Geniuses. To fully express the true self is at best a calculated risk. Nevertheless, giving the false self free rein is like tying your dreams to an anchor. We can't run away from the responsibility either to our potential or to our inner needs. Most of us long for the acceptance and endorsement of who we are and what we might accomplish. Yet we reside in the real world just as it is, not as it might be.

To varying degrees we all experience rejection. But when the criticisms assault our very nature, and when they grow up alongside us at every turn, they tend to attach themselves like barnacles, tainting the integrity of our self-image and the quality of our internal dialogue. Even in adulthood, whenever our ego takes a hit, the wind is knocked out of us and we strain to breathe, suddenly feeling weakened and vulnerable. Over the years ten specific criticisms have disguised themselves as our own opinions, censuring us in false-self voice. They tear holes in our self-confidence because we have forgotten they were actually created by others.

The false self is a powerful adversary, one whose sharp-tongued admonitions can be heard in every situation of self-doubt, a foe that keeps us from our true selves and sometimes distances us from others as well. Nonetheless, it is merely the accomplice of the real enemy. The real enemy—fitting in—wages a kind of guerilla warfare, shrouding itself in thick fog and dense underbrush, avoiding direct confrontation. This is why it is so important to confront false-self criticisms that often conspire to obstruct personal growth.

Unlike the larger, more diffuse problem of fitting in, we can learn to deal with the false self on our own terms because we can hear its voice. We can sensitize ourselves to its influence if we learn to recognize its tactic of carping at us in hushed tones like a talk-radio host of the mind, with propaganda that is as subtle and seductive as it is dangerous. Until we hear its critical attack for what it is, the internalized voice of disapproval, we are destined to go through life unwittingly duped by its lies.

What, then, do we do if we want to fit in and yet must remain true to ourselves? Is living a watered-down version of life possible when self-actualization hangs in the balance? In some respects it's true that Everyday Geniuses lead a curious life. Consequently we can expect that sometimes others will consider us curiosities. But wouldn't it be nice if we could go about the business of living that curious life without being bruised by hostile remarks and inaccurate labels? The following criticisms are external complaints that gifted adults routinely internalize. They are lifelong obstructions that interrupt the flow of burgeoning potential.

THE TEN CRITICISMS

There are ten primary criticisms that gifted people are made to repeatedly endure. Though these complaints are often intended as harmless "observations," they are not benign or easily dismissed because they pierce the susceptible skin of the evolutionary personality. They are written in descending order, number ten being the least destructive and number one having the greatest negative impact on your self-worth. As you read them take note of your feelings and any images that emerge. Then read the list again, mindful that these criticisms *are not* and *never were* facts.

10. "Why don't you slow down?"
 9. "You worry about everything."
 8. "Can't you just stick with one thing?"
 7. "You're so sensitive and dramatic!"
 6. "You have to do everything the hard way."
 5. "You're so demanding!"
 4. "Can't you ever be satisfied?"
 3. "You're so driven!"
 2. "Where do you get all those wild ideas?"
 1. "Who do you think you are?"

9

CONFRONTING THE
FIRST FIVE CRITICISMS

The most dangerous of our prejudices reign in ourselves against ourselves. To dissolve them is a creative act.

—Hugo von Hofmannsthal

A s we've seen, Everyday Genius can be both a blessing and a curse, a positive force and a negative force in our lives. Yet it is indeed a real force, conscious and unconscious. Far more than a set of distinct qualities, it is a state of being. Denying our ability makes us feel as though we don't exist. Consequently many find their fundamental character traits unwelcome even to themselves. This perspective is all upside-down, and in a very real sense we may need to stand everything on its head to see things correctly.

A choice to reframe old negatives into affirming positives urges us to remove the obstacles that impair our vision and impede the expression of our gifts. Trust is the key element. A rekindled trust in life and its opportunities enables us to avoid becoming a victim of cynicism. To that end, as Everyday Geniuses we are called to:

- Discover who we are and are not
- Make peace with our given nature, past and present
- Find new ways to let our gifts be assets in our lives instead of liabilities
- Avoid the anti-life forces of self-sabotage and oppression by others
- Make changes in how we apply our gifts

- Learn to trust and cooperate with our inner guidance
- Clarify and enact our life's mission

REWRITING PERSONAL HISTORY

There's magic to be done here that turns undeserved censure into valuable self-acceptance. It occurs when we risk looking at ourselves again from the other side of the norm pond, the well-informed side where our daring efforts will be rewarded with the gift of freedom.

We're highly adaptable and have learned to live in a restrictive existence. At the core we have been a bit like Merlin of Arthurian legend. Upon his unjust imprisonment Merlin cried out: "Without fresh air I cannot breathe. These four walls are suffocating me!" To correct this involuntary confinement, we can perform a type of wizardry. Essentially we must rewrite our histories through our imagination and reinvent ourselves on an important new plane. People rarely accomplish this prior to developing mature perspective.

We need to metaphorically retrain ourselves. If we develop a portable internal counselor, we can reduce the lingering ill effects of the past. Once we respond as chief advocate for our characteristics and reframe our "excesses" as our assets, we can replace the criticisms that stifle us and restrict us with more positive messages of love, trust, and self-acceptance.

Magically, when there is no enemy within, there are far fewer without. Waging needless wars with ourselves and others saps creative energy the way a faulty air conditioner sucks up kilowatts on a 100°F day. Frankly, we can't afford such self-sabotaging indulgences. Many of us have learned to defend ourselves against the Ten Criticisms with clever remarks or quick, embarrassed retreat. By learning what experts have uncovered about the gifted experience and by listening to our Genius, our inner guide, for confirmation, we can stop being hounded by internalized dogma that demands that we need to conform like everybody else.

The goal is not to toot our own horn, but to fortify ourselves with accurate information. When false stereotypes fall away we will begin to repair some of the damage and become revitalized and recommitted to individuality with a greater sense of freedom. Then it won't be so difficult to find the courage to express our gifts with authority, to say yes to opportunities when they are right for us and no when they are not. And should we ever again be hit with one of the old undeserved criticisms, we will meet the challenge with a confident yet respectful reply. There's no time like the present to begin.

CRITICISM #10: *"Why Don't You Slow Down?"*
NEW RESPONSE: *"Going Fast Is Normal for Me."*

It is imperative that we begin to apply the term *normal* to our ways. Most of us do think and move quickly at times, often to the confusion and frustration of others. It's as simple as this: Because we can, we do. "Jumping to conclusions" and "running from pillar to post," as we've heard so often, may seem disorganized and unnecessary to those around us. But we're simply designed differently than others.

When combined with powers of intuition, our thought processes and perceptual abilities allow us to surge through information to quickly detect the core problem, recognize patterns, and reveal possible answers. The process might be described as a right-brain, left-brain team with all systems working full speed ahead. Gifted adults automatically understand what President John F. Kennedy observed: "You can't depend on your judgment when your imagination is out of focus."

We need not deny that we process things differently and often faster than others. We understand that this does not make us insincere. It is important to be sensitive to the fact that to others our rapid pace may seem as though we are skipping over important factors in our analysis or may suggest a lack of earnestness about the topic at hand. Our critics wonder if our unconventional decision-making process is too superficial or careless when it doesn't take a year and a day.

Others may think we do a lot of "educated guessing." And they're right, because our cognitive style is a form of guessing that is synergistic and goes beyond the application of previously learned facts. Indescribable though it may be, we have learned to rely on our specialized methods of grasping concepts on multiple levels simultaneously.

Information from our multiple awarenesses and internal resources produces insights that can seem to come out of thin air. The fact that much of the work takes place in the subconscious does not mean our conclusions are without logic. Accumulated knowledge and speedy processing permit us to accurately sum up and characterize things with only a minimum of data, and we're used to that. Most of us don't know quite how it works ourselves, only that it does. Chastising us for proceeding in this way is like being in math class and being graded down for not showing all of our work. If we can do it in our heads, why do we need to do it on paper, too?

Complex Thinking is linked to our use of time in interpersonal situations as well as occupational projects. It offers us ways to quickly size up dynamic aspects of human interaction to find creative solutions for improved interpersonal encounters. We can ascertain important bits of communication at once (words, personality, goal, emotional state, body language). Because we are proficient multitaskers, we can simultaneously observe, respond, analyze, and predict what will come next. In no way are we mind readers, but we do seem to develop a sixth sense that helps us quickly understand how other people operate. This is why many gifted people are superb negotiators, salespersons, and diplomats.

Pace is linked to creative inspiration. I once knew a man who noticeably increased his speed whenever innovation and originality were required. He literally ran from book to desk to lab and back, nearly bowling over everything and everybody in his path. His brother, who had a history of butting heads with him on such occasions, wanted to avoid these encounters. He noted that his brother's wife seemed to take her husband's pace in stride. When he asked her, "How can you tell how fast he's going so you know when to get out of his way?" she chuckled and replied, "By the size of the flame!"

When creative juices start to flow, the hands of the clock follow suit and start to spin. Time streaks by in an instant as we run for the pen or brush to compose our vision. The force is so strong it fends off any attempt we may make to return to the demands of the real world. In truth, creativity is the keeper of the clock tower.

Activated creative vision redirects our attention and pace nearly every time, and often to its own dictates. Sally, a computer programmer whose part-time dream job was writing song lyrics, describes it this way:

> The days before I am ready to write seem colorless and slow, not bad, just different, minus the spark. Sometimes I sleep more than usual and feel sluggish. I read, I wander about in a mixture of things. I might spend hours in the garden or planning a party, or reading everything that catches my attention. Most of this looks like it has nothing to do with my

lyric writing, like I'm just goofing off. I do my regular job like I'm not really there some of the time even though I get things done. It's something I've adjusted to in spite of how strange it seems.

Then the clock seems to start ticking faster. My mind clears out some of the cobwebs and ideas start to surface, usually while I'm running or in the shower. There it is, right in front of me, but still like unformed clay. My feelings and thinking start to join forces and off I go, sometimes at the most inconvenient times. I hate that part, when I have to delay, but that's part of it, too. People like me don't have the luxury of a patron, so we have to respond to every vision and notion that pulls on us.

When it works out I notice that I'm in a strange space, neither good nor bad, and that time has been altered. I'm going into my work as if I were on the tracks of a roller coaster. I'm excited, afraid, nervous, and ready as the process builds. I wish I could just squeeze it out of my head because as soon as I put a pencil in my hand and get down to the business of writing the words, I know I'll lose some of the purity of my inspiration.

Then I go into some sort of trance and get pulled down into my ideas. It can last anywhere from a few seconds to weeks. Some of it is awful. Looking for that "just right" combination that only comes after several rewrites takes what feels like an eternity. People think creativity just blasts forth like a volcano, but that feeling of ecstasy, when I'm off the ground with inspiration, passes in a flash, and then the clock slows down again. I miss it when it leaves. When I land again I feel as though I'm somehow larger and I'm waking from a dream adventure.

For many of us, especially those of us born with a need for speed, urgency is a common sensation. In actuality, some of this may be tied to our heightened sensory system and innate need for stimulation. In any case, we are never far removed from the awareness of time since we have a sensory relationship with it, as if the passing of the hours were something we can almost feel, like the temperature of the air on our skin.

Beyond this vague impulse to keep things moving forward, economy of time is a major factor in our ability to be high achievers. As self-starters, once we are task-committed and determine our goal, we seldom waste a moment. This feels natural to us given our instinctive goal-directedness. As we've seen, goals have a way of pulling on us, almost whispering in our ear: "Every minute counts."

The commonly accepted image of the gifted adult is akin to the White Rabbit in Wonderland, always rushing about absentmindedly, caught up in thought, late, disorganized, and oblivious to matters of external consequence. True enough, when we are on a mission, we can speed about like five-o'clock shoppers on Christmas Eve. Many of us move along at breakneck pace every day out of habit, though it is a risky practice because it may keep us in a constant state of anxiety.

We go slow at times because we are lovers of theory who can easily drift off into complex thought processes, puzzles, fantasy, and imaginative inner games. The abstract commands attention as we build castles in the air, become lost in fascinating details, and at times find ourselves bogged down in a maze of our own making.

This tendency doesn't always sit so well with others, who may berate us for taking these flights of fancy. Our swings between tortoise behavior and hare behavior are indeed baffling to those around us. In part, their concern is useful because we must be certain that this kind of absorption is truly warranted and not avoidance in disguise. If we need to develop other aspects of our personality, we cannot afford to hide out in the inner world. Most of the time being lost in thought is simply the by-product of creative thinking, a rich resource for grounding ourselves and reviving our sense of well-being.

CRITICISM #9: *"You Worry About Everything!"*

NEW RESPONSE: *"Yes, I'm a Person of Deep Concern and Moral Conviction."*

Kimberly: If there aren't enough things going on to keep me fascinated, things that stir up my mind, it means trouble. My mind is like a hungry beast. If I don't feed it the right mix of puzzles and possibilities and questions—things to ponder and wonder about—it goes off on its own into worry land. And believe me, you don't want to know how upsetting and how far down the road a mind like mine can go with worry. If I don't pay attention and nip it in the bud, I can work myself into a frenzy in ten seconds.

Our very ability to identify problems, envision the best, and experience feelings at a deep level increases the likelihood that we will become accomplished worriers. The worry habit develops early. It is probably unavoidable, since in childhood we had few channels to express our serious concerns and certainly no way to solve issues of universal importance.

We had no authority to do otherwise because the only option was to roll our concerns around in our heads and worry.

Earnest concern for the welfare of others (endangered plants and animals, historic sites, natural treasures, and the disenfranchised of the world) is almost always included in the gift package. By the time most of us were in the second grade, we had already developed a strong sense of social justice and were deeply concerned by any form of inequality or injustice. Our awareness and sensitivity compelled us to be social monitors, a very important role.

> *Brendan: When I was six years old I was already a fanatic for fairness, monitoring the playground and stepping in when things went wrong to make sure everyone played fair. I was a little watchdog for the potentially abused, on the lookout for bullies who took advantage of the little kids. I don't know why they all paid attention to what I said, but when I meant business, they listened. Thinking back on it, that was really odd because I was at least three years younger than some of them. I don't know why, but I didn't give the fact that I was smaller than everyone else a second thought. Making sure things ran fairly was a job that just seemed to fall to me. It's always been like that. I don't feel okay unless everybody has an equal chance. I can't stand oppression and intimidation. That stuff makes me see red!*
>
> *I notice injustice all around us and it still bothers me a lot. But I can't go on anymore letting myself be undone by it. That's counterproductive. I suppose I'll always be a fighter for the wronged, but now I realize I have to manage my zeal in order for my concern to be effective and to keep me from feeling overwhelmed, like a one-man social justice army.*

Often when the rights of others are abused, we still react as if it were happening to us, because we have a strong connection to humanity on a higher level. Again, this is normal, as is our tendency to spend a significant time pondering life's most perplexing puzzles, such as war, discrimination, and famine. Who, one may wonder, will wrestle with such concerns if we do not?

In her writing on the characteristics and emotions of gifted adults, gifted-education expert Annemarie Roeper asserts:

> Many gifted people have strong moral convictions and try to use their specific talents, insights and knowledge for the betterment of the world.

These are the people who, for example, use their gifts in the service of the planet. It is the gifted who are global thinkers, who have an understanding of the complexities, the patterns and the interrelatedness of global affairs. It is the gifted who have the capacity to replace the world's shortsighted, short-term reactions with careful, overall solutions.[1]

Another manifestation of deep concern and moral conviction is our frequent difficulty with authority figures. These confrontations are to be expected and are not necessarily negative. At various times the existing rules need to be challenged and sometimes even rewritten. Roeper describes gifted adults as "independent thinkers" who "do not automatically accept the decisions of their supervisors. Their reactions may be based on perceptions of the fallibility of decisions or may relate to moral questions."

Our sense of justice and willingness to push at the boundaries of conformity are suited for the difficult work of championing social causes and breaking down the barriers of prejudice. Our ability to "see through" facades helps us to quickly identify the issue at heart in situations of moral conflict. Such gifts can help steer us clear of inauthentic people and involvements that may compromise our strongest values.

When I first met Graham I could see that he was a razor-sharp detective of pretense. The fact that he had a history of clashes with people in positions of authority was no surprise. Graham seemed to illustrate the Everyday Genius' uncanny ability to perceive artificiality and deception. He could not only detect hidden agendas and cleverly disguised untruths, he was a born master at sizing people up and being able to discern the true person beneath social veneers. Not everyone appreciated Graham's gift.

I just call it as I see it. That's what I've always done. My teachers used to tell my parents they hoped I'd go into politics so I could use my sharp tongue in some constructive way. There was more than one disorganized teacher that felt the sting of my disrespect. Even in college, if I thought the teacher was incompetent or biased—stand back!

It's taken me years to figure out that this ability of mine to see through fakery and pretense is only a gift when I have it under control. I think I used to spit out everything I discovered about people and their intentions—especially if they were trying to pull something over on me or someone else—because I felt obligated. It was as if I knew the truth about what was going on, so I was charged with setting things right. The other thing that occurred to me is that pretending I don't see or know what I can easily detect makes me feel like a fake, too, which is something I can't reconcile. And the last motive for my truth-telling habit is the realization that others' efforts to conceal or sidestep or whitewash things they don't want revealed feels insulting to me. I say to myself: "Do they really think I can't see through that? Do they really believe I'm that stupid?" It makes me angry enough to show them up, and it all happens so fast.

Sometimes it seems like I don't even have to say anything, or even make an exasperated face. Like last week. We were in a meeting at work and these two guys from the marketing department came in all puffed up with enthusiasm for their ideas about our new product. I could hardly believe it, but no one else in the room seemed to get it. It was so obvious to me that they hadn't done their homework. They had just reconstituted last year's game plan without doing any new market research. I was a lone wolf with my unspoken cry of "Sham!" Even though I kept my opinion to myself and tried to put on a poker face, they glared at me like I was a traitor when their ideas fell on deaf ears. I don't know how, but I must have communicated my feelings via some sort of negative vibration or something.

I want more than anything to be an effective team player. I honestly want to support my colleagues, not to undermine their efforts. I just don't know how to turn off my radar system—I can't help what I become aware of. And if that's the case, I need to do something different, change my approach or attitude in some way that will permit me to still be a seeker of truth and a straight shooter. But not one who just shoots from the hip all the time and ends up the bad guy.

Although we are prone to worry, worry by itself is rarely useful and can easily diminish our personal resources. Yet intense concern is the precursor of all evolutionary action. It is important for us not to berate ourselves for our watchful attention.

Reasonable worry can serve as a kind of radar that draws our attention to something that is painfully wrong. Although we cannot become involved in everything that gives us empathic pause, we need not feel singularly responsible, because we can rest assured that many others hear these alarms. Nevertheless, we are ever vigilant in the face of menacing threats to humanity. As those who can hear the faintest of alarms and perceive problems early, we are often the ones called upon to notify others and to take action.

> CRITICISM #8: *"Can't You Just Stick with One Thing?"*
> NEW RESPONSE: *"No, Probably Not."*

In our society there is great pressure to answer the question "What are you going to be when you grow up?" with a decisive and singular choice. We are usually presented with a small array of options, mostly in the form of a job list. However, those with EvI rarely benefit from the traditional career-planning methods because our underlying goals are not aligned with a simplistic job-seeking formula.

I chose my initial college major and first job in a most haphazard way, even though it was according to three seemingly reasonable criteria: (1) what others said I should do, (2) whatever fit with the mixture of things I'd studied thus far, and (3) the necessary training didn't take too long or cost too much. These were the requirements for getting a good job.

My friends and I understood that a "good job" was anything that would pay the bills and wouldn't raise eyebrows. A few of my acquaintances were more daring and took classes based on their interests and for fun. Most of them seemed to fare better in the long run, ending up in jobs more closely related to their gifts and passions. They somehow valued the wisdom of their inner voice over the prescribed voice of "reason." I discovered, as many of us eventually do, that my indoctrination in reasonableness was highly overrated.

Career misdirection was followed by yet another mandate: "It's not wise to change directions once you've selected a line of work." The gifted adult who lands an unfulfilling job often ends up suffering from intellectual and spiritual exhaustion. Those who brave an "unwise" new direction frequently do so with little support. Even if they find success in a second, third, or fifth career, their search may be rewarded with nothing better than "I knew you'd do it; what took you so long?"

The issue of what to be when we grow up is even more complicated for the multitalented individual. It is essentially a problem of too many options. In school such a person may have been excellent in mathematics, first-chair violin, captain of the track team, and a member of the student council—many talents, many interests, many choices.

Gifted people are also confronted with the need to select a direction from several possible areas of success that may hold equal interest. Rudimentary "do what you like best" advice doesn't make the sorting process any easier when most of us are interested in nearly everything, when our decisions about where we will invest our time and energy in the future are guided by our need to expand, not narrow, our horizons.

Andrew: Much of my energy comes from getting involved in something new that excites me. That's why it looks like I'm always switching gears and starting over. But what if that's normal for me? What if that's how I work?

Tracia: This may sound like I'm nuts, and I don't want you to take this wrong, but I feel like I'm a gathering of personalities. Not that I'm split off from them and disturbed by them, like people with multiple personality disorder. I seem to be a combination of characters. There's the playful, mischievous me who tends to stir things up and have a good time—sometimes at the wrong time. Then I can swing into the serious-minded, overbearing conventional me who rags on myself to get with it and stop goofing off. She's not so much fun, but I rely on her to help keep my nose to the grindstone. There are a whole bunch of these characters in me, and I think I need them all.

Kevin: I'm interested in everything—well, almost everything. Change is my friend, not the enemy my friends think it has to be. They've been after me for years to settle down. One of them even suggested I might be hyperactive. They just don't get it. There's so much to learn, to discover, so many places to travel and books to read. I can't imagine ever finding myself in a position with nothing to do. The truth is that even if I live to be a hundred, I'll be sorry that I didn't have enough time to do all the things I want to do. It bothers my friends that I'm on my fifth career, but that feels so normal to me. Every time I go to the theater I have the strongest urge to be in a musical production. When I'm camping I want to be another John Muir. When I watch CNN/FN I find myself wishing I had become a Wall Street money shark. I'm just not able to sit still in the status quo. Lots of stability might be the ticket for lots of other people, but not me. In fact, I tell my friends that if they ever find me just swinging in the hammock with no "passion du jour," that will be the time to worry about me.

Career-choice demands occur just as the world is beginning to open up to us, so that in many respects the timing couldn't be worse. The need to choose is like taking a child to an amusement park for the first time and saying, "Now, *just one* ride, no more. Choose carefully." Even later in life it may be quite difficult for us to match ability with highest interests, deepest values, and long-range life goals without skilled mentoring, which is always in short supply. Occasionally, even work that seems like a "good job" may fail to expand in concert with our need to grow. Unless we explore the larger issue of personal mission, we run the risk of becoming stuck for years in a life direction that starts to feel like a set of repeated, uninspiring tasks.

A career path suited to our needs must provide us with a sense of meaning and large-scale purpose. If our initial avenue is filled with dead ends, a change is often inevitable. For many of us it often takes years of varied experience to clarify a life mission and to find our niche. Frequently multiple interests and talents call for the creation of a tailor-made career. Sometimes the right path requires additional training, which is not proof positive that we "wasted time" in other endeavors, since the creative person is a great recycler of experience, good and bad.

> *Lionel: It's so confusing. People praise me for being so diverse and then turn right around and try to pigeonhole me. I've become known as the fun-maker, the one who lifts people's spirits and lightens things up when they get too solemn. Then I get cast as the silly one, the clown, even though I don't always want to be the one who provides the enthusiasm and zing. I can be as melancholy as the next guy. I'm odd in that I seem to be an introvert and an extrovert. I've become used to the many sides of me—soft and edgy, involved and aloof, in charge and in the background. Why is it so hard to understand that I'm as wacky as I am thoughtful and in some ways as conventional as I am different? Is it impossible for others to accept all the aspects to my personality—the changeable me?*

Change is a natural outcome of multipotentiality, self-directedness, and adaptability, not an indicator of instability. Many of us progress along a convoluted track of seemingly unrelated careers. As it turns out, such a course can make the necessity of earning a living a fascinating adventure that contributes immeasurably to the development of wisdom. In hindsight, many successful self-actualizers identify their career shifts as integral steps in the spiral of change. This is when they begin the story of their brilliant careers with "If it hadn't been for the time I had to . . ."

> CRITICISM #7: *"You're So Sensitive and Dramatic!"*
> NEW RESPONSE: *"Yes, My Senses and Feelings Are Heightened."*

Across the board, experts identify our heightened sensory awareness and perceptivity as markers of giftedness. This means we are serious experiencers. Life really *is* dramatic for us. Each part of our sensory system is magnified, so we operate in, around, and through all of the sensations of the moment. We react to things more because we feel them more and respond to the intricacies, patterns, tone, and color of situations. The gifted person understands on a sensory level the difference between a lavender velvet evening and a white satin morning.

Though we may think our life experience is not different from anyone else's, this is not the case. It may help to think of our gifts of sensitivity and perceptivity as the difference between listening to a digital recording of the Moonlight Sonata and sharing the piano bench with Beethoven as he plays it. Same music, different experience.

We not only live in a colorful world, we detect all the subtle shadings of experience and feel impassioned by many things. Everything in our surroundings seems to be endowed with an energy that can be translated through the senses. Because this is so, we need the validation of like-minded others to ward off sneak attacks of self-doubt and low self-esteem.

My gifted friends nod in unison when we discuss the "scent" of an inspiring melody, the "cry" that emanates from a sculpture, the "feeling" of the rhythmic pulse of the earth, or being "bruised" by the hostile edge of an angry look. This is not irrational. It is the normal result of a physiological hardwiring that contains a sensory system that is different—broader, deeper, and more intense.

Clinical psychologist Dr. Dierdre Lovecky, in an article on gifted adults entitled "Can You Hear the Flowers Singing?" informs us that gifted adult "may be unusually aware of the feeling tone of situations and of the more sensual aspects of the environment, such as color and shading . . . They hear the flowers singing, feel a unity with the universe, and want everyone else to hear the song as well." In addition, she observes:

> Adults gifted with perceptivity are those who can hear the flowers singing within others not yet aware of their own gifts. . . . [They are able to] understand the meaning of personal symbols and to see beyond the superficiality of a situation to the person beneath. . . . People who are gifted at "seeing" often seem to have a touch of magic about them. . . . Jane Austen, Langston Hughes, Anne Hutchinson, William Shakespeare, and Henry David Thoreau are all examples.[2]

As children, many of us had a strong connection with animals, rocks, birds, or flowers, engaging in a form of anthropomorphism that humanized objects with an animal, vegetable, or mineral "soul." This sensitivity and perception of the common thread of energy within the cosmos was spirit in action. You too may be someone who apologizes to plants for neglect or listens carefully when the birds in the park tell you their stories.

When others complain that we are "too dramatic" they are suggesting we are too expressive, too passionate, too connected to our emotions, and that our inviting them into the deeper realm of life frightens them. Gifted adults are often dubbed dramatic or crazy when they confront others with their intensity.

> *Charlene: When someone is in emotional pain I'm right there in it with them. I feel it right along with them and react deeply. Sometimes I think I feel what they're experiencing even more strongly than they do!*

The role of emotion is an integral part of our creative nature, and a gift to be treasured. It might even be said that we think with our feelings and feel our way through our thoughts. In other words, our intuitive, feeling mind and our logical mind work in concert. As one might guess, passion and the willingness to feel the highest crescendo and deepest decrescendo is the realm of the artist:

> *Nobody sees a flower—really—it is so small it takes time—we haven't time—and to see takes time, like to have a friend takes time.*
> —Georgia O'Keeffe

Many would prefer that we repress our awareness and emotional energy. But channeled appropriately, intensity can be exceptionally useful, as feeling and thought are reshaped into paint stroke, piano chord, or pirouette. It is also the source of enthusiasm, dedication, care, and devotion.

> *Marael: Do you know how hard it is to keep the lid on my emotions? Even when I do, people mimic me or scold me for being "so emotional," like expressing my feelings somehow makes me a lunatic or a drama queen begging for attention. I don't know what to do. In a world that tells us to acknowledge our feelings and express them to avoid becoming depressed or having headaches, I know I'm different and I'm not allowed to be that open.*
>
> *If I really let loose with my emotions I'd probably be either locked up in a psych ward or everyone would run away from me like I was a bomb about to explode. The only place where I dare to come close to fully expressing my feelings is with my family, not with outsiders. And even then I have to be careful not to scare everybody.*
>
> *Over the years I've had to put a lid on my feelings to fit into the world around me. I know I have to in order to be taken seriously. The truth is that my intense emotions are the center of my passion about things. Do people really think meaningful changes in society are brought about by the apathetic and dulled-out? It's a real dilemma. People love me for my passion, until they decide it's too much. Then they want me to do away with it like throwing ice water on a flame. And that's simply impossible.*

Our "dramatic" side reflects our intensity of mood. Often discredited, mood is the director of the idea process, playing an integral role in motivation. Otherwise, obvious musical art forms such as the blues would not exist. In fact, one of the quickest ways to change moods is to experience music, dance, or drama. Mood also makes us deeply human, which is the vital difference between us and the androids of science fiction.

Throughout his career, esteemed humanistic psychologist Abraham Maslow found that self-actualizing people dealt with emotional expression differently than other adults. Their feelings were unencumbered, their expression and spontaneity childlike in its freedom. His exceptional subjects, who were considered to be models of human evolution, might also be seen as dramatic. Their demonstrativeness and openness were obviously essential to their unusual progress in living successful and meaningful lives.

Maslow determined that self-actualizing people were not ordinary people with something special added, but dynamic people with nothing suppressed or taken away. In *The Right to Be Human: A Biography of Abraham Maslow*, author Edward Hoffman tells how Maslow challenged modern psychological premises by studying human exemplars rather than the "mentally ill or statistically average" to "devise accurate theories about human nature." Maslow's research indicated that self-actualizing people tended to demonstrate

> greater self-acceptance and acceptance of others, autonomy, spontane-
> ity, esthetic sensitivity, frequent mysticlike or transcendent experiences,
> and democratic rather than authoritarian outlook, and involvement in a
> cause or mission outside oneself. Self-actualizing people, too, seemed
> to possess a good-natured rather than a cruel sense of humor and an
> earnest desire to improve the lot of humanity. In addition, they tended
> to seek privacy and detach themselves from much of the petty and
> trivial socializing taking place around them. He also found that regard-
> less of their particular occupation or station in life, self-actualizers
> tend to be highly creative as an outpouring of their very personality, not
> limited to activities like writing or composing music. . . . Whatever one
> does can be done with a certain attitude, a certain spirit which arises
> out of the nature of the person . . . [and] although self-actualizing peo-
> ple are not emotionally flawless, they can serve as exemplars in the val-
> ues by which they lead their lives.[3]

In concert with our concerns here, Maslow sought to correct a "mis-understanding of self-actualization as a static, 'perfect' state in which all human problems are transcended, and in which people 'live happily ever after' in a superhuman state of serenity or ecstasy." Instead, he insisted, self-actualization is a "development of personality which frees the person from the deficiency problems of growth, and from the neurotic problems of life, so that he [or she] is able to face, endure, and grapple with the 'real' problems of the human condition."

Through his studies of excellence and fulfillment, Maslow discov-ered three important factors that contributed to the gifted reaching a higher level of human experience than other people: (1) liberated feel-ings, (2) openness to new ways of seeing things, and (3) fascination with the unknown:

> They were able to be more "natural" and less controlled and inhibited
> in their behavior; it seemed to be able to flow out more easily and freely

and with less blocking and self-criticism. This ability to express ideas and impulses without strangulation and without fear of ridicule from others turned out to be a very essential aspect of self-actualizing creativeness. . . . Their innocence of perception and expressiveness was combined with sophisticated minds.[4]

Aliveness is often described as "being in touch with feelings." Rather than labeling intensity as excessive, expanded sensitivities might better be defined as a major component of artful living. If you were to ask someone in the arts or sciences what feelings have to do with their work, most would reply, "Everything!" They will tell you that feelings and creativity are never separated.

Allan: I can be hit with emotional highs that are truly beyond articulation. Many times they come right out of the blue, like I'm suddenly bathed in a shower of light and energy and peace. It's fabulous. No, it's more than that. It's ecstasy! A gift from another realm, free and clear, and totally fulfilling. It's a great ride!

Personal experience is not the only value of intensity. Some experts in the area of leadership believe so-called dramatic individuals make the best leaders. They are charismatic models of loyalty to a cause who demonstrate unwavering commitment. One of our most valuable gifts is the ability to stir up enthusiasm in others. Mahatma Gandhi, Martin Luther King Jr., and Eleanor Roosevelt took the moral high ground and relied on emotional response to fuel their campaigns for justice.

Without our having an emotional response to them, our experiences are just commonplace experiences, and we in particular are equipped for what Maslow called "peak" experiences. We have, in his words, "this wonderful capacity to appreciate again and again, freshly and naively, the basic goods of life, with awe, pleasure, wonder, and even ecstasy, however pale these experiences may have become to others."

In short, we are *highly*, not *overly*, sensitive and perceptive, which means we see more and feel more. We are thereby more likely to be compelled to express ourselves more than other people, and none of this should be equated with excess. Intensity is a gift that allows us to know the meaning of rapture as well as of despair. Therefore, exceptional experiencers live more intensely than most people, live more acutely, with more color most of the time. We have a unique opportunity to be transformed by the spectacular revelations made available in each moment. Why would we want it any other way?

> CRITICISM #6: *"You Have to Do Everything the Hard Way."*
> NEW RESPONSE: *"Ah. I See You Understand That Excellence Is Difficult."*

The "hard way" is the habit of creation, and the creative equation cannot be completed on one side without involving the other. Innovation implies new construction or restructuring existing ideas in novel ways. The latter is, of course, the very hardest way, and yet in many situations it is the *only* way.

Innovation's restructuring process is often called creative problem solving, and happens to be Everyday Genius' forte. This form of problem solving is a strength that involves more than occasional searches for solutions because it is tied to our core directive—our First Nature— heightened receptivity and the urge to perfect. It comes as no surprise because on multiple levels we are here as delivery persons compelled to seek, know, and create. When we allow ourselves to be influenced by the creative field, we feel it, sense it, hear it, and respond to the urge to capture its illuminating effect.

Giftedness alone does not make the creative process easier, for "making new" is difficult at any level of ability. Simply being "creative" is also inadequate because many people have ideas they never develop, or give up when the going gets tough. The difference between a creative person and a creative producer is hard work. Those who actually produce the play, build the rocket, find the cure, and write the novel don't let their ideas collect dust on the "tomorrow" shelf. They dig in, often before they feel completely ready, and keep digging until they unearth what they are searching for. It is the unglamorous, relentless, dirty-hands effort that eventually turns a drawing into a masterpiece and a melody into a concerto. When excellence is the goal, nothing less will do.

Like so many gifted organizers, Claire had found both success and comfort in exactitude. Setting things straight—really straight—made her a top candidate for excellence in her career managing her city's botanical garden. She was proud of the obvious precision in the hedge maze, a place where she liked to linger over lunch whenever she could. Claire felt at home there amidst the flawless angles and bubble-perfect levels of green. Precision was a defining part of her world, and for the most part she was a shining star in it—that is, until she flip-flopped into a robotic procrastinator:

> *I'm hoping you can help me find a middle ground between my attachment to rules and order and my need to feel free and to enjoy my life. So far I've tried being one or the other—a compartmentalized, niche-maker fanatic, or a freewheeling blithe spirit. I can't seem to make a go of either one. When I start systematizing I don't know where to stop. If I let everything go, it makes me feel shaky and negligent. I want to regain my childlike sense of wonder and creative dash so I don't get myself stuck in rules and all-or-nothing motorized behaviors. But I also want to be on top of things because otherwise they come back at me with a vengeance and then I have to spend too much time getting things back in order. So there's the assignment: Become an organized easygoing person, or conversely, a go-with-the-flow finisher. No more getting perfectionistic to the point of stalling out. No more procrastinating because I always have to overresearch and get ready ad nauseum. No more boxing myself in so tightly that I become a stereotype instead of a person. And no more avoiding and letting myself be a lounger to the point where I have to race around like a chicken with its head cut off. I want to take the varying road in the middle that will never get me detoured to those extremes again.*

Everyday Geniuses' need to create the best that they are capable of is not something that goes away with time. It's not something we can excise, or a job from which we can expect to happily retire. To be sure, the intensity of creative pressure does ebb and flow, but like the tide, it always comes back. Unless we are extraordinarily hindered, sooner or later we must comply with the creative spirit's urgings, because it is more persevering than any attempt by our thinking mind to ignore our gifts. Living every day with the need to create is like sharing a room with a hyperactive little brother who elbows you, tugs at your shirtsleeve, and tweaks your ear repeatedly until you give him your undivided attention. You can't stand him, but at the same time you love him dearly.

Annemarie Roeper, founder of the Roeper School for the gifted and *The Roeper Review*, a highly respected professional journal dedicated to enhancing the understanding and education of the gifted, identifies the intense inner pressure to create as a hallmark of the gifted adult:

Gifted adults may be overwhelmed by the pressure of their own creativity. The gifted derive enormous satisfaction from the creative process. Much has been written about this process: how it works, the pressure of the inner agenda, the different phases it involves, the excitement and anxiety that comes with it, and the role played by the unconscious. One aspect, however, is not often mentioned. I believe the whole process is accompanied by a feeling of aliveness, of power, of capability, of enormous relief and of transcendence of the limits of our own body and soul. The "unique self" flows into the world outside. It is like giving birth. Creative expression derives directly from the unique Self of the creator, and its activation brings inherent feelings of happiness and aliveness, even though they may be accompanied by less positive emotions, such as sadness, fear, and pain. Underneath all is the enormous joy of discovery and personal expression. The creative experience is not unique to the gifted, but I believe that for them there are more opportunities for creativity, and that the experience is more alive and powerful. Just as the creative process creates a feeling of happiness, the greatest unhappiness can occur if it is interfered with or not allowed to happen. In that case the inner pressure cannot be released.[5]

Many Everyday Geniuses have talents that are designed to produce a creative end result, and they also have one thing more: a special capacity to explore in independent and imaginative ways and to generalize their findings on many subjects. In their atypical minds they turn reality on its head to view the world in fundamentally different ways. Beyond producing objects of value, the gifted create for the sole purpose of creative expression. They need to create and are rejuvenated by it. They often do so whether someone asks them to or not, regardless of payment or recognition, chiefly because they enjoy solving their own puzzles independent of external influence.

With this in mind, I can honestly say I have never seen a movie I didn't appreciate. Naturally, I have been disappointed when certain films didn't meet my expectations. When I overhear patrons leaving with nasty criticisms, I take offense on behalf of those who have put in the tremendous creative effort required to complete such a project.

First there's the effort of originating the idea in the first place, then recasting it so it makes sense. Then there's the writing and rewriting of the screenplay and the daring to offer it up to investors before surviving the sharp marketing claws of the industry gurus. The process continues from the title expert and the makeup artist who can incrementally age an actor fifty years to the special-effects technician who makes us believe it's really raining. All this effort is commanded for a public who pays ten dollars to sit in a soft chair and absorb the creative results for ninety minutes. If it grosses millions, I say, "Well done!" If it's a one-weekend fiasco, I say, "Well done!" It's the creative effort that matters.

Creative people can feel badgered by a sense that they must constantly deliver winning results, which is why many gifted individuals quit their artistic quests prematurely. In American society the creative process is rarely seen as its own reward, so the evolutionary must remember that the final product only hints at the aliveness and transcendent power of the process of innovation.

> Scott: Until you asked me I never gave it a second thought. But you're right. I do take stock of myself all the time. I'm constantly reviewing my actions and motivations. No wonder I'm anxious. I'm a person under nonstop scrutiny—my own. I'm no easy-to-please evaluator, either. That's for sure!

The gifted tackle complex problems, problems that at first glance appear unsolvable. This often looks as though we're doing things the hard way, and yet arduous effort is not evidence that the problem could have been solved more easily. This tolerance and preference for intricacy are the characteristics that often make the difference when someone must find creative answers in the face of growing complexity. Tolerance and perseverance work together because the Everyday Genius mind is built to tolerate a lack of structure until the pieces of the puzzles begin to line up in some understandable order.

We are not digging around for answers in a haphazard way, even though it may look that way. Everyday Geniuses come equipped with something like an internal mining crew that manages a well-organized home base so we can go off searching in different directions. It empowers us to imagine and wander about in creative thought without getting lost or straying too far from the intended goal. This is why creative producers seem so enigmatic. The system that keeps the work moving forward and organized on the inside is invisible in the midst of a desk that looks as though a tornado struck it.

It's a good thing that we are suited to work in a foggy maze, because that is where innovation so often resides. Though others may find it odd, apparent unfeasibility is inviting to us when it presents itself as a fog-covered labyrinth, a place where we can peek around unfamiliar corners and play with our intuition to see if we can make our way to the other side. Carl Jung grasped this when he observed, "The creative mind plays with the objects it loves."

However, there is a paradox in this, one of several that appear in the gifted person's life. Negotiating the problem maze is a fascination/repulsion contradiction that can be summed up in the remark: "Oh, how painful this is; I just love it!" Perhaps more than anything else, it is this love-hate relationship with challenge that stymies others who mistakenly conclude we choose to suffer unnecessary angst. It's true that until the creative product appears on the scene, we may be the only ones who have a solid idea of where we're going. Explaining one's vision to others is generally an exercise in frustration that is better avoided.

In truth, that vision is often nearly impossible to articulate, sometimes even to ourselves. We have an itch that needs to be scratched, a door that beckons us to open it, a want that turns into a must. The love-hate relationship with creative production is somewhat like a good horror flick—all the juices start to flow, the sensory system is on full alert, and the unexpected is expected. Courage and thrill in the murky engagement, relief and gratification in the conquest. The painstaking steps of the creative process always involve formulating and reformulating, retracing old steps, and taking new ones, then repeating it all until the final goal is reached. Then and only then can we permit ourselves to sit back and say, "There."

Sometimes we are inappropriately accused of being intolerant despite the fact that we tolerate one thing most people distrust and avoid: ambiguity. Defining ambiguity is not difficult; whereas obscurity stems from chaos and impossibility implies the unattainable, ambiguity is about quandary, about apparently irreconcilable contradictions about a multiplicity of options. The skill to confront complex meanings, however, complements our ability to approach all sides of an issue, and we are always fascinated with complicated riddles.

Like others, we find complicated situations troublesome, but the reason we are recognized as idea people is because we're willing to float on a sea of doubt longer than others. The moment when others are frustrated enough to throw up their hands in resignation is often when we are just getting going. The so-called hard way is really the long and slow and irritating way of excellence. Reserving the need to be certain along the way is a hallmark of Everyday Genius thinking. Even though we get frustrated, too, we understand that progress is almost never a rocket shot straight to the target.

The creative burst that has the power to change everything is the product of what writer Arthur Koestler calls the "sudden fusion" of two or more concepts. The Everyday Genius' ability to overshadow the average problem solver is in large part attributed to an exceptional ability to combine existing data with new ideas, to tame and harness paradox. This management of paradox—not being undone by it or running away from it—involves simultaneous problem-finding and problem-solving efforts.

We possess so many ideas primarily because we can allow seemingly disconnected elements to linger in our heads in a subconscious filing system that determines what is valuable and what is mental "junk mail." There they wait, stored and filed, until the right moment, when, as James Vargiu, founding director of the Psychosynthesis Institute in San Francisco, notes, the ideas are ready to "come under the influence of the creative field."[5] This filing method integrates the powers of learned experience, knowledge, and intuition by holding captivating notions in a state of readiness.

The creative thinker holds a different attitude than others, one that does not give way to the forces of turmoil and creative tension, but rather sees stress as opportunity for discovery. Certainly Einstein's discovery of the theory of relativity illustrates this point. In *Productive Thinking* Max Wertheimer describes Einstein's preillumination frustration:

> [A] certain region in the structure of the whole situation was in reality not as clear to him as it should be, although it had hitherto been accepted without question by everyone, including himself. . . . During this time he was often depressed, sometimes in despair, but driven by the strongest vectors.[6]

Einstein's struggle with his relativity theory continued for seven years, during which it might have been said little happened, that he was trying to do something "the hard way." Yet perhaps many of the greatest discoveries are by necessity the result of the greatest difficulties. Besides perseverance and tension tolerance, knowing when to stop fishing for a while to do something else is a critical factor in innovation. Einstein's sidetrack to reexamine his theories about time led to his new theory of relativity just five weeks later.

Like Einstein, we too rely on the knitting that is done by our unconscious minds when we are "off task." A problem or idea in incubation is free of the limitations of our conscious logic, at liberty to examine theories and relationships the thinking mind cannot. This is the territory of our inner creative artist, who is able to stretch out the problem in many directions, to pull together strands of silk, steel, ocean water, and cloud from remote areas of the cosmos, far beyond the reaches of educated knowledge. When the strands have been artfully and painstakingly woven together, illumination occurs.

Once the "aha" has occurred, we can switch back to our linear-thinking mode and make use of the newly designed fabric. Then the more mundane work must begin, the work of production, which many creative producers consider a frustrating necessity. Nevertheless, innovation is not all spark and sparkle, and it never comes easy; its challenges and demands almost always exceed the effort implied by the end result.

The so-called hard way is truly the way of evolution itself, which is creativity on the cosmic scale. Innovation is the direct application of our gifts as they are allowed to come under the influence of the Higher Creative Field. Throughout the process of creation we ascend and descend again and again, each time crossing the threshold between ground-dwelling human and transcending spirit. This is what Wertheimer meant when he referred to the "strongest vectors," because its unusual properties combine direction and force, both of which are inspired, not forced. This is the way creativity has always been.

10

GETTING FREE FROM THE
TOP FIVE CRITICISMS

We are the ones we've been waiting for.   —June Jordan

When the ten major criticisms are finally debunked, you will no longer need to question and requestion yourself in search of permission or approval. You can free yourself from the urge to repeatedly explain yourself, justify your ideas, and placate everyone in your path who seems confused about you. There's simply too much energy wasted that way, and usually for naught.

Affirming your true self on the inside does not, however, mean you can rest on your laurels. Nor does it mean you can forgo ownership of inappropriate social behavior, lack of effort, selfishness, or immaturity. Yet by ridding yourself of a few fundamental "Who am I?" confusions, the ones that nag at you and wear you down the most, you can face your life revitalized and ready to fulfill your potential.

If all this sounds like a Herculean assignment, stand by; there is good news. Self-empowerment tends to grow in curious stages, first in tiny "Can I really do this?" steps, followed by several "by George I'm doing it" upward strides, and sometimes in quantum leaps. This is accomplished by understanding yourself at the core level. This is necessary because every step of self-definition is a revolutionary act.

Remember, no matter how ready and willing you are, all change is inevitably interspersed with backsliding. Don't fool yourself into thinking this is not the case or that falling down is easy to take. No one does well with the discouraging stumblings that set things back a few strides, especially because they often seem to happen just when things are going along well.

Reclaiming the birthright of Everyday Genius takes practice. It's like learning to walk all over again. Occasionally, traversing the peaks and valleys of self-becoming can result in a wrong turn or a bruising fall. But we're built for that, too—to get up, brush ourselves off, and forge ahead, although it might not seem like it at the time. Everyday Geniuses are programmed to bounce back. Soon awkward steps become easier, and you find yourself moving forward with new confidence. That is when you will be free to deliver your gifts with determination. Consequently, when you turn around you'll discover most of your self-doubt has been shed. Now, with half of the obsolete criticisms dispelled and the momentum of 50 percent more self-assurance, let's face the top five.

> CRITICISM #5: *"You're So Demanding!"*
> NEW RESPONSE: *"I Do Know What I Want."*

Let's look at how being exacting is connected to our specialized way of doing things. When we *do* know what we want, we don't want anything else. After assembling the components of an important idea and reaching the point of crystallization, our conclusions are not easily budged. And yes, we can become very insistent.

Gerald: Everybody seems to think I'm a radical, that my primary goal in life is to be a nonconformist. That's not it at all. I just have this really active imagination that runs all the time like a movie marathon with overlays of ideas and news of the day and list of things to do. It's pretty busy up there in my head. When I get hold of the image of what I'm after on a project, I hold onto it like superglue. I have always had a sense of when things are done—done right, that is. I'm willing to take what's important to me all the way; I don't care what it takes. I just can't justify doing less. Everything I do I put my heart and soul into. That's what makes it worthwhile. Not just getting done, but getting as close as I can to the ideal.

Nadine: Persistence isn't a choice for me, it's a way of life. I vigorously pursue my goals, sometimes finding it hard to balance my life because of my intense commitment. I always have a goalpost in my line of sight. I simply don't feel good unless I can see that I am clicking off the yardage and getting somewhere. Trouble is, as soon as I reach the end zone, the yards gained behind me disappear from view. Then I'm on to the next problem or achievement: goalpost ahead, many yards to go. If only I could let myself accumulate some kind of internal praise or tribute to what I did before instead of dismissing it as nothing more than what was expected. I'd be much more content, much happier along the way from one end zone to the next.

Ralph: Whenever I'm really absorbed in a project—deep down into it— it drives me crazy if I'm interrupted. It breaks me out of my zone and I get really upset, especially if the interruption is for something I think is trivial.

Most people have a limited understanding of how personally laborious it is to plow through ideas toward the bumpy process of innovation. Though it's generally great to be creative, creative expression does not come without its price. The zealous and single-minded individual who supports a project until it reaches maturity and excellence is all too often interpreted as being incredibly demanding. It is not easy for us to accept that others do not share our zeal and are not willing to go to the lengths that we are to investigate, polish, and refine. This disappointing reality is just as difficult for us to handle as our exactitude is for others.

Case in point: In the course of the thirty-plus years of her indefatigable career, Barbra Streisand has been recognized as one of the most successful and talented people in show business history. Few, however, have been privy to her private world, a world that has included exhausting rehearsals and years of painful stage fright. In a 1994 article in *Vanity Fair* Streisand openly discussed her difficulty in returning to the concert tour after twenty-eight years: "I was really frightened in Vegas. . . . My heart was pounding. Why would I put myself through this agony? . . . I thought I really would disappoint people, that I wasn't good enough."[1] Yet, in true evolutionary style, she persevered, and there is little question that her willingness to overcome her anxiety to perfect her creative products resulted in much listening pleasure for her public.

Later Streisand was rebuked in the press for reportedly holding up the release of *The Prince of Tides* for more than three years by insisting on a series of meticulous changes. True, she seldom settled for anything less than what measured up to her high ideals. Perhaps, however, her fortitude and insistence on perfecting details was precisely what made the movie so successful.

Streisand's high standards have paid off specifically because the ideal she envisions is usually exactly what she delivers. She does know, clearly and in detail, what she wants. Even so, it seems reasonable that her high expectations might not always mesh with those of others.

It is true that over the years her perseverance has alienated a few colleagues. However, this is not about her being childishly demanding; it is about pressing for the highest artistic achievement. After all, how does an energized visionary push the creative limits without having someone occasionally push back? Although Streisand's commitment to her goals has sometimes annoyed her associates, there is little doubt that it has contributed immeasurably to the value of her endeavors.

Yet like all gifted adults, Streisand is much more than her list of accomplishments. By her friends' accounts, she is "curious, passionate, eager to debate, and quick to flit from subject to subject." Many also find her compellingly interesting and articulate. Currently, Streisand's need for balance in her life is said to receive top billing. By her own admission, her intensity and insatiable appetite for learning and truth are becoming more reflective and spiritual with the passage of time.

CRITICISM #4: *"Can't You Ever Be Satisfied?"*

NEW RESPONSE: *"Sure. I Derive Satisfaction in Many Ways."*

When others hear us complaining about the status quo, what we are really doing is comparing "as is" to our dream of a better world. For those of us who tend to say what we see, it must appear that we can't be satisfied. In a way we are always dissatisfied with the present because we are Apollonian in our aim toward goals, long shooters who dare to set our sights high and far. It is important for us to accept the fact that we will inevitably be frustrated some of the time. All the same, we must take care to avoid letting constant dissatisfaction alienate us from the joys of our journey.

Everyday Geniuses are not perennial malcontents unless they are deterred from self-expression. Though our satisfaction may not always be readily apparent to others, it does become visible as we find ways to become who we are intended to be. Then our looks of contentment shine through in spite of life's daily aggravations.

> *Charles: A lot of my "thinking" is picture and sound, and I process things by image more than words. In some respect I think it's my way of trying to shut out the world and relax. I'm a stimulation junkie, which means if I don't pull inside for a while, I suffer from stimulation overload. I'm like one of those sea anemones, those flowerlike creatures stuck on rocks that wave their little tentacles about in the ocean for food, except unlike me they have the sense to pull in when they've had enough stimulation. Me, I'm always on the go, like a stuck throttle.*
>
> *When I kick back in mental meandering I'm taking a break; the outside world and my inside agitation don't get to me. I can get lost in my own thoughts. I suppose sometimes that means I seem aloof or rude. And I know I need to watch out for that. But the truth is that I need that source of satisfaction, or at least something like it. Ten minutes in the park gazing at the ripples in the pond are worth their weight in gold. My fantasies and fascination with the little things make the humdrum parts of life richer, more exciting, more touchable. It's my built-in well of serenity, standing back from the details of everyday life to regain my sense of balance, to reconnect with the steady frequency of life itself.*

Many of us discover that conventional forms of satisfaction become less important as we gain access to higher yet simpler sources of fulfillment. We learn and relearn that small pleasures possess a much longer shelf life than material goods and public approval.

One of our most priceless gifts is our ability to uncover pleasures others often miss. No matter what the obstacles, our inherent craving for authentic experience is never destroyed. Opportunity for satisfaction is never lost because of three of our gifts: (1) a curiosity that revels in examining things closely in our mind's eye, (2) a deep understanding that we are part of a universal tapestry in which all things are interconnected, and (3) being purposely designed to wonder about the cause of this wonder in the universe.

What does all this have to do with contentment? Our sensitivities equip us to go about our daily lives within a virtual Epcot Center of discovery. Heightened awareness offers us a renewable resource of immediate experiences of seemingly disparate elements of beauty. Many Everyday Geniuses seem to have this heightened awareness and ability to appreciate what's most valuable from the start. Some gain it through life's turnabout events. After a heart attack, Abraham Maslow noted a profound change in his sources of satisfaction:

> One very important aspect of the postmortem life is that everything gets doubly precious. . . . You get stabbed by . . . flowers and by babies and by beautiful things—just the very act of living, of walking, breathing, eating, having friends, and chatting. Everything seems to look more beautiful rather than less, and one gets the much-intensified sense of miracles.[2]

Like it or not, we are grounded beings who have much on our minds and plenty to do. Everyday Geniuses are fitted from the start to perceive their world as a playground of fascinating possibility. Many times in our uncommon existence we parallel the experience of Lewis Carroll's wide-eyed heroine in *Alice in Wonderland* as we, too, exclaim, "Curiouser and curiouser!"

One way or another, from ants to Zoroastrianism, there's something that fires our ready interest, and interest is the instigator of satisfaction. Multiple interests become a problem only when we try to go down too many roads at once. If we take precautionary steps to avoid spreading our energies too thin, our broad range of fascination can serve as a lifelong source of fascinating adventure and ecstatic moments.

Self-actualizing people, who rely on flashes of surprise and wonder to liberate themselves from fear, self-doubt, lack of control, and feelings of isolation from Self, often have ecstatic experiences. We can learn to employ these invigorating time-outs to gather and refresh ourselves as we exhale the dross of everyday living. For a brief period the world is changed, fantasy and reality merging, while we take time to ride the mystical rhythms of a cello or skate over the intricate design of Jack Frost's icy etchings.

Another source of satisfaction that is particularly attractive to us is the future. The future is always a realm that beckons the evolutionary. Fortunately, here is an area in which we may delve to our heart's content with little fear of becoming bored or running out of puzzles to ponder. By midlife many of us begin to experience an escalating interest in the future, and not just in terms of what's going to happen next week.

For those of us who love to future-play in the labyrinths of human evolution, the subtle ins and outs of symbol, myth, poetry, dream, spirituality, and philosophy can be especially engaging. Our interest is more collective and focused on the farthest reaches of human experience. Here is where the future becomes deep, wide, and dramatic. Indeed, these are rich resources of well-being for nearly every self-actualizing adult. By most accounts self-realization and spiritual enlightenment progress simultaneously, requiring us to become seekers of the transcendent. Here is the second stanza of "On the Ineffable Inspiration of the Holy Spirit," written by German poet Catharina Regina von Greiffenberg in the early 1600s:

> *Never by its own power the soul is thus alight.*
> *It was a miracle-wind, a spirit, a creative being,*
> *The eternal power of breath, prime origin of being*
> *That in me kindled for himself this heaven-flaring light.*[3]

Fortunately, we also have a gift of appreciation for art and beauty and can rely on it as the rootstock for inspiration and energy. Just as our sense of purpose provides us with invigoration and renewal, our aesthetic consciousness serves as a wellspring of illumination. Vitality and joy increase when we allow ourselves to be influenced by art, both manmade and Divine.

It might even be said that a tryst with aesthetics is one way in which we "go home for a visit," a brief reunion that momentarily closes the gap between Self and soul. Experiencing art is like raising both palms with fingers extended upward until our hands are met by the hands of the Divine. Such "homecoming" encounters with beauty are depicted in the visionary words of many an Everyday Genius. For Kahlil Gibran, beauty was "eternity gazing at itself in a mirror." Ralph Waldo Emerson saw "God's handwriting" in beauty. And Jane Porter interpreted beauty as "the soul shining through its crystalline covering."

In her unique way, Georgia O'Keeffe possessed the genius to pull us directly into the heart and essence of her aesthetic universe. Her paintings capturing a single flower's magnificence immediately distinguish her work and underscore the innumerable marvels of nature that surround us every day. It is said that when O'Keeffe was six months old she was set outdoors on the grass upon a patchwork quilt. Many years later she could still see in her mind's eye the quilt of tiny red and white flowers on a black and white background exactly as it was that sunny afternoon. Above all she recalled the magnitude and splendor of the day, able to regain the joy she had felt so long ago in "the brightness of the light—light all around."[4]

In the symbolism of poetry, William Butler Yeats insists the creative mind must be at liberty to wander and wonder, to contemplate, to meditate:

> The purpose of rhythm, it has always seemed to me, is to prolong the moment of contemplation, the moment when we are both asleep and awake, which is the one moment of creation, by hushing us with an alluring monotony, while it holds us waking by variety, to keep us in that state of perhaps real trance, in which the mind liberated from the pressure of the will is unfolded in symbols. . . . I was writing once at a very symbolical and abstract poem, when my pen fell on the ground; and as I stooped to pick it up, I remembered some fantastic adventure that yet did not seem fantastic, and then another like adventure, and when I asked myself when these things had happened, I found that I was remembering my dreams for many nights. I tried to remember what I had done the day before, and then what I had done that morning; but all my waking life had perished from me, and it was only after a struggle that life perished in its turn. Had my pen not fallen on the ground and so made me turn from the images that I was weaving into verse, I would never have known that meditation had become trance, for I would have been like one who does not know that he is passing through a wood because his eyes are on the pathway.[5]

For us, deep satisfaction is rarely far away. It is even more accessible because of the legacies of Everyday Geniuses, renowned and unnamed, who have provided us through the years with the foundation to support our own life's work. We can draw on the very same source of radiant light as our predecessors, because we too possess special vision. It is the vision that allows us to peel away the outer coating of everyday experience to touch the transcendent.

CRITICISM #3: *"You're So Driven!"*

NEW RESPONSE: *"Yes, I Am Focused and Have Much to Do."*

Everyday Geniuses do, of course, derive immense pleasure from effort. Yet in order for effort to be fulfilling, a good part of it must be related to our unique inner agenda. Once Mandated Mission and Drive are connected, it is not easy to turn it off like a faucet, because a great part of our identity concerns goal direction.

At times our goal orientation makes us feel like a geyser, filling us with repeated rumblings of discomfort until the appropriate fissure opens a new channel for expression of the true Self. Most of the time the pressure gauge approaches the red zone well before we consciously know what our drive is about. Turning down the pressure would be easy if it were simply a matter of choice. It is not. For when effort is about calling, a personal duty, it is a powerful force that compels us to do what we are intended to do in the service of humanity.

The source of the pressure is the central point about being "driven." The key element in this equation is the fact that we alone are not the drivers. We are *driven* by purpose; we do not simply choose to *drive* ourselves toward our personal goals. If we heed the wisdom of our subconscious agenda as made known to us by our daemon, our guiding inner spirit or genius, and consciously reflect on our unique place in the scheme of human evolution, we can accept ourselves as responsive co-creators who merely collaborate with destiny instead of attempting to force it into place.

> *Calvin: I need to find a way to stop impersonating myself and have the inside me and the outside me match more often. I am smart and a go-getter, though I'm still human. I'm not perfect or inexhaustible—I have real needs and real doubts and as thin a skin as anybody else. But no one knows that, and I'm really scared that if they did, they'd either be glad to see me knocked down a few pegs or they'd be disappointed in me. Not much room for winning there!*
>
> *Accepting myself as a high achiever with killer drive is no problem. Opening my arms to the part of me that is imperfect, vulnerable, and fallible is another thing altogether. I've always expected myself to jump through hoops. When I miss, I can be pretty hard to live with.*
>
> *More and more I want to enjoy doing what I'm good at, and to excel without feeling like I need to apologize for it. I have so much to do; so many needs in the world tug at me for my attention. Being free to do something special with my life in my own way and to be supported in that is much harder and lonelier than people think.*

In a very real sense, we are guided by something akin to the migratory instinct of birds. Birds spend little time considering whether or not they should go north in summer and south in winter. When it's time, it's time, and off they soar, following their instinctive map. This is not so easy for us *Homo sapiens* with "advanced" intellect. Our imprinting is also strong, but much more difficult to sort out. It takes time, diligence, and a willingness to take that important leap of faith. We also feel the migrational force grow stronger as we close in on our authentic direction. Then our built-in will becomes more useful as it unites with our true purpose.

Perhaps like nothing else, the Everyday Genius' drive toward meaningful goals exemplifies the power of the individual. In today's impersonal business world, where there are so many people involved in projects that we don't even know their names, it's easy to forget that progress is all about individual effort, whether the work is done within a large network or alone. Many creative producers who make a positive difference put in innumerable unseen hours of labor long before their efforts come to light for the rest of us to see. The most effective of them are resolute, hard-driving individuals who are not overwhelmed by setbacks or others' skepticism. We can all be grateful that they dare to invest in and enact their visions and beliefs; they do so, in part, because their very being is permeated with their objective. The fuel that powers their initiative is their ability to suspend "common sense," which may render them "crazy" for a while—something they take in stride until their incredible striving produces something the world finds credible and creditable.

By the mid-1800s Cyrus Field had made a fortune in the paper business. In the face of one disaster after another, Field furnished both the capital and the drive to take on a project that today would be left to huge governmental concerns—to lay a telegraph cable across the Atlantic ocean. His determination and ability to arouse piqued the interest of scientists who provided the know-how to get the job done. In 1866 Field's perseverance paid off, and the United States and Europe were connected by electric signals. He was awarded a congressional medal. Yet he didn't stop there, and went on to spend vast amounts of money and effort to build New York City's elevated railway system. Field died in 1892—successful and poor.[6]

In a 1996 interview financial wizard Muriel Seibert, an admitted college dropout, said: "I think I've spent my life breaking down doors. When I see a challenge I put my head down and charge." Her drive is indeed legendary, taking her all the way from a $65-a-week position as a research analyst trainee at Wall Street's Bache and Co. to being the first woman to buy a seat on the New York Stock Exchange despite having the first nine men she approached to sponsor her turn her down. It was a long time after that day in 1967 before other women would join her, she recalled: "For ten years it was 1,365 men and me."

Seibert went on to become the first woman to own a NYSE brokerage firm. She has received numerous awards and honorary degrees, and is as well known for her philanthropy as for her business acumen and brass. The Seibert Entrepreneurial Philanthropic Plan gives 50 percent of its commissions from certain stocks to charity, with its cumulative donations nearing $5 million by 1997. Seibert explains her charitable work as her way of trying to create "a decade of decency."[7]

Maggie told her quite different story of contribution as an Everyday Genius:

> *Maggie: I don't think what I'm doing is all that special. I've been going to the neighborhood free clinic for thirty-two years now. It's just something that has to be done. Why me? Why not me? The homeless people there might be asking the same questions. None of us knows the answer to all our whys. My grandmother told me I had good hands for helping, and that's what I try to do—just to hold the hand of the sick and dying. It's such a little thing, really. But it's my work, my reason for getting up and on my feet in the morning. They expect my hands to touch theirs, and they need to feel cared about. That's all there is to it.*
>
> *I can still see in their eyes the dreams they once had for life. I'm not special, they are—fighting to hold on to their dignity, so quiet, asking for so little, yet deserving as much as the next person. If my hands can help by changing soiled sheets or feeding soup a sip at a time, I'm at my best. In some small way if I can help them have a dream of going to the end of life feeling worthwhile, then I thank them for honoring me with the opportunity.*

There is surely no point in being a person of vision unless we have the will to act. Daydreams and inklings about taking our personal mission seriously must be translated into action or be lost in the dust of "could have but didn't." As it turns out, we have repeated opportunities to discover our mission and have been favored with the asset of will to meet the challenge.

It is not will alone but *inspired* will that lifts us up and over discouragement. This is the same driving force that we see in acts of heroism and compassion, a sense of determination powerful enough to move tremendous obstacles while being able to withstand the ravages of repeated conflicts. Inspired will directs our driven nature so that we may attempt to turn the gigantic wheel of human progress ever so slightly.

CRITICISM #2: *"Where Do You Get Those Wild Ideas?"*

NEW RESPONSE: *"Straight from the Source."*

If you should ever encounter a gifted person who tells you that her or his creative ideas and meaningful living are the product of nothing more than intellect and effort, don't believe it. Such a belief in self alone may last for a while, especially in early adulthood. Yet sooner or later, some manner of reorienting experience or trauma shakes things up. When everything is turned upside-down we feel engulfed in chaos, which is always the seedbed of creative action. In such a weakened or humbled state we recognize the fundamental reason for our special gifts. Suddenly we come face-to-face with the absolute proof of a strength and purpose greater than our own.

Whether physicist, composer, Wall Street wizard, or caregiver, the vast majority of high achievers and self-actualizers throughout the ages have understood that their inspirations and abilities are gifts. Gifts can only be received, given by another, offered with care and good intention. In the case of the evolutionary, the Source who gives the gifts does so with an authorization to deliver them in the service of humankind.

One of my clients addressed the difference between intelligence and giftedness:

Jill: Would Hitler and the Unabomber be considered gifted? Certainly both men had high IQs. I guess the difference is this: Ability used for destruction is not a gift. It's more like a seductive curse that warps one's vision and destroys the soul.

I think giftedness implies that God was the giver. Maybe that's why I was so reluctant to acknowledge my own abilities and think of myself as "gifted." I guess it was because I sensed the seriousness of the responsibility that comes with them, the price tag that says I am supposed to use them well.

On the other hand, knowing this frees me from any self-consciousness I might have about being smart and talented, because I now realize I am just a vehicle. It's like my body and mind are being used to do what people need for the betterment of the whole, and I cooperate, but can't really take the credit. I like that because everything I do now has become a "we" thing, not just an "I" thing. That makes everything I try to do so much easier.

In many ways the top two criticisms that Everyday Geniuses endure are the most complex and require the most personally revealing and least defensive responses. As Jill had discovered, there is no need to try to manufacture intricate explanations of why we do what we do and how we do it. When faced with an irritating criticism about where we derive our ideas, especially inquiries connected to our divinely designed purpose, we simply acknowledge that we are mere "vehicles," point our finger upward, and smile.

> *Stuart: Looking back on my life, it seems so foolhardy that for so long I was a victim of my own ego. I truly believed I had to do all the work to come up with the ideas I needed as an illustrator of children's books. I remember so many times literally squeezing my head as if by doing so the ideas would squirt out the top.*
>
> *Now it's all so different, so very much easier! What's really interesting is that deep inside I don't think I ever really believed my best inspirations were self-propelled. When I was a kid I seemed much more comfortable with being receptive, doing my part and then waiting for the idea burst to come—which it always did. I don't know why I worried so much about it later on. I don't think I could stop having new ideas even if I tried. So now that I don't need to get so wound up about running out of good ideas, I can relax into my work, trust the process, and even glide more easily through the inevitable dry spells where nothing seems to be happening. Trusting the creative cooperative process has not only brought me to new heights in my work, it has also struck a chord within me. I can honestly say that I am a happy man—not just when things are buzzing along with energy, but in the quiet moments, too, when I can accept my role as creative vehicle and allow myself to be filled again with the creative spirit. I've been thinking a lot lately about a quote from Thoreau that I memorized when I was about twelve. For the first time it really makes sense to me: "If one advances confidently in the direction of his dreams, and endeavors to live the life which he has imagined, he will meet with a success unexpected in common hours."*

CRITICISM #1: *"Who Do You Think You Are?"*

NEW RESPONSE: *"A Humble Everyday Genius Called to Serve."*

"Who do you think you are?" is a fair question. Yet it is one most adults, even the best thinkers, have trouble answering. Perhaps this is because we are each a work in progress. Perhaps it is because we have been led to believe that who we are is equivalent to what we have to show for ourselves in terms of awards, possessions, and power. In part we are a product of our actions and achievements, our relationships and efforts. The self can also be imagined as those parts of us that are stable over time, the foundational aspects of our being that may or may not be observable on the surface of our lives. It is the bulwark and the pivot point from which the personality ventures forth.

In *What We May Be*, psychosynthesis teacher Piero Ferrucci speaks to the identity question:

> [T]he self remains the same in ecstasy and despair, in peace and turmoil, in pain and pleasure, in victory and defeat. . . . [S]ure enough, if we take a look at our psychophysical organism, our first impression is that there is no such pivot point, that everything is in a state of continual flux. To begin with, our body is sometimes tired and sometimes full of energy, healthy or ill, young or old, sleepy or awake, hungry or satisfied. It certainly isn't an immutable reality. Our feelings are not permanent either. Through some mysterious illusions they sometimes assume a character of changeless presence. But then they disappear and other feelings take their place, bringing with them the same old illusions of permanence. Finally, our thoughts are not permanent. They pop in and out of our minds, one after another, in a matter of moments.
>
> Yet if we look within ourselves carefully enough, we will find that there is a permanent element. Body sensations change, feelings fade, thoughts flow by, but someone remains to experience this flow. This "someone" is the self, the experiencer. . . .
>
> The self is not a reality to be experienced only with closed eyes. It is a realization that can be retained in the midst of daily life. While the self is by definition pure inner silence, it does not necessarily take us away from our everyday moods and activities; on the contrary, it can increasingly manifest an effective presence and self-reliance.[8]

The most effective way I know to fly free and release one's exceptional gifts is to detach from the ego long enough to join forces with the Divine. Humility need never be a prescription for either docility or total self-denial. As we know, Everyday Geniuses come in all types, from Mother Teresa to Michael Jordan. And they do so for a very good reason—

when they are on the right path, the ingenious creations and efforts of all of them are necessary for progress to unfold. By giving ourselves the freedom to be a "we" in our personal missions instead of a lone "I," fears that we hold in the conscious mind can be overridden. Self-doubt in the face of criticism can be disregarded. And we can learn to control our shaking when we find ourselves on uncertain ground.

By detangling ourselves from the tight knots that arise whenever we search for nods of approval by trying to explain who we are and why we are different and what we are up to, we set ourselves free. In many ways, embracing our smallness is the way past society's obstacles. It reminds me of what an unforgettable elderly client once told me about why she loved getting older. She smiled broadly with the glint of wisdom in her eyes and said: "Just you wait until you're seventy. It's the greatest thing! I can do whatever I want. I can sing in the grocery store, laugh out loud walking down the street, wear plaids and stripes together, and say what I want. I've never been so free in all my life, because I can be me, all of me, nearly all of the time. And if people don't like it, I don't care. Besides, I can be as different as I want because the odder I seem, the more everyone else is willing to pass it off as eccentricity. And that's where all the fun is!"

A fundamental discovery question for many Everyday Geniuses is this: Is it we who create, or is it in our creations that we are made? Furthermore, do we really have as much choice in the matter as we have come to believe? Composer Igor Stravinsky found himself set upon the path of the revolutionary:

> I was made a revolutionary in spite of myself . . . . [A]ll creation presupposes at its origin a sort of appetite that is brought on by the foretaste of discovery. This foretaste of the creative art accompanies the intuitive grasp of an unknown entity that will not take definite shape except by the action of a constantly vigilant technique. This appetite that is aroused in me at the mere thought of putting in order musical elements that have attracted my attention is not at all a fortuitous thing like inspiration, but as habitual and periodic, if not as constant, as a natural need. . . .
>
> The very act of putting my work on paper, of, as we say, kneading the dough, is for me inseparable from the pleasure of creation. So far as I am concerned, I cannot separate the spiritual effort from the psychological and physical effort; they confront me on the same level and do not present a hierarchy. . . .
>
> What concerns us here is not imagination itself, but rather creative

imagination: the faculty that helps us to pass from the level of conception to the level of realization. In the course of my labors I suddenly
stumble upon something unexpected. This unexpected element strikes
me. I make note of it. At the proper time I put it to profitable use. . . .
The faculty of creating is never given to us all by itself. It always goes
hand in hand with the gift of observation. And the true creator may be
recognized by his ability always to find about him, in the commonest
and humblest thing, items worthy of note. . . . The least accident holds
his interest and guides his operations. If his finger slips, he will notice
it; on occasion, he may draw profit from something unforeseen that a
momentary lapse reveals to him. One does not contrive an accident:
one observes it to draw inspiration therefrom.[9]

For most of us evolution is a concept of mammoth proportion and
difficult to contemplate without a ready supply of aspirin. Burrowing
through the classics and written legacies of the great minds who have
for centuries labored over the ways of creativity and the possibilities
of humankind might be suitable for scholars. It goes without saying that
study brings about more questions, which bring about more study, which
is just the right cup of tea for some gifted individuals.

Yet most Everyday Geniuses have little enough time to reflect and
contemplate, and may not be inclined to spend too much time in the library stacks in search of discoveries for the greater good. When it comes
to our individual part in evolution, our head can still feel as though it is
spinning off its axis.

We are all charged with the task of individual and collective evolution. We are called by name to figure out our place in the process and to
meet the challenge with respect and courage. When we're prepared,
seeking guideposts through meditation and inner discovery will reveal
our unique design and dictate our direction. It is not usually a loud voice
that pronounces what we are to do, so we must pay close attention to the
subtle details of communication.

Our whole self is awakened and expanded as the split between conscious and unconscious, dreaming and being, and soul and mind is
bridged. The evolutionary experience is more than excitement, achievement, or happiness. It is a complete integration of inner spirit and outer
action that fits like a lock and key with evolutionary purpose. Evolutionary actions go well with our gifts because they shift humanity toward
something future generations will applaud.

Each of us has a specialized way in which our gifts will be delivered.

The way we go and the style of our pursuits may be anonymous or public, traditional or unconventional, soft or hard, colorful or neutral, together or alone. But go we must, or face stagnation and loss of fulfillment. The height to which our potentialities are to be realized will be directly related to the development and expression of our individual nature, not someone else's. Obscuring and contradicting our intended fulfillment would be a fatal mistake and indeed an affront to the Divine.

Self-realization is by its very nature fraught with risk, yet it is a welcome risk because it implies unimagined adventures, particularly the adventures born of the mysteries of mind and spirit. The call of the evolutionary is not for the faint of heart, which is why we were created to answer it with our special gifts delivered to us for our development and offering to humanity.

11

MEETING THE FALSE SELF

One's real life is so often the life that one does not lead.
—Oscar Wilde

The dangers of denying one's true nature can be very serious, not only because self-denial is a bad choice that causes persistent feelings of frustration and anxiety, but because inauthenticity threatens one's quality of life at the deepest level. Inauthenticity is a cultivation problem. When high potential is treated like a neglected tree, underfed and pushed out of the sun, it does not die off entirely. Nor does it thrive and bear wonderful fruit. It merely survives in an atrophied form, its vibrancy aborted.

Though for a time ignoring one's gifts may seem the safer bet, in the long run trying to pursue a life destined for another offers only the meager comforts of pseudoconfidence and artificial belonging. Over time the security blanket of "blending in" begins to unravel. Because the Everyday Genius identity crisis so often occurs at times of personal injury or loss, or at midlife, it is easily misjudged as a factor of those experiences alone. Crises are an invaluable opportunity for the Everyday Genius to come to grips with the false self, because when we're vulnerable and confused, the false self rises to the surface in full force. This is exactly what Byron discovered when he was a victim of corporate downsizing and his thriving career suddenly caved in.

Byron: I'm so stunned about my job loss that I can't even think straight. I knew the company was in for a shake-up. But not in a million years did I ever think the ax would fall on me. Mostly I've been treated like the department wonder boy—"Ask Byron, he'll know what to do" was the chief problem-solving method. And what's really absurd is their choice about who goes and who stays. The head of personnel confided in me that as far as she's concerned it's only the idea people who have any starch in them who are being let go. How does that make any sense?

I know it won't be long before I find something else. So why am I so undone? Because I feel like I woke up yesterday and had no idea who I was anymore. I'm forty-three years old. How can I not know myself? I feel like I did when I was in high school after we lost the big game— slammed up against the wall with nothing to say for myself. The only thing that runs through my head is a diatribe that goes right back to what my father always told me: "Byron, you've got to get your feet on the ground and learn to go with the flow. Keep a low profile and you'll be all right. Stick your neck out too often and you're likely to get your head chopped off." That's exactly what I tried to do, and it made me miserable a lot of the time. And here I am in spite of my efforts to follow Dad's advice. Now what do I do?

At critical turning points like Byron's, if we look deep enough, we will reencounter the lost self underneath the facade of the false self. By going back through our histories on a rescue mission, we can rewrite the fictional account of ourselves that for so long we have thought was true. It is a mission of liberation fueled by our new responses to the old criticisms and the willingness to meet and challenge the false self who has been running the show far too long.

MEETING THE FALSE SELF

For many Everyday Geniuses, meeting the false self can feel very precarious. This is especially true for those who are accustomed to being the "other"—the ugly duckling self who insists we will be miserable unless we think, perceive, and experience the world the way everybody else does, the outcast who reminds us that we have no business believing in idealistic visions or following our inner agendas. If all else fails, we are often brought up by the short hairs for even daring to talk about our gifts. After a time it's nearly impossible to observe ourselves from an alternative frame of reference—to see ourselves in any other way than in the straitjacket of conformity. Without any argument from the external world, the false self has no trouble taking control.

An identity theft occurs without our even knowing it. It is this "other" self that has been given all the time, support, and experience to grow and develop habits, while our true self has remained hidden and dormant. It's easy to understand that when it's time to shed our surface identity and rescue the lost self, we can feel very unconfident. Often we are afraid that if we look inside, underneath the familiar false self, there may be no one there. This is exactly what the false self wants us to believe, because it was established for protection in the first place. Like many remnants of childhood, this defense is no longer useful and in fact is no longer tolerable.

Perhaps the most powerful weapon of the false self is its last-ditch effort to convince us that we need not bother to develop ourselves further since our gifts are nothing special after all, that they are commonplace and inessential. The confrontation between the true self and the false self takes on an increasingly negative and deprecating tone whenever we attempt to uncover its agenda. Eventually a full reckoning shows the false self for what it is: an all-out effort to bully the Everyday Genius back into conformity.

I had been working with Carl for about three months before he was ready to take on his false self. He was motivated by the fact that through years of superficial living he had neglected and dishonored his true self, frozen bit by bit over time until a brittle state of longing had become his most constant companion. Like so many Everyday Geniuses, Carl waited for some unexpected event that would force him to become more genuine and rescue him from his deepening depression.

Carl: I've been thinking about those Ten Criticisms a lot. It's hard to believe that I never saw them as incorrect or inaccurate. In some way I must have always known they were unfair because right now I'm experiencing feelings of anger and exasperation that are probably left over from my childhood. Of course, I don't say anything out loud because there's no one to complain to now about how I felt all those times when I was misunderstood and "quieted down," which was my father's idea of behaving properly. That doesn't mean I haven't felt the urge to express myself fully—basically throw a tantrum. I have been so afraid of how I might be perceived, so terrified of rejection that I ended up rejecting myself!

All that time, all those years of denial and self-blame. What a waste. It's done me a great deal of good to review all this in my journal, to make sense out of my childhood with new understanding and compassion. Without that I'm certain I would have just felt sorry for myself, like an embittered and immobilized victim. But by exploring my past from this vantage point, holding open the door to a freer future, I've found I could trade in my resentment for hope. Better yet, my anger and fear seem to have turned into motivation and determination. This may sound odd, but I think there's been a reunion inside of me. The suppressed free-spirited nature of my childhood has been reunited with the independent adult I am now.

FIVE BLOCKS THAT ENSLAVE THE SELF AND ECLIPSE THE SOUL

Blocks that bury identity beneath layers of prescribed "should" and "should not" behaviors enslave the self, veto its gifts, and ultimately eclipse the soul. Ironically, tolerating the false self for too long, remaining loyal to the given societal script, makes us feel increasingly invisible. The predicament is this: Which kind of invisibility is less damaging, more likely to cure chronic emptiness—hiding the Self's light under a bushel and pursuing the unfulfilling grind, or resuscitating the lost Self?

There are five primary blocks to recognizing and accepting the full breadth of Everyday Genius:

- Indulging the false self
- Denying gifts and talents
- Avoiding risk in the "safe life"
- Seeking approval
- Impostorism

Each of these blocks is equally debilitating, but with time and effort we can develop strategies to minimize their effects. As is so often the case, the first step entails identifying their presence.

INDULGING THE FALSE SELF

This first block to liberation requires considerable reflection and reframing. A staged life of scripted line reading may seem interesting and rewarding for a while. But it is a mismatch of inner and outer satisfaction. Typecasting can indeed feel less threatening, and may seem like less work, though what it really means is a life of repetition and limitation. What the "audience" commissions inevitably turns into a role of feigned normalcy. Challenging past false beliefs about the self is especially critical for the Everyday Genius because mistaken interpretation is so prevalent.

Left unchallenged, these myths will sabotage all future growth. Once we bring them to the surface they are available for conscious consideration. Energy tied up in festering old wounds can be restored. We must ask ourselves, "Do my beliefs about who I am and how I must operate in the world actually belong to me? Or did they simply become so familiar that I never questioned their origin or merit? Which pieces of my identity feel truly authentic in light of what I now know about the personalities of gifted people?"

This self-questioning dovetails with the demystification of the Ten Criticisms and goes even deeper. It's a necessary and cyclical task for those committed to self-actualization. The questioning and reshaping process solidifies confidence and supports our choices. After all, there is no way to be intelligently assertive unless we know who we intend to be in the world, what we stand for, and why.

Because life-span research shows that developmental shifts create identity upheaval about every ten to twelve years, we would be wise to become practiced in the lifelong habit of taking stock and reliberating the true self whenever necessary to avoid slipping back into old self-defeating habits. Simply recognizing the modus operandi of the false self goes a long way toward stopping the wholesale destruction its self-negating words and behaviors cause.

Study the differences between what you know to be true about yourself and the false-self myths that burden you. Look for signs of self-critical "shoulds," regrets, harsh labels, and shaming comparisons with invisible others who always seems to be one step ahead. As you listen to the voices that chatter in your head, try to make out the tone and attitude. Ask yourself what the hidden agenda behind such words might be. Is something in your subconscious truly trying to protect you or guide you? Or is what you're hearing the harping voice of shamers from your past? One of the strategies my clients especially like is the one I call "pin the tail back on the donkey." To do this, listen carefully to the words you hear; if they are not genuinely productive, useful, and positive, send them back to the originator. Eventually, when the Greek chorus of nay-sayers fades into the background, what does your true voice sound like, and what has it been waiting to say to you?

Challenge each of these misconceptions and misperceptions in turn by developing new, more realistic, and more compassionate comebacks, as we did with the Ten Criticisms. Do this when you are feeling pretty good about yourself, and put them in writing, because when you are once again overcome with self-doubt, the false self will not give way to counterattacks that are disorganized or flimsy. Select and use your own term for giftedness. Settle on synonyms that will allow you to get past semantics and get on with embracing the self-rescue mission at hand, such as *smart, capable, intuitive, visionary, talented, inspired, progressive, mindful, futuristic,* or simply *determined.* All are fine choices, particularly if they emancipate your thinking from the "superior/inferior" labeling that threatens your self-trust.

Stepping out of false-self disguise is considerably easier if you consider the fact that gifts of intelligence, intuition, vision, and creativity are not optional. They were given, entrusted to us with a plan attached. Even though acknowledging our gifts is a weighty responsibility, it also lightens our burdens when we accept that we are who we are with the gifts we were given. That also means we no longer have to feel guilty about having something special to offer. None of these gifts comes without a price. We pay as we go with risk, disheartening disapproval, and the emotional toll of making creative contributions in today's world.

DENYING GIFTS AND TALENTS

Determined though we may be, we have no method of ridding ourselves of our gifts and talents, much less eradicating their drive. Even by refusing to develop our abilities, we cannot hide from our responsibilities, because the mechanics of giftedness won't shut down. Nonetheless, to defend ourselves from undue prejudice, many of us protect ourselves by pretending to be without gifts.

The payoff is analogous to living in a witness protection program, a charade that provides a small measure of solace and refuge. The difference between witness protection and gift denial is profound, especially when we examine why we chose to assume this other identity. An informant consciously chooses this means of self-protection because remaining out in the open means that his or her life is in danger. This is simply not so when we deny our ability. Keeping potentiality under wraps is more dangerous, not less.

Mary Rocamora, a therapist who works with gifted and talented adults, writes about this common block. She observes that running away from the idea of exceptional ability is understandable because gifted people "find that description incompatible with their self-concept. For others, their resistance can be attributed to fear of failure to live up to the label. Those clients whose core identity is based in shame, or who polarize from anything that would tend to make them feel superior to others, also have a hard time being called gifted. . . . [S]hame is the leading cause of death of the potential for actualizing giftedness." However, Rocamora reminds us, "Once it is explained that giftedness is not identified by high intelligence alone, and that there is a personality profile attendant to giftedness, the resistance begins to yield and a new sense of identification emerges. . . . Simply knowing one is gifted opens a floodgate of energy."[1]

We learned to guard against criticism in ways that disguised us and dumbed-down our insights and ideas. This was reinforced by the approval of others when we did hold back, tone down, and keep quiet. One of the basic premises of psychology is this: Any behavior that is reinforced will thrive, while behaviors that are ignored or dismissed will fade. Subtle social reward and punishment methods encouraged us to silence our self-expression. Indeed, our denial habit was programmed so gradually and with such skill that it may not seem possible to operate any other way. But it is.

The genius mind loves metaphor; consequently it is often an invaluable tool in working with gifted adults. Sometimes denial of giftedness is so strong that the truth cannot surface in any other way. Thankfully, gifts and talents seem to have their own autonomy and frequently rely on the subconscious to present a story to disrupt the defenses of the rational mind. That's exactly what happened to Maureen.

At forty-two Maureen had shifted between many different career paths, mostly centered on the promotion of biomedical research scientists by either assisting them or raising necessary funds and obtaining grants. Throughout her professional life Maureen had abdicated her own authority by derailing her education, telling herself that her abilities weren't anything special and surely were not on par with those of her impressive colleagues. To her, the proof positive of her inferiority was in the fact that she had not obtained an advanced degree.

Maureen liked her work somewhat, but she still felt trapped and vaguely unsatisfied even in light of the changes she made within her field. Her substantial efforts to make herself satisfied with her situation were only fleetingly successful. She concluded that her dissatisfaction was a matter of selfishness rather than a denial of her inner agenda. To sidestep the powers of her conscious mind, which was still under the direction of her false self, I asked Maureen to recount a dream she had recently experienced. The dream she recalled was quite revealing.

> *Maureen: I'm walking along a dimly lit path in the woods. No one is there but me. I'm looking for something important, but I can't say what it is. I just know I'll recognize it when I see it. The road is unmarked and I'm not sure which way to go or even where I'm headed. I go on anyway. To my left and right I hear faint voices of warning, and occasionally I make out a haughty laugh in the distance. It unnerves me. I don't stop, though, I keep going. Part of me seems to know how to forge ahead. It's curious, but I feel like I can trust my sense of direction more than anything else. As the noises in the dark trees frighten me less and less they soften suddenly and then vanish. That's when I come upon a little box tucked away in the hollow of a tree. This is what I have been searching for. Something I alone am supposed to have and to care for. I think it is a legacy meant for me. Something special and friendly, and very personal.*

Maureen's session ended without further discussion. She had reclaimed her personal story and her Self right there. Very little ever stood in her way after that epiphany—not her lack of an advanced degree, her old fears, or anyone's idea of how she should conduct her life. Today she is the founder of a research institute dedicated to finding a cure for chronic pulmonary disease, which is itself quite a metaphor.

Gifts denied and delayed are not destroyed, no matter how many years have passed. Despite ongoing societal demands on early bloomers, it is quite common for long-repressed personal gifts to be revived and developed late in life. Sometimes the gift development is more effective when maturity provides a stabilizing foundation. Delayed growth is expected for anyone who grew up in an environment that criticized spontaneous unmaskings of the spirit or scoffed at inspired "wild" ideas and "emotional" zeal. At a more experienced stage of life we seem to be more willing to thumb our noses at society's expectations and others' opinions.

Catherine, a very bright seventy-year-old client, proclaimed with flailing arms: "At last there's no one alive anymore who has the authority to tell me what to do or how to do it!" Yet we need not wait until we are septuagenarians to make our move. If for no other reason than comfort, it is wise to correct our long-standing commitment to self-suppression.

Otherwise internal tension continues to rattle our well-being every time we settle back too comfortably into our socially prescribed role. Gifted people arrive with a built-in agitator that reminds them of one unavoidable fact: Only by emerging from behind ingrained blocks can we release our natural energy, the powerful actualizing force held hostage by self-doubt and negation. This realization is the beginning of serious inner exploration.

GETTING OVER GIFTEDNESS GUILT

To effectively reformulate our personal lives we must stop feeling guilty about our gifts. Guilt is destructive, corrosive, and an incredible misallocation of energy. This is why understanding our evolutionary and spiritual roots is critical to accepting our given characteristics and abilities. We were given our gifts at the outset for evolutionary reasons, which is why we feel a tug that tells us they were not given on the cheap.

As long as we allow guilt to weigh us down, we can't fully experience freedom and joy, and self-realization will be a distant and fast-receding goal. By having these gifts, we have done nothing wrong. So why feel guilty? Nor are we guilty for needing a fair amount of time to hear and understand our calling clearly enough to start ourselves down the right road in the service of humankind.

Generally people feel guilty or remorseful or culpable because of some wrongdoing. In our case we have not been doing wrong but have been seen as "being wrong," as being too far from the center of the bell curve. Guilt is an emotional response to discovering an unwanted behavior in ourselves, an error that caused upset or harm. In itself, guilt is not without meaning and purpose. It is a part of our moral fiber, a tool in developing a conscience, a guide that points out poor judgment and acts that go against our convictions.

But because we have such high expectations for ourselves as gifted adults, we often carry a burdensome load of guilt. In fact, if we are not careful to be compassionate with ourselves as well as with others, anything that we do that seems to fall short of the ideal can become grounds for judging ourselves "guilty." Moreover, since we are extrasensitive, guilt cuts very deeply and leaves painful scars that can keep our destiny immobilized.

Peter desperately needed to recycle his giftedness guilt. During his fifty years of living as an unidentified gifted person, Peter had experi-

enced a rich mixture of good, bad, and neutral. His journey's log included athletic awards, military honors, two marriages, four children, a
fairly profitable business, three patented electronic designs, repeated
anxiety attacks, and unexplainable feelings of guilt. After Peter had
spent several months in therapy his anxiety attacks were under control
and he felt much stronger. But he found even then that something continued to gnaw at him:

*Peter: I thought I would be rid of all those old feelings of guilt and
shame by now. I'm fifty years old, and look at all the things I've done.
Everyone I know thinks I'm pretty amazing. I just wish I agreed. And,
you know, sometimes I do. But not for long.*

*If anything is out of sorts in my life, that old slimy feeling of self-
hatred sneaks back in when I'm not paying attention. It's almost like it
seeps in through my pores. And what's so strange about it is my friends
and family tell me I'm usually generous about forgiving and letting go
of things others have done. My brother Jack tells me all the time how he
thinks it's so great that I don't ever hold a grudge. If he only knew that
the only person I have held a grudge against over the years is me!*

*I still feel remorseful about things that happened years ago, little
things that no one else would ever remember. I'm even carrying around
ancient embarrassments, blaming myself for things that happened when
I was in grade school! Like one time when some of us guys chased this
poor overweight kid home from school in the third grade. We laughed at
him and called him every awful name in the book.*

*What a terrible thing to do; that was really mean. And you know, I'll
bet I've gone over and over that same thing in my head at least ten times
a year since then. I figured it out the other day. That would mean I've
kicked myself about this at least four hundred times!*

*Then there's the guilt about being gifted, even though I never de-
fined myself that way. I realize I've felt guilty for most of my life for being
smart and creative, like it wasn't fair for me to have the talents I was
given. I tried hard to keep a low profile, but that didn't help because then
I feel guilty about being who I'm not. But when I do share my insights or
do something out of the ordinary, so many people react negatively, like
I'm trying to show off or show them up even though I'm just being who I
am and saying what I know. Worse yet, when I dare to voice my deepest
understandings and ideas about the future, I make a complete fool of
myself because nobody around me understands; then I feel like an impostor and begin to doubt myself. So what do I do with all that old guilt?
Do I ever get to feel bad about it for once and for all? I can feel guilty*

about a million things, but mostly I find myself in a trap: guilty if I go
my own way and stand up for my ideas and individuality, and guilty if
I don't.

According to experts in giftedness, talented individuals suffer from guilt to a greater degree when they are under stress. Gifted people's socialization tells them to label themselves elitist, arrogant, or self-serving when they achieve something important or express an innovative thought that others have not yet begun to consider. Essentially we have been taught to feel as though we've done something bad whenever we do something individual and creative that gets noticed. It's not too different from the feelings of guilt a person has when he or she has quit smoking and the former "smoker's club" members act as though a betrayal has occurred.

Since our sensory system is easily rocked by disturbing realities and injustices (such as human suffering, environmental destruction, prejudice, or cruelty to animals), feelings of concern often precede our capacity or authority to intervene. Hence we tend to bear an unsteadying amount of existential angst. This is probably unavoidable, since concern over the basic problems of human existence is a primary motivator of the evolutionary spirit. We must take care, lest such intense concern burden us with more discomfort than can be cured by the Revolutionary Action of even formidable individual effort.

Getting free of giftedness guilt requires us to clarify who owns which responsibilities. This analytical function must become a conscious part of our mental evaluation routine. Because our ability to envision the ideal collides with a reality that points to how dismally slow the progress of humanity can be, pangs of sorrow and frustration are inevitable, though they need not be confused with personal culpability.

Nor do we need to be naive about how to provide ourselves some relief from guilt. Though it may seem that if we just decide to ignore our guilt feelings, they will move on, there is another strategy that is more effective because it is less passive. By consciously identifying some of our feelings of guilt as unnecessary, shouldering its weight becomes a choice rather than an irrefutable obligation. Honest introspection may indeed lead us to conclude we have made a poor choice or behaved badly. Yet a simple sorting-out regimen may free us from a considerable amount of Self-hindering guilt and from the habitual acceptance of responsibilities that rightfully belong to others.

Here are the basic guidelines for getting over giftedness guilt:

- Honor good intentions and expect error; separate maliciousness from mistake.
- When you've said or done something mean-spirited that has insulted or harmed someone else, accept the regret, make amends, and use it as a catalyst for growth, resolving to do better next time.
- Appraise yourself honestly and humanely according to realistic criteria, remembering that no matter how learned gifted people become, few of us are like Solomon or a savant endowed with unflagging wisdom.
- Discard the myth of starting over, since history cannot be rewritten by believing that if you were given a second chance, this time around you would act with the benefit of all the knowledge since gained.
- Surrender to the reality that although you may accomplish a great deal and perhaps achieve eminence, some goals and possible contributions must be sacrificed in favor of others, for not everything that captures the gifted mind and sense of duty can be realized by one individual in one lifetime.

When you still feel guilty after taking each of these steps, any residual guilt that is no longer educational must go the way of yesterday's newspaper. Cognitive psychotherapy experts Albert Ellis and Robert Harper recommend:

> We really would like you, of course, to fully acknowledge that you have made some kind of error, if you actually have acted badly; realize that you handicap yourself if you keep acting in that manner; and work as hard as you can to minimize or eliminate this kind of poor behavior in the future.[2]

Yes, at times, no matter how smart or mature we are, we act poorly even though we may realize that we will keep getting the same unfortunate results if we continue to act that way. But it does no good to engage in self-flogging, punishing and denigrating the entire self for making such errors. Don't damn or remonstrate with yourself in any way, no matter how many times or how seriously you err. Your acts may prove foolish or reprehensible, but you need not be damned or vilified for performing them. If you need to do penance or make amends, do so, learn from your mistakes, and get on with things.

We saw how Peter had stockpiled guilt. Underneath it all he had learned to be ashamed of who he was and what he had to offer. His giftedness guilt left him without a sanctuary inside or out. There was no place where he could stretch out in the liberating air of unconditional regard and no way for his gifted inner self to reach him through the thick dross of his habitual self-reprisal. More than in the present moment, Peter's future was tainted in advance by projections of guilt onto upcoming events. In *A Woman of the Future*, Australian novelist David Ireland described a character whose "past was before him like a beacon; he would keep going in that direction and call it the future."

The important questions about guilt and failure revolve around the value of reliving regret for the sake of maturation, and preventing soul sickness. When we self-impose heartache, especially over being gifted, we must ask ourselves: "When will I stop mentally flogging myself for being different? When will I accept that my differences are the rootstock of my soul's design? Haven't I already crossed this same river of angst many times over? Am I brutally evaluating my performance, as evidenced by my tone and/or language? Unless we can free ourselves from protracted guilt, we are sure to be discouraged and weakened by our self-imposed sentence to a life of sackcloth and ashes.

THE "SAFE LIFE"

Risk is one of those paradoxical components of life, especially for the Everyday Genius—can't live with it, can't live without it. The words *risk* and *risqué* share a French etymological root whose definitions shed an interesting light on each other: a course of action involving uncertainty or hazard; exposure to the chance of loss or damage or disapproval verging on impropriety or indecency. We may as well get a grip on risk here and now, since there is no avoiding it in the realm of Advanced Development. Indeed, anything we do to find contentment and security—the "safe," "riskless" life—is sentencing ourselves to go through the motions of life like the walking dead. With the false self acting as judge, jury, and executioner.

Thinking clearly about our talents and urge to accomplish something creative and meaningful reveals that there is no safety in running away from risk. Then why do some people learn to live with the risky business of developing their full potential while others do not? Look back at the definition of risk. It's not at all surprising that anxiety goes hand in hand with taking a risk. After all, who wants to invite potential loss, damage, humiliation, or reprisal into their lives? Obviously there's no need to risk anything if we can convince ourselves that we want nothing more from our lives than what we have right now—no more change, no new horizons, no challenging bridges to cross. Let's be honest: Many adults do make an unconscious decision at the crossroads of their lives to do exactly that. As a result, as they age, they become a grayer, older version of who they were when they stopped becoming.

A predictable life of few risks may be just fine for many people. But it sounds like a death sentence to the Everyday Genius, who is designed for change. Nothing about taking risks is easy. Often we have to go it alone while others remain on the sidelines shaking their heads. So how do we get off the bench and into the game of risk? For starters, we must ask ourselves two pivotal questions: "What am I afraid of?"—embarrassment, loss of love or respect, feeling like a loner, making a mistake, becoming powerless?—and "Can I ever hope to fulfill my dreams if I hang back and take no risks?"

The answer to both questions depends on our definition of "necessary risks," which are not so much the kinds of risk involved in skydiving or climbing Mt. Everest, but rather the daring steps we must take into the land of uncertainty; these steps are inescapable if we are serious about leaving this earth one day without a stockpile of regrets. When we are honest with ourselves, we know for a fact that we are dyed-in-the-wool seekers. And seekers hunt, search, and track down what they are after, often without much of a map to guide them. So the same risk that makes us tremble is also the inevitable traveling companion who accompanies us as we journey toward our hopes and dreams.

There is little worth doing that doesn't include some risk. We hear all the time about risk and reward. Obviously, the greater the reward we seek, the greater the risk . . . or so many would believe. In fact, that's not always the case. We can manage risk to maximize reward. With preparation, practice, and patience, we can reduce what once seemed highly risky to necessary risk. After all, since progress leaps forward on the backs of extraordinary individuals who put themselves on the line, we are all risk takers.

To everyone's detriment, many Everyday Geniuses don't fulfill their potential because they are afraid of "coming out" about being gifted. To announce their giftedness to the world in loud or quiet ways would mean constant pressure to perform well. They believe that the demands of the world would increase beyond their reach and ability. They quake at their own thoughts, which suggest that whatever they do, every effort will have to be something fit for a magazine cover, especially if it involves putting their talents on the line. This creative block surfaces nearly every time we try something new.

Perhaps everyone marches through life fearing failure. Nevertheless, for gifted adults, these feelings are more intense than simple inhibition or the desire to avoid embarrassment, because we have been led to expect superhuman performance from ourselves. Our fear of failure seems to have two components: fear of humiliation and loss of future opportunities if others see our downs as well as our ups, and fear of subjecting our true Self to scrutiny or even exploitation.

These fears are not simple foolishness. Each of us has firsthand knowledge of how sometimes others ask more from us, offering less in return, when they discover what we have to offer. If we are unsure of ourselves or lack assertiveness skills, showing our true colors can lead to being exploited, a risk that unfortunately is inherent in "coming out" as gifted. If a demand for flawlessness has become internalized, daring to be original or unswayed by popular opinion opens the door to potential disapproval, a response that has often previously resulted in calamity.

By most people's estimation Warren was a genuine risk taker. And this was true in many respects, except he had never really put his most valuable asset on the line—his visual inventiveness. Sure, he experimented with new visual concepts all the time, but he never really stuck his neck out. He wanted to develop a software program that would present ethical/moral dilemmas in an appealing and thought-provoking strategy game for teenagers. However, he got only so far with his idea. Why? Because Warren could never find a way to hurdle his feeling of apprehension. This man who was fearless in the rapids and among the boldest of mountain climbers couldn't seem to transfer his courage to unleash his creative dream. Meanwhile, his ego took a beating every time he read or heard of some new software program that was taking the market by storm.

Warren: I know it doesn't make any sense, but I get weak in the knees whenever I try to make myself get serious about my idea. I think it has a pretty good chance of making it, or at least being useful in high schools.

I'd really feel good if that happened, you know? Not just because it might make some money. To be honest, I'm doing this not only for altruistic reasons, either. I actually want to help our future generation handle complex social and ethical judgments better. But there's something else I've come to realize. I want to contribute something that is a piece of me, of who I am, that I can be proud of.

I don't know why I've dragged my feet on this for so long. I think it's tied to being so important to me. That's pretty crazy, isn't it? I'm not applying my time and energy to the very thing that means so much to me. If it were a friend of mine in this situation, I'd encourage the hell out of him and press him hard about taking the risk. In fact, I think I'd expect him to do it, like he was obligated to give his idea a fighting chance. And I know just how I'd convince him. I'd scare him about future regret if he didn't try. You know what I mean? That image we all dread, sitting back at the end of our lives willing to give anything to have another chance to take a chance. Then he'd have to channel that future fear into here-and-now effort. Funny how it seems so obvious and easy when you think of it in terms of someone else's life. Maybe when we're afraid to stick our necks out for what really matters in our own development, our egos have a way of magnifying the risk so that we mentally jumble chance and failure and the possibility of looking foolish all together. Instead of accepting the fact that creative acts depend on risk, we wait it out, hoping there's another way. But, you know, I think in the long run it's the extended waiting that's the real risk. Quite a paradox, isn't it?

MAKING FRIENDS WITH RISK

The dangers of denying one's true nature can be very serious, not only because of frustrations and unavoidable anxiety, but because remaining off course threatens one's quality of life at the deepest level. Creative inertia is symptomatic of a failure to acknowledge and accept ourselves as we have been designed.

What is there to do other than to take charge of how we will work with our own qualities? Perhaps the best way to turn around outmoded ideas about success and failure is to get creative with our own beliefs. We can choose to believe in something other than all-or-nothing evaluations of worth that are based on observable achievement. We can put risk in a new light.

If we do not change our minds about how we value ourselves, we are destined to live entrapped in a double bind, because taking no chances and staying stuck feels just as bad as taking a chance and making a mistake. Once we understand that being exceptional doesn't mean performing exceptionally all the time, we can include our entire Self in our mirror's image. We must try, even against the demands of the outer world that cheers only the winners. Otherwise we prematurely accept a future of regret.

To exterminate the internalized fear demons who prey on us by flashing scenes of failure through our minds, we must hide our authentic identity for a while. That way we can adjust to it gradually, so our old fears won't escalate beyond control. With each step we take toward our genuine Self, we will be rewarded in some small way, most likely with the opening of a new energy source or with a sudden creative insight. This is often enough to keep us growing.

The emerging true Self brings with it so many rewards during its long-awaited return that we seize every opportunity to respect our abilities and ourselves in ways that provide a more suitable creative environment for our authentic Self. Exaggerated demands for instant expertise and mistake-free living soon fade as we build a friendship with our eccentricities and accept the necessity of error in every creative pursuit. In fact, it's laughable when we admit that our fear of failure is founded on a ridiculous learned pressure to be superhuman, boldly innovative, and a failure-proof achiever all rolled into one.

When we set this burden for greatness aside, we discover entirely new avenues for fulfillment. This is when the fun begins, in the playful freedom that emerges from the conscious decision to be not grand, not noteworthy, and not impressed by our gifts and achievements. This is eventually accompanied by an increasing disregard for the criticisms of others as we come to the conclusion that there is no room for the concept of "failure" when we engage the concept of "becoming."

SEEKING APPROVAL

All of us are creatures of habit, our behaviors and personalities formed to varying degrees around our responses to the approval or disapproval of influential others. Approval seeking is one of the most debilitating blocks to the liberation of self and our gifts, because when we overidentify with that aspect of our character, we leave ourselves unbalanced and vulnerable to limitation. Being too concerned about what others think of us, needing repeated nods of approval, warps our self-confidence. We develop tunnel vision, devoting all our energies to striving for acceptance.

This is a bad bargain for the Everyday Genius, whose long-range goal is self-realization.

For example, striving to be the most dedicated worker in the office might pave the way for advancement and the achievement of expertise and efficiency. In the same way that repeatedly hitting the same pothole with our car can put our wheel out of round, overattention to this goal in hope of gaining the approval of others eventually knocks us out of round, and our personality and life begin to reflect this. Real and imagined pressures to strive harder and move faster in a direction that is not in concert with our personal mission get us lost in reruns of the same experience: strive, strive harder, achieve, receive the nod, and repeat. Eventually that bent rim destabilizes other systems, and soon we're not handling like we used to. So we mash the gas pedal and grip the wheel more tightly, hoping to make up for precise handling with speed. The crash is inevitable.

There would be nothing wrong with this approach if conformist striving weren't also so frequently followed by feelings of hollow accomplishment. The Self we truly are gets lost in the "self" everyone else seems to want. Approval is a very potent aphrodisiac to a vulnerable ego, especially because many Everyday Geniuses receive little to no recognition. Others tend to see us as extremely stable individuals with unshakable confidence and endless sources of self-nourishment. Our obvious abilities and exceptional stamina often make us appear to be without needs. Perhaps this is the image we present; perhaps it is partially true. In any case, compliments and words of appreciation are few when excellence is expected.

Paul was the eldest of three boys. His parents held high expectations of him in nearly every endeavor, from school grades, baseball, and the violin to Scouts, a clean room, and modeling exemplary behavior for his younger siblings. They raised Paul in a way that linked love with approval, making his worth contingent upon praiseworthy actions. It was no surprise that the combination of this kind of parenting with Paul's obvious giftedness set him off on a path of award-winning achievement. The ladder he was on was steep and tall, with always another rung of "more" or "better" for him to climb.

Paul was hooked on approval, whether a raise in salary, a smile, or seeing his name in the paper for his latest community service. Underneath it all Paul rarely felt satisfied. He reached his goals with panache, set new ones that were often unrealistic, and revved up the engines for more striving. He could put his effort in harness and drive it forward in many valuable directions. Yet he often felt empty, absent in his own world, numbed out. He realized he was getting "sick" more often, staying home from work. Where had all his motivation gone? Striving had been able to fix things before, to fulfill what he thought he needed. Why not now?

No one, including Paul, would have considered him to have been a neglected or rejected child. Yet that was actually the core of the problem. What Paul had been taught as being "good and worthy" about him were his achievements, especially those that earned him the praise of others. He had heard his parents boasting of his accomplishments at church picnics and on the phone, and his teachers and coaches holding him up to the others as a prime example of "doing it right." Though they never consciously intended it, they taught Paul that the other parts of him were not worthy of attention. His need for unconditional acceptance, freedom to do things poorly or just for the fun of it, or permission to make mistakes without disappointing everyone were things that he could ignore for the time being. There was no room to find out who he was while assuming the role of the expected hero.

BREAKING THE APPROVAL-SEEKING HABIT

Ironically, because he could always "do better," the approval Paul received didn't last. The lost self that had been overlooked in favor of high achievement would not and could not accept approval because that would mean continuing to believe that Paul was only as good as his achievements. This also meant he could never slow down. For if he felt only this modicum of contentment with intense striving, how could he ever trust the feelings he would experience if he did less? Paul's job in therapy was to gingerly back away from the push/pull of striving and to get to know himself all over again, to let his latent gifts take form free of the stranglehold of relentless striving.

The result was remarkable; learning to proceed in an incremental, calm, and deliberate manner was far superior to frustration and confusion. He was able to resolve his inner conflict only when he took the sting out of disapproval or the lack of outright praise. No longer obsessed with accomplishments or approval, for the first time Paul began to enjoy his own company. He learned to play golf for the fun of it. By distilling out what he did from who he was, Paul could try new things and go back over old ground without feeling as though he was wasting his time.

Paul reframed his definition of success. He has become more judicious about his strivings these days. His first criterion for performance shifted from outer to inner approval, and his second criterion from traditional notions of individual success to collective service. He decided on his efforts instead of reacting to the real and imaginary demands of others. His achievements took on a new meaning, becoming different in form and substance, with satisfaction and sufficiency resonating throughout each of his days. Whether he was closing a multimillion-dollar real estate deal, pulling chickweed out of his tulip bed, or making paper boats with his sons, Paul became proactive, making his own choices about his allocation of effort. He was no longer cut off from himself, no longer empty, no longer lost.

IMPOSTORISM

The vast majority of gifted adults lack knowledge about themselves and are bereft of supportive peers. They are in a poor position to manage the gravitational forces of a culture that anchors genius and creativity. From the beginning we have received both stop and go messages from our families and other authority figures. Society at large confuses us with mixed messages about when it is safe and when it's not safe to be our creative, enthusiastic selves. To be supported in creative ventures, our ideas had to be channeled according to the unspoken rules of "not too far," "not too different," "not too intense," "not too fast." And learn we did.

But we are not impostors in terms of faking ability and intellectual power, or purveyors of snake-oil intent on conning others into believing that we have the new cure for humanity's ills. Ironically, in one vital sense we are indeed "impostors" if we continue to swap the call to actualize our potential for a gilded invitation to a neatly prescribed existence. True impostorism is exactly that—the perpetuation of the false self, the one who covertly agrees to hunker down and conceal the true self in an assumed identity.

Why, we might ask, would anyone do such a thing? What would compel a person to forgo the development of exceptional ability that would also fulfill the heart's desire? There are many reasons. Mostly we retreat into self-sacrifice and self-denial because those were the first tools we picked up early in life that actually worked. Since they were the salve that stopped the pain of having our ideas and creations defiled, we applied it liberally and often. And to our delight, though the relief was temporary, we were slow to build up a tolerance to it.

As adults, we find that any discrepancy between inherent ability and obvious "proof" of accomplishment by net worth or celebrity status reinforces a negative self-image. Perhaps this might explain why so many gifted adults who have no external evidence to substantiate their belief in their thinking and creative skills continue to drown in low self-esteem.

Frequently, the window of opportunity for creative expression is opened according to whom one knows and society-sanctioned credentials (awards, titles, years of experience). There is little room for late bloomers, and less still for highly ethical truth tellers who take risks to change things or fast starters who don't require years of experience to gain expertise.

Elaine, a brilliant overachiever, found her experience as a first-time author quite a revelation.

Elaine: One of the first people I consulted about writing a novel was a well-published author who publicly promoted the artistic endeavors of beginners. His response to my inquiry about publishing a book was: "Well, good luck. But, you know it's nearly impossible to get anything published these days, especially if you're a newcomer. Are you sure you want to try this? It's such a long shot. Really, the way things are right now, if you're not already a published author, chances are slim to none that you'll ever break through. Maybe you just started too late. You could try to write a little magazine article, I suppose. Maybe you'd have some luck there."

Needless to say, I wasn't encouraged. But I couldn't help but notice the lack of logic in his remarks. And to my own amazement, I replied: "Well, I guess that means everyone who's ever going to be a published writer has already signed a contract and every writer worth reading has already been discovered. Better inform the publishing houses and literary agencies so they can plan for their eventual obsolescence." Poor fellow. He caught me at the exact moment when I no longer needed external permission or approval and I didn't have to pretend to be anyone but myself!

UNLEARNING IMPOSTORISM

Dr. Lee Anne Bell, assistant professor of educational studies at SUNY-New Paltz, conducts research on gifted females, and here are some of her practical tools for unlearning impostorism:

- Decide what is worth your best effort, and don't persist in less important matters.
- Learn that it is competent to ask for support.
- Own your own accomplishments instead of dismissing them or giving them away. Keep a written account of all your accomplishments.
- Give those who recognize your abilities credit for knowing what they are doing.
- Talk openly about the fears, confusions, and misunderstandings that are a normal part of creative work.
- Introduce and support mentoring programs and networking.[3]

Impostorism is always toxic, not only to the gifted but to those who would reap the rewards of their abilities. We Everyday Geniuses may produce what the world wants, and may in many respects succeed, yet our soul will not sing as long as we are expected to live an inauthentic life. By giving in, we become mannequins. We have the look, the pose, but the eyes are lifeless and our feigned self-actualization is as hollow as we are.

Each of us who is gifted must become a champion of the possible and act courageously on our own behalf. Hesitant and afraid or not, we cannot afford to sit back and cower in our thin gifted skins and wait for society's invitation to fulfill our potential. Each of us is obliged to sit down, listen very deeply, and recall the promise we were given and the one we must declare to ourselves.

Can we afford to procrastinate, hoping that the wished-for patron will pave the way for us, introduce us to all the right people, and provide us with a literal or metaphorical canvas and studio with the finest paints? Or is it wise to wait for the "right" time, when we're "really ready," when it "feels right"? Do we wait for the sea change that will transform the culture, so that America will suddenly respond to the gifted person's plea for support while indulging the pursuit of excellence? As the sprawl of the global economy promotes and necessitates the artless life of the worker bee, can we dislodge ourselves from the swarm? How can we not?

Achieving excellence in creative ways and perfecting ourselves and the human condition with deep commitment and resolve are not tasks set for only those few we deem true geniuses. Many Everyday Geniuses will not be rewarded for their efforts. Yet the rewards that stand the test of time are here to be claimed in spite of the challenging atmosphere in which creative trailblazers live.

If and when our attention becomes less preoccupied with persistent negative evaluations of self-worth, we discover our energy is more easily directed to what is needed in the world, and not so much toward what we fear. Gradually we notice we are no longer unsteady. This is when the joy of life's travels replaces the joy we once expected only upon the fulfillment of an achievement. This is the authentic moment when "heaven on earth" begins to make sense for the first time.

The lucid insights of Mother Teresa of Calcutta remind us that our gifts were not frivolously assigned. To embark on a path of self-actualization with any chance of fulfillment begins by acknowledging that Special Abilities are a mixed blessing, for we must shoulder accountability and advantage in equal proportion. Ironically, humbling oneself in the face of constant opposition is the gateway to courageous, revolutionary action.

When conceit and inflation no longer present stumbling blocks, we can harness our creative powers rather than rein them in.

We can do no great things—only small things with great love. . . . You can do what I can't do. I can do what you can't do. Together we can do something beautiful for God. . . .

I am unique, Lord—You have made me unrepeatable . . . and you have bestowed upon me talents and graces. . . . We are but instruments that God deigns to use. . . . The wire is you and me. The current is God.[4]

12

HOW ASSETS CAN
BECOME LIABILITIES

To confront a person with their own shadow is to show them their own light. —Carl Jung

Fulfilling the promise of Everyday Genius has always been, and may always be, a difficult balancing act. Like everyone else, we can overdevelop certain characteristics while we underdevelop others; we can misuse our talents in disadvantageous and even destructive ways.

What does this balancing act mean for us? Just as we are beginning to make friends with our true nature and all its intensities, must we learn to hide it all over again? No, not at all. It can take years to come to grips with the challenges of living out the promise of high potential. After taking such painstaking steps toward liberation, it's unlikely that anyone would willingly turn back to repeat the process.

Once the swan has made the first move away from the duck yard, there is no going back. We can't turn on ourselves again in ways that enslave our very being. We can tolerate and manage betrayal and abandonment from others. But none of us can bear self-abandonment; only when the inner and outer forces of Everyday Genius work together in concert as a team, "you and me against the world," do we have the daring and stamina to move forward with resolve.

To increase the probability of having it all—accomplishment, meaningful contributions, joy, and right relationships—we cannot sweep negative tendencies under the rug. In our newfound relief that we were not wrongly constructed in the first place, it's imperative that we not overlook potentially ruinous misapplications of our genius. In fact, it is only when we have learned to stand up for ourselves, inside and out, that we can take the next step forward.

Besides, the Everyday Genius balancing act is a hand-in-glove operation: We work all sides to integrate mind and body and soul and action. Improving what's flawed or incomplete is just as consequential as perfecting obvious gifts. Remaining committed to making the necessary adjustments to preserve the developing personality is the never-ending business of Advanced Development. It is as though we have to develop new homeostatic systems to promote the continued growth of this fledgling authentic self. The resulting self-confidence we earn when those new systems come on line and function properly permits us to defy our fears and to abandon old behaviors that were intended to protect us but which in the end backfired and harmed us.

How, then, can we be free to be ourselves, like ourselves, and like and respect others, all at the same time? This is perhaps the greatest challenge of Advanced Development. The good news is that the process of self-actualization is the way of the gentle giant, where power and compassion operate interdependently. It's a tough task, to be sure, because we are called to simultaneously tear down old habits as we build up new ones. This is why as we practice mustering out old self-criticisms we must construct a new set of psychological defenses at the same time.

Instead of guarding our sensitive psyches and vulnerable emotions by hiding out in risklessness and denying our gifts, we can learn sensible new ways to be forthright about what we think and how we conduct our lives. We are only truly liberated when we can step forward into fully expressed creativity without arming ourselves with unsociable cynicism, sarcasm, or passive-aggressive subterfuge. This critical shift goes a long way toward increased happiness, because Everyday Geniuses are always adversely affected when they are reduced to words and actions that hurt others.

So let us take the second giant leap toward liberation by plugging our noses and diving right into what gifted assets look and sound and act like when they become liabilities. If we are to do well by our reclaimed abilities, we must learn to harness their power, not to let them run wild. Otherwise we will surely fall prey to our own missteps, losing ground by getting caught up in things that distract us from important endeavors, throwing away precious time and energy by riding roughshod over those who annoy us. The Everyday Genius must learn to choose battles wisely, to expend energy judiciously, and to keep high potential from becoming weapons of unnecessary relational wars.

THE SHADOW SIDE OF
EVERYDAY GENIUS: DISORDERLY CONDUCT

Let's reconsider the ambient factors of Everyday Genius that are unquestionably assets. Since every good thing can become a bad thing if unwisely directed, we need to be familiar with how intelligence can be mismanaged. The aftermath of diverted intelligence is disorderly conduct, which can leave a messy blot on our character and rip holes in our significant relationships.

When Independence Becomes Inflexibility

Self-motivation and autonomy are certainly valuable and necessary traits for any inventive achiever who has dreams of making a real difference in the world. Indeed, the fierce curiosity of the Everyday Genius is not to be denied. Yet when intense pursuit takes over and becomes a veritable holy quest for understanding and mastery, autonomy can quickly go awry.

The seeker on such a mission can resist input from others, dodging external suggestions and cautions by classifying them as uncreative or envious wet-blanketing. While those characterizations may be true, chronic refusal to consider others' opinions tags us as someone who's "not a team player." We can potentially become what we often criticized others for—being someone with a narrow vision. We can become victims of our own enthusiasm by refusing to take a look at potential problems or other solutions that may be worthy of our attention. Without intending to, we may be creating obstacles for ourselves and undermining the success of our projects. Sometimes it's too late to go back over the same turf to rethink our decisions, and we lose out altogether. Worse yet, we may be in line for a much-deserved "told you so" lecture, something no Everyday Genius can tolerate very well.

Victor had always been someone who had confidence in his ideas. He was respected for his leadership and visionary plans, which mostly met with great success. His gifts of rapid understanding and intuitive ability to penetrate problems made him a master of difficult situations. He owed a debt of gratitude to his advanced reasoning ability, for he could persuade even the most uncompromising champion of the status quo to support his ideas.

In spite of his creative problem solving and expertise in selling his ideas, Victor struggled to work with others, preferring to work alone whenever possible. Most of the time this was justifiable when it didn't impede the flow of his projects. But now and again he'd lose sight of the part others played in the overall task, letting his headstrong nature have its way. His intolerance often coincided with an increased stress level, which gave him even less control over his inclinations. Things just seemed to happen that not only disrupted his good standing with his peers, but thwarted his efforts and wreaked havoc with his exacting timetable. To put working relationships back into good functioning order, Victor found he needed to spend quite a bit of time mending fences after he had posed embarrassing questions, backed a colleague into a corner, or squared off with his boss without extending her a way to save face.

Victor: Honestly, when I get into the thick of a project at work, I don't start out with an intention of hurting anyone's feelings or making them look like asses in front of the others, but I get frustrated and out it comes. Like I'm obligated to "set things straight," to enlighten in biting detail anyone in my way, especially anyone who seems to bog things down. And when I'm under pressure, I find the slowness of others to be absolutely insufferable.

Just last week I set my relationship with Susan, my boss, back about two years. I was working along swimmingly on my latest project—restoration of a great old mansion in the city—and I simply lost it when she started asking questions. Of course she had a right to ask about how things were going, and I was okay with that. I have no problem about keeping her up to date. But she wanted to go back over some old ground we'd already covered a long time before. I couldn't see the sense of it and I thought she was just wasting my time. I suppose I felt insulted to be questioned at that stage, and I baited her by sarcastically asking her if she'd been hit on the head and lost her memory. I drove the knife in a little further by recounting our previous discussion on the subject nearly verbatim.

I didn't let her get a word in edgewise, or even slow down when I noticed her face turning pink and her jaw tightening. I just kept going like a harping schoolteacher lecturing a naughty kid. She was so embarrassed. I was the one who should have been embarrassed, going off like that. I just couldn't tolerate her after-the-fact interest and her irrelevant questions. She wasn't interested at the beginning of the project. And I guess I've always been pretty dismissive and hotheaded with others who seem less motivated or enthusiastic than I expect. But what a kick back in the teeth I got. For three weeks no one was willing to cooperate with me. And Susan avoided me like the plague, right when I really needed her to sign off on final contracts. So if working alone was what I was

*after, cutting remarks were the swiftest way to get there. Too bad for me
that the discourtesy I sowed ended up being discourtesy I reaped in full
at a time when I could least afford to be the office pariah.*

When Systematizing Becomes Fixation

Everyday Geniuses love to turn chaos into order. They have an uncanny
capacity for sniffing out patterns, inefficiency, and obstacles to successful completion of their goals. Better-working systems just seem obvious
to them in ways that are often invisible to others. This ability is truly an
advantage in situations that call for organization and innovative restructuring. Especially valuable is a related faculty for synthesizing, or bridge
building, that has the power to bring together abstract concepts and concrete answers. This is the underlying marker of outstanding, creative
leadership, and must never be underrated. Yet it can also become overblown and misshapen, especially in ways that rob one of spontaneity and
emotional expression. In brief, a life of too much systematizing can grow
dull and overly predictable, to say nothing of the legitimate exasperation
felt by friends and loved ones.

When anyone wanted something organized, they automatically
called upon Tanna. One way or the other, she became the resident answer
person and self-propelled coordinator of events in every group she
joined. There seemed to be no end to the innovative ways in which she
could reshuffle the deck so things would run more smoothly, and Tanna
derived much approval and self-satisfaction from this over the years.
Tanna had a love affair with "facts," especially those that were compati-
ble with linear thinking. Nothing pleased her more than cause-effect
investigation—complex, unsolvable mysteries being the best of all possible challenges.

There was never a "can't be done" dare that Tanna couldn't beat—
that is, until it dawned on her that in some way she was missing out, that
while she had been busy reorganizing and systematizing her world she
had become mired in deadening routine. Things were indeed in order, all
except her sense of adventure and vitality.

By overdeveloping her system-oriented skills, Tanna had inadvertently become overattached to rules and procedures. Others began to
find her a bit rigid and even controlling. "It's her way or the highway" was
the behind-the-scenes watchword in her group. She found it more
and more difficult to accept the fact that others could come to the same
conclusion—or sometimes a better one—in ways that were considerably

different from hers. Having always considered herself an egalitarian progressive, Tanna would have felt her face turn ashen had she known that people referred to her as "the little dictator" behind her back. She had no idea her rules-oriented style had turned into outdated patriarchal behaviors, and that her capacity for exceptional leadership was disabled by her immature approach.

Too often others turned down Tanna's suggestions and circumvented her opinions because her excessive reliance on facts and logic made her impervious to influence. Her whole personality became associated with the word *problem* because she tended to point out every possible flaw in every situation. Her response to every challenge was the same, which meant she was prone to overresearch topics of relative insignificance and to avoid the simple solution in favor of one that was unnecessarily complex. It was difficult for others to trust Tanna when her concerns seemed inflated, vague, and fixated on doubt. She too found it difficult to trust others because it seemed they were apathetic, carelessly poor observers who underestimated the potentially adverse effects of a neglected predicament.

Ironically, Tanna's need to get things organized down to the nubbins, to marshal everyone's energy for the sake of unrivaled efficiency, had enslaved her. Gradually it had put her creativity under lock and key. Life simply wasn't fun anymore, neither for her nor for those around her. Not only was she missing out on opportunities for pleasure and growth, but her exactitude had turned her into a procrastinator. More often than not, before she could embark on a task she had to take several steps backward to "get things ready," which turned her projects into menacing behemoths. Striving to do things right and then even better, Tanna had allowed her all-or-nothing thinking to develop into a programmed, self-imposed system that rendered her a problem-focused, cheerless woman. Ultimately Tanna found little consolation in her hard work because the same systematizing that made her a good starter now rendered her a bad finisher.

When Humor Becomes Biting Sarcasm

Life is quite a bit more fun and funny for many Everyday Geniuses because of their ability to detect the absurdities of situations. Their perceptive natures allow them to laugh at themselves and enjoy the foibles of human nature. Natural abilities earn them the reputation of the "enthusiast," the one who brings the energy to a group. Many are charismatic, with effervescent personalities that have the power to light up a room and introduce a touch of magic to any encounter.

Don't we all rely on these spirited souls to make us smile, to bring us out of the doldrums, to help us make light of otherwise unbearably sorrowful situations? How could such a wonderful gift ever go astray? How could charm and frivolity and playfulness turn sour? Norrine had puzzled over those very questions for nearly thirty-six years:

Norrine: I was always the class clown, the funny one in the group, because I was the third-born in my family. I think that's part of it. But now that I know more about what it means to be gifted—even though I still bristle at the sound of the word—I realize I just naturally find life amusing. My sister used to tease me about being so easily entertained, like when I mimicked animal sounds or danced around the house like a bad ballerina. She claimed I was the only person on the planet who could have a good time tucked away in a closet by myself.

I'm generally glad that everyone loves my enthusiasm and zest for life. I have the distinction of being known as the one who brings the fun to the party. And that's okay by me. I'd be fidgety and bored otherwise. Life would be colorless if I just sat back and watched the world go by without jumping on and waving my arms about right in the thick of things.

I never thought it would be true, but lately I've discovered a bad side to being so animated. It's a matter of what you might call typecasting. For one, people expect me to be lighthearted all the time. This wasn't so bad when I was a kid, but as an intelligent adult, I want to be taken seriously. But instead of other people seeing that I have many sides to my personality like everybody else, I'm not supposed to ever be quiet, or pensive, or angry. No one seems to want to be around those parts of me, so I feel trapped. Sure, I'm generally a happy-go-lucky sort of person, but not all the time. I have deep concerns about the world, and I get just as upset as the next person. Only some way or another I'm not allowed.

It's taking a real toll on my career and even on my friendships. At work I'm having a hard time being heard or treated like I have something important to offer. Outside of work I'm beginning to feel used. I've always been there to support my friends when they've lost loved ones, been fired, or needed a shoulder to cry on. But no one seems to think I ever need any of that. Last week I called my best friend when I felt lonely and sad, and dared for the first time to cry openly. She didn't know how to act. I felt foolish when she finally said, "I don't know what to say, Nor-rine. Why don't you take some time to calm down and call me back when you're feeling more like yourself?"

But I was being myself. Over the years I have held back serious com-ments and expressions of my intelligence in favor of entertaining others.

I'm tired of keeping my disagreements pent up, acting like every-thing rolls off me like water from a duck's back. I'm also fed up with being worn out by subtle and not-so-subtle demands to buoy up the downhearted, to power up passive coworkers, to energize the lifeless party. Maybe that's why my sarcasm seems to be going through the roof.

WOUNDS AND REACTIONS

It's not easy to accept the truth about ourselves, especially about the na-ture of our deepest wounds. Self-truth explorations are rarely painless, which is why many of us need a large measure of adult experience under our belts before we are emotionally equipped for such an undertaking. So why look back at all? Why not just forge ahead with our customary deter-mination and will? As many of my clients propose, "Let's just leave the past in the past."

And yet we cannot leave well enough alone because the liberation of our potential calls for completeness. All of our resources must be fully functional and available if we intend to take our abilities seriously. No matter how smooth our upbringing may have seemed, without mending the splits and self-doubts we bear, we cannot be as fully alive and power-ful in our creative endeavors as we are intended to be.

The goal is not to revictimize ourselves by opening up old wounds merely for the sake of feeling bad all over again. Blame is not the point, either—not toward ourselves or toward those who raised us, loved us, or worked with us to the best of their ability. At first, most Everyday Ge-niuses resist the idea of dredging up old wounds and revisiting the detours they wish they'd never taken. No one wants to reexperience emo-tional pain and regret. Yet the wounds of Everyday Geniuses are not the kind that heal with the mere passage of time. Luckily, most Everyday Ge-niuses are practiced in recycling their experience. Their innate optimism and tenacity help them find creative ways to make use of all of their expe-riences, even agonizing setbacks. To give meaning to what happens in their lives, they look for ways to turn bad into some form of good.

LOOKING BACK TO MOVE FORWARD

Charlene, a thirty-nine-year-old materials engineer and mother of two sons, explained her resistance to looking back: "I can't stand whining—not in my children and certainly not in me. My family wasn't any better or worse than anyone else's. I don't need to scrape up a bunch of reasons to feel bad about my parents or to cry over spilled milk. That's just not my style. Besides, I don't have time for all that. I have real things to do, right here and right now—today's business, not yesterday's."

Indeed, many adults have ventured down the paths of their personal histories before, but to no avail. There was a lot of bad therapy in the 1970s and 1980s that indiscriminately glorified the inner-child/wounded-child philosophy. Inadvertently the very process that was supposed to free people from their pasts tended to hold them captive, accentuating their feelings of blame and regret. Without the proper measure of insight and analysis, they were incapable of coming out on the other side of their pain, healed and revitalized. Instead, many became fixed in self-defeating behavior.

Uncomfortable though it may be, our pasts were not so benign that we can afford to leave them untouched. At some point in the course of self-discovery, most gifted adults are struck by a sting of regret as they ponder possibilities that became detoured. For many this happens around midlife, which is also an opportune time for goals and abilities to crystallize.

At forty-six, underneath his authoritarian demeanor, Jason struggled with inner conflict. He had fought hard to make peace with himself after abandoning his dream to be a theater director. He dutifully joined the ranks of business to do the work of "a real man," as his father had insisted. Outwardly, Jason's eventual success as a venture capitalist was undeniable. Yet he secretly carried the scars of a forsaken dream. He was very resistant to the idea of revisiting this issue.

Jason: I don't see the point in dredging that up all over again. I've worked too hard to forget those old pipe dreams. I made my choice long ago and now I have to live with it. My family couldn't see any value in the theater. They were good people and I don't hold any grudges against them. Truthfully, it's just too upsetting to think about what might have been. Every time I've done that—just think what I could have done, who I might have become, if only . . .—I get all worked up for nothing. You'll have to convince me that it's really worth my while to get me to go down that road again.

In the same way that we have opened the door to our true identities by recognizing ourselves as gifted people, we must also come to grips with the fact that giftedness is often paired with self-denial and constraint. Even if we had known we were different for a very valid reason, most of us felt like a minority of one who didn't feel safe revealing our true nature. In our early, most vulnerable years, far too many of us used our brains to hide our feelings, to constrain our wild ideas so others wouldn't be shocked or reject us. We turned down our intensities and lived up to the expectations of others—essentially to earn their love and approval. Being prized by others came at an extraordinarily high price, because when you're inherently different, looking for approval becomes a mandate for self-exile. The rules of the fitting-in game call for someone to lose. And more often than not, that someone was the true self.

EVERYDAY GENIUS—
THE SECOND TIME AROUND

Ironically it was our own characteristics, not our failings—our versatility and extraordinary adaptive skills—that allowed us to intelligently shift and refashion ourselves whenever situations of approval or disapproval arose. No child who meets with "the look" of displeasure, no matter how smart, ever concluded that the givers of the look were wrong. Consequently, the only remaining conclusion they could draw was: "I am doing it wrong. I am wrong." Approval—contingent on getting good grades, hitting home runs, being elected class president, and charming grown-ups—becomes the most reliable security blanket, and sometimes the only one.

Any thinking person knows we cannot change the past. However, we can change our view of it, and especially how we see ourselves and our behavior. This is all we need to move forward with renewed confidence and freedom of expression. By taking a second look, we have the advantage of reviewing the "rules" by which we have lived to see if they still fit, and indeed if they are our rules or the internalized rules of others. In adulthood it is we ourselves who hold the key to our prison. Alice Miller stresses the importance of correcting and healing old wounds as an indispensable act in the reclamation of self:

In order to become whole we must try, in a long process, to discover our own personal truth, a truth that may cause pain before giving us a new sphere of freedom. If we choose instead to content ourselves with intellectual "wisdom," we will remain in the sphere of illusion and self-deception . . . . We can repair ourselves and gain our lost integrity. . . .

The true self cannot communicate because it has remained unconscious, and therefore undeveloped, in its inner prison. The company of prison warders does not encourage lively development. It is only after it is liberated that the self begins to be articulate, to grow, and to develop its creativity. Where there had been only fearful emptiness or equally frightening grandiose fantasies, an unexpected wealth of vitality is now discovered. This is not a homecoming, since this home has never before existed. It is the creation of home.[1]

In previous chapters you have been offered a new perspective on some of the fundamental criticisms. Now we need to explore how these criticisms, when taken on by the highly vulnerable, highly sensitive gifted child, were internalized as the truth. Because there was no alternative message, Everyday Genius traits were labeled as problems or character defects. These "defects" were always subject to attack or censure, and the child began to internalize "I have a problem," which soon translated into "I am a problem." This is just as difficult for the gifted child to endure as it is for the real "problem child."

As the criticisms are repeated over and over again, they combine and fester to become permanent wounds—but the Everyday Genius is smart enough to defend against the criticisms by either hiding the behavior to avoid disapproval or defiantly accelerating the behavior in an effort to make the critics wrong, that is, collapsing the wound in on itself, or "acting out" beyond the control of disapproving others.

Early defense against character attacks tends to be a polarized choice between two extremes, neither of which is effective for very long in adulthood. For example, the hypersensitive gifted child is told he or she is "too thin-skinned," a "crybaby," "overreacting," "out of control," or "melodramatic." The child learns that being sensitive—an inborn trait—is a problem, something unacceptable that must be dealt with either by yielding to and expressing every feeling in knee-jerk fashion in an effort to make the world adjust, *or* by closing off the feeling channel and pushing emotions away or sidetracking them into icy logic. In other words, in this case the polarized defense would offer two options: ride it out in the wilds of Emotion Land, or retire feelings altogether and settle aloof and detached into the background in the Land of Repression. I define these two equal and opposite reactions this way:

> *Exaggerated false-self reaction:* Indiscriminately indulging the trait's expression and forcing everyone else to deal with it.
> *Collapsed false-self reaction:* Developing an impenetrable armor to hide the natural expression of the trait, deadening awareness of it by choking off its inner signals.

The false self is limiting in that it is stranded in outdated reactivity and lacks clear judgment. Furthermore, the false self is a serious impediment, whether its reactions to the hostilities and misunderstandings of the external world are exaggerated or collapsed. For many Everyday Geniuses the false self presents an exponentially more difficult hurdle when its reactions swing back and forth like a pendulum: first exaggerated expression, then collapsed repression, back and forth over and again. They are two equal and opposite forces that tend not to cancel one another out but to cancel out the true self.

For example, Trisha was an endlessly curious child—the quintessential detective in miniature—who was regularly chided, "Stop asking so many questions! You're wearing me out." Her defensive reaction was to indulge her truth-seeking nature indiscriminately. She learned to ignore people's sighs of irritation, but she never learned to regulate her candor. In middle school she posed probing questions in class and was scolded: "You are out of line, young lady. You'd better watch your step!"

When she went to college Trisha was determined to turn over a new leaf—to be silent in the face of falsehood, to withhold the unasked but necessary question, to just go along and get along. To her surprise, when she graduated and landed her first important job, her supervisor told her: "Listen, Trisha, you're playing in the corporate big leagues now. You're going to have to learn to speak up and show people you've got something to contribute. Otherwise you'll just be pushed aside, and I know you're too smart to let that happen."

Trisha was totally confused about how to be effectively assertive. Soon after this conversation, her false-self reaction reared its head once again, but in its opposite form, when she felt obligated to stick up for a discredited colleague in a meeting: "Excuse me, but let's give credit where credit is due. That was Ruth's idea, Linda. Just because she brought it up in the midst of a budget crunch, the plan was dismissed.

But now that we're into a new financial year, you're suddenly the hero who's getting applauded for all of Ruth's hard work."

Despite the fact that Trisha's insights were quite correct and her intentions virtuous, her remarks created a terrible backlash. Her freewheeling need to be the champion of justice instantly banished her to the company's no-man's-land as everyone rushed to Linda's rescue. The event also cemented Linda's position as the office wunderkind, which only added insult to injury. And to make matters worse, after the meeting Ruth lambasted Trisha: "Who asked you to be my crusader? I was *so* humiliated in there. How dare you!"

THE "TEACHABLE MOMENT"

Both false-self reactions—exaggerated and collapsed—are inadequate. Yet, we ask ourselves, what other alternatives are there? No authority figure ever explained our choices to us at the teachable moment—the very moment when the opportunity for understanding is at hand. That is when a wise teacher is needed, especially one who can help us see that there was nothing wrong with the innate characteristic, and who can make it palatable for us to hear that we need to learn to handle things differently. Well-done tutoring is Socratic in nature, not domineering, shaming, or stifling.

Imagine a time when as a chatty, inquisitive youngster, Trisha's kindly grandmother witnessed her being scolded. As her grandmother extended an understanding hand, Trisha might have heard:

"Trish, honey, show me your new books, will you? I'm so interested in what you're learning at school these days. Your mother tells me you're crazy about astronomy. Is that right? You know, Trish, you and I are quite alike. When I was your age I was so full of questions, I think it drove my parents and teachers crazy. I wondered about everything, and questions kept coming to my mind. It's really too bad that people get annoyed with questions. But in some ways I think people like you and I move so fast with our thinking that others can't keep up. That's why they're bothered. Our questions are just fine—no problem there. But I learned something a long time ago—a secret—that I want to share with you that you don't have to tell anybody else. No one will ever tell you, but it's true. People have about a two-question limit at a time. Smart girls like you and I have loads more than that. But just between you and me, we can tell by the look in their eyes when we've zoomed past them and

they've reached their limit. That's when we go to our journals and write down all the secret, unasked questions. I brought one for you today, and here it is. It's your very own secret question book. You don't need to share anything you write in it with anyone else. But whenever you like, Grandma will be happy to listen to any question you have."

Insightful guidance in the form of the teachable moment is priceless and rare. Regrettably, the teachable moment that could empower Everyday Geniuses in the face of criticism is very hard to come by. Parents, teachers, and siblings play the hands they were dealt, and for the most part they do the best they can. Yet many gifted children's development is inadvertently impeded by those who, despite their love and good intentions, either don't seize the teachable moment or are turned to the wrong page in the lesson plan.

Parents and advisors have asked me how to nurture and shore up the gifted child. Business leaders want to know how to help the gifted adult live up to his or her potential. Much of the answer lies in the art of the teachable moment—not lecturing or propagandizing for conformity, but offering pragmatic insights that help eliminate obstacles without undermining the genius spirit. Whether as a parent of a gifted child, a spouse, a friend, or the mentor of a gifted adult, we all get countless second chances—more "teachable moments."

Everyone benefits when we pause and respond by artfully and diplomatically hitting the nail on the head. These are indeed the magic moments eminent people identify as making all the difference. Applying the art of the teachable moment has a threefold reward. By extending the best of ourselves through a restorative gift to another, we (1) heal our own wounds, (2) support and strengthen the liberation and maturation of other Everyday Geniuses, and (3) create a constructive ripple effect in the evolutionary pond.

For the vast majority of Everyday Geniuses, suitable how-to instruction for navigating the rough waters of actualization is scarce. When we are no longer children at home with parents, or students in school, to whom can we look to remedy this lack of good instruction? Our penchant for self-sufficiency comes into play again as we discover one of the basic remedies for past wounds is the development of the art of the teachable moment in ourselves. Doing it over—relearning from an adult perspective—defies false-self reactivity and liberates Everyday Genius in its development tracks.

THE REACTIVITY PENDULUM

We unconsciously invited the false self into our lives for a very good reason: to defend our vulnerable, highly sensitive, and intense selves from disapproval, rejection, self-blame, and feelings of isolation. It was a smart and resourceful subconscious move that worked for us for a long time. Because its initial mission was to protect us, in adulthood it's hard to fully rid ourselves of false-self influence, though to be free, that is exactly what we must do. In much the same way that we trusted a loyal and devoted dog to protect us and our property, the false self stands guard. Unfortunately, it often lacks the power to adequately discriminate real from perceived threats. Also, we've come to implicitly respect its judgment, refusing to believe that it would ever be too zealous, blaming others who, despite our assurances that the dog is nice, shy away when it bares its teeth or raises its hackles.

Even when our confidence is somewhat restored, we still face the false self every day. When we're not paying attention, it's easy for the false self to sneak back into our attitudes and behaviors. If we feel the urge to keep our ideas to ourselves, to anesthetize our language to avoid glares of disapproval or berate ourselves for not being omniscient, the false self is present. When our reactions are far more heated than the situation calls for, the false self is probably there. When we feel helpless and timid like a lost child, the false self is most likely loitering just around the corner. Unless we stop, look back, and reconsider our experiences, the chronicle of our lives will be distorted by the propagandizing of the false self. In our favor is the fact that our heightened awareness, the same adaptive gift that suggested we should conform at all costs, is now the tool we can use to give the false self the boot.

Identity has consistencies, but it is not a stone face. Identity is dynamic and fluid, especially for Everyday Geniuses, who are always in the process of reinventing themselves. The voice of the true self will be heard and its energies will be manifested, one way or another. The truth always seeks the light of day. And when the true self begins to reemerge, it is an epiphany that evokes a bevy of emotions that range from anger to panic to rapture. This is the way all prisoners react when they are finally set free.

Recovering the vitality of the true self motivates us like nothing else, because the real opposite of despair and emptiness is vitality of spirit, which is far more than momentary pleasure or the illusion of never-ending happiness. The imagined reunion with your full-potential self will be enough to encourage you to look again to see where and your past wounds occurred. You will then begin to understand why you needed a false self to protect you in the first place.

Liberation of Everyday Genius must begin at the beginning, the place where our true selves were detoured—the place where we learned to reject ourselves in order to fit into the world around us. This occurred at the time of identity formation, when we made our first decisions about what we would and would not show of ourselves, what parts of ourselves we would love, and which attributes we would distrust and loathe. There we will discover the picture within the puzzle that was previously hidden from our awareness.

Other paradoxes of Everyday Genius are that we cherish our atypicality, and that we are internally motivated, creative, and energized by life's challenges while simultaneously knowing that we have few with whom we can truly relate. At the very least we must be able to honestly relate to ourselves. We are tired of looking for ourselves in all the wrong places. We suffer battle fatigue from misreading our habits and attributes, because the dual nature of giftedness was never fully explained to us. To undo the tangled knots that tie us down, we must review our lives, going back to the basics of our development before we can make complete sense to ourselves and make conscious choices for productive change.

By honoring the original meaning of genius, we form a new bond of security: genius as our guiding inner spirit revived, made real again, to breathe free as it was in childhood. Suddenly we remember. Fondly we reunite, no longer feeling alone or like strangers in our own house. Once again we realize there is someone who really "gets it," someone who will not abandon us, who has always been and will always be alongside us on each risky venture toward the completion of our intended role.

Bear in mind that the personal experience of giftedness is not about being better than anyone else. Rather, it is a history that centers on exceptional awareness and sensitivity. In childhood this raw awareness translates into intense vulnerability. For the budding Everyday Genius, the pores of impression are wide open, and consequently whatever the sensory, emotional, or relational experience, good or bad, it leaves a profound mark. In many ways the gifted child is like a butterfly—fragile, remarkable, inquisitive, and yet capable of enduring the most extreme environmental hazards.

THE UNBECOMING EXTREMES

Let us turn our attention to the major domains of Everyday Genius, this time focusing on the rise and rule of the false self. Very early in our lives the traits that characterize these domains are eye-catching and different, often eliciting disapproval from others. Naturally we tend to internalize this feedback, often carrying it around inside us for a lifetime, as if it were a valid belief that we ourselves conceived. And because the psyche is prepared to defend us against disapproval and rejection, in its child-like wisdom it chooses either to magnify the trait, in an exaggerated false-self reaction, or to go underground and camouflage the trait, in a collapsed false-self reaction. Remember, each of the primary factors of the gifted personality is a foundation of excellence and an invaluable asset. In fact, these traits are essential for all who wish to go beyond expertise into the tumultuous frontier of becoming a creative producer— those who will not settle for being an expert, but who must ask the new question, turn the status quo upside down, and ultimately bring about a valuable transformation in his or her field of endeavor.

Domain: Intensity

> EXTERNAL MESSAGE: *"Why don't you just slow down and stick to one thing?"*
> INTERNAL MESSAGE: *"I'm so impatient. I've got to settle down, or I'll never amount to anything!"*

> FALSE-SELF REACTIONS:
> EXAGGERATED: *Pushes self into constant state of physical and emotional exhaustion; intolerant of the natural rhythms of things; overstimulated, scattered, and burned out*
> COLLAPSED: *Anesthetized by lack of challenge; resigned to inactivity, boredom, and a single-task existence*

Chad possessed the energy of five or six people rolled into one. He had been an excitable, energetic kid, and recalled people referring to him as "Dennis the Menace." His nervous system worked like the most advanced radar, which made his life experience radically different. Chad's father had always called him a "hot reactor," because he was so easily aroused by sensory input and the slightest emotion. He was always on the go, changing directions from one things to another depending on what caught his interest. Once engaged, he was a voracious information seeker whose focus was laser-sharp.

Through the years Chad maintained a kaleidoscopic array of interests that varied from gourmet cooking to building grandfather clocks. One could almost hear the wheels turning in his head, his intense curiosity and amazing comprehension bounding from one thing to the next. In fact, he compared his shifts of attention to an accomplished channel surfer. Chad was indeed intense. He was a stimulation seeker extraordinaire who seemed to thrive on novelty and challenge.

Yet having been brought up in a family that equated stability with success, Chad's passions were considered to be a sure sign that he was destined for failure if he couldn't settle down. Because of this, Chad was constantly criticized for being flighty and hyperactive. He recalled his father's protests:

> *Chad: From the beginning I was always exploring something; my parents called it "getting into everything." It nearly drove my father crazy. He still talks about how when I was little I hardly ever slept—no naps, hardly ever sat still. When he was really fed up, he'd shake his head and yell: "Chad, one of these days you're going to give me a heart attack!"*
>
> *I was a big-time risk taker. I just had to see and do things for myself—like the time I nearly blew up the basement with my chemistry set. I grew up thinking I was a pretty mixed-up kid. By the time I was a teenager I bet I'd heard my father holler at me a thousand times: "You keep that up and mark my words, you'll never amount to anything!" Still, I tried one sport after another, looking for just the right one. I didn't want to miss out on anything. My dad had a fit about that too: "I'm not made out of money, you know. We can't afford to be buying you a new batting helmet and baseball shoes one week and then skis or track shoes the next. For once in your life just pick something—anything—and stick with it!"*

The term most often applied to Chad in his youth was "all over the place," which is often translated into the external world as hyperactive, flighty, or out of control. As a young adult, Chad could have been the poster boy for the slogan "So many choices . . . so little time." Yet to many adults Chad's versatility and excitability could be seen only as an inability to harness his energies and focus on one thing at a time. Although Chad had an enormous capacity for concentration in things that interested him, young people like Chad are often regarded as scattered and impulsive, perennially judged as being unable to focus their attention on one topic for very long.

Chad's high-school counselor was exceedingly frustrated when he attempted to "help" Chad pin down what he wanted to do in the future. As Chad recalled:

> *My counselor had me take all these tests. You know the kind—those either-or tests that ask you things like "Would you like to be a landscape architect more or less than being a zoologist?" I about drove Mr. Wainright nuts because I kept on interrupting him as I was doing the tests to complain that I couldn't really answer that way. It was like this. I was excited about nearly everything. When I went to the zoo, I wanted to become a zoologist. When I read a great article in a magazine, I wanted to be a journalist. After we went to the state championships in baseball and I pitched one of my best games, I was sure I'd want to turn pro one day. And nobody knew this one: that I've been a closet poet since I was a kid. I think I've memorized at least half of Emerson's work by now. So this poor guy who was making every effort to guide me through the wilds of career choice didn't stand a chance of hitting the nail on the head.*

Chad was well-liked, engaging, and vivacious. And without a doubt his excitability and multiple interests were sure markers of giftedness. It was highly unlikely that Chad would go through life bored or inactive. Yet what had stuck in him deep in his gut was the ongoing criticism that being the way he was meant that he'd never amount to anything of consequence. Whenever he faced criticism or lack of obvious approval, Chad was plagued with self-inflicted attacks, his mind gushing with fatalistic self-talk like a storm-swollen river:

> *What a screwup! Always switching horses in midstream. Can't follow through on anything. Great starter, rotten finisher. No wonder you never get ahead. Excited about this, excited about that! All over the place like a Mexican jumping bean! No one respects that, Mr. Impulsive. No one has a chance to take you seriously when you never stay with anything long enough to look like you know what you're doing.*

No one had ever explained to Chad that many gifted people struggle with the impossible choices presented to them because of their multiple talents. Which ones do they give up for the sake of others? It's an experience of loss, because for multiply talented individuals, many gifts must remain underdeveloped. No one had ever approached Chad at the teachable moment during his key developmental stages with a kindly and accurate portrait of his true self. If that right person had appeared at just the right time, it might have gone like this:

> *Chad, I see that you are excited about so many things. It's hard to have so many interests. It's a real challenge, and yet it's also a gift. I've had four different careers by now, and I'm not sorry about any of them even though my colleagues think it's crazy. Don't ever forget that when you learn something in one area, it nearly always has some value in another. You know, like Michael Jordan's switch from baseball to basketball— both require speed, agility, teamwork, and concentration. It's just that for him close wasn't close enough. Baseball was good for him, but basketball was great. When you find something you love, you will still need to find the courage to stick it out in the hard times. Once you've attained a nugget of expertise, your credibility will allow you to really do things your own way. You've really got something, Chad. Don't let your enthusiasm run you; learn how to run your enthusiasms.*

Since this teachable moment had not happened for Chad, he was left with an exaggerated false-self reaction that continued to create obstacles in his adult life. Losing girlfriends in his early twenties didn't bother him much. But now at twenty-nine, Chad had finally found a woman he loved and with whom he thought he might like to make a life. However, as a stimulation-seeking adult, Chad paired intensity with high risk, venturing off into rock climbing, parachuting, and mountain bike racing, and just as in childhood, Chad still found that no one, including Sarah, was willing to play his way all the time. Lately Sarah had been complaining, "You're all go and no show!"

Chad's intense personality and high activity level had created a powerful barrier to intimacy. Sarah loved Chad, and she too hoped they could make a life together. But her trust in the relationship was repeatedly undermined by Chad's exaggerated false-self reactivity. She interpreted his discomfort with intimate talk as unresponsiveness, which made her feel unwanted. When Chad balked at strolling in the park, quietly holding hands, or just "being together" without a structured agenda, Sarah took Chad's urge to "do something" as an indicator that he liked what they did together more than he liked her:

Sarah: I can't get close to you, Chad, because you're such a fanatic. When you get into one of your hot new projects, either I have to jump in headfirst with you or I'm left out in the cold. To be with you, I always have to move into your world. First it was the box seats for the hockey games, then the ski lessons, and now you're talking about hiking the Sierra Nevada this summer. You're so intense! No, it's more. You're always hooked on pumping adrenaline. It comes down to this, Chad—if you don't find a way to settle down, I'm going to ask Dr. Hokenson if he can put you on Ritalin!

Chad had all the undeveloped features of an exemplary mate— dependable, loving, passionate, fun. But he had learned to protect his sensitive nature and vulnerable self-image by staying busy, directing nearly all of his energy into challenges that kept him from being fully known by Sarah and from fully engaging in emotional closeness. Chad didn't know how to transfer some of his energy to the less active parts that were essential building blocks of a close relationship. He needed to learn how to be intense in different ways—intense serenity, intense listening, and intense patience. Perhaps the greatest irony was in the fact that Sarah complained about Chad's lack of passion with her.

Triggered by insecurity, Chad's false self resurfaced with a vengeance. He was fooled into believing he had to make a horrible choice: be an enthusiastic go-getter who wears people out, or tie himself down like a caged lion. Beyond this, without addressing the problems caused by Chad's lingering wound and the defensive false self, Chad's many talents were likely to continue to be diverted into a series of time-consuming trial balloons. Ultimately, Chad had to discover new ways to feel good and find satisfaction in the completion of goals that were important to him.

Chad had always set up his life like Disney World, activity being the "drug" of choice. Over and again nongifted snipers would challenge Chad to "dare to be average." In truth, Chad needed someone on his side who would challenge him to know himself fully; he had to learn the art of staging; and he had not only to dare to start, but to dare to finish. He needed to dare to exercise different ways to stay motivated and achieve without relying solely on newness as the incentive. He didn't yet know it, but there was no need for him to try to turn himself into a dull, single-track guy. He just needed to channel his energy and enthusiasm so that his own unique process worked for him instead of against him.

Annette is the polar opposite of Chad's false-self reaction. Her defensive style turned intensity in on itself. Her earliest memories were experiences of being shushed. More than anything she had been taught to loathe boisterousness and any behavior or appearance that would draw attention to herself. In Annette's family individuality was about on the same par as conceit. In elementary school Annette was praised many times for being such a "good girl." At conference time her parents beamed when her teachers commented on how "well-mannered" and "mature" she was. It was crystal clear that any attempt at expressing her unique self would be met with disdain. The cardinal unspoken rule: blend in to the wallpaper. Or, as Annette later said in therapy, "Get in line or get invisible."

By the time she was in high school, Annette knew she had secretly agreed to tie down her exceptional gifts and anchor herself to her mother's idea of security: "Pull your head out of the clouds, Annette. Nobody in this family has ever been a star, and you're no exception. Just get yourself a good job so you can count on having a secure life."

Annette's early adult life as a secretary may have been secure in terms of constancy and a steady income, but it was anything but secure emotionally. Over the years Annette's dissatisfaction became more difficult to ignore. She felt estranged from the picture she had once had of herself as a dynamic woman who was in charge of her own life. Her life had become so predictable that she felt like an automaton, anxious and fatigued at the same time, going through the motions according to schedule, one month more or less like another.

When I first met Annette, she appeared lifeless, indifferent, and depressed. There was no sparkle in her eyes, and at twenty-nine she looked much older. When I asked her what she really wanted from life, Annette rotely replied: "I just want to have a good job and feel secure." I leaned forward, looked her straight in the eye, and softly said, "No, Annette. What do you really want?" Several minutes passed while Annette sobbed. Then, when she looked up, her eyes had a bit of a glint in them. "You know what, I don't think I've ever allowed myself to think about my life that way. All I know for sure is that I've felt like a large part of me has been dead. And I don't want to be dead anymore!"

Gradually we began to unravel the false self that was so prevalent in every aspect of Annette's life. She was on the verge of discovering something all Everyday Geniuses need to know: Symptoms of ill health and emotional distress are caused by lack of challenge and boredom just as much as by overwork and scattered energy. Her depression subsided as she realized the effect her false-self reactions had on her. If she was to get free of its clutches, she would have to dare to take charge of her life and create an alliance with the unpredictable frontiers—the zone where all the possibilities she had left behind awaited her. Annette found that she had been falsely indoctrinated with a belief that predictability equals security. A routinized life stuck in a pose of security is a dangerous choice for the Everyday Genius when life as an adventure and the fulfillment of high potential hang in the balance.

Domain: Perceptivity

> EXTERNAL MESSAGE: *"You're so concerned about everything and everybody. Stop looking for trouble!"*
> INTERNAL MESSAGE: *"Why can't I just mind my own business?"*

> FALSE-SELF REACTIONS:
> EXAGGERATED: *Overly responsible; absorbs the troubles of the world like a sponge; feels resentful and burned out; outspoken truth telling backfires*
> COLLAPSED: *Paralyzed by feelings of self-doubt, alienation, and despair; highly distrustful of others or slightly paranoid; conceals creativity to avoid exploitation*

Sandra was eight years old when she first noticed the boy down the street in leg braces. She was painfully aware of how difficult it was for him to function. Each time she went out to play she caught sight of him standing on the sidelines, watching the other boys his age chasing each other in a game of tag or speeding around on their bicycles. She felt crushed when the neighborhood kids made fun of him, calling him "the gimpy metal kid."

When his mother planned a birthday party for him, Sandra was the only child to attend. The day after the party Sandra asked her friends, "What happened? I thought you'd be at Larry's party." She was outraged when one by one each of them stammered out a flimsy excuse. "Well, uh, I came down with a fever and my mom made me stay in bed," replied Joanne as she ran in from the playground after recess. "Party? What party?" Rob fibbed. "I thought that was next week."

Years later, Sandra remembered this experience as one of the first times when life seemed painfully unfair. She recalled being so upset that she cried about the incident all night. Her young psyche was so absorbent that she felt responsible for righting this wrong, especially because others around her seemed indifferent. She made sure Larry didn't sit alone at lunch for the next three weeks, and walked home behind him to fend off the bullies' stinging insults.

Sandra had become a fairly accomplished cellist by age fourteen, a confident veteran of numerous recitals and school performances. In fact, she had never held any position in the various school orchestras other than first chair. She practiced hard and had won the respect of her music teachers and friends alike. Sandra was thrilled when her teacher told the students the school had received an offer to perform for the governor's inauguration celebration—a small ensemble would be chosen within the week. That same afternoon as she left school Sandra realized she had left her music folder behind and went back to retrieve it. Hearing hushed voices, she hesitated before she entered the room. Mr. Mann, the orchestra director, was talking to Jimmy Sanderson's father, a member of the school board. Sandra overhead Mr. Mann say, "Well, Mr. Sanderson, I understand why you would want Jimmy to have this opportunity. But you know that Sandra Ellsworth has been first chair for a very long time. It would be pretty awkward if I had to try to explain to her why Jimmy was chosen over her." Mr. Sanderson replied, "I'm sure I can count on you to do the right thing, Mr. Mann."

Thinking little more about what she heard, Sandra decided to run for the bus without her music. She returned to Mr. Mann's room the next morning before class. As she was about to leave with her music folder, her teacher stopped her. What he said nearly took her breath away: "Sandra, lately I've noticed a lot of effort and improvement in Jimmy's playing. So I've decided to let Jimmy take first chair in the ensemble this time. I know you'll understand." Sandra was mortified, unable to utter a sound. She stewed about it all day, hardly able to concentrate in class. After school she made a beeline for Mr. Mann's office. The confrontation was fueled by intense feelings of betrayal and anger. "When I came back for my folder, Mr. Mann, I heard what you talked about with Jimmy's dad. You tried to make me believe you had a good reason for picking Jimmy for the ensemble over me! How could you?" Her teacher felt backed into a corner and rushed to put her in her place: "Sandra, you've got a lot of nerve talking to me this way! Don't be so immature! Life isn't always fair, you know."

As she grew into adulthood, issues of injustice continued to hit Sandra like a freight train. She was often troubled by the social intolerance and hypocritical agendas around her. When Sandra heard the news that she had been passed over for the new project manager position in favor of one of her coworkers, she was irate. She headed straight for her boss' office. Without knocking, she launched into her protest: "I can't believe you gave that job to him, George. You and I both know I've earned that position. My ratings are higher, and I've been here three years longer— three years!"

Unfortunately her boss was not at all equipped to offer Sandra any kind of guidance at this teachable moment. Adding insult to injury, he laid it on the line: "Look, Sandra, I gave the job to Ron because he's a real team player, not always stirring things up. He just does his job and that's what we want here. We don't need someone who's always second-guessing management. In case no one informed you, bluntness is not a management tool. If you wanted to defend the truth so much, maybe you should have gone into the justice system, not real estate management!"

Frequently, perceptive and concerned gifted adults are involuntarily set up by society to be the truth tellers and the whistle-blowers, even though it is not an effective way to win friends or move up the corporate ladder. Since childhood Sandra had struggled with inner conflict because she expected everyone—especially herself—to practice what they preach. No matter what the situation, Sandra's internal compass always pointed in the direction of the whole truth and nothing but the truth. Consequently, she was incapable of choosing her battles wisely.

As we explored her dilemma in therapy, Sandra challenged: "Why would anyone *not* want to know the truth?" Ironically, Sandra's great concern for the truth worked against her whenever she chose to be candid without allowing the other person a way to save face. No one had ever taught Sandra that she need not be the sole guardian of the truth. Over several months of work to reduce the impact of her false self, Sandra was able to realize that opinions differ because there are many ways to arrive at the truth and truth is never simplistic.

Sandra's task was a balancing act—artful advocacy for the truth balanced by respect and controlled compassion. What troubled her most was that criticisms first voiced externally had now become an endless flow of internal carping. It fueled her profound self-doubt and emotional pain. Maybe her critics were right, she often thought. Yet once Sandra was able to identify the true source of her internalized shame as voices from her past and not the voice of her own psyche, she could begin to hear the difference between her own values and will and the objections and criticism of others.

This made a huge difference in Sandra's self-belief. Just knowing that the condemnations of the past were rooted in mistaken opinions began to liberate her. With a new option to be selective about how or when or if she chose to share what she knew to be true, she felt reenergized and far less burdened. She began to understand that it was possible to find a middle ground between her own judgments and apathetic indifference.

The same lightbulb might have gone on during Sandra's adolescence had a discerning mentor appeared on the scene at a teachable moment. Perhaps one of Sandra's teachers—one who had taken the time to build a trusting relationship with Sandra—might have responded to her complaints about tripping herself up by blurting out the truth:

> *You are dealing with one of the most difficult problems gifted people confront, Sandra. You really do detect falsehoods, and your exceptional ability to see through the veneer of any given situation means you really can see what others do not. That's a gift, Sandra, and don't ever let anyone convince you otherwise. Not everyone is comfortable digging to such depths. And, as you are discovering, when you pull back someone's coverup to reveal what they want to keep hidden, you're in line for an all-out attack. Give yourself permission to pause a bit to do some consequential thinking and perhaps to say no to some of your truth-telling inclinations. Ask yourself two things: (1) Is this piece of truth directly tied to one of my most important convictions? (2) Am I willing to go to the wall for this, no matter what the outcome? If the answer to both of these questions is yes, then off you go, full speed ahead.*

Gifted children tend to agonize over the difference between right and wrong. Many have trouble adopting a flexible method of dealing with issues involving truth and justice. Strangely, this is precisely as it should be, since Everyday Geniuses are designed to uncover and confront the most difficult concerns of humankind. Their underlying mission is to advance truth and to overturn oppression. Yet in order to fulfill this task they must learn to trust themselves and to choose their battles wisely.

By reevaluating her childhood experiences with injustice, Sandra learned to transform her deep concern into effective action. She understood that there are many defenders of justice in the world; this fact would not excuse her from doing her part, but it also meant that she didn't need to go on feeling overwhelmed, because she was no longer the only soldier in the army. Railing against every perceived enemy of the truth was an outdated and immature strategy. When Sandra learned how to merge negotiation and compromise with her moral principles, she was liberated of her self-doubt. She didn't need to sell out by remaining silent alienating others with her sharp tongue because now she knew how to advocate for them in ways that were most likely to make a real difference.

Contrary to Sandra's reaction, the powerful perceptions of Everyday Genius powers can be overwhelming and cause a very different false-self reaction. When voiced perceptions are met with glares of disbelief or disgust, there is a natural tendency for the expression of the trait to give way. The false-self reaction attempts to get rid of troublesome impressions and intuitions. Feelings are intellectualized—forced out of the zone of emotion and up into the mind. Rather than validate what is intuited or discerned, every effort is made to make "sense" of awareness by formulaic methods of reasoning. The ultimate outcome is unexpected insecurity and self-doubt. When commanding perceptions are cast aside or buried under the weight of oppressive logic, trust of self and others is nearly impossible. The overall effect of replacing emotional reactions with reasoned, intellectualized responses is that life loses much of its color, becoming a comfortable, if dingy, shade of gray.

This collapsed false-self reaction can lead to feelings of alienation and despair. Perhaps nothing is more painful for the Everyday Genius than the secret feeling of being alone in the world. It is an experience of involuntary exile. It is a formidable task to come to grips with this, which was something Miles had begun to realize as he recounted his history:

When I think back, it seems like I've always felt alone, even when I was right in the middle of my family or with my friends—like I was an observer from a different planet or something. I've also realized how much my older sister's experiences had to do with the way I handled being different. Kim was so bright—really gifted. And I saw what it was like for her when she was honest about her insights. One time she predicted my aunt's divorce and got sent to her room for being insolent—although that's exactly what happened six months later. If she dared to point out when my father was being a hypocrite, she got the belt. The worst of all was after Kim let it slip to my grandmother that she'd had some sort of psychic or spiritual event. In private she and I had shared those kinds of secrets, because I had them, too. Not ghosts or creepy things. More like being washed over by an image or presence of something divine. But when my grandmother told my parents about what Kim had said, they

dragged her off to the family doctor and I didn't see her for a long time.
They put her in the hospital and I wasn't allowed to visit her. When Kim
came home she looked like all the life had been drained out of her.
Everyone said she was "so much better." I kept my mouth shut, but I
didn't agree then, and I still don't. I suppose I made a vow to myself that
I would never be in her situation.

By the time Miles had graduated from elementary school he was already a veteran skeptic. Yet rather than channel his doubts into a debate club or even a class discussion, he went inward. He closed off his natural conduit to second-sight information, which only served to increase his distrust. As happens so often, Miles was rewarded for his self-denial, especially by his parents: "Miles, you're becoming such a grown-up. Thank God at least one of our children has his feet on the ground!"

Without any way to verify that his experiences and insights were normal for gifted children, Miles grew to hate everything that represented the aesthetic or ethereal. As a teenager, he was resolute about being "normal," which for the most part meant keeping his distance from anyone who might get to know the real Miles. Once again his peers and teachers commended him: "I always know you'll come up with the reasonable solution, Miles. You're so levelheaded." What no one knew was that in trying to find a ground for his being in "reality" alone and by refusing to indulge the creative aspects of his personality, Miles was existing in a lifeless void. To justify to himself his rejection of his perceptions, he chose to be a nonbeliever in nearly everything. He saw the world as a completely dangerous place, and had no faith that others could be close to him without exploiting him. He held back his ideas, distanced himself, and under stress slid into paranoid thinking. There was no one to trust on the outside, and no one home on the inside. His distrust became a self-fulfilling prophecy that kept him going around in circles of hesitation for more than twenty years.

Miles went a long way toward recovering his emotional self and his ability to connect with others by using his gifts of perception to review his past. Nonetheless, distrusting his ability to read people correctly continued to plague him and turn him away from intimate relationships. He saw the damage the false self had done, and in typical style tried to think his way out of his loneliness, which was yet another false-self tactic. After considerable urging Miles agreed to keep a notebook of perceptions: sensory and emotional material, daydreams, night dreams, memories, and "gut feeling" reactions to others. He augmented this by taking an art class, having loved watercolors when he was a young man. There, from behind his back, his instructor fulfilled the guide's role that he had been seeking:

> *Ah, Miles, I see you are beginning to trust your eyes to direct your hands. How wonderfully you paint when you check your intellect at the door. What you reveal on paper is so much more real than "reality." Don't ever let anyone convince you otherwise. What you see is real . . . for you. And when you dare to reveal that you make it real for us too. That's when you create the art that your soul longs for.*

Early in their lives gifted children are willing to accept popular opinion as infallible, even if their exceptional perceptivity tells them otherwise. They may know better than the adults around them, but they don't know that they know better. This explains why convictions of the most headstrong, even acerbic bright child can suddenly wither under the weight of opposition and self-doubt. Over time maturing Everyday Geniuses come to mistrust what their discerning minds tell them, blaming themselves for being poor thinkers who either make things up or cannot rectify perceived problems without being ostracized. Worse yet, as in ancient Roman times, the bearer of bad news is still considered the source of the trouble, and though today heads are not lopped off in actuality, metaphorically this is exactly what happens. In such cases it is not much of a stretch to understand how such individuals come to disown their own intuitions and insights.

Are Everyday Geniuses vulnerable to exploitative others? Must their openness and creative risk taking make them easy marks for authority figures? To some degree, yes. If one is to be a true creator who leaves his or her mark on the world, there is always a certain amount of toughening that must take place. One has to be resilient enough to sell the creative idea to the doubting gatekeepers in any field. In adulthood, personal skills, drive, and the personality traits of Everyday Genius are far more important for breakthrough achievement than a truly extraordinary IQ score. True, world-changing creators do not easily accept the popular view of things. For Miles, a blend of skepticism and trust in what seems unexplainable was the answer. He discovered he needed to be whole himself if he was to reasonably expect to live a whole life. And in his case, his unfettered artist's eye brought him back to his true self.

Domain: Sensitivity

EXTERNAL MESSAGE: *"You're just too sensitive!"*
INTERNAL MESSAGE: *"I feel too much. I have to learn how to toughen up!"*

FALSE-SELF REACTIONS:

EXAGGERATED: *Emotion-dominated behavior; overreactive to the point of being judged as moody, hyperemotional, or hysterical*
COLLAPSED: *Compartmentalizes feelings and lets the intellect rule; seen as being cold, indifferent, or apathetic*

Before Elsa was two years old she displayed a level of sensitivity that astounded nearly everyone, including her mother. She reacted to the slightest noise, change in room temperature, or aroma. Turning on a bright light made Elsa shrink into a ball. She couldn't sleep with the wool blanket her aunt had knitted for her because her face broke out in a rash. And if her older brother was even mildly scolded, Elsa would run into her room and hug her teddy bear as though something horrible were happening. Her relatives began to refer to her as "The Princess with the Pea." A tactless uncle suggested her father build her a padded room so the world wouldn't bother her so much. Even though her mother tried hard to understand Elsa's delicate nature, it sometimes baffled her completely.

One morning as Elsa sat in her highchair fingering her breakfast, her mother put an empty milk carton on the floor to flatten it with her foot before she threw it away. Just as her foot began to crush the carton Elsa burst into tears. Her mother looked over immediately, wondering what had happened to little Elsa, having no idea it was the "killing" of the milk carton that had triggered Elsa's staggering compassion. Elsa's suffering in this moment was an incident that most children would not have responded to at all.

Most everyone blew off Elsa's exceptional sensitivity as touchiness, something they prayed she would "grow out of." When she was in the fourth grade, she experienced something she couldn't explain during art class. She waited, hoping the sensation would go away, because art was her favorite subject and she didn't want to go to see the nurse. But her feeling that something was terribly wrong didn't subside. The nurse was more than a bit skeptical when she took Elsa's temperature and found it to be normal: "Not a thing wrong with you from what I can see. I'm not so easily fooled, Elsa. Now back to class you go." On her way out the door,

Elsa turned and announced: "I didn't mean that I was sick right now. I meant to tell you that I'm going to be sick next week."

No one believed in Elsa's built-in early warning system. Although her mother was much nicer about it, she thought Elsa was exaggerating, too. Yet exactly one week to the day, Elsa suffered a serious attack of appendicitis and was rushed to the emergency room straight from school. In fact, she barely survived the night. The school nurse called Elsa's mother the next day, contrite and flustered: "I don't know what to tell you, Mrs. Bertram. I couldn't see a thing wrong with Elsa when she came down to see me last week. I'm really sorry. There was no way I could have known."

In the best of worlds, this experience would have offered Elsa a poignant teachable moment. The guiding voice might have told her:

> *Elsa, you have an ability that is very rare. Over time you will grow up and learn how to trust your powerful senses. You'll be able to handle things that are upsetting now. The world will probably always feel too loud or seem too harsh in countless ways. So you'll need to protect yourself from that by insisting others turn down the volume on the radio or taking yourself out of the most dissonant or distressing situations as much as possible. For now, I want you to know that I'll believe you if you tell me you hear a train in the distance. It's just that no one else hears it like you do. If you feel upset after sitting next to someone who's sad, I know that's real for you. Just because others don't react the way you do, Elsa, doesn't mean they're right and you're wrong. Remember that.*

Sadly, this conversation never took place. And so Elsa defended her highly vulnerable self by collapsing the trait. To keep herself on the straight and narrow, she told herself: "You're so thin-skinned! Every little thing bothers you. There's always something wrong with you!" Because no one had instructed Elsa in better methods of self-defense and no one showed her how to respond to disturbances with graduated levels of upset, every negative experience resulted in a disaster-level reaction. In college, she recalled with embarrassment, one of her friends had complained: "I swear, Elsa, if somebody was hit by a donkey cart in Borneo, you'd feel it and start worrying about it."

To counteract these criticisms, Elsa did a complete about-face. She closed off her feelings and pushed them up into her intellect. Going on to graduate school made it even easier for her to do this, since intellectualizing was a socially reinforced virtue. To the surprise of her family and friends, the Elsa who had always reacted to every shift in the wind turned into an unflappable ice maiden. It was the only way she knew to protect herself from her own sensitivity.

It wasn't until Elsa was a successful attorney in her late thirties that fate delivered her an opportunity for change. Acutely aware of a younger associate's inability to rebuff the unwanted advances of a fellow lawyer, Elsa remembered how precarious the position of an associate was. No associate could afford to offend one of the managing partners, yet when she stumbled upon her licentious colleague trying to grope the young woman in the law library, she was in a terrible quandary. Because of her history of overidentifying with the plights of others, she had a difficult time deciding whether or not she should take up the young woman's cause. For so many years she had been training herself to steer clear of entanglements.

As a therapy client, Elsa worked hard with me to revise and correct her history. Though in many ways Elsa's sensitivity was her most outstanding characteristic, she had come to see it as her archenemy. The problem now was that the cost of feigning emotional detachment was increasing. She had never been told that her sensibility and loving kindness were the bedrock of who she was designed to become, or that it was possible to balance sensitivity with selective detachment.

Elsa had reached a turning point. To undo the knots of the past, she faced a two-pronged problem: to learn the difference between feeling with and feeling for others, and to learn to love her sensitivity without letting it rule her life. Most of all, she needed to stand up for her depth of compassion and exile the old voices that branded her a "crybaby."

Initially Elsa struggled with the strangeness of making conscious choices about how she would display her sensitivity. With time and practice she learned to manage her extraordinarily tuned-in nature by judiciously stepping back for a while or stepping out altogether. She also learned to determine when and where and to whom she should extend her empathic involvement. Elsa became skilled at discernment, and her sensitivity no longer led her around on a leash. For Elsa, unbridled expression had cost too much.

This is not always the course false-self reaction takes. When not outwardly expressed in exaggerated ways, heightened sensitivity can implode, turning in on itself. Rather than manifest itself authentically as warmth and caring, the collapsed reaction is one of cold aloofness and seeming apathy. Liang was a textbook example of this reaction to gifted levels of sensitivity:

Liang: From the time I was very young the only thing anyone seemed to like about me was my ability to toss out quick answers and facts. I guess you could say I was a fact junkie. And that suited my family and teachers just fine. All the way through high school and college I stuck to the tried and true. If there had been a contest for chemistry lab queen instead of homecoming queen, I might have won. I arranged everything in my life like an equation. As far as I was concerned, if it couldn't be proven, it couldn't be. I was a walking, talking encyclopedia, and people admired me for that. I had no idea how much that self-protection plan would cost me. I'm lonely, and everybody thinks I'm aloof. My boyfriend tells me I'm a cold fish. I suppose that should bother me, but it doesn't. In fact, nothing much bothers me, so I'm not sure why talking with you is going to help.

Unlike Elsa, Liang was so removed from her own feelings that she couldn't even talk about them, much less express them. If I asked her how she felt, she responded with "I think . . ." When I stopped her and asked her to specify what she was feeling, she looked at me as though I were speaking a foreign language. Indeed, feelings *were* a foreign language. Because she was so bright and otherwise articulate, it was maddening for Liang to feel incompetent in the realm of emotions, so she had learned to denigrate emotion. She also came to realize that as a female intellectual in a male-dominated field, some of her denial of feelings was prudent.

To undo the choke hold the false self had on her feelings, Liang set about the task of first learning to identify and label what she was feeling. Though she was convinced it was silly and a huge waste of time, she consented to take note of her feelings several times throughout the day over a period of weeks. When she was at last able to use feeling talk to describe her emotions, reserving thinking talk to describe her ideas, she discovered that others misread her less often. It was still a steep climb to the place in her life where she would be able to express her feelings openly to anyone, even to me. We are still working on that, and making some headway. A while ago she jokingly remarked: "Well, I must be progressing, I cried in a movie last weekend. I thought my boyfriend was going to fall into the aisle. I'm glad we're doing this, but it's really hard. I may have earned a Ph.D. in chemistry, but when I earn even a GED in emotional expression, I'll feel like I've finally arrived."

Domain: Goal-Driven Motivation

EXTERNAL MESSAGE: "You're such a driven perfectionist! Why can't you just accept things the way they are?"

INTERNAL MESSAGE: "I guess I'm just too picky. I wish I could just lighten up and let go!"

FALSE-SELF REACTIONS:

EXAGGERATED: Relies on achievement as the only legitimate source of motivation and satisfaction; rigidly holds out for the ideal no matter what the cost or consequence; gets lost in unimportant details and misses the window of opportunity

COLLAPSED: Avoids opposition and disapproval; lowers standards and "dumbs down"; gives in prematurely, pretending not to know what he or she does know; feigns contentment with status quo to fit in and make others feel comfortable

The Everyday Genius' instinctive urge toward perfection is directly connected to goal-driven motivation. Like all Everyday Geniuses, as a little girl, Amanda didn't do things without reason. Painstakingly arranging and refining every drawing, every shelf of storybooks, and every hairdo on every doll was an early marker of giftedness. Like all young Everyday Geniuses, Amanda held out for the ideal she envisioned in her mind for two reasons: she had an internal set of aesthetically pleasing standards to which she felt responsible, and simply because she had the ability and concentration to do things exceptionally well.

As a child, it was nearly impossible for Amanda to grasp the fact that satisfaction and success share a curvilinear relationship with painstaking effort—too much nitpicking arouses feelings of distress, and settling for second-rate arouses feelings of distress. To be effective, aiming for excellence and holding out for the imagined ideal need to be intelligently balanced with insightful acts of letting go. Everyday Geniuses always wrestle with this because lowering the bar on their naturally high standards reduces motivation and excellence. On the other hand, raising the bar too high too soon and perfecting things in too many directions increases the likelihood of feeling like a failure whose talent and energy have become so fragmented and scattered that they've become impotent.

When Amanda was six years old, for several weeks her rapt attention centered on finger painting. She spent hours each day after school covering paper after paper with paint. She loved playing with the unexpected color mixtures that appeared, and she was fascinated by the direct connection between her hands and the movement suggested by her unschooled art. When it was time for dinner, Amanda's mother found it very hard to convince Amanda to put her paints away. "No, not yet!" Amanda would protest. "Can't you see that it's not finished?" In her young mind's eye, Amanda held a vision of what she wanted to create on paper: that exact vision, nothing else.

Her mother took Amanda's resistance as a sign of defiance: "Amanda! We are about to have dinner. Your paints aren't that important. They can wait. Now put your things away and mind what I tell you this instant!" As her frustrated mother reached down to pick up the paints, one of them spilled on the paper she had been working on in tiny strokes of rainbow colors for the last two hours. Amanda went off like a volcano: "Oh, no! Look what you've done! It's ruined! It can't be fixed. I hate it. I hate the whole thing, and I'm never going to paint again!" She ran from the kitchen in a flood of tears, leaving her mother dazed and perturbed.

The teachable moment passed. Had Amanda's mother been aware of the importance of this seemingly insignificant event, and had she understood the developmental nature of the gifted child, things might have gone differently. Amanda continued to be easily frustrated. As with most Everyday Genius children, Amanda could picture in her head what she wanted to accomplish long before she had developed the skill to actually produce it. Though asynchronous development of talents nearly always accompanies giftedness, no one helped her adjust to the frustrations of not yet having the skills to bring her ideas into reality in a satisfying way.

In adolescence, Amanda tangled with the flip side of perfectionism: procrastination, a form of avoidance that is rooted in holding out until things are "just right." Whenever Amanda had a school project, she was off to the Internet, sleuthing every related Web site and information link available. Before long, she was off on some irrelevant tangent and grossly behind schedule. Fortunately, she was smart enough to pull a rabbit out of the hat at the last minute. Yet earning good grades for being off task only reinforced her habit of delaying and then going into crisis mode.

Her astute biology teacher failed to offer Amanda complete guidance, though she did see what was going on:

Okay, Amanda. You win. I can't give you anything but an A minus on this project. It is just about the best in the class. But I know you threw this together burning the midnight oil. You may be able to get away with that in high school, but one of these days your procrastination will land you in a mess that no miracle will save you from.

Amanda continued to have trouble with unbridled goal-driven motivation. Too often she failed to see the big picture when she obsessed over some trivial refinement. Her mental agility and powers of concentration carried her through college and graduate school, but as a research scientist in her early thirties, she was struggling. Amanda knew herself well enough to declare: "I'm simply not satisfied until I'm satisfied."

Initially Amanda came to therapy complaining that she felt taken advantage of at work. She was the resident expert when it came to exactitude and put in more lab hours than anyone on her team. Yet she was not happy. She had come to realize that in her hardworking style an unhealed wound continued to cause problems:

This may sound petty, but this same thing has been going on since I was a kid. Those of us who work the hardest and do the most get no credit when we knock ourselves out because everybody expects an outstanding performance from us every time. But if I slow down or mess up even once, the fireworks go off. At the same time certain people get boatloads of approval for doing as little as possible. Everybody expects me to knock myself out without any praise. Even if I am recognized for my achievements, the thrill is immediately followed by my own insistence that I have to do something more—sooner, better, farther. It's like a bank account that keeps getting depleted even though I keep making deposits.

Often in adult life, if left to its own devices, the perfectionism wound can show up as sharp-tongued intolerance of others, self-degradation and loathing, grudges that eat away at happiness, punishment of the body with substances or food or neglect, and almost always a chronic lack of self-acceptance. The unmanaged gifted trait of exceptionally high standards was becoming exhausting for Amanda. It was painful to work under an umbrella of unremitting self-demands. In nearly every endeavor she was a one-percenter, expecting more of herself than others expected of her and more than she expected of them. She truly believed that not only could she do better and better all the time, but that she must. Long ago her sense of self-worth had become riveted to achievement, and little else.

Amanda's unhealed wounds had primed her to spiral downward in a self-defeating vortex each time she felt she was falling short of the mark. This was how her false self invaded her life. She was plagued by an overwhelming sense of urgency if she felt as though an important dream might be slipping away. In response, she would push herself relentlessly, become bossy and impatient, neglect important relationships, ignore essential tasks, and sabotage her own health. Although she generally came out of this all-or-nothing driven effort being seen as a winner, the price was sky high. She may have achieved the desired goal, but she was left a wreck who felt discredited time and time again.

Outside of work things weren't much different. For eight years Amanda had been a loyal, hardworking member of a volunteer organization to help battered women. Her creative ideas, zeal, and drive were respected and appreciated. Amanda was convinced she was a shoo-in for president-elect and was shocked when she was passed over. Heartbroken, Amanda confided in another member she trusted. A close friend rose to the daring position of compassionate mentor and carefully told Amanda:

> *I really don't know how to say this, Amanda. I hope you won't take it the wrong way. Cynthia may not have earned the position the way you did, but I think she was elected over you because she's so easygoing. In the president's job we have to have a leader who's not so intimidating. When you get your eyes set on a goal you drive yourself long and hard. But we've all seen what it's like when others are involved. In all honesty, Amanda, your style is pretty abrasive and domineering. An organization like this calls for a leader who can pull the best out of people without riding roughshod over them. I'm sorry, Amanda. But that's how it is.*

Though very hard to hear, Amanda's friend's remarks were humane and helpful. It was a teachable moment that turned the tide. Amanda was a natural leader, but her rigid, exhausting style was immature and ineffective. She needed to find ways to nurture herself and to deal with the realities of working with less driven, less gifted others. She needed to make a pact with her demand for the ideal and learn to laugh off her tendency to straighten every tilted picture and to pick up all the leaves the rake had missed.

More than anything else, Amanda needed to find a more reliable security system than achievement. Otherwise she was destined to live out her life as a frantic striver whose self-worth and inner peace were perpetually at risk. One researcher summed it up beautifully when he said unmanaged perfectionism takes a constant toll because "[y]esterday's success has no meaning in the lexicon of the perfectionist. Indeed, they walk through snow without leaving tracks."[2]

From time to time Amanda would have to remind people around her of her triumphs as well as let them see her sweat and make mistakes. She also needed to keep pressing ahead while not abandoning her high standards, because indeed she was destined to alter her field of endeavor. Here and there she would struggle with the temptation to throw in the towel or loiter in procrastination. She would need to become a skilled manager of this tendency, permitting herself some time to peruse catalogues or surf the Net to recoup, but not for too long or as a place to hide out and create unnecessary crises.

Lionel's story was quite different. He too was exceptionally bright and intrinsically motivated. To fit in, his false self took over by avoiding opposition and disapproval, pretending to have mediocre standards and dumbing down to be "one of the guys." Lionel had been repeatedly rewarded for making everyone around him feel good. People loved having him around, especially when things were getting a bit dull. Even as a very young boy, Lionel had been the designated fun-maker. His ability to see the absurdities of life provided him with a natural wit that the growing false self quickly put to good use.

Lionel had learned to use his wit as buffoonery in school to ward off classroom boredom. One of his fondest memories was of the time he persuaded his physics partner to help him fill the huge oblong lab sink with water all the way to the rim. When his teacher arrived Lionel talked his way out of trouble by explaining his antics as a serious experiment in surface tension. While the students smirked, the teacher bought the story— and this was what usually happened. After a while, Lionel found that his role as the resident comic prevented him from fully developing his multi-faceted personality:

Back in my senior year of high school I remember making a conscious decision to stop being the class clown all the time. I had a serious side to me, and I was sick of covering it up. And you know what happened? All my friends got mad at me. I remember them asking me over and over again, "What's wrong with you? Are you sick? Are you mad at someone?" It was pretty obvious that I had been assigned my role—no one would take me seriously.

Lionel's advanced sense of humor later made him a top-level sales rep in the competitive market of communications technology. Yet when he didn't feel like clowning around, others became agitated, as though in some way he had betrayed their definition of him. This was where we began our work—allowing others to define him. To permit Lionel's scripted persona to go in some different directions, we made good use of therapeutic improvisation. These methods raced past Lionel's inner critic and allowed him to break through ingrained false-self reactions. His ability to laugh at absurdity also allowed him to laugh at himself. That was the easy part. It was far more difficult for Lionel to express the pain of having to play the jester, remembering all the times he felt like crying on the inside while he was grinning on the outside. Then he had to dare to be taken seriously by others and to allow those close to him to see the diverse aspects of his complete personality. He and I talked about how others might react, how some might not like the more serious or unhappy side of him. We also discussed why he needed to take the risk if he wanted to be able to share more of himself with others than entertainment, especially if he hoped to let others bring joy to him as well. "What a concept," he exclaimed. "I can be as serious as I can be funny. I like this new me!"

Domain: Complex Thinking

EXTERNAL MESSAGE: "Where do you get all your wild ideas? Stop rocking the boat! Who do you think you are?"
INTERNAL MESSAGE: "Me and my big mouth!"

FALSE-SELF REACTIONS:

EXAGGERATED: Seen as troublemaker; constantly butts heads with authority figures; stubbornly resists input and advice from others; poses embarrassing or threatening questions; turns verbal ability and humor against self and others
COLLAPSED: Denies self and sells out to be seen as a team player; distrusts own intuition and opinions; holds back visionary contributions for fear of being ridiculed

Everyday Genius always comes down to being different, which, as we have seen, all too easily translates into being seen as out of step, stubborn, wrongheaded, or weird. Yet genius is like a complex engine, built and rebuilt over time. The differentness required to make a real difference in the world is fueled by independence of thought, daydreaming, making up new rules, and fidgeting with gadgets. Because gifted children often have trouble finding same-age peers who think and wonder like they do, or who share their unusual stick-to-it-iveness, they delve into their interests with gusto, not in an effort to be oppositional, but because they must.

When Stephen Hawking was growing up in England his teachers considered him smart but nothing special. In the sight of others, his genius abilities emerged gradually. Yet perhaps one of the earlier indicators of his brilliance was the type of game he enjoyed. Like so many developing gifted children, Hawking liked to devise his own games, making up rules complicated enough to challenge himself, but so intricate that his peers gave up in frustration. He gathered around him some of the more intelligent students who could share his incredible instinct for mathematics. When he was just sixteen he and a buddy concocted a working computer from a grab bag of used parts from a telephone company. Today, despite the toll amyotrophic lateral sclerosis (Lou Gehrig's disease) has taken, though he is bound to a wheelchair and forced to communicate via a voice synthesizer, Hawking continues to hold the world's top spot in the field of astrophysics.

For Everyday Geniuses, having a head chock full of ideas, images, questions, and words is like living inside a buzzing beehive, a marvel of nature that when well managed can work exceedingly well in all its complexity. Everyday Geniuses are often in the process of reading five or more books at a time. They think on multiple planes simultaneously. In an instant, the Everyday Genius mind can fly about in all directions on one tangent after another, most of which are useful detours in thinking. Yet mental detours are not always beneficial. Sometimes the nomadic original mind illustrates the adage "Many a train of thought carries no freight." Worse yet, when the fast-moving mind of an Everyday Genius is headed down a negative path, it can quickly turn into a lethal internal attack force. This is how it came to be for Jack.

In his early childhood Jack was exceedingly shy, saying only what was absolutely necessary. Most of the time he was content exploring his own thoughts, indulging his insatiable curiosity on his own—that is, until someone got in his way. Despite his quiet manner, it was clear from the outset that Jack had a mind of his own and wanted to do things independently and do them his way. One of the first indicators of Jack's gifted blend of autonomy and creativity was his insistence that he do things for himself. When anyone attempted to show Jack how to do something, like tying a shoe, halfway through the instruction he would cry out, "I want to do it! I want to do it!"

Then it all changed. When Jack was about nine years old his powerful mind and strong will surfaced like a nuclear submarine. Jack found he could no longer contain his ideas and comments. Instead of being criticized about being quiet—"What's the matter, Jack, cat got your tongue?"—now he was a constant target of criticism for being a "motor mouth."

By the time Jack was a sophomore in high school he was labeled the "rebel with a constant cause." His gifted ability to size things up quickly and understand things on multiple levels, his talent for bridging seemingly incompatible concepts, and his exceptional command of powerful language made him an ace on the debate team. Off the dais, it also made him several enemies. No one had ever taught Jack the difference between being correct and being politically correct. When he thought he was advancing knowledge and showing people the light, more often than not he was being rude or insulting. Jack's coach tried to make him see what was happening:

> There's no doubt, Jack, you're one of the finest debaters I've ever coached. You're quick as a whip and you zero in on the weak points of the other side like a cruise missile. But I don't think you're winning any points with your teammates, and that matters, too. Think about that. And while you're at it, think about this—I wish you'd learn to take advice now and then. Even in our team meetings, when I say "up" you say "down." It's bad form to show up the coach in front of the others, Jack. Didn't anybody ever teach you that?

Jack did think about it, but just as quickly dismissed it. And so it went. Others continued to be offended when he squirmed impatiently to indicate his irritation if their way of processing things was different or slower than his. In fact, he found nearly everyone to be insufferably slow. In class, he went so far as to start snapping his fingers at people, as though to say, "Hurry up and get on with it, will ya? Let's get to the point here!"

Although he was a fierce and successful adversary on the debate circuit, Jack left a trail of affronts behind him and failed to see how or why others disliked him. He was deeply hurt when he overheard two teammates talking about him: "That Jack guy is such a big-headed jerk! He thinks he's so special and the rest of us are a bunch of dunces. I get so sick of him telling everybody to hurry up all the time. Who does he think he is, anyway? He may be the star on the debate team, but as far as I'm concerned, he's a conceited bully!"

In group situations Jack always felt like a pressure cooker, always trying to restrain himself, to do as his teachers and parents had said: "Be patient and make room for others, Jack. Stop pushing your way of doing things onto everybody else." That's how it continued for Jack all through his school years and on into his career. Lacking specialized guidance, he continued to be an "in-your-face" kind of guy, as his colleagues complained. He shrugged off hurt looks from others, telling himself, "If they can't swim with the sharks, they'd better get out of the water." Jack honed his innovative and verbal skills along with his persuasive talents and became a top marketing guru in the automobile industry.

One fateful day, in a meeting with his marketing managers, Jack started off as usual with a full head of steam, tapping his watch and rolling his eyes if discussion ever went beyond a few seconds per topic. His near terror of wasting time blinded him to the value of group process. He had no idea that by cutting people off in midsentence and saying things like "Just give me the bullet points," he was killing off the very creative energy he sought.

Having had to fend off the bitter complaints of Jack's subordinates more than once, the company president decided it was high time he paid Jack a visit. It was indeed the teachable moment, and although his boss handled it quite well, Jack was in for a powerful dose of reality:

Jack, if I didn't value your incredible creativity and enormous talent so much, I'd be tempted to go along with your manager's pleas to fire you. I'm really on your side—our side, Jack. And maybe it will help you swallow this pill a bit better if I tell you that when I was in your shoes I heard from one of my bosses what I'm about to tell you. Not everyone is as quick and creative as you, Jack. And that doesn't mean they're wasting your time. Life isn't a thirty-second TV commercial. Ideas have to be developed, sometimes by going over the same ground many times over. You can't shove your timing and style down their throats and then turn around and expect them to dare to offer some new ideas. Creativity only

*thrives in an atmosphere that makes it safe to express one's opinion—
even if it's half-baked.*

Possessing the trait of Complex Thinking means processing information on multiple levels simultaneously. This is a powerful tool and part of
the bedrock of excellence. But as we've seen with Jack, there's a catch.
While leapfrogging through problems to quickly detect problems and
cause-effect relationships, we can look as though we're either immovable
dictators or irresponsible guessers who move forward with incomplete
analysis. Gifted children cannot explain how they understand things so
quickly, and their comments are therefore often met with slack-jawed
disbelief or ridiculing laughter.

In the psychological literature, this trait is called "divergent thinking." In general it is a preference for, if not a need for, the unusual. Essentially this means the Everyday Genius typically comes up with the
atypical response, tending to look at things from unusual angles and seek
out original solutions rather than repeat the same-old, same-old. Because
Complex Thinking follows novelty down whatever road it seems to take,
the exceptionally creative child can appear absentminded, off track, or
even obstinately defiant. Unusual responses of gifted children rarely sit
well with adults, who praise their innovative products while wagging a
finger at the lack of conformity.

Traditional methods of structuring concepts and approaching subjects in school in strictly linear fashion often do not fit the comprehensive
processes of gifted children. Hence they may appear to be slow learners
who can't seem to get organized. Even though such children may be considerably brighter than their classmates, they see themselves as anything
but bright. Instead, they feel incompetent, dull-witted, and alienated. It
stands to reason that under such conditions they have trouble finding
value in their unique style of thinking.

For Jack, moving forward into Advanced Development meant learning
to deal with others in new ways. He needed to boost his skills at eliciting
creative idea building, which meant developing the type of think-tank atmosphere with his staff that he had dreamed of for himself when he was a
kid. He had to learn how to pull the best from others instead of driving
them toward what he determined was the one and only goal. Now it was
Jack's turn to make room for other creative thinkers and to mentor them
as well.

I urged Jack to find creative ways to foster confidence in others by planting the seeds of ideas and letting them grow of their own accord, by pruning and carefully shaping others' ideas, and by focusing more on the process of creative thinking and less on the ultimate product. Through the development of others Jack could heal his old wounds and reunite his true self with the headstrong child whose imaginary pastimes had been channeled into productivity over process with emphasis on speedy over sufficient. Over a period of several months, Jack came to relish the change, realizing for the first time that uniqueness need not be sacrificed in order to create teamwork, and that he could lead by following the inspirations of others. The ad campaigns were better, everyone was getting along better, and, amazingly, life was much easier when he didn't have to do everything himself.

Felicia's false-self reaction led her in quite the opposite direction. It's not hard to imagine how this would play out—too much compromise, too little conflict, and entirely too much self-imposed complacency. The collapsed false-self reaction is no easier to correct than the exaggerated version. In either case, the answer lies in finding the balance—flexible autonomy and respectful methods of rocking the boat without swamping the entire crew as the goal sinks out of sight.

Felicia ran a bakery near the train station. Though she was quietly brilliant and exceptionally insightful, people tended to think of Felicia as an ordinary person who was special because she really cared. In her community she was respected as a woman who made a real difference in the lives of others. Felicia had never put in anything short of 100 percent personal effort, with one profound exception—the fulfillment of her own dreams.

A quick observation of Felicia's routine revealed a very pedestrian life that appeared satisfying and meaningful enough. In some regards this was true for her. When her parents died in a tragic car accident she felt compelled to leave law school prematurely and run the family bakery, though she feared she might never find a way to go back. For a while she wondered where her choice of conscience would lead her, silently worrying about lost opportunities and anguishing as her hopes for the future began to fade.

Yet Felicia was not the self-pitying type. Because she was determined to live out her "responsibility," she found a pseudoniche for herself. Her decision to make the most of her situation hinged on her capacity to provide the energy, support, and encouragement lacking in the lives of those she encountered every day. Each morning she saw the same faces passing by the bakery window, too many of them sad, lonely, and troubled.

Felicia didn't see the parallels between what she was doing and her shelved dream of becoming a lawyer who advocated for the powerless members of society. Though she was applying the right intention and making good use of her natural talents, Felicia's life had become deadened because she was enacting someone else's dream. Her own visionary ideas about the "good society" were shoved aside. She sold herself out for two very powerful reasons: she felt indebted to her family, and she felt indebted to those who looked to her for support.

Over the next ten years she expanded her family's business, opening two more shops near transit depots, insisting on the same welcoming atmosphere from everyone she employed. Her success was due in part to her natural business acumen, but more to her exceptional capacity to see and deliver the exact thing her customers needed to get their day off to the right start. In her heart she felt good about what she had done. In her secret hours she mourned what she had given up, settling for what her community seemed to want of her instead of taking chances with her own future. Felicia was quite sure she would never be disparaged for being selfish or unappreciated. Yet she never said a word to anyone about her deep-seated pains of regret.

At Felicia's funeral several years later, a huge crowd of mourners overran the church. Nearly all were from the train station, customers who, unbeknownst to her, had sometimes driven miles out of their way to be greeted by her. These were people who had made new friends and treated each other better because of her, workaday folks who shared something special at the bakery—a sense of belonging, worth, and enthusiasm. In their eyes, Felicia had been a huge success.

Did Felicia do it wrong? Can a life so clearly beneficial to others and yet so sacrificial to the true self be considered a victory? Who is to say? Yet we can imagine how many overly responsible individuals like Felicia with exceptional gifts have gone a similar route. Family, neighbors, and society at large may indeed be grateful for people like Felicia. In many ways these are the Everyday Geniuses who forgo developing their full potential to support and complete the rest of us. Yet what of their personal sacrifice? What of the gifts that were never developed? What do we all lose when potential creators such as Felicia become sidetracked in a life that is only half of the possible picture? Moreover, what harm is done to the very soul of the Everyday Genius who settles for less simply because others seem to have a stranglehold on what they can become?

Now we can see what fosters the false self and how it can betray high potential when left to its own devices. Unfortunately, the rise and rule of a false self is probably unavoidable. Fortunately, Everyday Geniuses have what it takes to heal old wounds, to see things from a new perspective, to evaluate their own motivations and behaviors, and to reformulate themselves over the life span. By liberating their creative potential and promoting the best in themselves, the advanced "sanities" they develop can create a ripple effect in the universal consciousness. Their freedom to self-actualize may indeed be the linchpin of progress upon which our collective future turns.

Unhealed wounds and ignored false-self reactions penetrate to the very heart of the matter: who we think we are. Wouldn't it be something if it were smart to act as smart as one truly is? If that kind of liberty were feasible, wouldn't far greater numbers of society's Everyday Geniuses fulfill the promise of their high potential—the arduous trek toward self-actualization that leads to the revolutionary contributions our world so desperately needs? They would be equipped to decide for themselves which sacrifices to make. Think of what all the bright, creative people who are now in private exile could accomplish if the differences that are fundamental for revolutionary contributions were differences we could all learn to live with.

PART FOUR

MANAGING THYSELF

SELF-MASTERY AND INTEGRATION

13

THE BIG THREE DIFFERENCES:
INTENSITY, COMPLEXITY, AND DRIVE

Those who are victorious plan effectively and change decisively.
They are like a great river that maintains its course but adjusts its flow.
—Sun Tzu

As we have seen, the assets of Everyday Genius are powerful, and when managed, they can fulfill their intended role as the effective foundation for Advanced Development and excellence. However, when unregulated, these same forces can turn against us by becoming unnecessarily *exaggerated*—needlessly inflaming situations or causing time-consuming detours, either of which can trigger crippling bouts of self-defeating reactivity or self-doubt that make us appear hopelessly out of control. When Everyday Genius energy is *collapsed* or overregulated, the force of gifted ability becomes inverted and stifled or seriously weakened.

Expressions at either extreme can set into motion a pendulum swing of self-defeating behaviors and divert the dynamic flow of high potential from its intended course. Clearly, Everyday Geniuses cannot allow such loss of valuable time and energy to persist if their missions are ever to be fulfilled.

MANAGING THE FLOW:
NO TRICKLES, NO TORRENTS

How can we be fully dynamic in our authentic expression of self in the real world? Liberation matters. But proportionality also matters, because none of us lives or works in a vacuum. To be truly efficient we must learn to allocate our energy and influence. How, then, can we be liberated and regulated at the same time?

The answer lies in embracing the fact that we are different in three fundamental ways. Everyday Geniuses are *quantitatively, qualitatively,* and *motivationally* different. This is simply how our circuitry is designed. There's no reason to either pat ourselves on the back or fake it, pretending we are the same as everyone else. Our unique characteristics are as cumbersome as they are creatively potent, each admirable quality being infused with promise. They are never grounds for arrogance. We need only know how to make our quantitative, qualitative, and motivational differences work for us rather than against us.

Intelligently regulating the force of Everyday Genius is like balancing the flow of a surging underground river. Although its mighty current is mostly invisible, its dynamism is ever moving and ever present. Because of this, we need a conscious plan to oversee and guide its unseen forces. Damming the current of Everyday Genius can divert it to a channel that leads in the wrong direction, slowing it down to a trickle, stagnating its flow. Letting the current of Everyday Genius energy run wild may flood potentially vital regions of our lives and personalities while keeping other areas drought-ridden.

Years of investigating the psychology of the gifted as well as working with my Everyday Genius clientele have repeatedly revealed how gifted adults struggle at the extreme ranges of behavior that occur when no energy is flowing through and around a given trait, or how its flow can become overwhelming and out of control if not managed correctly. Both expressions are hazardous. Only by learning to balance and regulate the powers of Everyday Genius do we stay steady, moving forward into the waters of Advanced Development and the expression of Evolutionary Intelligence.

Mismanagement is very costly. A close monitoring of giftedness helps us to avoid errors in judgment and expression that can make us look anything but smart. Self-mastery is the basis of Evolutionary Intelligence. The amplification of giftedness over the course of a lifetime is possible primarily because, like the river, the powers of Everyday Genius endure. With time and attention, these powers can be consolidated into a network of energy resources capable of fueling Revolutionary Action. As we shall see, taking the step from being gifted to being an evolutionary is at once gratifying and empowering, since our three major differences correspond to the Advanced Development markers of Driven Effort, Humanistic Vision, and Revolutionary Action.

Learning to navigate in two worlds—the daily grind and the evolutionary domain—requires this new level of self-awareness from which we may develop an individualized balance plan to make the most of our abilities. We must avoid the temptation to sell out or hide out. We must also learn to integrate our special abilities wisely. This marriage will take everything our talent and resolve can muster. To be fully present and undiminished in today's society, the Everyday Genius needs to acquire the artful agility of a tightrope walker. Let us never forget that this very tension—the tightrope walk of being our true self, who we are meant to be in the real world—is the power source of creativity and breakthrough Evolutionary Intelligence.

CHARTING AN EVOLUTIONARY COURSE

The principal umbrella traits that set gifted individuals apart are Intensity, Complexity, and Drive. To manage the commanding influence of our powerful assets, we must accept the fact that Everyday Genius is grounded in being quantitatively different, qualitatively different, and motivationally different. And because this is so, whether the sum of our efforts will amount to a worthwhile legacy depends on how well we manage these three pivotal differences.

In order to gain a clear understanding of how the dynamic energies of Everyday Genius play out in real life, examine the charts on pages 259–262, 268–273, and 280–282. Each primary characteristic is divided into three categories: *collapsed* (the flow of energy is dammed up, turning in on itself), *exaggerated* (the energy flow is uncontrolled and results in "flash floods"), and *balanced* (the energy flow is on course, liberated, and dynamic because of self-mastery).

Think about a recent difficulty you experienced. Did an imbalance in one of the three traits——Intensity, Complexity, or Drive—either create or exacerbate the problem? Do you think the problem occurred because of an imbalance in a particular subtrait within that trait? If so, in what form was your expression made, collapsed or exaggerated? Now, consider the balanced expression, a prerequisite for Evolutionary Intelligence.

Advanced Development demands regularly taking an honest inventory of our behavior—especially our habit and reaction patterns. Remember that the expression of your special abilities must be reckoned with. One way or another, these dynamics will make themselves known in our lives. The only wise course of action is to manage the underground river ourselves—neither slowing it to a trickle and letting it stagnate in resignation nor allowing it to rush unchecked, overrunning its banks at every change in the weather and ultimately eroding our most important goals.

The sense of urgency that we feel upon knowing ourselves, understanding ourselves, and managing ourselves comes from the awareness that we are the true caretakers of our exceptional gifts. We are the only ones who can learn to intelligently adjust the inward flow of stimulation and the outpouring of our energy. Only through conscious management under an informed and watchful eye can our gifts be expressed in ways that do not harm those around us or jeopardize the expression of our Evolutionary Intelligence.

Reconsider problems you've had in the past, especially problems that are recurrent or elicit strong emotional reactions. Many times the most heated response to a given situation—a reaction that in retrospect seems over the top—is the royal road to self-understanding and growth. Don't be afraid to delve deeply into these areas, using the chart as a backdrop against which you can measure your own plan for self-regulation.

For example, take the subtrait of verbal agility. In its collapsed form, when little or no energy is flowing through this characteristic, words lose their power and become bland or colorless. Hence the Everyday Genius appears to be dull, uninterested, or someone who can never get off the fence and take a stand. When the forces of verbal agility are allowed to run wild, they become exaggerated and potentially harmful, and Everyday Geniuses who fail to heed the signs that their verbal agility is overflowing its banks are stunned when they are criticized for being domineering, insensitive, or politically incorrect. Many careers have sunk under the weight of one of these imbalances.

In the area of *excitability* we are generally concerned with issues of stimulation. Visualize someone who seems exhilarated by life and energized without being harried. Determine if the person is vitalized by stimulation rather than burdened by it. This is a person who can judiciously regulate stimulus input and outflow to avoid becoming overwrought by sensory overload or addicted to risky stimulation seeking. Collapsed, this trait becomes weakened by boredom, monotony, or understimulation. Exaggerated, excitability becomes hyperkinesis, which is an inside-out expression of the trait, seen in perpetual restlessness, hot reactions, or demanding to speed things up. The collapsed form of excitability is an outside-in problem. This is a person who deals with penetrating stimulation and heightened sensory inputs by turning off all of their receivers. The result is someone who looks anything but excited by life. What we see is listlessness, a distant look in the eye like a dim flickering flashlight powered by weak batteries. No stimulation is being absorbed, so no stimulation is being released.

When it comes to emotional sensitivity, there are many things that can short-circuit the healthy expression of this trait. Authenticity, for instance, is difficult especially for Everyday Geniuses who must live in a society that glorifies the norm. When the energies of emotional sensitivity are turned in on themselves, nothing authentic is allowed to flow free. The result is someone who feels isolated and appears inhibited. The identity is blurry, both to the Everyday Genius and to others. Although this may be a person of tremendous capacity for unique individuality, that is not what we see. We're not sure of our perceptions, since we are constantly trapped in fears of being an impostor. The collapsed version of this trait is similar to the chameleon who changes color as an adaptive instinct to survive in potentially hostile environments.

At the exaggerated end of the spectrum, the artificial Everyday Genius who makes a conscious choice to masquerade as somebody else may do so as a way of refusing to manage or believe in his or her true self. In this exaggerated form there is a repetitious "trying on for size" of endless personas—acting all the time. However successful the impersonation, it is enormously hard work because of its counterfeit nature. It requires nonstop vigilance and an inordinate amount of energy because it is based on second-guessing what others "want." This energy could be allocated to Advanced Development and meaningful delivery of exceptional gifts if its flow were artfully administered.

As you use the chart don't forget that one of the best ways to learn is by making mistakes. Often when the lesson is very hard to learn, we make the same mistake constantly. That is how all human beings are designed, no matter how smart or talented. There's no shame in needing to plow the same ground repeatedly as long as we continue to consciously recognize the problem, own our part in it, and assertively push for improvement. For the Everyday Genius, this is paramount when self-actualization hangs in the balance.

Do not forget the value of your keen observational skills, exceptional memory, and ability to draw fitting analogies. When we are attempting to change a trait in ourselves, we need to have something else at the ready, an alternative way of reacting to situations. Look around you for signs of balanced Everyday Genius. There are lots of examples from which to draw, whether in real life or fiction.

For example, if you observe someone handling a difficult situation with finesse, make note of the body language, facial expressions, tone, and so on that made the person's strategy work to everyone's advantage. In fact, many of my clients actually create a new "script" for themselves so that they are prepared for the next challenge. This action accelerates the process of self-directed growth and gives more control to the individual seeking change.

Of course, there are gradations between the extremes that are not listed here. However, the charts will offer you a way to spot your strengths and weaknesses. They will provide you with a specific blueprint for change and assist you in your effort to give yourself credit for the areas in which you have already modified your behaviors to achieve greater success.

As you review the charts a second time, reflect on relationship issues or situations in which you upset others if they didn't tell you outright what you did that bothered them. Ask yourself which traits seem to be at the heart of the matter. Consider the range of choices you have at your disposal. Imagine the different ways in which you could aim for a more balanced expression of a specific trait. Also review the charts to locate particular traits you have that are not properly governed, and consider how the imbalance prompts your own self-judgment or criticism. Think about how your internal world would improve if you consciously worked on this area. Remember, even though the flow of energy is strong and it has found a comfortable groove over the years, it is not immovable. A small shift can make a huge difference.

INTENSITY: QUANTITATIVELY DIFFERENT

Considering how we are quantitatively different from others allows us to bring together the gifted subtraits of sensitivity and high excitability under the single category of intensity. Intensity is primarily a matter of increased arousal. It is the result of a sensory, neural, and emotional network that is more receptive and more responsive, extending higher, deeper, and farther than that of the average person. This umbrella trait encompasses verbal agility, excitability, a strong sense of humor, exceptional concentration, empathy, emotional sensitivity, and high energy.

INTENSITY: QUANTITATIVELY DIFFERENT

Collapsed	Exaggerated	Balanced
EXCITABILITY		
Listless	Wired	Exhilarated by life
Numbs out with substances	Thrill seeker; addicted to excitement	Frequent peaks of experience
Understimulated and bored	Raw and overstimulated	Enriched by the five senses
Depressed or sullen	Overwhelmed or harried	Robust
VERBAL AGILITY		
Dodges controversy; steers toward popular opinion	Intractable opinions; dominates conversations	Engaging conversationalist; comfortable with intense discussion
Dull and unimaginative speech; can't hold the floor	Embellishes the truth; poses embarrassing questions	Colorful storyteller; sincere spokesperson
Vague; spineless fence straddler	Coercive; lectures and corrects others	Persuasive

Collapsed	Exaggerated	Balanced
Substitutes mindless banter for in-depth conversation	Caustic; uses words as weapons	Articulate; stimulating

STRONG SENSE OF HUMOR

Collapsed	Exaggerated	Balanced
Silly and inane; never serious	Clowns for attention; obnoxious prankster	Quick-witted and exuberant
Whiny or peevish	Sarcastic; cynical	Skillfully navigates life's tragedies and comedies with appropriate expression
Prim and drab	Inappropriate hilarity; feigns happiness	Appreciates life's absurdities and human foibles
Deprecates self as laughingstock	Jokingly mocks and humiliates others	Joyous; congenial

EXCEPTIONAL CONCENTRATION

Collapsed	Exaggerated	Balanced
Dabbler; cannot sustain focus or momentum	Automaton; consumed by projects	Discriminatingly attentive

All plans and no progress; dreams fade away	Exhausted and burned out	Accomplished and fulfilled
Noncommittal, indifferent, or capricious	Bitter workaholic with a martyr complex	Committed
Scattered	Preoccupied or obsessed	Contemplative and conscientious

EMPATHY

Insensitive, hard, or merciless	Self-destructive martyrdom	Compassionate
Self-absorbed and distant	Invasive; "feels others' feelings" for them	Concerned
Detached loner; fears intimacy	Promotes codependency	Interdependent; capable of healthy intimacy
Apathetic; materialistic isolationist	Carries the weight of the world	Humanistic

EMOTIONAL SENSITIVITY

Cold and remote	Doting and smothering	Warm and caring
Closed off; rationalizes feelings away	Too trusting; easily wounded; transparent and gullible	Open and receptive

Collapsed	Exaggerated	Balanced
Inhibited; blurred identity; impostorism	Artificial; impersonates to camouflage true self	Authentic; expressive
Melancholic and despairing	Crisis-driven alarmist	Emotionally fluent; comfortable with wide range of emotion

HIGH ENERGY

Collapsed	Exaggerated	Balanced
Restlessly inactive; squirrelly	Frenzied risk taker in perpetual overdrive	Full of life; animated
Creates obstacles; wet-blankets vitality and possibility	Provocateur; wears others out	Inspiring; uplifting; charismatic; revitalizes people and situations
Devitalized; drained or indolent	Randomly disperses energy; capabilities ungoverned and squandered	Artfully allocates energy
Overcontrolled; trapped in deadening routine	Out of control; self-indulgent; defies authority and ducks responsibility	Knows when to control and when to let go

Intensity means that many things command our attention and call for a response. This sensitivity shows us things that others seem to ignore or miss altogether. We are qualitatively different in this way because we are *more* energetic, *more* emotionally reactive, *more* excitable, *more* passionate, *more* responsive, *more* self-aware, *more* committed, and *more* empathic. In other words, our extraordinarily sensitive nervous systems require us to make our way through life with all the advantages and disadvantages of being endowed with an ultrasensitive body, mind, and spirit.

Intensity can be seen in many forms of expression, including high levels of activity and animation, deep emotional reaction, a display of what looks like impulsivity, rapid speech, nervous habits, complaints about sound or small discomforts, and strong reactions to the problems and feelings of others. It is not surprising that until we find effective ways to manage our intense natures, we run the risk of wearing ourselves and others out.

Everyday Geniuses are constantly penetrated by life. It's fascinating, yet not surprising, that studies of the physiological characteristics of gifted children indicate a greater incidence of allergies.[1] Our internal and external worlds are raining stimuli constantly. Even though I categorize the intensities of giftedness in quantitative terms, they make a huge qualitative difference as well. Our expansive arousal system makes us walking, talking electronic detectors. As one researcher put it, being so very sensitive makes for an entirely different sort of life experience: "vivid, absorbing, penetrating, encompassing, complex, commanding—a way of being quiveringly alive."[2]

One of my clients described his experience with intensity this way: "Lots of people around me seem to passively observe a lot of things that get under my skin and set off reactions. It's always been like that for me—awareness in, reaction out. When it's bad I feel like I've been hit by an anvil, shattered like cartoon characters but without the instant recovery. That's the deep pit where I feel lost and alone. But when it's good, it's as if all my nerve endings are deliciously electrified; I'm on fire inside and swept off my feet by the passion and energy that washes over me. That's the pinnacle where I am truly alive and at my best."

In ordinary circumstances the same form of vitality needed to create transcendent moments can turn in an instant and produce unpleasant events. All Everyday Geniuses know exactly what it's like at that instant—time is suspended, the tone shifts dramatically from positive to negative, and the looks aimed your way tell you loud and clear that you've gone too far. Though intensity incorporates a powerful set of potential assets, when unchecked our natural excitability and emotionality can overpower or repel others. Although they would not be overpowering in a group of their peers, even quiet Everyday Geniuses are sometimes very dominant in a setting of people who are naturally less intense.

Everyday Geniuses who dare to talk fast and express much more than "normal" individuals are quickly educated in social rules about this form of intensity, verbal agility. They are just being themselves, and they are confused when others pull away from their emotional depth. Yet in the real world such rejection comes with the turf. When our intensity is running at full throttle, there are always those who rapidly reach their saturation point and show it with the roll of an eye and a sigh. They have had all they can take for now. If we fail to heed their signals, it soon becomes obvious that those around us who feel trodden upon can and will turn against us, especially if our exuberance makes them feel inadequate or left out.

For some people more is not better, especially when it comes to expressions of emotion. Everyday Geniuses' empathic interest and unusual capacity for closeness can easily miscarry if other people feel the protective walls of emotional distance closing in before they are ready. To them, getting too intimate too soon stirs up anxiety, which is often followed by a hasty retreat. Without understanding why this happens, it appears to the fast-paced gifted person who feels secure that others are either emotionally disconnected or disinterested in what they have to say.

Like it or not, the same thing that makes us stand out and apart also requires us to hold back at times, to make room for others' styles of expression and slower pace, as well as lesser degrees of comfort with passionate feelings. One Everyday Genius defended himself this way: "Sometimes the people who think I'm overmuch are the ones I find *undermuch*—less sensitive, less responsive, less spirited. To my way of thinking, that's simply less alive." Yet these kinds of self-justification are unnecessary when we understand that no one is really over- or underintense; rather, individuals simply fall on different places along the broad spectrum of intensity.

Consciously gatekeeping intensity to manage and direct its flow is critical to the fulfillment of our entrusted personal missions. Yet none of us will find it easy to face the shadow side of Everyday Genius until our admirable side feels grounded and reasonably secure. After several months of counseling, Glenda came to know and accept herself as a gifted adult, which made it possible for her to see herself in a new, more welcoming light. This, of course, was a prerequisite for her to be willing to delve into the shadow side of giftedness, to see more clearly how her intensity played out in her daily life in ways that kept her from reaching her potential.

Increasingly Glenda became aware of how she had never managed or protected her highly sensitive constitution. Without realizing she had any effect on her exposed level, she had become used to chronic vulnerability and the exhaustion that accompanies stimulation overload. For Glenda, life had always been a high-volume pitch-and-roll escapade, like living at Great Adventure during high season. Moreover, being as porous as a sponge to every visual, auditory, tactile, aromatic, emotional, and internally produced twinge of stimulation, Glenda's exceptional gifts were increasingly underpowered. The catalyst that caused a breakthrough for Glenda was a reawakened childhood memory:

> *Glenda: When I woke up this morning it hit me like a ton of bricks. All the things we've been talking about, especially the piece about intensity, reminded me of one afternoon twenty years ago. It was the day I decided to try on the world with my senses dialed way down. I stuffed my ears and covered them with earmuffs, put on an old pair of glasses to make everything fuzzy, sucked on some alum to numb out my mouth, and insulated myself from head to toe with mittens and sweaters so I could hardly feel anything from the outside. I even put on the nose plug I used for swimming. Then I went out to the backyard and walked around. I'll never forget it. It was surreal, like floating around in a cotton cloud. At first I liked it—it was so quiet, so undisturbed. I remember thinking: "This must be what it's like for everybody else."*
>
> *Of course, covering up my sensory radar didn't work for long, then or now. But it struck me that when things get to be too much I can put myself on "mute" for a while. I can even stay away from things like upsetting movies and pushy crowds without having to explain myself. I can adjust the amount of my exposure as the situation demands. I'm the one in charge of my intensity, and not the other way around. Until now I never thought there was an alternative to the extremes—anesthetized or emotionally raw. Now I can see how critical it is for me to protect myself from too much stimulation—especially invasions of negative energy.*

Excitability and sensitivity are genuine gifts. However, like all valuable commodities, gifted intensities must be monitored so it can be allocated wisely. This is why one of the essential parts of self-mastery is to find others like us with whom we can be open and authentic without fear of judgment or reprisal—a peer group in which it's acceptable and normal to go fast, far, and deep. Such validation will make it easier to regulate the outer expression of our intensities with those who don't share our hardwiring. In the same way that we are offended when our intensity is criticized as "too much," we must not disparage others who experience life less intensely. Acceptance is an equal-opportunity issue. Besides, our natural preference for diversity makes this adjustment an unavoidable rung on our ladder of Advanced Development and personal evolution.

Impulsiveness and flightiness have traditionally been confused with a subtrait of gifted intensity: excitability. It is often laced with judgment and misinterpreted as being restless, high-strung, or emotionally combustible. But for the Everyday Genius who manages it, excitability is an invaluable source of enthusiasm, motivation, and empathy that is key to humanistic accomplishment. The importance of excitability cannot be overstated for two fundamental reasons: (1) it is directly and inexorably tied to creative productivity in a cause-and-effect relationship, and (2) it is both a trait and a need. It is because Everyday Geniuses are relentlessly curious, easily aroused, and perennially open to new experience that they are equipped to passionately pursue a wide range of interests. And it is because they feed their need for stimulation that they constantly revitalize their indomitable spirits.

Intensity makes Everyday Geniuses stimulation seekers more than simulation avoiders. For them, life is brimming with possibility, endless avenues of discovery and excitement. With an entire system that is energized and engaged, the life of an Everyday Genius is filled with an unshakable sense of urgency—so many options, so little time.

When the Everyday Genius is well-informed and a prudent self-manager, life can be a series of exciting events that evolve within a deeply meaningful process. Although it rarely happens according to our schedule, mastering our assets puts within reach our willingness to go the distance to achieve our goals. By learning to discriminate between meeting challenges and reckless risk taking, we can make better decisions about when and where to say "stop" or "go" to ourselves. Learning to feel *with* instead of *for* others gives us a chance to be fully and intimately involved without being drained dry. By giving ourselves the authority to protect our sensory systems, we can prevent stimulation overload without the deadness that comes from taking refuge in monotony.

Remember, intensity is not equivalent to being touchy. Rather, it is about being profoundly in touch. If we are too afraid of rejection or betrayal, we can rein in our intense personalities for the sake of conformity. If we throw caution to the wind and let our intense natures run wild, we may find ourselves alienated and sabotaged by our own actions. Unless we learn to regulate our intensities and skillfully channel them, we play a dangerous game of chance, and in the end may lose the chances we deserve.

COMPLEXITY: QUALITATIVELY DIFFERENT

Brain research informs us that it is a random assortment of genes that makes gifted individuals different by design. However, although genetics is a major factor in intelligence and creative abilities as well, "DNA cannot *directly* influence behavior."[3] It is clear that one need not have brilliant parents to be brilliant. Many geniuses emerge from utterly undistinguished families. Underscoring this data is the fact that "[o]f the two dozen most famous mathematicians in the history of the world, all but two were born into families not containing any mathematicians."[4]

There is also a strong link between genetics and all the variables of exceptional ability, including high intelligence and the personality factors of giftedness. When general giftedness is supplemented by special talents, the likelihood of successful application of abilities increases. But here we are faced with an interesting problem. Many gifted children grow up and go through life without demonstrating any unusual creative accomplishments, their exceptional gifts failing to be corroborated by real-life creative contributions. Something else besides raw talent needs to be present if valuable achievement is the expected outcome. And that something else is exceptional motivation or self-contained drive.

Everyday Geniuses have minds that are *qualitatively different* in that they rapidly assess, integrate, and employ information from multiple domains—facts or theories, images or symbols, feelings, intuition, and Divine illumination. Perhaps more than any other trait, complexity makes the internal life of the Everyday Genius dissimilar to that of others. Complexity is the realm of multiple interests, keen self-awareness, intuition, perception, exceptional memory, originality, and compound thinking.

On the positive side of complexity, we find creative thinkers who are high achievers, often in more than one field. Their independent natures allow them to think differently and come up with innovative solutions to break down the barriers of antiquated practices. At the same time, these "idea people" can be socially adept bridge builders, drawing out the best in others and pulling their talents together to achieve a goal.

COMPLEXITY: QUALITATIVELY DIFFERENT

Collapsed	*Exaggerated*	*Balanced*
MULTIPLE INTERESTS		
Feigns fulfillment on a single track; endures monotony	Pressured and overextended in every direction	Renaissance-level creativity; skilled "switch-hitter"
Resists change; stuck in the tried and true; wedded to the obsolete	Information junkie; seduced by novelty	Energized by ideas, research and problem solving; lifelong learner
Talents underdeveloped; tinkerer	Superman or superwoman syndrome; Jack-of-many-trades and "master of all"	Ingenious; excels in several areas; blends skill with finesse
Limited; constrained; stagnant; imperturbable	Erratic or unstable; never finds a niche	Versatile; trailblazer; entrepreneurial
SELF-AWARENESS		
Self-negating or self-loathing	Distorted self-image; grandiose	Honestly introspective; self-knowledgeable
Superficial or shallow; avoids self-examination	Thinks there's no need to change or grow, though others should	Can objectively assess own behaviors and motivations

Fatalistic view of mistakes and failures	Minimizes failings; blames others; doesn't learn from mistakes	Optimistic; accepts self and others as works in progress
Unable to protect self; assailable; prone to self-injurious behaviors	Anxious hypochondriac; compulsive self-evaluation; chronic mental torture	Monitors and maintains health and well-being

INTUITION

Restricts knowledge to what can be "proven"; all-or-nothing thinking	Bypasses common sense; acts on half-baked hunches; distorts reality	Trusts and applies ways of knowing beyond the rational
Distrusts and dismisses extrasensory abilities	Manipulative and unscrupulous use of extrasensory powers	Utilizes integrated extrasensory abilities
Fears the intangible and irrational	Paralyzed by elaborate images, unrealistic ideas, and fanciful pursuits	Appreciates that life doesn't always make immediate sense; honors paradox
Takes everything literally; bounded by concrete experience as ultimate verification	Dwells in figments of the imagination; obsessively superstitious; seduced by false mysticism and occult powers; delusional	Comprehends the seen and unseen worlds; relies on gut feel and a priori knowledge

Collapsed	Exaggerated	Balanced
TRANSCENDENT EXPERIENCE		
Soulless; empty; inner battles between body, mind, and spirit; unprincipled	Neglects real life in favor of the ethereal—lost in the cosmos; excuses bad behavior with spiritual rationalization	Spirit-centered; integrates body, mind, and spirit; dedicated to higher principles
Stunted growth; follows path of least resistance; unfulfilled	Self-improvement junkie; obsessed with psychospiritual "glamours" and power	Enlightened; self-actualizing; steadfastly pursues wisdom
Hollow; lacks inner life; seeks external validation for internal experience	Indiscriminate spiritual faddist; overdependent on spiritual or religious authority figures	Cultivates and values inner guidance; spiritually mature
Unimaginative rationalist; bureaucrat who manufactures red tape and unnecessary policies and systems	Too far out to be trusted; ungrounded magical thinker	Visionary; grounded futuristic thinker; pragmatic idealist
PERCEPTION		
Clouded awareness; distrusts own observations; slow to catch on; tunnel vision	Hypervigilant; trusts no one; randomly scrutinizes everything	Penetrating awareness; keen observation; seasoned discernment

Prosaic; unrefined and uncultured; indifferent to aesthetic forms or motifs	Promotes art for art's sake; settles for bargain-basement appreciation of the arts; discounts and destroys nature or creativity	Prolific creator; appreciates the arts and aesthetics; revitalized by nature and beauty
Stuck in the past; out of step; possibilities immobilized	Fixated on the future and uninformed by the past; misses signals and overlooks the obvious	Fluid processing; integrates past experience with future possibility; one step ahead
Slanted or naive perceptions; unprocessed or incomplete insight; culpable	Exploits awareness of others for own gain; manipulative or Machiavellian	Uses insights for the collective good

EXCEPTIONAL MEMORY

Mind clogged with minutiae; Trivial Pursuit master or detail-obsessed; flood of data camouflages lack of knowledge or truth	Pompous and pontificating know-it-all; mental pack rat	Extraordinary and wide-ranging knowledge base; sharp recall serves as powerful reference tool
"Walking wounded"; constantly relives the past and reopens old wounds; keeps repeating same mistakes	Shuns responsibility; all problems are someone else's fault; projects rage onto others for disappointments and hurt; blames past experience and relationships for current problems	Enriched by reminiscence and introspection; capable of self-healing; values life lessons derived from past experience

Collapsed	Exaggerated	Balanced
Avoids in-depth analysis; Pollyannaish; unrealistic or incomplete thinking	Consumed by racing or overwhelming thoughts; fretful worrywart	Skillfully manages thought processes; expert synthesizer
Trifling or narrow-minded; selective memory; valuable ideas dismissed prematurely	Flooded with random ideas and images; unable to identify salient information	Reexamines history and retains key ideas for future application

ORIGINALITY

Collapsed	Exaggerated	Balanced
Threatened by uncertainty and unpredictability; rushes to restrict or suppress emerging ideas	Indulges tangents or confuses distraction with productive process	Comfortable with ambiguity; willing to let ideas evolve and mature
Constantly revisits same ideas; goes round and round	Hooked on novelty—"the latest thing"; fosters whim without wisdom	Advances and implements innovative ideas
Dogmatic and demands instant results; undermines innovation with impatience	Thrives on chaos and confusion; feeds off perpetual drama	Accepts process; understands chaos is prerequisite for creative accomplishment
Wedded to mindless simplicity; distrusts fresh ideas	Overcomplicates everything; rushes ahead with undeveloped ideas	Distinguishes "different and valuable" from "simply different"; artfully applies the simple and elegant solution

COMPLEX THINKING

One-dimensional or dead-end thinking; repetitive or illogical	Analysis without end; no closure	Outstanding problem solver; enjoys research, analysis, and theoretical constructs
Relies on uniform solutions for *all* problems; glosses over complex interrelationships; cannot detect or analyze complex analogies	Assumes faulty connections; forces connections and premature closure; demands for consensus result in mediocrity	Detects patterns and relationships; efficiently stores huge amounts of data; bridges the abstract and concrete
Slow to process; more cogitation is always better; exasperated decisions	Finds problems everywhere; careless analysis and hastily drawn conclusions	Naturally inquisitive; rapid conceptualization; draws sound conclusions; effective truth seeker and problem finder

The force of complexity comes from a mixture of multilevel thinking and penetrating insight that reaches far beyond hard facts and visible evidence. In many ways the foundation of exceptional insight is the strength that comes from having second sight or intuition. The transpersonal and spiritual realms are therefore naturally inviting, if not irresistible, areas of exploration for the gifted. At the gut level they know that there is more than meets the eye.

Before we delve into the more abstract regions of Everyday Genius thought processes, let's examine their fundamental analytical style. Scientific studies reveal that gifted individuals process information differently. In short, their minds operate more efficiently—less energy is needed for them to operate without sacrificing high performance levels and accuracy.

Research on "gifted thinking" identifies seven overlapping ways in which the gifted differ from others:[5]

- They recall more information and know it better than others, adeptly referencing and selectively applying prior knowledge.
- They are more "mindful" in that they expertly monitor, correctly evaluate, and effectively steer their own thinking (metacognition) for fewer errors and greater performance.
- They require less time to identify the task at hand and find problems, which means they have to spend less time on lower-order planning (basic operations) and can spend more time on higher-order problem solving.
- They do better at excluding irrelevant data, work with less need for assistance, and master skills more quickly.
- They employ intricate strategies (for example, shifting between verbal and visual procedure or right brain/left brain) as warranted to avoid trial-and-error methods or guessing.
- Their thinking is flexible (which many researchers consider the central factor in creativity), permitting them to reinterpret problems by "seeing" alternative strategies, especially when success is dependent on change. This is one of the most notable characteristics of outstanding mathematicians.
- They prefer complexity and demanding problems, and welcome ambiguity, which allows them to go farther with innovation and the development of expertise. Gifted people often introduce complexity to games and stories to enliven their experience. Many

eminent architects and artists seem to thrive in a rich, busy, abstract atmosphere.

Let me mention here that there is little evidence to support the popular belief that the more creative or brilliant one is, the more neurotic one inevitably becomes. Contrary to common cultural myths, geniuses are not destined to be eccentric or crazy. Yet with of all the media-driven stereotypes of the mad scientist and temperamental artist, gifted people secretly harbor a fear of falling into madness (or being judged mad) if they allow themselves to live authentically. It is little wonder so many gifted adults go to great lengths to conceal or deny the depth and breadth of their abilities.

In fact, the "smart = crazy" notion makes little sense given the fact that psychosis destroys creative productivity. Studies confirm that highly creative, bright people are very inclusive in their thinking, layering ideas with a much broader brush than others. They like to play with remote concepts, abstractions, and unusual associations. But there is a finite difference between stimulating creative thinking and abnormality. While the disturbed mind cannot differentiate, healthy Everyday Genius minds maintain the ability to review thoughts and creative products critically, declining to further consider anything too far-fetched or senseless.[6]

Complexity means having a mind that is always pondering ideas and images. This is good, because originality is an inextricable part of complexity, which in turn is essential for innovation. Having a memory like a video recorder may be tremendously valuable in a classroom, courtroom, laboratory, or brokerage firm. Yet such strengths of mind are not always the qualities that are assigned social merit. Besides having excellent powers of recall for even remote details, Everyday Geniuses also have keen powers of perception. They can see all the layers of meaning in situations and detect undercurrents, falsehood, and symbolism. They readily figure out the motivations of themselves and others, and can be very skilled at helping others understand themselves.

All of these things made Wesley a human reference desk:

Wesley: People come to me for answers and information all the time. Sometimes I'm rankled by others who tend to use me as a walking, talking reference library. It's much easier for them to come to me for a quick fix than to do the work to find out the answers themselves. Mostly, though, I am and will continue to be generous. I don't really mind it except when others think I'm infallible, expecting unflagging competence

*from me. Ironically, because I'm smart and competent, I'm permitted
fewer mistakes than others, and if I don't have all the answers, I'm
looked at like I can no longer be trusted.*

Another subtrait of complexity, *perceptivity,* is an exceptional ability to
cut through the veneer of situations to see the "truth" beneath. Everyday
Geniuses readily comprehend the intricacies of other people's personalities and intentions. Everyday Geniuses with higher levels of perceptivity
rely on their intuitions to inform and guide them. They tend to be open,
honest, outspoken people who are irrepressibly curious and perpetually
analytical, unless they are exceptionally introverted or very wounded.
Their uncanny ability to penetrate the outer layers of people and situations
make them excellent religious leaders, therapists, poets, playwrights, biog-
raphers, and photographers. This intuitive force may take them far in their
own development when they apply it to understanding themselves and determining what they really want their life's journey to be.

On the downside, perceptive acuity can make social defenses like
lying and pretense seem unbearable. Nevertheless, the danger is that not
everyone wants to be "known" as quickly or as thoroughly as the gifted
person can size them up. People caught in the Everyday Genius' penetrating awareness can feel uncomfortably exposed. This is especially the
case if less-than-honorable intentions are laid bare by their piercing insight. Hypocrisy and gifted perceptivity are a bad mix. Chloe, a fashion
designer, explained the dilemma:

> *Chloe: Maybe the only thing I'm supposed to be is an invasive news re-
> porter. But in my line of work, being really aware and perceptive isn't al-
> ways a blessing. I get confused when I can "read" things about people that
> are contradictory. It bothers me, and I don't know if I should trust their
> outer face or what I pick up behind it. Besides, even if I hold my tongue, it's
> like people who put up a false front figure out that I know more about them
> than others do. I guess I'd feel threatened, too, if I thought I was that
> transparent, especially if I had something to hide. So what do I do? Pre-
> tend I don't see the whole picture and give some trite response, or drop the
> bomb and reveal what I know? When I'm spontaneous, I tend to stir up
> trouble. If I'm not, I'm the one who feels like a hypocrite.*

Constant demands for honesty and truth can get in our way; so can a
freewheeling intolerance for each and every form of unfairness. If our defenses are too penetrable, acts of injustice take us out of the game. They

sap our strength and cause stressful breakdowns in our emotional stamina, stifling productivity and even impairing our health. By fighting every battle that presents itself, much-needed vitality is drained, often in defense of trivial concerns. Plans and dreams can be stalled by impractical or untimely loyalty to high ideals. Sometimes when we jump onto the bandwagon of "let's make things right," we lose perspective and fail to set important relationships right. This doesn't mean we must throw our convictions out the window. But it does oblige us to make sure our convictions don't burden us with excessive worry, an unwieldy yoke of universal guilt, or existential depression.

Versatility and adaptability are hallmarks of high intelligence and giftedness that also belong to the domain of complexity. These features makes it easy to change directions and reinvest energy whenever something new and intriguing comes along. However, as with all the potent characteristics of Everyday Genius, within this asset lurks the prospect of becoming scattered and depleted. Though an adaptive nature is indispensable in creative excellence and advanced human development, it can also lure one into becoming a jack-of-all-trades and master of none. Juan was very familiar with the hazards of unmanaged versatility:

> *Juan: I detest the word* victim, *but I am one, though not of anyone else's maltreatment. I'm a victim of my own enthusiasm and versatility. I get so interested in things, so eager. It's like being on fire inside. I love that feeling—it's addictive! The energy that comes from being caught up in something new makes me feel like an adventurer who's just made a monumental discovery. When my curiosity takes over, I'm hooked. I love to learn new things and to develop fresh ideas. It's a big part of what makes me who and what I am.*
>
> *But there's this problem; sometimes my energy goes spinning off in a million directions at once. That's right where I get sidetracked, and my hot idea ends up being nothing more than unfinished* soupe du jour. *Likewise, I can be victimized by my own enthusiasm whenever I go off half-cocked to spread my ideas around. Sharing isn't always the best course of action, though for me it's the most natural. I can't tell you the number of times my brainchild proposals have been co-opted by someone else. I don't seem to do a very good job of detecting unscrupulous others who are capable of running off with my ideas for their own profit.*

Reflect on the domain of complexity that consistently upends you as discussed in the previous section. Personalize it, and be careful to credit yourself for the strengths you already have. Remember, each of these traits is an endowed energy source and a powerful asset. Each simply needs to be observed and managed, not eradicated.

Considering this group of traits from the perspective of Evolutionary Intelligence, let's now look at *intuition*. In this context intuition means the ability to see beyond what is rational, obvious, or "provable." Everyday Geniuses are naturally inclined to do so, and need to remind themselves that this is normal. In the past few decades we have been especially mesmerized by laboratory methods, statistics, and hard facts. Fortunately, in recent years we have come to realize that we shortchanged ourselves when we threw out second sight in favor of tangibility.

In the realm of Advanced Development, intuition is a vehicle that can take us deep and far. It takes hunches and gut feelings to new heights and in many ways intuition emerges as a complementary form of intelligence. Nearly every eminent scientist, philosopher, artist, or world leader admits to a strong reliance on their intuitive powers. In this sense its development is a necessary component of Evolutionary Intelligence because it informs our inner vision. Yet, as with all the forces of Everyday Genius, we need to take precautions. Exaggerated reliance on intuitive abilities can trick us into minimizing important facts and logical thinking processes. We can become expert fantasizers drowned in the figments of our imaginations. We can even go so far as to override our sense of responsibility and manipulatively convince others to join us in false mystical practices or acting on half-baked ideas.

And just as intuition allows us to see into things, perception allows us to see through veneers. Here too we must take care to protect ourselves and others. For example, an Everyday Genius with exceptionally penetrating insight who fails to govern it wisely could see innocuous social facades as an abomination, the result being an inability to trust or respect anyone. On the other hand, the collapsed form of this trait might result in someone who is repeatedly thwarted because of blind spots that arise from perceptions that are constantly discounted or overruled. Such constraint not only weakens a powerful asset, but does extreme damage to the self-esteem and confidence of the Everyday Genius' exceptional insights.

As you review the last section of the chart, think back to the beginning of the chapter where these traits were defined as keys to self-mastery. Complexity is perhaps the most profound and distinguishing characteristic of Everyday Genius, and must be fully understood and accepted in order to make the most of its extraordinary powers. Look for yourself in these descriptions. Think about particular events in which they come to the forefront of your life. Then, once more, consider how you might make the shift from either the collapsed or the exaggerated form of expression toward the balanced form, which is the key to self-mastery.

DRIVE: MOTIVATIONALLY DIFFERENT

If the traits we have just discussed are the fuel and the flame of Everyday Genius, then drive is the spark that makes it blaze up and venture out into the world. Drive is much more than being unusually ambitious. It is rather a self-contained daemon or guiding inner spirit. Drive is the domain of insatiable curiosity, high standards (perfectionism), perseverance, independence, and self-motivation. The same Sir Francis Galton we met in our earlier discussion of the development of IQ described this motivational difference with penetrating insight when in 1874 he said that in a person of genius, "the ideas come as by inspiration; in other words, his character is enthusiastic, his mental associations are rapid, numerous and firm, and his imagination is vivid, and he is driven rather than drives himself."[7]

The Everyday Genius trait of being a self-starter is usually evident *very* early in children who ask endless questions, stick their fingers into everything, seek out challenges without urging, enjoy and often prefer self-directed learning, and seem to relish competing with and besting themselves. Many gifted children are driven to explore their world and the inner landscape of their creative minds in solitude. While the parents of the gifted child may be upset about this—fearing the child is miserably lonely or sure to become a recluse—research tells us the child is quite content.

Even when the Everyday Genius is a youngster, it is obvious that there is always a goal just ahead. For all but those who are severely thwarted in their development, the drive to discover, learn, develop expertise, and produce creatively continues throughout life, even when the finite goal remains unclear for many years. A commanding sense of personal destiny propels even the most perplexed Everyday Genius forward. For many, it takes years for this cycle to reach the turning point, or crystallizing experience, that codifies special abilities and clarifies a personal mission. And yet, despite the obscurity of the intended path,

DRIVE: MOTIVATIONALLY DIFFERENT

Collapsed	*Exaggerated*	*Balanced*
INSATIABLE CURIOSITY		
Indifferent and lax	Impulsive; invasive or nosy	Versatile and engaged
Ineffective decision maker; avoids information gathering	Overresearches and can't decide; ruminates after decisions are made	Adventurous and inquisitive; capable of doing many things competently
Uninformed; narrow	Overextended; lacks expertise	Innovative; diverse competencies
Involves nobody; underestimates collaboration	Involves everybody; overestimates collaboration	Good collaborator; knows when to work together and alone
HIGH STANDARDS		
Chronic procrastinator; wavering and unprincipled	Chronic perfectionist; stubbornly holds out for perfection and loses ground	Holds firm to visions of the ideal; discerningly pushes for excellence; lives by solid standards
Uncertain; acquiesces prematurely	Constantly critical and dissatisfied; intolerant; demands instant gratification	Broad-minded; acquiesces; accepts the step-by-step process of success, excellence, and wisdom
Disorganized and inefficient; erratic or aimless	Obsessed with systems and orderliness; trapped in methods and overplanning	Master of organization and discipline; order is balanced with creative freedom

Self-denigrating; lowers standards to fit in	Governed by strong opinions; self-serving and unbending	Takes a stand; willing to go against the grain when necessary

EXCEPTIONAL PERSEVERANCE

Good starter, bad finisher; low self-esteem; underachiever; chronically behind schedule	Rushes to finish; self-worth directly tied to achievement; constant one-upmanship	High achiever; internal sense of self-worth; supports achievements of others
Terrified of setbacks; doesn't know when to start	Terrified of wasting time; doesn't know when to quit	Resolved and ready; superb time manager
Gives up too early; lacks competitive edge	Sticks it out no matter what; neglects health and relationships	Manages obstacles and setbacks; knows when to persist and when to let go
Too malleable; easily defeated	Can't shift in midstream	Resilient and self-directed
Avoids hard work; trades actualization for ease	All work and no play; confuses labor with life—"I work, therefore I am."	Balances work and play; achievement remains part of larger picture

INDEPENDENCE

Dependent and conforming; limits own independence	Rigid and controlling; limits others' independence	Self-reliant; regulates needs of self and others
Easily controlled; buries beliefs and aspirations	Resists input and advice; insists on reinventing the wheel	Selectively autonomous

Collapsed	Exaggerated	Balanced
Codependent and needy; avoids autonomy to feel protected	Solitary and obstinate; avoids closeness to maintain control	Mutually independent in relationships; individuality enhances intimacy
Fears risk; hides out in the safe life	Reckless and confrontational; mistakes the risky for the creative	Flexible and unconstrained; takes reasonable risks

SELF-MOTIVATION

Collapsed	Exaggerated	Balanced
Needs permission and continual reassurance; chronically doubtful	Never seeks guidance; chronically overconfident	Guidance from within; able to reassure self and others
Self-sabotaging; lacks internal resources	Contrary or obstinate; lacks external resources	Resourceful; skilled at sustaining energy and renewing enthusiasm
Waits to be pushed and then resents it; lacks initiative; frustrates others	Pushy and headstrong; jumps in too soon; demoralizes others	Confident self-starter; skillful motivator of others
Distrusts self; operates via external rule	Egocentric; operates via rigid, self-serving rules	Self-trusting; operates via inner rule

the daemon seems to have something specific in mind, which is why we go forward on leaps of faith. As soon as one goal is reached, another is set.

In this sense, being driven is a good sign, since it means our personalities and talents are beginning to become more integrated, and we are learning to cooperate with all of our forms of insight and direction. This particular kind of motivation not only brings the best of Everyday Geniuses to the forefront, but also often means that their zeal to achieve is infectious. Everyday Geniuses high on this trait tend to be vibrant people of substance who make outstanding teachers, such as Helen Keller; social reformers, such as Florence Nightingale; or physicians, such as C. J. Peters, whose work at the Centers for Disease Control is dedicated to studying the world's deadliest viruses, including Ebola.

Perseverance is an important part of being motivationally different. Everyday Geniuses tend to stick to tasks long after others would settle for lesser results. There seems to be an internal yardstick that measures efforts, sounding the all-clear only when the inner vision is realized, and not a moment before. To balance the forces of exceptional drive and to stay the high-potential course, several management tools are required. Perhaps the most critical adjustment comes from learning how to stop being our own worst critic. The internal damage done by self-criticism is enormous, as insufficient self-confidence is a heartless assassin of creative contribution. Nothing vigorous or daring stems from an interior plagued with misgiving and self-inflicted censure. Like so many Everyday Geniuses, Harriet was cognizant of the fact that she could be her own worst enemy:

> Harriet: I know it's bad for me, but I can't seem to help it. The slightest setback or blunder and my mind is racing with a wild flow of cutting remarks from me about me—"You stupid jerk! Why don't you get hold of yourself, take a little advice now and then? Always have to do everything yourself, don't you? Perfectionist one minute, dawdler the next. Get real! If you're going to be such a procrastinator, forget about all those pie-in-the-sky dreams and plans." That's how it goes, only a whole lot faster. No wonder I wallow in self-doubt all the time.

At first, even though they may have a vague sense of calling or personal mission, most Everyday Geniuses don't know the source of their drives. Whether they're moved to design houses, invent, compose, save lives, or produce Nobel prize–winning economic theory, they have a need to know and a need to go. Sometimes they are motivated by the same things that draw out the efforts of others—awards, money, prestige, power. More than one gifted adult has heard, "You're supposed to be so smart, so why aren't you rich and famous?" Truth be told, fame and riches are hardly ever the primary goals. The actual goal is rather enigmatic, and the closest we get to articulating it may be found in the exhilaration of discovery and mastery—locate the mountain and then climb it—and the distinct sense that some paramount sense of accountability has been satisfied.

As always, there's a catch. Unmanaged drive can swallow us whole. Unless we are consciously aware and in charge of ourselves, it is all too easy to let our single-minded zeal keep us awake all night, too busy to eat or talk to friends or family, even too absorbed to know what day it is. Sometimes with a lot of caffeine or by deliberately overriding other stimuli, this kind of total engrossment can go on for days, weeks, and months, until the project is finished.

Often Everyday Geniuses are overwhelmed by their own drive, especially if they can envision going down multiple paths of endeavor and have the talent to match. They are indeed pressured from the inside by an odd mixture of excitement and anxiety. In many respects we are happiest when we are making forward progress in our latest theater of operations, and miserable or short-tempered if our mission is interrupted or terminated against our will. Underneath it all, untapped motivation produces tension, and hostility builds toward whatever impedes the process. As one of my clients said: "When this happens, it's pressure-cooker time—all heated up with no release valve. It's awful! But when it works, when creative juices flow and the pieces of a project come together, it's heaven on earth."

Though for most of us our exact life mission is obscure for a long time, pressure from our inner agenda does not disappear. This pressing inner agenda is both commanding and seductive. It is analogous to the enchantress or the captivating hero, and it contains the allure of the love affair. In a very real sense, to scorn it is to wantonly disown our very destiny. Unclear and unavoidable the goal may be, but its realization is not effortless. On a good day, setbacks can be taken as challenges, hurdles to be conquered.

Harvey experienced the motivational pull of setback. He also found that a steady mix of drive and frustration on the bad days could be the harbinger of burnout. It wasn't until he hit his mid-forties that Harvey realized even he had limitations. Over the years he worked for a large manu-facturing company, Harvey had managed to develop a human resources division that focused on human ecology—the support and development of individual talent within the organization. Maintaining management support for his team's objectives in today's bottom-line market was no small feat. Harvey was increasingly obliged to lobby for his interests and those of his coworkers, who knew their satisfying careers could easily turn into the chores of a bean-counter.

Harvey's low frustration tolerance for obstacles had never been a se-rious problem in the past. He always prevailed in the face of problems, usually with reasonably small amounts of personal angst. Lately, he had been uncharacteristically bothered by interruptions and questions. He felt invaded by the same associates who had at one time been his office buddies. Although his mental dedication to his goals remained strong, Harvey's private world was crumbling. In the face of faltering company support for the humane and ultimately cost-effective objectives of his group, he redoubled his already ardent concentration. He had always been able to throw himself completely into a project, pressing himself to stay on task long after others had gone home.

Contrary to his gospel of balance, Harvey's intensified response side-tracked him. He began to neglect his wife and children and resigned from his community hospital board position to spend more time at work. He convinced himself he had to override his health needs and family re-sponsibilities. Since he had never hit the wall before, Harvey believed he could push his colleagues and his family as far as he could push him-self. Nothing and no one would get in his way. By blindly persevering, Harvey let his powerful goal orientation take over. He couldn't let go, and he couldn't see the red flags.

The only one who was surprised when Harvey's wife filed for divorce, his health began to fail, and his world fell apart was Harvey. His relent-less drive had driven out his happiness. In aching despair, Harvey im-plored: "How can this be? What happened? How could all my hard work and good intentions—doing it right—turn out so wrong?"

As you review the chart on drive, think about how the Everyday Genius subtraits of drive explain the impetus of the push for excellence. Drive is fundamental to Advanced Development particularly because the journey is often long and hard. Yet in terms of Evolutionary Intelligence, even excep-tional drive alone is never enough. As you look over the chart and plot where you are in terms of overregulated and underregulated expressions of energy, ask yourself questions that will form a framework for the higher level of drive needed to make the leap into Revolutionary Action.

Think about the difference between basic drive and Mandated Mission, the latter being powered by the integrated forces of the combined elements of Multiple Intelligences, Gifted Traits, and Advanced Development. As you determine which subtraits hold you back from the fulfillment of your potential, you'll want to review the first two sections of the Big Three Differences, considering how they interact in your daily life. You may even decide to target the top three subtraits whose imbalanced expressions require your most immediate attention. After you prioritize, allow yourself time. Important changes are never quick or easy—even for Everyday Geniuses.

14

SELF-MASTERY: MANAGING INTENSITY, COMPLEXITY, AND DRIVE

I get up every morning determined both to change the world and have
one hell of a good time. Sometimes, this makes planning the day
difficult.   —E. B. White

We have now learned how Intensity, Complexity, and Drive operate as the primary forces in the Everyday Genius personality. We have seen how these traits can be played out in a wide range of behavior. Since Intensity, Complexity, and Drive are the springboard for Advanced Development, we have no reasonable choice but to learn to consciously harness the tremendous power of these characteristics.

The inner, not outer, rule is our true objective, so self-mastery is the only vehicle that will allow us to fulfill our promise. Intensity, Complexity, and Drive become personal strengths not through self-denial, self-willed overcontrol, or self-aggrandizement, but through understanding the underlying dynamics that drive these characteristics.

No matter how you approach it, the Everyday Genius' innate drive for perfection and heightened sensitivity affects everything we think and do. Underlying every dimension of who we are, at the very core of our being, is our attachment to perfection. We cannot help but see what's wrong when compared to what could be because we feel more intensely than the average person. When something strikes us as not quite right, we experience a myriad of emotions. In turn, these powerful feelings command our attention and trigger our impulse to react more strongly and more often than others.

Mastering Intensity, Complexity, and Drive is rooted in our ability to understand the relationship between our traits, abilities, needs, feelings, and impulses. Mastery is at the heart of our commitment to self-management. And because self-mastery rests on managing the forces of ICD, we need an efficient working model and specific tools to shift from being emotion-driven to becoming the master of our feelings. To start and to finish the process of self-mastery, we must revive our natural optimism.

THE DRIVE TO
PERFECT VERSUS PERFECTIONISM

We may be able to master our ICD traits, but we must also learn to simply accept our First Nature traits—heightened receptivity and the urge to perfect. Since our natural ability to envision the ideal initiates exceptionally high standards, and because the pressure to improve is the central line of our being, our First Nature is a force that must be both understood and honored. Although no Everyday Genius honestly expects to reach ultimate perfection, each of us is so hardwired to identify problems and see solutions that we can push ourselves harder and farther than most to bring our dreams into reality. Contrary to some psychological theories, a perfection orientation is not dysfunctional and not equivalent to compulsive perfectionism. A wholly negative view of the drive toward perfection is a troubling distortion of its original meaning, the definition that describes this trait in the Everyday Genius.

The descriptor *perfect* is perhaps best defined by the maxim "A thing is perfect insofar as it is actual." Striving for relative perfection here on earth is an old idea. It goes all the way back to the Latin root of our word *perfection*, meaning to fully or thoroughly carry out, make, or do. By extension, this accounts for our persistence toward fully developing our distinctly human capacities. In the Aristotelian sense, perfection is a powerful goal orientation or personal mission called *entelecheia*. Hegelian ethics of the nineteenth century redefined perfection as being intent on wholeness, not unlike our focus on fulfillment of high potential. The individual mind is considered an instrument of the universal source, which presses forward from potential to actualization, from separateness to union with the whole of existence.

In dictionaries of psychological, religious, and philosophical words, *perfect* means "complete in all respects; whole; having all the actual qualities and good attributes that are proper to its nature or type; fully actualized; fulfilled; finished; at its proper and natural end; without qualification or restriction." The aim of perfection is to fill in what is incomplete—to apply knowledge, wisdom, and power toward a meaningful and rightful purpose. Perfection is the consummation of all the unique properties of one's true nature, enacted toward its intended goal.

Research shows that pathologically perfectionistic standards are *not* directly related to being gifted. Instead of being pathologically obsessive or compulsive, perfectionism can be the basis of excellence. It can also be viewed as being loyal to the development and fulfillment of one's special gifts. When personal motives and high standards are intended for the greater good, the objective is laudable even if their realization may be subject to ignorance or human limitation along the way.

Perfectionism can easily become a curse when it takes high standards out of the realm of the ideal and into unproductive excess. Unhealthy perfectionism is really a variation on the all-or-nothing theme. No matter how difficult or great the accomplishment, it isn't enough. What we do is *never* good enough, according to perfectionistic criteria.

When relating their histories, Everyday Geniuses with unmanaged perfectionistic tendencies tell their life stories in terms of disappointment, unfairness, and emptiness, throwing in only a few glossed-over winning moments here and there. Although this might be an accurate assessment for an unfortunate few, it is unlikely the majority of days in most people's lives have been so negative. In fact, when these same clients are asked to look back over their lives and recall the number of uneventful or average days, they are consistently unable to do so. Selected superior achievements and mistakes are marked with neon yellow, while start-and-stop progress and small accomplishments get rubbed out. With such a faulty memory bank, they may falsely conclude they have accomplished little.

When high standards are always on the rise, goals become unreachable. When perfectionism rules, we increase self-restraint instead of expanding our freedom of action and expression, believing the answer to every problem is more rigid self-discipline. Our lives become predictable and limited, too tight on the outside and on the inside; a great deal of satisfaction is cast aside when daily pleasures are denied because they do not contribute to visible accomplishments.

ENDING THE PERFECTIONISM/PROCRASTINATION
SEESAW: READY, SET, GO!

Everyday Geniuses may be experts at systematizing but are often over-attached to rules and order. This trait is not the security blanket it appears to be. Rules and order alone cannot bring stability to the uncertainty of our lives. A more solid approach is to develop a method of working that sidesteps obsessive overresearching and overpreparing. Structure does possess the almighty jurisdiction to control all uncertainty and doubt, but it can destroy creative freedom, enjoyment, and, strangely, even achievement itself. Whenever there is too much structure, there is stricture and rigidity.

Perfection is an honorable goal, though it is rarely found in the real world. Perfectionism problems emerge when we forget this and try to force perfection into situations where it will not occur. Waiting for the perfect answer, the comfortable decision that will please everyone, frequently raises anxiety and lowers self-confidence while real choices dwindle in number. Franklin Roosevelt once commented: "One thing is sure. We have to do something. We have to do the best we know how at the moment. . . . If it doesn't turn out right, we can modify it as we go along."

Skillful decision making is an antidote to perfectionism and an ally for our drive to perfect. Mastering our drive to perfect requires us to retain ideals but get off the perfectionism/procrastination seesaw. To consciously master our perfection desires, we must repeatedly ask ourselves three big-picture questions that force us to concentrate on the essentials—*purpose, quantity*, and *quality*:

- "What is the overall goal?" State this goal in a clear single sentence.
- "To what degree will more preparation or fine-tuning help me meet the desired deadline?" Estimate how much your chances of delivering in a timely manner will be increased.
- "How much would I bet that doing more at this stage will strikingly improve the outcome?" Assign a dollar amount to your projection.

The specific formula for ending the perfectionism/procrastination seesaw does not permit us to get trapped in "ready, ready, ready" mental gymnastics, putting our dreams on the "someday" shelf. Nor can we sit around in "ready, set, set" like a racehorse held at the starting gate. However, springing off at "go" without being ready or set is like jumping off a cliff and expecting a miracle.

Skillful decision making moves us out of the feeling and impulse range that often entraps us in pointless rumination. To help us objectify the problem, we can outline the essential factors and apply numbers. A skillful decision can usually be accomplished in just three stages: (1) determine essential factors in the decision, (2) assign each factor a weight, (3) do the arithmetic: multiplication + addition = decision. READY, SET, GO!

Most decisions are so inconsequential we don't even label them decisions. We have no trouble with that kind of choice. In fact, when the pros and cons to each option are about equal, "yes" can seem just as reasonable as "no." Instead, we can borrow principles from complex decision theories, simplify them, and use them to make quicker work of deciding, thereby minimizing the "ready, set" phases and saving our vigor for the action stage. One such method is suggested in Mary Kellogg's *Hard Choices, Easy Decisions*. It's a good fit for the fast-paced Everyday Genius life.

READY . . . To get ready, start with the information you have at the time. Gather more information only if it is absolutely necessary. Start by identifying the important factors. Be sure they are the factors important to you, not someone else. List the factors in priority order, with the most important at the top.

SET . . . Next, assign each prioritized factor a numerical value from 1 to 10, depending on how important each is to you, with 10 being the most important and 1 the least important. Question the value you assign to each factor, making sure you are being true to your own needs, preferences, and convictions, not just to socialized rules. Then, using what you have learned from the data you gathered, consider the first of your options and what you think it has to offer in terms of the first of the previously determined factors. Assign that first option a number from 1 to 10 in that regard. Continue assigning each option a number for each factor. When you have done this, you are now set to finalize your decision.

GO! . . . When you have finished assigning values, multiply the original weight for each factor by the number you have assigned each option for that factor. Add up the new, multiplied totals. (See the example below.) You can then objectively compare the outcomes. You may be surprised at the results, choosing to reconsider the weights you assigned, or you may become even more confident about your original choice. This method allows you to stop the pendulum of "maybe yes, maybe no." You'll also run less risk of running out of time and rushing a decision that may backfire.

If your results seem inaccurate, check your original priorities. Maybe you've been fooling yourself about what is important to you. If so, try again with adjusted factors. Usually through this process, or a similar procedure, the goal—that is, the decision—surfaces. Rather than worrying about the process and going in circles, you're able to fire with the greatest accuracy you can muster, without missing the target of opportunity altogether.

The ready-set-go method is similar for examining problems related to each ICD trait. For practice, let's look at a problem rooted in a subtrait of intensity, excitability: "This job offer that came out of the blue seems so exciting—I need a change—but I'd have to move and the pay wouldn't be much better."

READY . . .
List the most important factors in random order.

> Opportunity for increased career challenge
> Opportunity for career advancement
> Interesting work
> Close to relatives
> Interesting colleagues at work
> Positive work atmosphere
> Salary and benefits package
> Positive work relationships
> Safety of location
> Access to important amenities and resources
> Cost of living
> Beauty of surroundings
> Availability of suitable housing

List the most important factors in ranked order.

Most important factors in ranked order	Factor weight (0–10)
Safety of location	10
Positive relationships	10

Cost of living	9
Availability of suitable housing	8
Interesting work	8
Positive work atmosphere	7
Salary and benefits package	6
Close to relatives	5
Opportunity for increased career challenge	5
Opportunity for career advancement	4
Interesting colleagues at work	3
Access to important amenities and resources	2
Beauty of surroundings	1

SET . . .

Assign each factor a number (0–10) to indicate its relative weight of importance. (See right-hand column above.) Then provide a column for each option (two in this case: #1—stay in the current situation, #2—move to accommodate the new job). From what you know of about each option, estimate (0–10) what each option has to offer you for every listed factor.

Factors in ranked order	Factor weight	Option # 1	Option # 2
Safety of location	10		
Positive relationships	10		
Cost of living	9		
Availability of suitable housing	8		
Interesting work	8		
Positive work atmosphere	7		
Salary and benefits package	6		
Close to relatives	5		
Opportunity for increased career challenge	5		
Opportunity for career advancement	4		
Interesting colleagues at work	3		
Access to important amenities and resources	2		
Beauty of surroundings	1		

GO!

Now that you have finished assigning values, multiply the original weight for each listed factor times the values assigned to each option by going across the columns. Multiply each factor in the same way, entering the products next to each of the two option columns.

Factors in ranked order	Factor weight	Option # 1	Option # 2
Safety of location	10	$\times\ 7 = 70$	$\times 9 = 90$
Positive relationships	10	$\times 10 = 100$	$\times 3 = 30$
Cost of living	9	$\times\ 4 = 36$	$\times 7 = 63$
Availability of suitable housing	8	$\times\ 9 = 72$	$\times 9 = 72$
Interesting work	8	$\times\ 6 = 48$	$\times 9 = 72$
Positive work atmosphere	7	$\times\ 4 = 28$	$\times 8 = 56$
Salary and benefits package	6	$\times\ 8 = 48$	$\times 7 = 42$
Close to relatives	5	$\times\ 3 = 15$	$\times 9 = 45$
Opportunity for increased career challenge	5	$\times\ 2 = 10$	$\times 7 = 35$
Opportunity for career advancement	4	$\times\ 3 = 12$	$\times 5 = 20$
Interesting colleagues at work	3	$\times\ 7 = 21$	$\times 9 = 27$
Access to important amenities and resources	2	$\times\ 9 = 18$	$\times 5 = 10$
Beauty of surroundings	1	$\times\ 8 = 8$	$\times 4 = 4$
		486	566

Add the products listed in each of the two column options and enter the sum below each. Now you have relatively objective, weighted data analysis to assist you in making a decision and move on. If the results are a toss-up, let your intuition guide you. If the numbers seem incorrect, go back through the steps to ascertain if you prioritized and assigned values as accurately as possible.

Even if you decide to discard this analysis and follow your gut instinct, you've still put indecision to rest. Perhaps this is the best way at times. Last year a client agonized over whether to accept a promotion and move to Denver, or marry and stay in Minneapolis. After months of indecision, she agreed to use this systematic approach. She discovered she was trying too hard to please everyone and hoping to avoid the discomfort of choosing. When we last met, she exclaimed with tremendous relief and confidence, "As soon as I saw those numbers at the bottom, I thought, 'Forget all that.' I knew I had really decided a long time ago. I was just trying to be totally sure. I don't care how all those logical factors add up, I feel good about my decision, and I'm getting married!"

Never confuse busy activity with meaningful action, or contemplation with efficiency. Business writer David Mahoney sums it up this way: "There comes a moment when you have to stop revving up the car and shove it into gear."[1] Remember, individuality and autonomy cannot exist in the Everyday Genius life without coming to terms with the fact that no matter what we do someone will not like it. We must determine our own individual standards that feel right for us even if others disagree.

MANAGING FEELING

As we know, Everyday Geniuses are hot receptors. That's just the way it is. But we can learn to consciously decide when to react, how much to react, and when not to react at all. It is up to us to adjust our lives and temper our reactivity to avoid unnecessary conflict, burnout, and wasteful allotment of our much-needed energy reserves. Though thousands of years of instinct and genetics have shaped our acute responsiveness and intense emotions, we can learn to separate impulse from automatic reactions.

First, it helps to learn how to accurately label what we feel—to apply the right words to our experience. This is often difficult, however, since feelings tend to come in packages. But with practice, we can use our analytical minds and verbal acuity to distinguish between more than "glad, mad, sad, or bad" feelings. By being clearer about our feelings, we greatly increase the chance that our emotions and our actions will be in agreement, not at odds with one another.

For example, if we feel something strongly, instantly interpret it as anger, and immediately act out our emotions, we may indeed be expressing ourselves authentically and appropriately. Upon further self-inquiry, we may realize that we have learned to respond to fear with anger, acknowledge our feeling as fear instead of anger, and therefore decide to choose a new and more appropriate response. By pinning down our emotional responses and choosing how or if to respond, we develop an accurate match between inner feeling and outward expression, a positive sign of both authenticity and Advanced Development.

Review the following list of feelings and notice the category each emotion falls into. Then look back over the list as you ask yourself: "Which emotions are easiest for me to express in mature ways?" Also select feelings to which you respond to in a less mature, reactive fashion. Be certain to note which feelings you suppress entirely.

Event-driven hurt feelings: sorrow, grief, hopelessness, loss, abandonment, loneliness, sadness, rejection, depression

Self-directed hurt feelings: shame, regret, guilt, self-loathing, worthlessness, self-degradation, loss of energy, depression

Angry feelings: irritation, annoyance, frustration, hostility, rage, hatred, disgust, submission, resentment, rivalry, defiance, condemnation, contempt, depression

Fearful feelings: panic, dread, suspicion, distrust, jealousy, worry, nervousness, foreboding, butterflies in the stomach, muscle tightness, tension headaches, muddled thinking, powerlessness

Heartwarming feelings: fondness, affection, closeness, trust, common bond, empathy, joy, serenity, confidence, eagerness, transcendence, insight, compassion, appreciation, wonder, love, respect, honor, gratitude, reverence, universality, benevolence, determination, purpose, value, meaning

Reflect on the internal messages you experience related to these feelings. Are some of them still distorted in false-self thinking? Be especially mindful of the following automatic reactions: defensiveness, isolation, silent contempt, tantrums, coercion, and disowning feelings by intellectualizing them. Review Chapter One to get a clearer picture of how the subtraits of Intensity, Complexity, and Drive are manifested in you and how you tend to react. Then ask yourself what it would take for you to achieve the balanced version of each subtrait. Look for new ways to respond instead of simply reacting—modified responses that could make you feel better, more in control, and yet allow you to be open and available to others without being naively vulnerable.

It is clear to us that our zest for new experiences can make life an exciting adventure. But unmanaged feelings and impulses exaggerate our need for intensity and send things quickly spinning out of control. Only when we understand how we become victims of our own enthusiasm can we come to grips with the fact that our energy reserves are not bottomless. We must admit that our legendary verve can leave us burned out, and that scurrying about can detour us from realizing our most important dreams.

An effective measuring tool for examining reactivity is the "marshmallow test," devised by Walter Mischel. In *Emotional Intelligence*, Daniel Goleman employs Mischel's test as a method of measuring the essence of emotional self-regulation: the ability to deny impulse in the service of a goal, whether building a business or pursuing the Stanley Cup. Goleman explains the need for goal-directed self-imposed delay of gratification this way:

> Just imagine you're four years old, and someone makes the following proposal: If you'll wait until after he runs an errand, you can have two marshmallows for a treat. If you can't wait until then, you can have only one—but you can have it right now. It is a challenge sure to try the soul of any four-year-old, a microcosm of the eternal battle between impulse and restraint, id and ego, desire and self-control, gratification and delay. . . . There is perhaps no psychological skill more fundamental than resisting impulse. It is the root of all emotional self-control, since all emotions, by their very nature, lead to one or another impulse to act.[2]

Rather than be overwhelmed by our passions, or steamroll others with them, we must become the masters of our gifts. We must school our feelings, impulses, and perfection orientation and allow them privileges in our lives, not free rein, if they are to serve as the powerful assets they are designed to be.

IMPULSE MANAGEMENT

What is an impulse? It is a sudden and spontaneous urge or inclination that is usually triggered by some short-term change in our external or internal circumstances. The difficulty with impulses is that we are inclined to *act* on them without regard for long-term consequences. Often when we act strictly from impulse, we react in an automatic, irrational manner.

Impulses are directly linked to motivation and drive. They are the activating forces that move our perceptions and ideas forward into reality. Obviously we cannot do without them when they are essential to the realization of our Evolutionary Intelligence. However, we do not want our sensitive nervous systems to compel us into reactivity at every possible whim. Automatically responding to everything that strikes a chord within us turns impulse into potentially harmful impulsivity.

How we handle our daily stimulus overload is a true indicator of how smart we really are. The fact that we are constantly bombarded with both internal and external stimuli—emotions, sensory input, the traffic, interactions with others, and so on—makes us susceptible to reactivity exhaustion. It is too easy to be overwhelmed by this torrent of stimuli. Our ability to identify with the pain of others becomes weighed down by the violence, tragedies, and strife in our world. This cannot be overlooked if we are intent on self-mastery. There are indeed times when we must protect ourselves, especially to avoid carrying the weight of every negative thing that moves us to respond.

Instead of always questioning the impulse behind the reaction, we must do the opposite—understand and accept the impulse yet challenge and question the response before we act. This is the consequential thinking that is key to impulse control: the conscious and rational interpretation of feelings and events, which is also the cardinal rule of cognitive psychotherapy. Events happen and stimuli collide with us all the time; this is something we can only partially control. We must take greater control of how we interpret what triggers and stirs up our emotions. In fact, the mental interpretation of what is happening is frequently the *only* point at which we have any control over our subsequent response. Consequential thinking—the questioning of our reactions—depends on distinguishing *automatic* responses that are irrational from rational responses that reasonably fit the situation at hand. For example:

Consequential Thinking

IMPULSIVITY
> Event: Jack walked by your desk three times today without acknowledging you.
> Automatic Mental Interpretation: "He must be mad at me."
> Corresponding Reaction: Avoid Jack and think badly of him and yourself.

IMPULSE MANAGEMENT

Event: Jack walked by your desk three times today without acknowledging you. [Event is exactly the same]

Automatic Mental Interpretation: "I wonder why Jack didn't say anything. Maybe he's really preoccupied today. Maybe he doesn't
feel well. Perhaps he's annoyed with me for some reason. I really
don't know."

Corresponding Reaction: As soon as possible express your concerns
to Jack and check out his response to the situation. Do not react
at all until you have better information.

Examine the hot reactions that have acquired a familiar pattern in
your life (for example, jealousy, anger, distrust) and which activate deep-
seated feelings that have a particular theme (such as abandonment, rejection, inferiority). For the example above, you might realize you often
react hot to situations that *could be* and *tend to be* interpreted as rejection. That is the central theme, and it is probably tied to old emotional
wounds, which is why those reactions assume control over your psyche in
an exaggerated manner. When you recognize a core theme to your hot reactions, especially if they repeatedly incite self-defeating impulsive behaviors, ask yourself a question like this: "Does this have to be about
rejection? Would ten other people in the same situation see this the same
way I do?"

We owe it to ourselves and others to filter our impulses through rational analysis. Our analytical minds must stay on course and not become illogical or indulge habits of thinking that create unnecessary
dramas. Remember that our emotional state, the viability of our relationships, and our physical well-being are the direct result of our daily
thoughts. None of us can afford to translate merely irritating events into
disasters. We cannot permit such waste of our valuable inner resources.
Our self-mastery must be trained to maintain an optimistic viewpoint by
developing our ability to rationally interpret what we experience both
within and without.

REVIVING YOUR
NATURAL OPTIMISM

Well-developed skills of consequential thinking help us avoid unnecessary upset. This also reopens the channel to the natural optimism of the

Everyday Genius, which often seems to disappear under a layer of emotional wounds or negativity. As healing old wounds renews our strength, confronting adversity is a question of who gives up and who does not. Fortunately, whether we like it or not, giving up is not a part of the Everyday Genius' character. Maintaining the course of full potential is all about staying power. If our high potential is ever to be realized, we have to develop and faithfully maintain an internal style of optimism. In many respects, durable optimism is the source of our staying power.

Fortunately, a sense of optimism is a natural component of the Everyday Genius personality. After all, it is the hope for something better that is the foundation of our Intensity, Complexity, and Drive. Every day in every circumstance we must have access to optimism as a part of our resilience scheme. Optimism is vital to Advanced Development because the barriers to fulfillment of high potential are notoriously fear-based: distrust of self and others, fear of failure, fear of rejection, fear of being hurt, fear of having to admit a mistake, fear of being outdone by another, fear that our most inspired products will be overlooked or exploited in the real world. Yet fear is only as powerful as we allow it to be. Facing fear must be part of our liberation plan, since we can only be truly alive and free to become our Selves when we insist upon viewing our experience through an optimistic lens.

When our ideas take a beating in the external world, we feel alone and unsure. When others misunderstand who we are, we feel alone and unsure. When we are snowed under with projects that are not challenging or interesting, we feel alone and unsure. And above all, when we dare to forge ahead into the new frontier while others around us think we've lost our minds, we feel alone and unsure. These are the challenging times when we must call upon all of our powers of resilience. And these are the times when we are in no position to invent a process. The only smart move is to be proactive—mentally prepared for both positive and negative experiences with new, more resourceful responses. By realistically and optimistically assessing where we are and what we are doing in an integrated way—being both realistic *and* optimistic—we are more likely to stay the course of Advanced Development. We cannot afford to let the pessimistic view prevail, because it reopens the door to the false self and creates another barrier to our progress as we struggle to rid ourselves of its influence.

Resilience in the face of adversity is essential because Advanced

Development cannot occur without encountering obstacles. Peace of mind and purpose depend on being able to attribute meaning to our experiences creatively and positively so we may enjoy the process. Optimism has played an indispensable role in the lives of my clients because they recognize it as the key to future accomplishments and fulfillment. Unfortunately, many of us have lost touch with our natural optimism and need a concrete plan to revive it and keep it alive in our lives.

Martin Seligman, a professor of psychology at the University of Pennsylvania and past president of the American Psychological Association, has studied resilience and the difference between those who cope well with adversity and those who do not. In his groundbreaking book *Learned Optimism*, Seligman shows us the value of understanding adversity and explaining it to ourselves in optimistic rather than pessimistic ways. The critical distinction is one of hope versus depression and can versus can't. Seligman asserts:

> Whether or not we have hope depends on two dimensions of our explanatory style: pervasiveness and permanence. Finding temporary and specific causes for misfortune is the art of hope: Temporary causes limit helplessness in time, and specific causes limit helplessness to the original situation. On the other hand, permanent causes produce helplessness far into the future, and universal causes spread helplessness through all your endeavors. Finding permanent and universal causes for misfortune is the practice of despair. . . . The optimistic style of explaining good events is the opposite of that used for bad events: It's internal rather than external. People who believe they cause good things tend to like themselves better than people who believe good things come from other people or circumstances.[3]

The following chart illustrates the range of Seligman's optimistic and pessimistic styles—the two opposing ways in which we explain adversity and success in our lives. First review the chart, reading from left to right. Compare the differences between the two styles, and look for your own habits of reaction. In the face of obstacles, setbacks, or criticism from others, how do you typically explain events to yourself? When you are successful, how do you explain that to yourself? Don't forget what you have learned about the self-sabotaging role that impostorism plays in the lives of Everyday Geniuses.

Next, reread the chart from top to bottom, starting from the right with the pessimistic viewpoint; then reread it a third time, top to bottom, beginning with the optimistic style. Think about the difference this would make in your inner life if the optimistic way of explaining events prevailed. Consider how it would change your outlook on the future and your view of the past.

EXPLANATORY STYLES
IN THE FACE OF ADVERSITY

OPTIMISTIC STYLE	**PESSIMISTIC STYLE**
Externalized and Impersonal	*Internalized and Personal*
"Other forces were at play here."	"It's my fault."
Temporary	*Permanent*
"This is a small bump in the road."	"This will last forever."
Limited Effect	*Pervasive*
"This won't affect other areas of my life."	"Everything in my life will be negatively affected by this."

IN THE FACE OF SUCCESS

OPTIMISTIC STYLE	**PESSIMISTIC STYLE**
Internal and Personal	*External and Impersonal*
"This is the result of my effort and creativity."	"This was just a lucky break."
Permanent	*Temporary*
"This is one of many successes."	"This is a one-time fluke."
Pervasive	*Limited Effect*
"The effect will ripple through and uplift my life."	"Nothing in the rest of my life will be uplifted by this."

Imagine how much stronger we would feel if we never again badgered ourselves with pessimistic explanations, and how quickly we could spring back into action from setbacks and disappointments. What a difference it makes when ordeals that accompany self-actualization are not exaggerated into catastrophes that undermine our self-confidence and resolve. We must never underestimate the destructive force of negative self-talk. *Learning to manage what we say to ourselves in our head is essential.* Otherwise our normally high Everyday Genius standards and expectations can turn against us, becoming the enemy within. The critical difference between inner encouragement and respectful self-coaching versus self-condemnation or self-abuse is this: No matter how disappointed you may feel, never say anything to yourself in your own mind that you would not say face-to-face to a respected friend.

SMARTER THAN EVER:
BECOMING SUPERCONSCIOUS

One of the hallmarks of physical maturation is gaining mastery over our environment and becoming less dependent on others. The same is true when our gift of self-consciousness matures into superconsciousness. Superconsciousness is a Self-honoring pledge that allows us to gradually shift from *external control* to *inner rule.* If we are determined to assume responsibility for our gifts and our life's work, outer forces can never be the primary control force in our lives. Rather than simply exist as reactionaries with a life plan based on random action, we can adopt a premeditated superconsciousness that promotes the development of Self rule.

Inner rule implies that the integrated Self is more than the sum of its parts. Since each of us has multiple subselves (for example, the arguer, the striver, the thinker, the romantic, the nurturer, the player, the helpless one, and so on), an inner rule must emerge. This inner rule manages the often unruly competing parts of ourselves by choosing who takes center stage at any given moment. Under the liberation management system of inner rule we no longer need to be outwardly defined. The energy that is necessary for creative living need not be wasted on lesser matters. If I *feel* anxious, it no longer means that *I am* powerless; if I *think* I've lost, I am not *a loser.* Should my *body* develop diabetes, *I don't allow* the condition to overtake my identity.

The inner-directed person is always more than mind, body, or spirit could ever be separately. For example, a highly trained, competitive football team understands the value of running certain plays and utilizing the talents of certain players in a given situation. A similar process is employed when the integrated assets of Everyday Genius outperform nearly everyone's expectations. This selective process prompts efficient use of resources and ultimately a synergy of effort that seems to take on a life of its own. The integrated Self feels like and acts like a one-person power-house because its multiple gifts are galvanized in harmony to surpass its own limitations.

Contrary to what might be expected, gifted adults often report feeling as though they are "coming apart." Yet they often fail to understand the origins of their distress. It is frequently a direct response to external rule—changing masks among the different selves to meet the pressures of external demands. During this constant shifting, we often stop short of self-mastery, overlooking the inner self crucial to maturation and effective inner rule. Our potential to influence evolution is hampered by the unfinished business of individuation. For example, if our *feeling* self—intensity—is underrepresented in our daily lives, it follows that we'll experience few sensations. If our *thinking* self—complexity—is under-emphasized, we are set upon a life of stagnating boredom. When the *doing* self—drive—gets short shrift, we do not reach our potential. It is likely that we will come to the end of our lives with a disproportionate share of regret and underachievement.

If we fail to find our inner rule and heed its guidance, we are easy prey to illusion, to maintaining a false view of ourselves, which only guarantees that we will be entangled in mistaken-identity poses for many years into our future. Continuing to shape our opinions and behaviors to fit the conventional mold only avoids conflict with others temporarily, and it dangerously increases our internal conflict because all of our false-self poses are ultimately unfulfilling.

As we piece our divided identities back together, we become reacquainted with our various gifted selves. These fascinating dimensions of ourselves must be allowed to reemerge if we are to intelligently create and maintain inner rule. In a sense, we are holding auditions and viewing tapes of past performances to see which part of ourselves is best suited to take center stage. Inner rule is the host of our *superconsciousness*, the means by which we may strike a balance in our everyday affairs.

Each dimension of the gifted self possesses its own pattern and ultimate purpose, none of which can be decided by another. The pressures of the world that attempt to bind us into a posed self lose their persuasive force with the emergence of healthy inner rule.

No one whose true vision is clear and whose intended mission is undertaken with trust and fervor is ever lost. Gifts of ability and talent need not be doubted or hidden because they follow the instructions that came with the package. The true vision of ourselves is enacted in a decision to perfect the match between *being* and *doing*. A finely wrought marriage of ability and endeavor is feasible for those seekers of self-actualization who are prepared to cooperate with the Creator's blueprint for evolution.

FROM STRESS TOLERANCE TO STRESS MANAGEMENT

Business writer Joel Rutledge investigated the "uncommon path to success," observing:

> When life begins, God takes this huge jigsaw puzzle with a zillion pieces in it, messes it all up, and throws the pieces into a box called "your life." Most think the object of life is to painstakingly put that puzzle together with great solemnity—thinking that there is only one way to make it fit. We're all hoping to get that big prize at the end of the rainbow.
>
> But the truth is, there are a zillion ways to put your puzzle together—and you get to make it up as you go along! From what I can tell, God often throws two or three puzzles in the same box, depending on what you need to learn at this particular point in time. . . . And if we're not having any fun putting it together, then it's time to mess it up one more time and put the fun back in.[4]

Your mental, physical, relational, and spiritual furnace needs to be stoked with more than tasks and paychecks. To live with passion while eluding the tragedies of heart disease, debilitating anxiety, severe headaches, back problems, hostility, depression, and sleep disturbances—to name a miserable few—you will need to get serious about loosening up.

If that sounds contradictory, that's because it is. The easiest way to bring your life into balance is to think in terms of opposites. In fact, this investment in balance parallels Sir Isaac Newton's third law of motion, which generally states that for every *type* of action, there needs to be an equally intense and opposite *type* of reaction. For example, if you do physical labor all day as a construction worker or sculptor, it stands to reason that your hands and body need a rest while your mind and spirit revitalize. Consider rejuvenating through a game of chess, a dance class, or listening to music, instead of watching hours of mindless TV after dinner. If you're a trial lawyer who is besieged with words, debate, and adversarial gamesmanship during work hours, a quiet and unstructured trip to the local nature center may fill the bill.

Remember that neither sleep nor couch-potato inertia reduces stress in any real way. If you take your unresolved stress and imbalance to bed or the couch, it will still be there when you get up. But you will become an expert at managing stress rather than tolerating it if you release your stress and replace it with revitalizing situations that complement your customary routine.

An accomplished businessman, Earl, came to my office one day, quite ashamed of asking for help. He was a proud man of sixty-two who had worked for many years to establish his lucrative hardware business. Recently he had been sleeping poorly and worrying a great deal. His physicians declared him to be moderately fit, but they warned him of potential depression or stress-related physical illness. Going against the grain of his self-reliant, Scandinavian background, Earl decided to take a chance on professional help to regain a sense of balance in his hectic life.

> My wife and friends all think I should be retired and playing golf or gardening. And you know, I'd love to be doing just that. But I can't. The business has been so much a part of me that I can't imagine not being there twelve hours a day. Who could manage it the way I have? I have terrific managers, and my son is doing a great job, but they're not as detail-minded as I am. There's a right and wrong way to do things, and it's hard to trust anyone else to handle things.
>
> My wife wants to travel and see our other kids more often. But I just can't seem to slow down. In our business, if you look the other way just once, somebody else will have the competitive edge. The worrying I can understand; I've always done that. But lately I haven't been able to stop, and I haven't really felt good for a long time.

Earl had lost sight of the big picture and betrayed his personal mission. He became confused about what to hang on to and what to let go. He was unaware that taking charge of life is an ongoing process of reevaluating and revaluing. To feel good and to get off the slide into burnout, at times we have to relinquish some of the culturally supported notions of success in exchange for serenity. True successes, the gains that last a lifetime, are what Earl craved. Those credits are about meaning, contribution, creative individuality, and satisfying relationships, not merely notable achievements.

Later, when Earl knew himself much better and learned to respect his temperament and needs, he realized that he had to move from stress tolerance to self-directed stress management. This is the task that grips the Everyday Genius who has advanced beyond the point where relentless striving alone is the key to happiness. Balance is the key to the fulfillment of Evolutionary Intelligence. Imagine your life as a sailing voyage. When you are like a well-crafted, fully equipped boat, feeling sturdy and confident, you can forge ahead in life. When the waters are calm and the winds and currents are with you, you can go even faster and can afford to take more risks.

You can be daring and sail into the uncharted waters of innovation so long as your boldness is balanced by maintaining your energy reserves. Remember not to confuse unnecessary risk taking with necessary risk. Being steady in thought and action is the way of success in the face of life's unpredictable upheavals.

We get into trouble when we forget this useful rule. Often when we don't know what to do, we act before we think and do something foolish. On the other hand, when we move forward with courage, we are able to respond appropriately in various situations, directing our course instead of being at the mercy of external circumstances.

Success is never an all-or-nothing venture. If you fail to insist on balance as you move forward, you may end up having "succeeded" in a way you will come to regret. What a relief it is to do less at times, to set limits, to defy disapproval, and to say no. How pleasing it is to discover that discernment still allows you to accomplish important goals.

Learning to balance the multifaceted personality of the gifted personality is true genius. We will need to develop our own ways of doing it, since each Everyday Genius has a slightly different package of gifts. Think of your resources as the scales of justice. To do justice to the potential we have been given, we must consistently evaluate our relative state of balance. At times we may want one side of the scales to rise, and at other times we may want them even. Too much on either side of the scales is an invitation to imbalance, and too much imbalance brings despair. Remember, we can always move our gifts from one side of the scales to the other and balance as we see fit.

THE LIFE BALANCE PLAN

Mastering Intensity

In many ways, intensity is the razor-sharp edge upon which we must balance most of our lives. Too much freewheeling expression of intensity can come with a very high price. Mastering intensity is critical because it facilitates the fulfillment of our goals, enhances our relationships, and keeps the juices flowing in the right direction. We have learned that we must retain an optimistic outlook in the face of adversity and success. We have learned that our Everyday Genius intensity needs someone to manage the floodgates. We need a plan that spells out how to balance the various subtraits of our intensity. Whenever we feel something strongly and have an urge to react, we can consciously and quickly decide how to keep ourselves on track without stifling the best of what we are.

A BALANCE PLAN FOR MASTERING EVERYDAY GENIUS INTENSITY

- Protect your biological and psychological sensitivities. Speak up or take evasive action when the noise level is too loud, the temperature of the room is too uncomfortable, the light is too bright; tell your physician that you are especially sensitive to medications and may need to ramp up slowly. Avoid overextension and burnout.
- Manage your allocation of energy like a shrewd banker. Take care to distinguish between tolerating stress and managing stress.
- Remember that your intensity can overpower some people and your excitability may be mistrusted as false or careless zeal. Allow others time to catch up with you. If you must go it alone, monitor and adjust your stimulation load wisely.
- Never allow stress to build up pressure past noon on any given day without deliberately neutralizing it with exercise, play, meditation, music, or a relaxation regimen.
- Don't accept someone else's balance method wholesale—find out what fits *you*. Do the work to outline the balance routine that suits *your* personality style; for example, determine if you are an introvert, extrovert, or ambivert, and know what you need physically, spiritually, intellectually, and interpersonally. Work within your unique style and needs, not around them. Reevaluate your plan every three to six months.

- Never use your persuasive powers for badgering or intimidation. Being engaging is not the same as engaging in verbal battle.
- Discipline yourself to find satisfaction in routine and necessary mundane tasks; think of them as supportive time-outs for your more creative work.
- Eat well; sleep the right amount *for you*, and try to maintain that schedule without much change. Exercise the right amount every day, and recapture the joy in movement that you had as a child. Allow no more than two days off per week unless medical advice says otherwise.
- Under extreme stress, when out of town, or when in high-demand situations that present multiple changes, create in advance a plan to conserve energy and effectiveness.
- Find like-minded others with whom you do not need to hold back or pretend and who enjoy your sense of humor. This will help you to balance out the real-world times when you must temper your intensity in order to get the job done.
- Practice the difference between caring about others and being an overwrought caretaker.

Mastering Complexity

As a rule, Everyday Geniuses wince at the idea of finding a middle ground, fearing that striking a balance in their lives is equivalent to granting too many concessions or settling for an agonizingly mediocre existence. Their fears are not entirely unfounded, particularly in light of their powerful inner drive and unwillingness to accept the status quo. Their much-needed energy is often subverted by their resistance to new strategies that could help balance their natural complexities and intensities.

This is the fundamental reason for learning to manage the busy mind that is the center of the Everyday Genius complexity. The brain needs a manager—not a punitive critic, but a permission-giving director who calls for a time-out whenever it's needed for our own good. It takes practice to clear the mind and to be selective about our focus. We do not need to become Zen masters to reap the benefits of daily attempts at mind calming and thought transfer. Fortunately, just the act of acknowledging and practicing stillness is of great value, even if it takes us a while to master the skill. Mastering our minds allows us to endure painstaking effort and not feel overwhelmed.

If you ever played the game of trying to "not think," you understand how resistant the mind is to being shut off. Simply telling ourselves to "stop thinking" is usually a wasted effort. It is a well-researched fact that negative thoughts are the forerunners of upsetting emotions. The therapeutic strategy of thought stopping relies on the connection between the imagined and the felt, aiming to reduce tension and free the mind for more constructive work through thought control.

It is my firm belief that panic attacks, chronic tension, and preoccupations with fears of inadequacy and failure are common afflictions that arise from the complexity of the gifted adult. This correlation first began to appear in my work with gifted people as members of my long-standing panic attack and anxiety treatment groups. The parallel effects of heightened sensitivity and an active imagination can produce horror tales in the fertile Everyday Genius mind. Flights of miserable fancy demonstrate how critical it is for the person of advanced intelligence to develop mental management skills. If insidious thoughts can be interrupted and the mind set on a better course, overall stress can be reduced significantly.

For example, if you are in an automobile and afraid of driving on the freeway, the pitted road straight ahead would be filled with thoughts about crashing or not being able to breathe or get out. As you approach an exit, reading the sign aloud in your head, you will also see that the way to the left offers you opportunities to think about magazine articles you've read, the plot of the novel you brought along, conversation with the person next to you, or a crossword puzzle. If this looks like a good choice, take it. If the apprehension is too strong for distraction, go to the right, which is perhaps a favorite meditation or song or poem. Or make up a detailed picture of a pleasant and safe place that is also a bit surreal or Disneyesque. Focus on each and every detail, including the colors, the sounds, the aromas, the feel of the air, the nature of the people and plants and animals. The buildings and the cloud formations are there for you to notice and describe. In your imagined scene, listen in to a conversation, perhaps between two children, a frog and a dragonfly, or a couple of computers. Do what you need to do to become fully engrossed on the right road, and stay there until a new road appears. Don't go back over dusty old turf. Then repeat softly and reassuringly to yourself: "I'm fine, this is okay, things have a way of turning out."

Remember, you will not be completely successful on your first attempt. Keep trying. Habits of thought are hard to break, and fearful thought patterns can be quite resistant to extinction. Go for the earliest intervention point possible. Remember, persistently upsetting thoughts head straight to the emotions, much the way music does. If you don't want to feel it, don't listen to it. The success of thought stopping and thought transfer depends upon early intervention. It's like being in a rowboat on a smoothly running river. When you notice some white water and your speed doubles, you don't simply ignore these facts and wait until you see the looming waterfall before you start to row toward the shore.

Pay attention to your thoughts whenever your mood goes sour or your energy level drops. Remain in charge. Change direction. Stop the flow. Save yourself the unnecessary agony of going over the falls and then having to resurrect your natural optimism. There will be times when you must stay out of a particular river altogether. Individuals with high Intensity, Complexity, and Drive must be very prudent about how much time they spend around pessimistic people, the amount of upsetting news they absorb, and the types of stories and movies that bombard them with negative images. If you practice thought management with determination, you can cultivate the most positive aspects of your Everyday Genius complexity.

A BALANCE PLAN FOR MASTERING EVERYDAY GENIUS COMPLEXITY

- Remember that your emotional well-being is directly connected to what and how you think all day. Be mindful of the themes and content of your wandering thoughts. Do not believe you can think or analyze your way through every problem. When you feel ill-equipped, remember that you have a right to seek the input of others.
- Indulge your multiple interests while still becoming an expert in a particular domain. Take the time necessary to master essential building blocks when you are learning something new. Try not to take yourself too seriously or get caught up in minutiae. Start every day with a creative view of the big picture.
- Avoid becoming overinvested in facts; stay connected with art, beauty, nature, and spontaneous sources of pleasure.
- Enjoy the process of growing and gaining new skills and insights. Laugh at the jokes that trip you into new awareness as a natural part of Advanced Development. Resist rigidity, especially as you gain expertise. Those who truly know a great deal are never know-it-alls.

- Never underestimate the rationality of your intuition. Learn to tell the difference between a hunch, a feeling, and inner guidance.
- Get rid of your old habits of all-or-nothing thinking and a fatalistic view toward mistakes. Explore and accept different ways of knowing.
- When you react with "hot thoughts," ask yourself three things: (1) "Am I reacting strongly because this experience represents some unfinished emotional business?" (2) "In two or three years, how important will this be?" and (3) "Is this worth such a large allocation of my attention and energy?" Practice thought stopping and thought transfer to manage your mental and energy resources.
- Know which convictions are so important to you that you are willing to go to the wall to fight for them, and distinguish them from other injustices that grab your attention.
- Always stay on some course of self-assigned education. The busy mind of the Everyday Genius gets into trouble when it is not fed properly.
- Never force yourself to feign expertise early or allow your exuberance to rule completely. By wisely regulating your enthusiasm, you can avoid some very irritating backpedaling. Do not insist on being so original that you underestimate the value of teamwork.
- Learn a mind-clearing meditation technique that suits you, and make it an integral part of your daily routine. Do not let your exceptional memory become merely a storehouse of minutiae.
- Never discount the value and power of your guiding inner spirit. Learn to become an artful, grounded visionary.
- When you feel lost or hollow, become spirit-centered in ways that take your mind, body, and soul into a transcendent state. Apply your insights for the collective good.
- Do not be dismayed by the need to repeat certain of life's lessons. Wisdom and Advanced Development are treasures that require excavation and polishing. No amount of intelligence will change this.

Mastering Drive

As we have seen, drive is also a prerequisite of Advanced Development. Drive in all its forms is indispensable no matter how high the intelligence or how astonishing the talent. Plain old hard work is always necessary to perfect one's talents and to pragmatically apply them in real life. Yet it is nearly impossible to separate drive from another marker of Everyday

Genius—the natural devotion to the envisioned ideal. It is a force in and of itself and a significant part of the three umbrella ICD traits. As we have seen, the call to perfection greets the Everyday Genius very early in life. Sometimes it can be a warm and exhilarating companion. Sometimes it wears us down until we wish it would disappear.

Whenever our impulses are triggered, we are faced with a decision. Our natural drive presses us to act quickly, although being backed into a corner is not the occasion when our first and most automatic reaction would necessarily be our best. Under stress we tend to react by making "protective decisions," attempting to convince ourselves we can't decide until something occurs, filling our heads with fearful propaganda: "If I can't be 100 percent certain, then I'd better hold off." "Why should I have to make this decision?" "Maybe I haven't done enough investigating yet."

In the lives of Everyday Geniuses, hesitation can give birth to a whole new set of tensions. On one hand, we press ourselves to get on with things and take the daring plunge, because we pursue the ideal and are willing to work for it. We also want an assurance that we will not have to look back with regret, criticizing ourselves ad nauseam: "I should have known better! I should have waited!" In a similar manner, our ability to look at things from every angle, the foundation of visionary insight, helps us make astute choices. Yet it also tends to promote vacillation when no single choice stands out as the incontestable great idea.

Effective decision making is a matter of skill, the product of learning something new about the process of deciding. Here's an instance where going for the complex, as is our nature, is not always the best approach. Although we tend to race right past anything simple, the easy answer is often more intelligent and takes far less time and cogitation than one requiring a procedural manual. There are all sorts of decision-making charts, formulas, trees, or computer programs that appeal to our sense of thoroughness and our love of a good puzzle, but we can get lost in these overcomplications.

Review and evaluate every misstep through the learning model. All setbacks retain some value, and have the potential to be recycled if we consider them learning experiences. Be stubborn about this. If we constantly strive to avoid foolish-looking mistakes, no growth can take place. Maturity requires growth, which is usually accompanied by error; there is no other way to move forward.

I was an alpine ski instructor for several years during and after my days as an undergraduate, teaching both children and adults. What I noticed among my students then still seems valid. The students who made the most progress were those who were willing to fall down, to look a little silly, to tolerate some snow up the nose. Sometimes these achievers even got bruised in the process. Yet those who refused to crash once in a while, afraid of embarrassment or pain, stayed at the same level, looking on with envy at those who had been willing to fall a lot to get ahead. Falling and failing are different. It is essential to learn the art of falling down on the way to moving up.

A BALANCE PLAN FOR MASTERING EVERYDAY GENIUS DRIVE

- Set realistic goals and learn to let go of ideas that may be someone else's to develop.
- Do not expect others to share or even understand your high standards.
- Distinguish between your perfection-oriented vision and energy-robbing perfectionism, and learn to override the latter. Finish what you start with as much attention as when you began.
- Monitor your natural sense of urgency; don't let it drive you and others crazy. Resist getting caught up in every little distraction, minor irritation or injustice, or low-payoff interest.
- Guard against allowing your mind to get bogged down in circular worry patterns. When you let your curiosity turn against you, you are inviting unnecessary anxiety and depression into your life.
- Find a variety of ways to experience time. Not everything works at top speed.
- Learn the difference between overstimulation and understimulation, and aim for equilibrium.
- Never allow your life to become overspecialized.
- Know your first signs of burnout, and never let stress build unchecked in the foolish belief that you have no limits. When you are in the throes of a project, remember to lift your head occasionally and step away from work for a while. Learn to make necessary midstream shifts and to let go of things when they have a very poor chance of working out. Not all hills are worth climbing.
- Master artistic shifting from one domain to another; become an expert at the timely change of attention from one intense area of focus to its opposite; remember my corollary to the "law of action and reaction." Count on your Everyday Genius abilities and natu-

ral resourcefulness to pull you through when you feel anxious or overwhelmed.

- Trust your self-directed motivation without becoming egocentric or always waiting to be pushed to perform by someone else.
- Honor your need for independence, but learn to collaborate. Few things succeed without the involvement of others.
- Use rules and systems judiciously. They are tools to enhance your life, not to control it. Finish what you start.
- Make friends with necessary risk. Rely on your resourcefulness to carry you through.
- Choose your battles wisely. Champion ultimate truths and minor injustices within reason. Curb your desire to fix everything that seems faulty. Remember, there are millions of other concerned, capable Everyday Geniuses who also take these things seriously.
- Balance work and play, and learn to accept that step-by-step process of excellence.

FIVE STROKES OF GENIUS FOR BEING SUCCESSFULLY DIFFERENT

1. *Link individuality with collaboration.* Often, Everyday Geniuses are not well suited to teamwork. By the end of middle school, most of us had our fill of involuntary group projects where we ended up doing most of the work or tolerating uncreative methods and mediocre results. Yet doing everything yourself is time-consuming, often unnecessary, and occasionally arrogant. Others can and will assist you if you give them a chance. Resist sabotaging their efforts with criticism and hawklike oversight. It's really a delicate matter of recognizing one's strengths and avoiding the things that entrap us in unnecessary energy depletions. Perhaps one reason our complex society has so many roles is precisely that we can each have a niche of our own, which, in order to work well, requires each of us to participate in the roles of the assisted and the assistant.

If you *could* be an effective office manager but your heart is not in it, give the task over to someone whose is. If you must paint or sing, or raise charitable funds, let self-sufficiency be your guide, not your ruler. Find your place honestly, without the need for undue compromise; don't behave as if you were specially entitled; and don't be a perennial one-man show whose glory is limited to claims of rugged autonomy.

2. *Do things in order or differently for good reason.* Many wonderful

stories and musical scores have been started at the end or in the middle. Who said things have to always be done in a particular order? Many creative people put systems, lists, and planners to very good use. Others systematize everything else in their lives and leave their creative acts to their own devices. Consider marrying structure with flexibility and ponder precisely how you might put such a union into practice. Being open to new avenues of getting to the desired goal can provide unforeseen benefits. Question your habits often in an effort to stretch your thinking; experiment with unexplored ways of approaching your innermost need to express yourself daringly.

It might help to invest in one of those books that describe how individuals have discovered one thing while planning for something else (e.g. the 3M Post-it note, ice cream cones, the telescope). Take your explorer self seriously, giving him or her freer rein and a broad turf.

3. *Practice creative self-coaching*, particularly when you have a close encounter with uncertainty. Lack of confidence in your ability to perform perfectly or better than everyone else will keep you frozen in procrastination. Get annoyed with inner demoralizing. Chase down and tackle your self-hindering scare tactics; they're no more powerful than the bogeyman in your childhood closet.

When you are hammered with mental alarms of "wrong" or "that's not the way to do it," still your mind and inquire within more deeply. Calmly assess whether it's really imperative that you turn around before you allow yourself to be dissuaded from your direction. Remind yourself daily that apprehension and unknowns are intrinsic to progress. Learn to wear ambiguity like a comfortable old sweater. Try new things with less fear of appearing foolish, mindful that no matter how brilliant your action, someone will disapprove. Intelligently persist in your efforts the way Albert Einstein did. When asked how he worked, Einstein replied, "How do I work? I grope."

Reward yourself for initiating and staying with boring tasks. Mundane duties are rarely enjoyable but often necessary if there is to be joy in other domains. Value the good feelings and positive gains that come from being a finisher. Remember that a large percentage of success comes from attending to the mundane aspects of a job. Creativity and productivity often depend on drudgery. The wish to be a writer, for example, doesn't put one word on paper. Pride in your product comes from the ordinariness of the process and stubborn pursuit. Well-known author

Gloria Steinem, in reflecting on her success, has noted that she dislikes writing but loves having written.

Know the enemies that can prevent you from accomplishing what you need to do, those "I can do this later; it won't matter" thoughts that sometimes invade our consciousness. Guard against tantalizing distractions, thoughts, feelings, behaviors, and cues from your surroundings that pull you off task. Find new ways to fend off the old nemeses. If it takes ten minutes of meditation to calm down and refocus, do it. If it means closing your door and temporarily transferring your calls to voice mail, do so. Are you stirring up trouble in one area merely to avoid dealing with another? Are you scheduling your day to invite procrastination? Perhaps meetings just before lunch will be more productive than early-morning planning sessions. Free yourself up to rearrange your schedule and environment to your advantage.

Beware of magnifying and catastrophizing habits. Take to heart the words of mythologist Joseph Campbell: "The ultimate dragon is within you."

Because you tend to gravitate toward complexity, you may be mushrooming duties and responsibilities until they seem overwhelming. Thinking exponentially, in terms of "and then . . . and then . . . and then . . . ," may be distorting your tasks, turning them into formidable monsters from which you must flee. Remember, moving from one place to another is a series of small strides, not one giant leap. Focus on one aspect of your goal at a time. When the job you face seems bigger than life and impossible, put on imaginary blinders and laser-beam your attention onto today's portion of the job only.

Use your talents to invite personal progress. Lead yourself into tasks by identifying what you would do first *if* you were to move ahead (for example, make *one* call to a prospective client; offer *one* suggestion at today's meeting; take *one* class). Utilize what I call the Five-Minute Method, a strategy to invite yourself to persist when the going gets tough. Most of us are willing to tolerate unpleasant things (such as a less-than productive meeting) for several minutes, so do the same with your task.

To use my Five-Minute Method, make an agreement with yourself that you will stay with the project, really focused, for five minutes, knowing you can then quit if you must. At the end of the five minutes, take a moment to evaluate. If nothing disastrous has occurred, do five more, and so on. Tell yourself, "I'm getting somewhere. This isn't so bad." You'll be surprised how those five minutes turn into hours of accomplishment when you repeatedly allow yourself *permission* to shut down. Avoiding is always a choice; no one can make you do what you don't want to do. Somehow knowing you are in charge of the decision removes the stubborn oppositionality that gets in the way of progress.

Watch out for beliefs of the "more is better" variety. Investing all your energy toward productivity will actually render you less productive. This is a scientific fact. Don't fool yourself about this. Some of the most effective "work" is done in our free time when our mind is allowed to synthesize information and to operate creatively. Practice putting up with the initial anxiety of being off task in order to be more effective overall. Recharging your battery is as important as one more hour spent trying to squeeze out that extra mile on the current project. Bear in mind that balancing helps to keep you from stumbling. Go for the middle position: not too much, not too little.

Forget faultfinding and blame, because blame always diminishes your ability to creatively solve problems. If you need a report done or your car fixed, don't give yourself permission to get sidetracked with tantalizing squabbles and annoyances. Shouting and complaining have never yet typed a report or repaired a muffler. If you need to work on preventing problems with others in the future, do so by negotiating *after* the current project is finished. And do not allow yourself to plug your ears against unpleasant information you may need. This selective deafness may feel better at the time, but it will make problems worse later on. Keeping an open mind and remaining approachable about unexpected obstacles will actually enhance your sense of control once you get used to it.

Wisely apply successive approximation by giving yourself credit for all small efforts at becoming who you might be. Buy yourself a thank-you card when you initiate and stay with a goal-oriented task in a balanced way. Or take yourself out for a nice dinner or buy yourself a new CD. At the end of each day, make note of all your accomplishments. There have probably been more than you are aware of. Use your scorekeeping skills to approve of every detail of your productivity. Do not give much attention to slips. Keep in mind that a setback does *not* equal failure.

4. *Find supportive peers*, fellow Everyday Geniuses, to team up in the fight against procrastination and self-doubt. You're never too grown-up to make use of the buddy system. Feeling understood and encouraged by a fellow perfectionistic avoider will offer you extra added support and a

way to check against unreasonably high expectations and irrational notions that try to convince you that delay is the answer. Agree with your friend that you will check in on each other's task status with encouragement at least once a week. Help each other overcome fear-producing thoughts that cause you to stall out. Laugh together about old tendencies, and praise each other's successes generously.

5. *Give inner-directed action preferential treatment.* Self-actualization is an action thing, even when the action is passive meditation. Leadership experts Tom Peters and Robert Waterman recommend an "action bias" in their suggestion "Do it, fix it, try it." All the preparing, systematizing, and analyzing in the world is not going to get the job done. Act, then react, change directions, and act again as you go. Feel free to teeter on the edge from time to time, the exciting place where innovation resides. Refuse to allow yourself to become stuck for long periods of time. People who truly excel understand that the hard work of goal attainment cannot be successfully avoided.

What business gurus Tom Peters and Robert Waterman have observed about successful organizations is just as true for the Everyday Genius: "The most important and visible outcropping of the action bias in excellent companies is their willingness to try things out, to experiment. If you wait until you believe you are safe, sure to be without occasional foolish feelings, you've most likely waited too long."[5]

15

THE EVERYDAY GENIUS
IN RELATIONSHIPS

Creativity and love come from the same source.
—Laurens Van der Post

S uccessful and satisfying relationships are possible only when the false self and its outmoded defenses no longer reign. Often it is the persona we present to which people attach. Consequently, any relationship between the false self and an unsuspecting other is destined to only resemble true connection. One of the keys to intimacy is the development of an emotionally safe atmosphere in which being fully known and vulnerable is the reasonably expected norm for those of us who have hidden so much of our genuine nature. We open ourselves up to the customary risks of real relating only when we feel safe. Relationships are not a matter of resolve and willpower, but a matter of finding equilibrium—how to care for others and feel cared about in return—without diminishing the character of our Everyday Genius.

Everyday Geniuses are prone to heartache until we learn to balance our excitability, emotional openness, capacity for deep concern, and sense of responsibility. We must adhere to a balanced regimen of monitoring other people's demands and curb our own eagerness to become overly empathetic. Being open and vulnerable is one of the most valuable assets of Everyday Genius, but it too must be managed for our own protection.

The stronger our sense of identity and autonomy, and the more skilled we become at setting boundaries, the better we are at allowing ourselves to take risks and explore all avenues of relationship. When our true Self is solid and resourceful, we no longer need to constantly anticipate others' reactions, always ready to "make nice" and overcompensate. We can tolerate rejection and setbacks and be selective in our efforts to bring a false stability to tenuous situations.

Trust is built and earned more easily when we recognize the real strengths and weaknesses of the people we allow into our lives. Championing others is often balanced by championing ourselves with the same confidence. Instead of spending exorbitant amounts of time trying to second-guess others' expectations of us, we can be more authentic across a range of situations because we know and value who we are. No longer do we need to beg or clown for attention or burn ourselves out taking care of everyone else. Others in our lives will learn that relating to us is a healthy exchange—a two-way street. Although people in our circle may have trouble adjusting, if they value us and our contributions, they will eventually accept our need to set limits.

Similarly, if we have maintained our sense of security and protected our vulnerability by maintaining an emotional wall or intellectualizing our feelings, our friends may become somewhat unsettled as we start to use feeling words to describe our experience. But soon they will come to see our animated faces as truthful, sincere expressions and not disguises. If we have always worn our heart on our sleeve, we can retrain ourselves to guard against being too accessible too soon to the wrong people. We can learn how to question our disclosures and temper them so that they're less revealing until trust is built. It's useful to recall occasions in the past when people have embarrassingly revealed too much about themselves to us. It was a matter of getting more information than we needed or wanted to know.

We must always bear in mind that our three primary differences—Intensity, Complexity, and Drive—are forces central to our personalities and shape everything we think and do. As we have seen, we must learn to be prudent with our expressions, managing them to be respectful to ourselves and others. Management of ICD traits is paramount in relationships of all kinds and perhaps the most difficult balancing act of all. We are different, situations differ, and the makeup of each relationship is unique. The fine line of relationship success exists between being true to ourselves and simultaneously being true to those around us, and we must wisely shift the weight of our expressions here and there to keep things from toppling over.

For example, Justine discovered that many of her relationship problems stemmed from exaggerated expressions of the subtraits of Intensity: "I never saw it from the other person's side until now. I realize that whenever I get excited about something I take over the conversation. I wish I could always talk a million miles an hour when I'm bubbling over with enthusiasm. But it's something I really have to watch at work." Justine's assessment was right. The fact that her thoughts and verbal agility could outrace those of everyone in her work team didn't give her license to override the others. She needed to practice selective and timely interjection of her thoughts and opinions so that people could take in what she was saying without feeling as though they'd just been hit by a truck. Justine was brilliantly persuasive only when she was the master of her intense reactions and enthusiasm, not the other way around.

Chet's relationship problems centered more on his difficulty managing Complexity. He tended to express this subtrait in the collapsed manner, and his exceptional memory was clogged with minutiae. Until he began to see his Everyday Genius traits as powerful assets that require masterful adjustments, he simply let his penchant for details rule his attention:

> When my girlfriend sat me down the other night for a heart-to-heart talk, I was hurt by what she said. I didn't get defensive right away. I just listened and tried to see the problem as something between us, not just about me being wrong. She told me that she felt lonely even though we spend a lot of time together. When I put her feelings together with what I've learned about how my mind works, I see what she means. When I'm really caught up in something, mulling over the fine points of some problem, it's like she said: I'm not really there with her.

Fortunately, Chet's self-awareness had advanced to where he could allow himself to hear a complaint without denying his true Self, overly defending his behavior, or counterattacking as a diversionary tactic. Instead, he began to recognize the difference between simply "being there" and "being fully present" in a relationship, the latter requiring his conscious self-mastery to allow their attachment to deepen.

Lisa was a chronic perfectionist whose exaggerated form of Drive was directly linked to her exceptionally high standards. For her friendships to thrive, she needed to be more aware of her tendency to voice her critical opinions too much, sounding constantly dissatisfied. She had a history of friendships that never seemed to last more than a year, and gradually began to see why: "My friend Joan was ducking my calls and didn't have time to get together anymore. It was really scary to be direct with her about what was going on between us, but this had happened to me before, and I didn't want to lose her as a friend. When she got to the bottom of it, Joan admitted she felt burdened by my complaining and was uncomfortable sharing confidences about herself because she was convinced I would be critical of her, too. What a painful but important revelation!"

Six months prior, Lisa probably would have let her friendship with Joan slip away. But when strengthened by knowing herself better and by some new self-management skills, she felt confident enough to face up to the problem. She started to pay close attention to what she said out loud, knowing that her tendency to quickly evaluate everything and measure it against the ideal prompted her to find fault. She discovered that her habit of voicing a string of "what's wrong with" statements distorted other people's view of her, making her seem unapproachable and untrustworthy. In order for Lisa to be interpreted correctly and to be allowed into another's private world, she needed to express her interest, joys, and sorrows more honestly. Then others could see through to the softer, more inviting side of her true Self.

NOT PHONY AND NOT LONELY

One of the first actions in our effort to balance our lives more satisfactorily is to truthfully assess the part we play in the relationship game. As we have seen, the heartfelt sensitivity of giftedness is an essential component of compassion, benevolence, and service to humankind. Like all the assets of Everyday Genius, this key element, too, can swing between exaggerated and collapsed expression. Not only are wildly varying emotions and attitudinal changes unsettling to us, they can be the undoing of our relationships with others.

Becoming tough and impervious to feelings is hardly the objective. Again, we must come to grips with a need to take charge of this trait, to harness its strengths and consider how its possible excesses could turn a relationship asset into harmful liabilities. With candor, we can admit that others have no way of knowing that we have the resiliency to spring back from the full expression of the extremes of our emotions.

Lana, one of my most articulate clients, tried to manage her sensitive nature by reining her feelings in so tightly that she trained those around her to believe she was emotionally cold, nearly imperturbable. Nothing could have been further from the truth. She took her healing process seriously, which aroused a wide range of emotions—tremendously painful grief, rage, and moments of soaring hope and transcendence. Her efforts to be herself were honorable and overdue, though by bulldozing the guard walls of her self-restraint all at once she threw her family into a state of alarm.

> *Lana: It had been a horrendous week. Work was out of control, the kids were at each other's throat, and my husband, Geoff, was out of town at a convention. I thought I was losing my mind. It was really hard to untangle all of my emotions and to find a way to express myself without becoming a melodramatic spectacle.*
>
> *I was like a pressure cooker by the weekend. So poor Geoff walked in from the garage after a long day and an exhausting flight to find me sobbing my heart out in bed. He had no idea of what was going on, and neither did the kids. Here I was thinking I was really being myself, letting it all out. I knew I wasn't falling apart. There was never a doubt in my mind that I would bounce back into action after a good cry.*
>
> *In retrospect I probably scared the wits out of Geoff and the kids. Never before had they seen me so distraught. For years I'd led them to believe I was unflappable, and then I suddenly turned on the waterworks. I was shocked when Geoff leaned over the bed and nervously said, "Honey, I'm really worried about you. Maybe we should consider taking you to the hospital."*

Though Lana was right to express her feelings more openly, she forgot to account for the possible reactions of others. She was unprepared for the level of anxiety in Geoff's response. Sometimes we are so used to our depth of feeling that we fail to understand how our profound emotional reactions can appear to our significant others. If our emotions reveal themselves with a new strength or depth, it can look as though we're falling apart. But that is not often the case.

Failure to be responsible for our sensitive natures in intimate relationships can turn against us in three ways. First, as Lana discovered, letting the emotional genie out of the bottle can easily shock others, leaving them feeling anxious or unsure of how to respond. Second, our deep concern over nearly everything and powerful transition from inner emotion to outward expression can overwhelm others. We tend to be talkative and demonstrative, which means that if we're not careful, we leave a wake of exhausted listeners behind us. Dreaded rejections can result, which only compel us to conceal our emotions and ideas, feeling betrayed, angry, and alienated.

Additionally, the hypersensitive perceptions of Everyday Genius can foil us when we defend ourselves with grandiosity, become rebellious, or both. Grandiosity in the Everyday Genius is the contradictory expression of emotional pain. It is developed early in life to cope with painful feelings that arise when we are deemed different in a society that resists embracing diversity. It is also a defense mechanism intended to compensate for what is lost when admiration is equated with love. This unmet need explains the compulsive pursuit of admiration and the relentless striving to meet the expectations of others; in fact, these are attempts to feel loved and appreciated. It's no surprise that a person of depth and intelligence whose need for love is unseen or unmet will resort to the next available commodity—public adulation and attention.

Alice Miller describes grandiosity and its tie to depression in gifted people this way:

[G]randiosity is the defense against depression, and depression is the defense against the deep pain over the loss of the self that results from denial. The person who is "grandiose" is admired everywhere and needs this admiration; indeed, he cannot live without it. He must excel brilliantly in everything he undertakes, which he is surely capable of doing (otherwise he just does not attempt it). . . . The collapse of self-esteem in a "grandiose" person will show clearly how precariously that self-esteem has been hanging in the air—"hanging from a balloon," as a patient once dreamed. That balloon flew up very high in a good wind but was suddenly punctured and soon lay like a little rag on the ground, for nothing genuine that could have given inner strength and support had ever developed. . . .

The grandiose person is never really free; first, because he is excessively dependent on admiration from others, and second, because his self-respect is dependent on qualities, functions, and achievements that can suddenly fail. . . . As long as the true need is not felt and understood, the struggle for the symbol of love will continue. It is for this very reason that an aging, world-famous photographer who had received many international awards could say to an interviewer, "I've never felt what I have done was good enough."[1]

The underdeveloped Everyday Genius often embarks on a frenzied search for love by substituting admiration for achievement. Having been denied consistent love while being told repeatedly how special we are, our capacity to trust relationships diminishes. We feel emotionally fragile when we expose inner thoughts and feelings in the process of getting to know someone else. This is all complicated by our past experiences with rejection of our ideas and expressions. Trust is something that is earned, not demanded. Rather than repeat a failed effort in relationships, we can hide out in nonconformity just as cleverly as the false self hides from disapproval by conforming.

Rebellious Everyday Geniuses appear to be aloof, uncaring individuals whom no one regards as needy or as having deep feelings. Although they can be effective advocates of a cause, or even support someone else's creative efforts, rebels resist applying such regard and nourishment to themselves. Hope for true intimacy lies in strengthening one's own identity. When the core of our individuality, our very being, is not on the line, there is less to risk and more to gain. There's less need to be cautious or avoid intimate attachments. Feelings need only be shared when we are certain that we're not too vulnerable. We can say no with certainty and without justification or apology. We can say yes with certainty to emotional closeness by effectively discerning who's exploitative and who's not.

The solution is self-affirmation, with the assistance not of grandiosity but of an assured combination of inner strength training and a broader support network of like-minded others who understand us without explanation. The first part of the self-affirmation prescription can take root in our lives as we promise ourselves never to return to false-self living. The second part, finding true peers and become more selective in our close associations—not avoiding them altogether—is typically a natural occurrence once our true identity is restored.

THE EVERYDAY GENIUS IN LOVE

We may be able to fool ourselves in other settings by denying our intense and demanding characteristics—the realities of our ICD personalities—but close personal relationships expose us. Terrified of being known and fearing mistreatment or rejection, we simultaneously desire and avoid intimacy. Often we approach intimacy like a beautiful rosebush: We reach out because it is enchanting and appealing, but we hold back because it is potentially painful. Although it may not be obvious to others, intimate relationships often frighten Everyday Geniuses. Succeeding in important relationships requires being able to bend in the right places and managing our thoughts and behaviors so that we can experience the benefits of loving and being loved in return.

Often we have agonized about intimate relationships over what's too close or too distant, too much agreement or too little compromise, because we have been utterly unsure of how to proceed. Vacillation lands us in interpersonal quicksand. When we repeatedly evaluate our partnerships, we create a perpetual style of anxiety by our inadequate all-or-nothing measurement system. Neither extreme, conquering master or submissive slave, gets us what we really want, an egalitarian relationship that provides loving support for our individuality.

Maggie Scarf illuminates the measurement fixation in *Intimate Partners:*

> Such a person can relate to someone else in a superior-to-inferior mode *or* in an inferior-to-superior mode, but has a great difficulty in relation to another individual on the *same* level of power and authority. This need for hierarchy makes the formation of an intimate relationship with a cherished peer an impossible, if not unthinkable, dream.[2]

PARTNER WITH THE PERSON, NOT THE POTENTIAL

We use terms like "crazy in love" and "lovesick" to describe the intoxication of early courtship. Anyone who has ever been caught in the throes of intense passion knows this zone is not noted for detached, rational thinking. If the average person can feel and enact love with ardor, the gifted person has a genuine flair for expressing the most profound aspects of intimacy. Some Everyday Geniuses marry as a false self, only to discover one day that their revived, more genuine self is not what their partner truly desires. Conflict arises unless there is a very mature meeting of the minds and hearts, for a newly liberated Everyday Genius is more than a little reluctant to retreat into denial.

Often the visionary capacity of the Everyday Genius gets activated in relationships that have only a slight chance of working out. Falling in love with another's *potential self* is a dangerous enterprise. To some degree we all do this, and it's perfectly normal. But when the Everyday Genius coats a romantic relationship with an idealized perception of their partner's potential, look out! After years of hoping, prodding, and waiting, gifted adults who expect their partners to feel the pull of self-actualization frequently find that their other half has become complacent and wants to grow no more. The resulting disappointment is profound.

Jeremy had always regarded himself as a conscientious and practical man. As a child, he easily connected with older children and grown-ups, and came to trust his perceptions of others. He was keenly aware of un-fulfilled potential in other people, quickly able to discern who they might become if they focused on self-realization and hard work. Jeremy was never totally content with the status quo and expected the same from those he admired.

Chloe, a warm and imaginative woman, also seemed to be filled with the dreams of love and mutual accomplishment that could be found in a committed relationship. She believed she had found this with Jeremy. That hope was never realized. Six years after their wedding Jeremy was disturbed by his growing emotional alienation from his wife. He felt mis-understood and found himself criticizing her and pressuring her to take classes or get a new job. Jeremy was convinced that Chloe was unhappy, too, and that it was primarily due to her lack of personal growth. Where, he asked himself, was all the teeming potential he had fallen in love with? What would become of them if Chloe remained stagnant and stayed exactly the same? Who would be his partner in advancement?

With all his perceptive powers, Jeremy couldn't see that he had mar-ried an image of his own making—the dream woman he wanted as a life partner. He failed to realize that he had no right to insist that Chloe live up to his vision for their lives. Jeremy felt betrayed and angry. Chloe felt badgered and rejected. They were confused, sad, and stuck. Each was a fine individual, but neither was at fault, really. Indeed, they had reached a stalemate. Love is built upon acceptance and respect. They would have to rediscover this truth in light of their real values and individual goals, or they would face the grim realization that their love would probably die a slow death.

Could this unfortunate drama have been avoided if Jeremy had been more realistic up front? Can we learn to accept the fact that potential in others may not ever be developed? Moreover, can we understand that others have a right to pursue their lives as they see fit, to grow and change or not? That people indeed have the right to live their lives badly and exist outside the confines of our neat prescriptions? Above all, we must recognize that even a failed relationship is a mutual relationship, and that we are accountable for no more than our 50 percent. If the greater part of our 50 percent is being misled by a belief in our partner that is stronger than his or her own, that is not the most dishonorable error of love.

A satisfying intimate relationship can never be reduced to a simple one-size-fits-all formula. There should always be an element of mystery to it. Nevertheless, it is important for Everyday Geniuses to honestly assess just how critical it is for them to be involved with someone who is like-minded so that the partnership will endure long after the heat of infatuation wears off. Studies of gifted adults reveal the same kinds of relationship problems that others encounter. We are all looking for that special someone who will make our lives feel really complete. Yet there is a fundamental difference for the Everyday Genius. Intimate relationships that are unequal with respect to intellectual ability and drive for Advanced Development tend to splinter at some point, one moving ahead while the other is content to stay put.

This lack of parity in personal growth in intimate relationships can often be linked to a lack of self-knowledge. Knowing ourselves and learning to manage our ICD characteristics are especially important to the process of forming intimate relationships, because when our identities are unclear and the forces of our personalities run wild, it is far too easy to partner with the wrong person for the wrong reason. After all, we cannot be certain about what we need in a relationship until we know what makes us tick and where we are headed. As one of my clients put it:

> Some people might be just fine settling down with someone agreeable and simply getting along. But I need someone who always has growth and new experiences in mind. Life as a whole would be an adventure of learning and becoming, all the way to the end. Most of all, I need someone with enough substance so we each support the other's full development. And it seems that kind of two-way support requires a similar drive and need to push past the status quo, only getting there together. I don't want boredom, and I don't want a battle. I just want to be me with someone smart enough to know who she wants to be too. And now that I know myself, I think I'm ready.

THE ACQUIESCE/ACCUSE PENDULUM

The qualities we really long for in our intimate relationships—respect, acceptance, equality, and mature love—are found in the balanced middle, the place where the power pendulum remains reasonably stable. However, when feelings of powerlessness arise, they frighten us, throwing an internal switch that sparks us into reactivity. We either become an acquiescing victim or an accusing perpetrator. Whenever we are in danger of being betrayed or emotionally abandoned, it is easy to lose all perspective and become defensive, blaming or going overboard in an attempt to please.

Fear and anger merge whenever we feel controlled by another or unable to gain a perceived upper hand. Until now, our tendency has been to react at such times either like a hysteric on a crashing airplane or like an innocent hardened by contempt and suspicion. There's no denying that unresolved anger takes on a life of its own in many instances, writes Scarf: "Anger, like nuclear waste, is nondegradable. Unprocessed and therefore undischarged, it simply remains where it is—but the threat of its emergence is constant."

Frequently, important relationships have been damaged by our own lack of awareness. At first, two people may feel quite comfortable attempting to "Osterize" their strengths. We congratulate ourselves for being "accepting" and making a real effort to improve compatibility. However, the warning signals of differing needs often begin to demand our attention. By not recognizing the power of the covert agreement we have made to merge with another in order to compensate for our individual deficiencies, we set ourselves up for disappointment.

Like most couples, we naively hope we can make up for our individual shortcomings by joining our attributes with our intended partner's in the blender of a committed relationship. As our frustration increases we wonder: "What happened to that agreeable, sensitive, intelligent person I fell in love with? Did I pick the wrong partner? Where's the nearest exit?" Yet we continue this ill-fated experiment, keeping our inevitable disillusionment to ourselves for fear of ending the magic spell.

As English poet Samuel Rogers observed, "It doesn't much signify whom one marries, for one is sure to find next morning that it was someone else." During the sunny initial phase of infatuation, partners tend to agree on most things. Consideration and compromise take the lead. We have drunk the love potion and are happily under its spell. We project the idealized persona onto our partner, a god or goddess projection that makes our newfound love appear to be everything we have always wanted. For a time, the unfailing lover of our dreams seems quite real. For a while we are walking on air, even though we ultimately crash back to reality and the unspoken disappointment that we love a mere human being.

For most couples, the sequel to falling in love is "Cinderella—Part II," where a non-fairy-tale struggle emerges within each partner to find ways to be more open and get closer without feeling claustrophobic. When we need personal space or more meaningful attachment, instead of working out our internal conflicts or negotiating with our partner, we expect our "other half" to automatically respond with everything from lacy red lingerie to applause. Although we rarely admit it, we have been carrying around scenes from our personally directed movie of how our relationship *should* function.

Since most partners are both very poor mind readers and prisoners of their own needs, battle lines are drawn. Suddenly disappointment blooms as the former god or goddess is transformed into a villainous enemy. The more extravagant our expectations, the greater the disappointment. Not only do we berate our partner for failing to live up to the scripted role, we berate ourselves for not being able to manipulate or command a fulfilling relationship into existence.

Rather than shifting from acquiescence to accusation, we can locate a midpoint, a place where we can be more stable and genuine. This new position, the one that offers the best chance for a successful intimate relationship, depends on skillful balancing, standing firm at times and bending at others. All the while, we must consciously manage our ICD tendencies. The two most important skills necessary to achieve disarmament and mature interdependence are respectful listening and effective assertiveness.

LISTENING FOR LOVE

Most couples participating in my relationship counseling work have entered therapy complaining about a "lack of communication." However, what is soon revealed is quite the contrary. There's plenty of communicating going on, but much of its intent is tainted by disrespect and assumption. The emotional environment of these disillusioned couples is very hazardous to the relationship's health. In our treatment plan we start with "how to listen for love" rather than "how to talk to each other." If respectful listening is not established first, no amount of "communicating" will result in understanding.

In school we learned to listen for *content*, taking notes on what was said so we would be able to call forth the concepts when it was time to take the test. We became accustomed to hearing words and silently paraphrasing what they meant in our minds. That type of listening is exactly as it should be in the world of education. Listening for content alone is sometimes appropriate in close relationships as well. For example, if a woman calls her husband to say she'll be home an hour late, she is merely relaying information. All her husband needs is a brief conversation in order to understand he'll being seeing her face a little later than usual that evening. Yet there are times when content-driven communication is quite limited.

Intimate relationships can resemble a building with a hidden basement. Although we clearly see the facade, the critical foundational structures remain out of view. The unspoken meaning, and the mental interpretations we assign to a significant other's words, are often both veiled. Nevertheless, it is this submerged foundation that can serve to either support the relationship or undermine its strength if it is faulty. Although we may hear every spoken word and parrot it back like a Memorex tape, we often miss the real message entirely. Instead of opening our eyes, ears, and hearts to the subtleties of tone, feeling, and body language, we hear the words and little else.

If the husband of the tardy woman silently received her phone call with the thought "This is the third time this week she's been late! She doesn't give a damn about me," when she arrived home she would be confronted with a scene far different from the one she had anticipated. It may seem elementary to learn the art of listening all over again, but most of us have never been trained in relationship-enhancing listening skills.

The first order of relationship business is to recognize that most of our assumptions are erroneous and need to be discarded, especially those that are repetitive and emotionally charged. Successful intimate relationships are founded on accurate interpretations. Any assumption that we *know* things about another in advance is arrogant and not very wise. Nothing drives a painful wedge between two people as deeply as preconceived notions. In fact, if we're not extremely careful, the problem with assuming too much increases over time. Before we know it, we're not communicating at all because we think we "know each other so well."

The truth is that because Everyday Geniuses are dynamic works in progress, we need to get to know each other all over again every day.

Ungrounded assumption is a poisonous by-product of our unmanaged complexity—an amalgamation of our rapid conceptualization, perceptivity, intuition, categorization, and interpretation gone awry. Sometimes we can even go beyond this into pseudoclairvoyance. We think that because this person is so familiar to us, we no longer need to pay attention to what is being conveyed. Halfway through the other's first sentence, we are certain we *know* what is meant, and often stop listening. The "I know what he [she] is going to say" and "I don't care what he [she] says because I already *know* what he [she] *means*" system is not high-level mind reading, but a destructive game. When we rely on assumption as truth, it is little wonder that our interpretations frequently miss the mark and backfire because we fail to allow our partner the respect of being fully heard and understood.

Difficult though it may be, we need to begin listening with the premise that no matter how perceptive we are, we *don't know* what our partner is attempting to communicate. It is critical to maintain one golden rule: Whatever our partner says is valid from his or her point of view, *no matter how it may sound.* If the woman arrives home late unaware of how her husband has interpreted the call, his disgruntled behavior would make no sense to her. Nevertheless, if she hopes to resolve the misinterpretation of her actions, she should begin with the belief that his reaction was reasonable *for him.*

When you are listening for love, you will need to reflect back like a mirror what is being communicated to you. Do this by giving your full and undivided attention, nodding occasionally, and, above all, allowing the speaker to maintain the floor. A casual conversation may go back and forth like a tennis match, but a meaningful communication is mostly open talk on one side and open reception on the other. Above all, this type of listening is not meant to be a debate or an opportunity to prepare a rebuttal or to impart solutions. When you're the loving, interested listener, your only job is to compassionately receive what is being shared and to do everything in your power to help your partner feel understood.

If your mind strays and you get sidetracked, make every effort to comprehend and respond to the underlying *feelings.* Should you find that your mind is busy preparing a criticism or thinking about anything other than what is being said and the attached feelings, you are missing the boat. You can expect to hit the rocks and sink. When that happens, briefly apologize—instead of justifying—and try again. Sometimes we have to rewind the tape a few times before understanding can take place.

To listen respectfully, you will need to respond once in a while with a very brief remark that indicates you are tracking the exchange, such as "I see" or simply "Mmm-hmmm." It is essential to assure your partner that you are not misinterpreting what is being said and to offer support that indicates you "get it." You might say, "Oh, that must have been difficult for you," or "Really? Tell me more," or "What did that mean to you?" However, interrupt rarely and only with care, avoid asking lots of questions, use very few words (try a gesture whenever possible), and always be sincere. Remember, it is your partner's agenda, not yours.

Here's a place where Everyday Genius empathy can shine, because you can put yourself in your partner's experience, all the way to feeling his or her emotions. Reflective listening is one way to dismantle the barriers between you and significant others. It lets them know that they are valued and accepted. Most people don't expect or need to be advised or agreed with all the time. They simply want to be heard and to have their experiences validated. As one of my Everyday Genius clients once admitted: "It took me forever to realize that I was having trouble getting close to people because I was always giving out information when all they really wanted was a little consolation and encouragement. It finally dawned on me that being heard and accepted is the very first thing that should happen between two people. Debating and sharing new information is fun, but it's not enough to serve as a solid relationship."

Remember that reflective listening does not license us as psychologists. Steer away from any tendency to analyze and sum up the other person's experience. Refrain from giving unsolicited advice about the need for change or how to do it. This is particularly important for smart men, since many have been socialized to be "fixers." As I advise many of my male clients, "You may indeed have the answer. Just keep it to yourself until you're asked. Your job is to listen for understanding and to reflect back your partner's feelings."

REFLECTIVE LISTENING

Mastery of reflective listening takes practice. The following suggestions may assist you in becoming an expert reflective listener:

- When another invites you to be a part of his or her private life and emotional world, handle this "gift of self" with care.
- Intimacy-building listening should not be considered a conversation. Allow the speaker to keep the floor until he or she is finished.
- The time you spend actively listening is money in the relationship bank.
- Validating feelings does not require agreement with a different opinion, but feelings are always legitimate, even if you think your partner's ideas are off base.
- Judging is for judges, not loving partners.
- Unsolicited advice can feel like a slap in the face; the sting is not soon forgotten. If you are unsure whether advice is wanted, ask.
- If the goal is loving understanding, then finishing other people's sentences, changing the subject, focusing on something else, telling how you see it, correcting grammar, and comebacks that begin with "Yeah? Well, one time *I* . . ." are all disrespectful and guaranteed to backfire.
- You can grasp another's point of view without giving up your own.
- There's room enough in a good relationship for both of you to be heard.
- If you must ask a question to clear up your understanding of what is being communicated, ask it briefly and go right back to active listening.
- When you acknowledge another's experience and feelings, you give them a much-needed emotional message of acceptance; you can expect one in return another day.
- It's okay if your partner doesn't make sense at first; especially for highly verbal types, clarifying thoughts often require a sounding board.
- Predominantly visual types often need to diagram or draw out what they're trying to communicate. Motion-oriented, active types may do their best communicating while walking about. Both are normal, even if your communication style is different from your partner's.
- When you are eager to say something back or share your own experience, the reflective listening comes to an abrupt halt.
- You will know you have done a good job of reflective listening when your partner looks and sounds understood, the interchange

comes to a natural conclusion at your partner's discretion, and you perceive that the two of you have moved closer together.

To thrive, intimate relationships need to be nourished. Listening with patience, consideration, and interest deepens intimacy, making a good thing even better. Being able to reveal yourself with an expectation of being respected is also the basis of trust. More than any other factor, trust must be preserved if the relationship is to last. It is a matter of kept promises, especially keeping the promise not to inflict the kind of criticism, misinterpretation, and control tactics that resemble the wounds Everyday Geniuses strive to heal in themselves.

ASSERTIVE INSTEAD OF DEMANDING

We would all like to live as if relating well were a natural occurrence. Wouldn't it be wonderful if our needs were clearly known and automatically fulfilled just because our partner professes to love us? Many couples struggle to hold on to this myth, believing such a glitter-dust fantasy works out in the real world. Every intimate relationship needs a little prince-and-princess glow, but expecting this illusion to sustain intimacy over the long haul is foolish.

The unvarnished truth is that loving relationships have a business dimension, a fair-trade policy. We all have specific and changing needs, and we must learn how to negotiate to get them met. That also means we must be prepared to compromise with a win-win attitude when our partner makes a reasonable request. If we can do so, we might eventually say with confidence that in our closest relationship we feel satisfied about 75 percent of the time.

In her sessions, Rosalie admitted she had always held fast to her unrealistic expectations and "love conquers all" beliefs:

Rosalie: I used to think Carlos would magically know how I felt and what I needed from him. I thought that if he really loved me, I shouldn't have to tell him or ask for anything. And if he let me down, even though he didn't know what he had overlooked, I would turn on him like a rabid Doberman. He never seemed to know what set me off. When I think back on it, that was pretty dishonest of me. Today, if I need something from him or have something to share, I just say so. I've found I make more sense to him now. When I'm upset or sad or quiet he doesn't look at me like I'm nuts, and he's starting to be more direct, too. The amount of time and energy we spent in the past on guesswork and guessing wrong was such a waste. I'll never again believe that negotiating is just for the conference room at work. It's for the living room and kitchen and bathroom, too.

Negotiating is intended to replace badgering, wishing, orchestrating, pleading, and commanding. Once we have mastered reflective listening we can work through any difficulty with respect and negotiate a workable resolution. Yes, we will still fall prey to misinterpretation over time. Disappointment and open conflict will occur. However, the odds will be greatly increased if we are able to settle our differences maturely. In order for this to happen we must learn to fight fair.

Another fundamental underpinning of negotiation is promise keeping. If love is built on respect, then the wrecking ball of intimacy is broken promises. When we expect to be loved and treated well, we must bargain fairly, making a clear distinction between a promise and "best efforts." In the classic *Mirages of Marriage*, William Lederer and psychiatrist Don Jackson explore the need to bargain in important relationships:

> The best kind of bargaining behavior is that which is not immediately "time bound." That is, the couple recognizes that if one spouse does something for the other, the benefited spouse need not *immediately* turn around and pay off his [or her] debt. It is assumed that there will be an opportunity for paying back in the future.
>
> This kind of arrangement is ideal, but unfortunately, as with most things, it sometimes also carries the seed of its own destruction within it. It is quite possible that A may keep encouraging B to believe that he [or she] will do something in the future, but never gets around to it. This sort of unkept promise is the material for marital disharmony and bitterness. . . . Marriage [or any significant relationship] is a series of adjustments, some of which may be best achieved through debate.[3]

Assertive refusal—the setting of limits—allows us to be free in relationships of all kinds. By establishing boundaries, we reduce our fear of being victimized or of acting the bully ourselves. Saying yes when we mean no is dishonest. If we ever hope to be free enough to reveal our true selves in important relationships, we must strive to create a match between inner feeling and outer expression. Every relationship requires the occasional acceptance of our partner's shortcomings without taking them to task. Yet effective assertiveness means we have to fake it less often; we feel stronger in our ability to be true to ourselves when we can be direct, so long as we do so respectfully.

Assertive messages offer us a way to say what we mean and mean what we say without inciting an interpersonal riot. We are less likely to be misunderstood and more likely to feel empowered. Assertiveness is a matter of how to speak up. It takes a conscious effort to make it a natural part of your relationship repertoire. The delivery of an assertive message is quite simple and usually requires only one sentence. Although we may have intense feelings about what we are saying, our tone must be as neutral as possible. This is where many of us get into trouble—we erroneously think *more* explanation and *more* justification, followed by *more* persuasion, is the ticket. Nothing could be further from the truth, because the more we explain, the greater the likelihood that it will sound as though we're whining and seem as though we are defensive and unsure of ourselves.

Effective assertiveness in close relationships has three parts:

1. Point out the issue of concern.
2. Succinctly describe the relevant feelings.
3. Identify the consequence.

For instance, if a friend repeatedly fails to return your phone calls, you might say: "I've noticed that you are not returning my calls [the issue]. I feel disappointed and confused [relevant feelings], and lately I've found myself wanting to avoid you [consequence]."

An assertive statement is not an insurance policy guaranteed to protect you from unpleasant responses. But it increases the odds for an amicable solution because it is (1) not overloaded with emotion that might set off a counterattack, (2) clear and concise, lending itself to less misinterpretation, and (3) delivered with respect and confidence.

Sometimes we may be quite certain a positive outcome is unlikely, but it may make a world of difference just to hear ourselves say what we mean and how we feel even when it might change nothing. This is one way we can validate ourselves, though it is something that may have been difficult to come by during our childhood.

In our efforts to be effectively assertive, we run the risk of amplifying our internal critic, who may pressure us to return to our old ways by injecting us with several milligrams of anxiety. But we can borrow a suggestion from the title of Susan Jeffers' book on anxiety management: *Feel the Fear, and Do It Anyway*. The best defense against nerve-torturing thought is a good offense based on believing in ourselves and our relationships enough to be assertive when we must.

Don't let things that bother you fester. Don't jump on every irritation like a nervous cat. Learn to tell the difference between a temporary annoyance and something that needs to be resolved by giving it the forty-eight-hour test. If after forty-eight hours you are still stewing about the problem, it is probably not going to go away unless you confront it directly. More relationships have been ruined by unresolved issues that neither partner wanted to bring up than can be counted. Unresolved issues have a way of becoming toxic and eventually contaminating the whole relationship.

When something bothers you, especially when you feel upset, check it out instead of assuming your interpretation is correct. The only respectful way to clear up false assumptions is to confront the problem directly. Had early radio listeners who tuned into Orson Welles' radio play *War of the Worlds* questioned what they assumed, they might have figured out it was merely theatrics and not a real alien invasion. Accurately identifying relationship fictions and nonfictions means less misreading of the interpersonal communication involved in intimacy. This offers a far greater chance of avoiding unnecessary conflict.

The false self would prefer that we stick with our well-intended fictions, but neither we nor our important relationships can tolerate such an oversight. Here are some common relationship fictions that can block effective assertiveness and create chaos. Learn to recognize them as false-self fictions and act assertively on your personal truths, which are the nonfictions—your Everyday Genius truths.

FALSE-SELF FICTIONS	EVERYDAY GENIUS TRUTHS
I must have an answer for everything.	It's okay to say, "I don't know."
It is selfish to put myself first.	I need to put myself first sometimes.
I must convince others to see things my way.	I can tolerate different points of view.
I need to keep my problems to myself.	I have a right to express my feelings.

If someone needs help, I must give it.	I don't always need to rescue or be the caretaker.
I must always have a good reason for what I do.	I do not need to justify myself to others.
If I don't accommodate others, they will dislike and reject me.	Sometimes I need to say no.
I should just leave well enough alone.	I do not need permission to negotiate.

The form of assertiveness explored here relates to limit setting—holding our ground to avoid giving ourselves away. However, there are two other types of assertiveness that are equally important: *request assertiveness* and *commendatory assertiveness*. Request assertiveness is just as it sounds—asking for something in a short and direct way (for example, "I am moving to a new apartment on Saturday and would like very much if you could be there to help me"). This takes little training for many people, but it is a considerable hurdle for Everyday Geniuses who prize their self-sufficiency and fear being seen as vulnerable human beings. Nonetheless, others feel uncomfortable when they receive but are never allowed to give in relationships. Imagine how you would feel in a relationship in which nothing was ever requested of you. Wouldn't it be likely that you'd feel unimportant or shut out? An important part of relating is trusting enough to ask for input or assistance once in a while. Reasonable requests or sharing confusions and doubts with someone is one of the primary reasons for developing closeness—so we don't always have to go it alone.

Unfortunately, in the popular literature and assertiveness-training programs, the first two types of assertiveness get top billing. But it's just as important to offer type three—direct commendatory messages. To be effective, commendatory assertiveness must be direct and genuine. These messages consist of encouragement, compliments, praise, and gratitude. Commendatory messages are spoken with meaning, using expressions that clearly match what is being conveyed—a warm smile, a nonthreatening posture, and a soft tone ("I really like the way you do that"; "I'm glad you're my friend"; "Thanks for listening").

Early stages of close relationships are enhanced by this kind of positive attention and recognition of Self all the time—a tender hand to the cheek here and a verbal hug there. Later on, commendatory behaviors often disappear, as in the old joke about the Scandinavian husband who complained in couples therapy, "I already told her I loved her twenty years ago. Can't she remember?" Long-standing relationships require repeated and fresh commendations. Repeatedly falling in love with the same person takes thought, time, and effort, just as it does during courtship. In fact, if any of the three types of assertiveness are to get short shrift, let it be the first two. Words of validation and valuation are more than casual remarks; they are a vital part of what makes us feel wanted and appreciated. When they are discarded in important relationships, we soon feel betrayed, angry, and distant, as if we had suddenly become devalued.

THE SELFISHNESS THAT
ENHANCES INTIMACY

Couples who are really close live in a relationship that has plenty of elbow room for individuality. Neither sacrifices his or her individual uniqueness or personality to be attached to the other. Rather, individuality is cherished and honored. In *A Couple's Guide to Communication*, John Gottman offers an intriguing and useful framework for building intimacy: Gottman and his colleagues have studied distressed and nondistressed couples for many years, demystifying much of what we generally believe about successful close relationships (such as "Only couples who are very much alike stay happy together" and "Only couples who work out all their differences directly stay happy together"):

> There are two general things you need to do. First, you have to begin by caring about yourself, by thinking of what *you* need, and about the kind of life *you* want for yourself. You must be selfish, not selfless. This means a commitment to your own personal growth and enhancement, your own creativity. It means finding out who you are and what you need. And that usually means you have to like and respect yourself.[4]

Although partners may spend a lot of time together sharing intimacies and personal secrets, the successful relationship is similar to that of running buddies: if they run too close together, they can trip over each other; too far apart, and they would miss the fun and support of moving forward together.

Intimate relationships that thrive, Gottman discovered, have a very interesting common ingredient. Regardless of the styles, ages, personalities, or backgrounds involved, intimate relationships that work out over time operate on a five-to-one ratio of positive encounters to negative ones.[5] Think of it: A five-to-one ratio means that for every *one* negative or relationship-damaging interaction, *five* constructive, relationship-building interactions occur. This may sound easy enough, but in actuality it takes concerted and persistent effort even to approach such statistics.

By contrast, what you experience as a positive encounter may elicit a neutral or even negative reaction in your partner. Remember, he or she is an individual with distinct personality traits. For example, one person may consider a check-in call during work a thoughtful and loving gesture, while another finds it invasive or even smothering. With couples in my therapy sessions we take the time to determine exactly what is positive and negative to each partner. It's imperative that we know our partner's possible interpretation of our words and actions. Why bother to send flowers, write a note, hold open a door, or buy tickets to the basketball game if we're just assuming that is what gives our partner pleasure? We know where unbridled assumptions get us. Rather, we need to know firsthand what makes our partner smile and feel good, aiming for behaviors that produce a feeling of being loved. Otherwise we may be guessing, or worse yet, we may make things worse instead of better.

We use reflective listening skills to determine what our partner truly wants and needs. Then we employ our newfound assertiveness skills to check out our beliefs and to share our own wishes and needs. Commendatory assertiveness can help fulfill and sustain our relationship dreams. Indeed, one of the most satisfying aspects of an intimate relationship is daring to ask for and receive what we really want.

What else do we know about successful intimate relationships? These dedicated pairs spend time together, not just going over the news of the day or solving problems, but dreaming, wishing, playing, and planning the future together. Their creative sides repeatedly fall in love with each other. They explore, listening to each other's fears, hurts, hopes, and fantasies. They reminisce, reminding each other of what they value in being together. They learn about each other's childhood as a way of better understanding the essence of each other. They share traditions and build new ones, whether it means returning to the same bed-and-breakfast each anniversary or shopping for garden supplies on the first day of spring every year.

Intimacy is really an extension of friendship. Getting and staying close often involves surprise, silliness, secret communications, permission to be alone, and enjoyable conversation about "nothing." Showing interest in your partner means you take responsibility for drawing him or her out, respectfully inviting your partner to say more and go deeper. Couples can easily become stuck in the mire of familiarity, reenacting the same conversations, same gestures, same stories. Some routine and task-oriented interaction is, of course, necessary, but too much of it drains away the joy that keeps intimacy alive. We must endeavor to maintain a "date" mentality. When there is no excitement, we must create some.

When there is nothing to look forward to, plan something. When you find yourself uninterested, ask yourself if *you* have become uninteresting. According to my close friend Betina Krahn, a best-selling romance novelist, intimacy depends on personal growth which each partner must undertake as a vital contribution to the relationship. Take charge of your part of the intimacy promise. Reignite the fire in your relationship instead of simply waiting for your partner to fan the flames. Let your inventive and playful nature have a say in it. Leave the safety of the familiar and try something different together. Overpredictability can be extremely detrimental to a relationship. Get back in touch with the joy of spontaneity; remember that joy is its own reward and needs no justification. At least once a week, ask yourself what you might do to earn the label "a romantic." If you think your partner could speak for you and knows your every move, you've probably become dull. It's not much of a leap from lack of variation to a relationship that is boring.

Let's not forget the physical aspect of intimacy, either. Although it may be the modern age of openness and sexual freedom, most couples maintain the old taboo "Don't talk about sex." It's helpful to remember that men often want sex to feel close, while women often want to feel close to have sex. In the continuum of pleasuring, the twain will have to meet, or a standoff will result. If you and your partner routinely ignore the S subject, go to a good bookstore and find a well-written book on intimacy, one that seems reasonable to you both and takes into account the full range of closeness, not just sexuality. Read it either separately or together and then discuss it. You may find out something new. Your may hear your partner say, "I never knew that."

However, the vulnerability of sexual intimacy must always be kept in mind. Be willing to give your partner encouraging, sensitive feedback, and share responsibility for initiating physical touch. Be honest; ask for what you want, but never give in to requests that make you feel unsafe or too uncomfortable. Feel free to talk about your sex life, inside and outside of the bedroom.

Far too many of us are touch-deprived. We go about our busy days within reach of people, but inside our own protective bubbles. It not only feels good to feel good, it is a necessary part of a reasonable balance plan to achieve closeness. For those who live a relatively isolated lifestyle, therapeutic massage and other nonthreatening opportunities for touch exist. Caress is simple. Even if you're out of practice, you know how to touch softly and lovingly. Pay attention to how your partner reacts. If you're not sure your touches are welcome, ask: "How is that for you?" Engage in a variety of caresses: face, foot, hands, head, and body. Physical intimacy occurs on a broad palette, and there's always a new shade or variation available to paint an appealing and satisfying experience. Remember, touch and sex are only a part of the larger intimacy picture, and never a replacement for the rest.

REAL RELATING

The tie that truly binds is a bond of trust. Real intimacy reduces unnecessary differences of opinion. Partners in constant competition both lose in the power struggle game. The tie that binds is not a win/lose competition, something strong-willed Everyday Geniuses need to remember. A former client once told me:

> I used to avoid social events because Pam was so much better at meeting people than I. Everyone seemed to like her more, and I got angry and felt like a nobody because she was the center of attention. When I was in the background I felt mistreated. The resentment grew and grew, and I blamed her for it. But that's all gone now. What a difference it made the day I decided our relationship didn't have to be a contest.

Learning to relate maturely involves putting forth more of yourself as a human being. Underneath it all, what we want out of closeness is someone who truly knows us. We also want them to allow us into their lives deeply enough to truly know them. People who care about us are more interested in how we see things and how we feel than in getting an earful of

information. For others to feel close to us, we need to practice seeing ourselves as worthy of love, blunders and all. We need to get over the alienating false-self and perfectionistic beliefs that we have to earn our way to
love and that no matter what we do, we will never be quite good enough.
This doesn't mean settling back and being adored. Real relating is a
working contract. It means that we can expect to be loved for who we are,
not just for our accomplishments.

When you think of it, we all attach most easily to those who are honest about their humanness. We can relate more effectively to others by
uncovering our own flaws and ridding ourselves of counterproductive displays of bravado or one-upmanship. We can also relate better to others by
daring to take a stand and refusing to be compulsive about creating harmony in every situation.

Relearning how to relate will cause insecure moments at first, especially as you dismantle the thickest parts of your false-self wall one brick
at a time. Be patient with yourself; remember it's a virtue. Becoming less
defensive may require your best effort thus far. A top executive remarked
during the final therapy session:

> *Building an idea into a successful, publicly traded conglomerate was
> easier than becoming less defensive in my intimate relationships. A year
> ago if someone told me I'd benefit from counseling and mastering my In-
> tensity, Complexity, and Drive, I would have thought they were mis-
> guided. I had already mastered everything I needed to be the king of the
> world. Now I realized that I wasn't as competent as I thought. I wasn't
> capable of managing my reactivity. And I wasn't free enough to be open
> with anyone, which meant I wasn't free to be loved, either.*

Successful intimacy may require shedding some old emotional armor
and unlearning some unproductive habits. Stick with it. You deserve
positive relationships and can have them. Don't ever believe you're too
different to be loved. And don't be afraid to get out of your own way to
make room for intimacy. It's not too late, and it's not as risky as you may
think. Individual development is an integral part of building intimacy,
and what you are doing is just that.

RELATIONSHIPS IN THE WORKPLACE:
WORKING TOGETHER, PRESERVING INDIVIDUALITY

Everyday Geniuses generally love the challenge of good competition. There's nothing wrong in that. But what about when competition is less than healthy or inappropriate under the circumstances? What about when we need to work with and not against others? How might we behave in ways that are not at cross-purposes to our goals?

Sometimes Everyday Geniuses confuse passionate work with worth. Believing we are the keepers of the true standards, our idealizing heads get too big and we can go so far as to label as slackers those who operate differently. If others judged us so harshly, we would complain that it's wholly unfair, and unfairness is something we rarely tolerate in ourselves. We must recognize that our marathon work style has often led us to disrespect others while branding them as uncommitted. Although sometimes this may be a fair assessment, it's rarely useful, since none of us can change other people's behavior.

Everyday Geniuses often discount others who are unable to accomplish extraordinary amounts of work or stay on task into the wee hours. Frequently our coworkers, supervisors, and subordinates fail to live up to our sky-high expectations and miss the mark. Sometimes we try to appease ourselves by molding others into Xerox copies of ourselves, only to discover they resent us. Lisa Kanarek, president of an organizational consulting firm, writes in *Executive Excellence*:

> Everyone has different working styles. Some people work slowly, making every effort to avoid mistakes. Others act quickly and rely on their instincts when making decisions. They may share the same company goals with you, yet have different ideas for reaching those goals. It may take something drastic, from a decrease in sales to a mass desertion from your staff to make you realize that your standards are too high. Your staff's frustration level will reach a point where nothing they do is acceptable, so they stop doing anything.[6]

When others act independently—which is what we need if we are to become less burdened—we run the risk of feeling irritated by our perceived lack of control. If we're not careful, this is when we alienate others by instructing or giving too much unwanted advice. We justify this invasion of privacy by concocting a rule: "If I can't make mistakes, no one else is allowed to, either."

After all, it's not a race. We constantly think that we must stay at least one step ahead of everyone else. This keeps us locked into a no-win situation of self-created paranoia. Being part of a team doesn't automatically mean one is destined to work as a nameless drone. You can be unique and a team player at the same time. With group effort, individuals can stand out while the team offers support, both in triumph and in defeat. As we have seen, one of the most problematic side effects of perfectionism is feeling isolated and unsupported. Joining forces with others can give us a sense of strength and belonging. A good support system can act as a sounding board, which is especially valuable when the work climate involves high-pressure responsibilities.

Other people may have good ideas. We don't need to come up with them all, or have to strive to prove ours is better. It isn't necessary to always have the last word. Often we can save ourselves from needless overload by remaining quiet in meetings, developing our supportive and listening skills at the same time. Remember, the one who speaks up is usually elected to chair the committee. Leadership advisor William Rogers offers a word to the wise, suggesting it is sometimes prudent to "say as little as possible while appearing to be awake."

Others will respect you for recognizing that many approaches can lead to positive outcomes. Diversity offers the advantage of a broader perspective and new angles to our limited vantage point. As you step away from one-upmanship you will find that joint effort relieves you from the pressure of having to be an expert in everything. The contributions of others do not make your ideas wrong or less useful. To work well with others—a true indicator of success—and to get the best from those who work with you, respect is crucial. Instead of trying to bullwhip others into action to reduce your own anxiety, you can learn to enjoy the opportunity teamwork affords. Listening more and advising less is a good beginning. Instead of assuming others are not doing things correctly, see if you can notice the variety of ways in which people are creatively productive. Put yourself in their shoes. How does your behavior look from their vantage point?

Excellence is rarely a solo effort, and it does not require exhausting martyrdom. The trophy of success can be awarded to more than one winner. You can learn to get ahead *along with* your teammates, not always *instead of* them. In an award acceptance speech, the first thing any real winner usually says is, "I want to thank so-and-so for making it all possible." Support and joint contributions are worth acknowledging. You can and will do special things all on your own. Yet special performances are not what's special about you. You are special when you are individual, and that includes being a creative individual within the context of team efforts and relationships.

A BALANCE PLAN FOR MASTERING INTENSITY
IN EVERYDAY GENIUS RELATIONSHIPS

- Avoid assuming automatic roles based on second-guessing what others want from you. Ask yourself if you're stuck in a pose instead of being authentic.
- Set parameters and mean it. But be sure your borders are permeable enough for trusted others to enter your life. When you need to set limits with others, avoid overjustifying.
- Get rid of unresolved anger, resentment, and loathing. Your destiny can't bear the weight of it. Dole out compassion extravagantly, including toward yourself.
- Avoid limiting your interactions to giving advice, becoming a walking, talking reference library, or fixing others' problems. Ask things of your relationships from time to time or you will train those around you to give you nothing and take everything.
- Don't expect everyone else to go at your pace. Use your conversational skills and verbal agility appropriately. Find some true peers with whom you need not hold back, slow down, explain what you mean, or curb your humor. In other situations, respect the differences and needs of others and never punish them because they "don't get it." Never fool yourself that verbal shredding from you is for someone's "own good."
- Remember, love is built upon respect. Insist on respectful treatment, and give it away in equal proportion.
- If you are very excitable, be mindful of how your high energy and enthusiasm can overwhelm others.
- Be careful with your sense of humor. Biting sarcasm and clowning for attention can be relationship killers.
- Watch your focus of attention. When you are with another person, endeavor to stay fully engaged and present, not adrift in your thoughts.

- Do not allow your empathy to rule you. Workable intimate relationships are a two-way street. Martyrdom only breeds disrespect.
- Learn the difference between being spontaneous and impulsive. Self-mastery is the key.

A BALANCE PLAN FOR MASTERING COMPLEXITY
IN EVERYDAY GENIUS RELATIONSHIPS

- Build a broad support network. Gifted adults need many types of friendships (including intellectual, sports-minded, playful, and spiritual ones, and those with business colleagues, people older than you, and people younger than you) for their lives to feel rounded. Strengthen your core identity within the context of these relationships instead of overadapting to them. Don't expect one relationship to fulfill all of your emotional or social needs.
- Let people see all sides of your personality, and share the responsibility for continued enjoyment in relationships.
- Never hide out in feigned conformity unless it is absolutely necessary. Endeavor to be yourself when you begin new relationships; this will avoid a setup for disappointment later on.
- Learn to use your inner resources and spirituality to fill in the gaps that occur in human relationships. Revel in solitude; just don't stay there.
- Be careful about avoiding intimacy by intellectualizing your feelings.
- Honestly assess how much your multiple interests take away from primary relationships.
- Others may not share your powerful inner drive for self-growth. Allow them their own agenda. However, do not indulge in wishful thinking and partner with someone's potential, which may never be realized.
- Use your self-awareness skills to your advantage. Neither avoidance of self-examination nor a fatalistic view of mistakes will contribute to your well-being.
- Seek out trustworthy others with whom you can share in your transcendent experiences.
- Realize that your exceptional memory can turn disappointment into a storehouse of resentment. Be prepared to let go of petty judgments and grudges. Ask yourself every day what's really important.

- Everything original and new is not better. Learn to keep the best of tradition and blend it with novelty.

A BALANCE PLAN FOR MASTERING DRIVE
IN EVERYDAY GENIUS RELATIONSHIPS

- Although you have experienced a great deal of misinterpretation and even rejection for being different, keep pressing forward with your efforts to get close to others.
- To avoid using drive as a control method, practice using all three types of assertiveness: limit-setting, request, and commendatory.
- Overextending yourself is always a threat to balance and an invitation for burnout and estrangement from others.
- Hold on to your desire for the ideal, but never confuse the *ideals* of perfection with the demand that others behave perfectly.
- Perseverance is one of your best attributes, but there is an art to knowing when to let go.
- Remember that procrastination is the flip side of perfectionism, and any decision to *not* decide is still a decision.
- Good relationships are built on promises that are kept. Use your natural drive to challenge yourself to be as good a finisher as you are a starter.
- Use systems and organization for your benefit; do not let it govern your life or others.
- Never underestimate the value of your own methods and timing, but don't impose them on others.
- Never underestimate the value of collaboration and teamwork. Very few things of consequence are created in a vacuum. Aim for principled work, while validating others' views.
- Neither recklessness nor risklessness is a form of self-liberation. Accept reasonable risk as an effective tool for self-actualization.

PART FIVE

LIBERATE THYSELF

EVOLUTIONARY INTELLIGENCE
IN ACTION

16
SELF-LIBERATION

Life shrinks or expands in proportion to one's courage.

—Anaïs Nin

At this stage of our development we know who we are, why we are different, and why we are intended to deliver our exceptional gifts in the service of something greater than ego, broader than individual accomplishment, and deeper than external approval. Liberation and responsibility are inseparable. Everything changes when we accept that we can propel ourselves forward with full force only if we move from the very core of our being. To take this leap of faith in ourselves when we are not properly balanced will only make us spiral out of control. Freedom demands that we must learn to operate according to our inner directives. So far our mastery has been incremental and our maneuvers performed at low altitude. Now, like any pilot eager to really fly, it's time for us to solo.

We have explored the following essential steps toward achieving the fulfillment only freedom can offer:

- Identify thyself
- Understand thyself
- Reveal and heal thyself
- Manage thyself

Now we must put all of the pieces together and integrate our differences so that our abilities can take their rightful place in the larger plan. We are ready for our final step:

- Liberate thyself

SELF-LIBERATION

What does "liberate thyself" mean for us? It means taking ourselves seriously, embracing our differences, maturing our choices from outer control to inner rule, and doing the work and making the sacrifices necessary to live from the inside out. We don't reveal ourselves to gratify our ego, nor are we naive sacrificial lambs ready to be exploited for the wrong purpose. Rather, we are on our own, wholly free for the first time because we have reached the point where we no longer need to seek permission from anyone or anything outside of our own soul.

This is the point of realization we've been working toward, when we have achieved both self-definition and self-mastery. We are finally safe to reveal ourselves, because our gifts of ability have been tested by experience and tempered by what we have learned and what we know we must do. The apparently random revelations that have occurred in seemingly unrelated moments are now clearly connected to our very center. What was once an unconscious pressure to reach a goal is now a conscious strategy to fulfill a distinct purpose. Before, we were fainthearted in the activation of our gifts; we stopped and started many times over the years, uncertain of our destination and purpose.

Because we have come to accept our First Nature traits, we can also accept the fact that Everyday Geniuses cannot escape the pull of personal destiny. The subtle messages of our inner agenda call us in quiet moments of the night and echo in scattered moments during our busy days. They call us to liberate our thoughts and abilities and to free ourselves from the glamours of the ego so that we may carry out the revolutionary acts of which we are capable. We sense this guiding presence and know it has immense power. Now that we've accepted our Mandated Mission, we're more focused than ever before. Over the years we come to recognize the mysterious force that provides us with direction whenever we get too far off course. Sometimes the wake-up call is like a practical joke. Oftentimes it is painful—the voice of truth that can be heard only when we've wandered into the wilderness.

Although we learn to accept the puzzling course of our destiny, even when we increase our consciousness and listen with great willingness to the soul's intentions, we are repeatedly frustrated by how unclear these revelations are. We get bits and pieces here and there—images, powerful emotional reactions, disappointments, and dreams. We may reasonably wonder why the path of destiny must be so full of detours, especially those bumpy side roads we seem to travel until we learn to heed the stop signs. Wouldn't it all be so much easier if each of us came into the world fully assembled and with a toe tag that carried explicit directions? "This is a Type XZ300-4K Model. The purpose of this model is . . . For best results . . . Never . . . Handle with care."

And yet nothing so vital as personal destiny could ever be so simple. Which means there is no use in waiting to go forward until we are absolutely sure of our direction and filled with confidence, for as breakthrough thinkers called to stick our necks out and change the status quo, we never obtain that level of certainty. Uncertainty is the draw. It is the future. It is the realm of possibility.

We know this, and yet we all want to have it both ways—to forge ahead daringly in our creative acts and yet proceed without fear of failure. To fulfill our high potential autonomously we are quite willing to take on the challenges of the world if we can do so comfortably, and with a reasonable promise of success.

Many times we feel just like my seventeen-year-old Everyday Genius client who complained: "If I'm supposed to be using my mind and talents to do something important, what's the point of having to grope around in the dark all the time? I'm listening, I'm willing, so why can't we just get on with it? Hand me the outline or a map or something, so I don't have to waste time looking in the wrong places and doing the wrong thing. I don't get it!"

We don't get it, and it does seem chaotic. It must be chaotic because the flip side of dynamic creativity—Revolutionary Action—is filled with confusion, uncertainty, and momentary despair. The journey of self-actualization is never an easy one. It is a long, unpredictable, and arduous trek, not a simple trip to the corner wisdom store, and certainly not a destination with reserved seating.

EVOLUTIONARY MOMENTS:
A PREVIEW OF LIFE'S COMING ATTRACTIONS

It's always fascinating to hear high achievers talk about their lives. Some seem to have plotted their lives like chess grandmasters and others have hopscotched their way to eminence, while still others seem to have engaged in a kind of demolition derby, leaving behind a trail of ruined vehicles until they finally climbed into the one that got them moving on the speedway in their chosen field. No matter how we might describe how they've lived their lives, each of them experienced several key moments along the way that helped shape their lives. I call these Evolutionary Moments. We all have them, but what sets liberated Everyday Geniuses apart from everyone else is that they experience a more profound and more intense Evolutionary Moment that brings the purpose of their lives into sharp focus. I call these events catalyzing Evolutionary Moments.

Every one of us has probably glanced skyward and seen a jet rending the fabric of the sky, and wondered where it departed from and where it was headed. Like a jet creating an evanescent vapor trail, sometimes Everyday Geniuses leave behind indicators of where they've been and where they are going, but these signs soon drift off and disappear.

Whether as Everyday Geniuses we have the flight logs we've kept to tell us what stopovers we've made, what our intended flight path was, and what landmarks we used to plot our course, whether we've been on a non-stop direct flight or have been barnstorming our way across the landscape of our lives, one thing remains true: At various points, whether by apparent whim or by design, we've made course corrections. Whether we received navigational aid from someone else or our own inner compass guides us, whether the winds blew us off course or we diverted to avoid a storm, when we're finally back on the ground we can all look back and see when those moments took place.

These Evolutionary Moments may be one event or a series of seemingly disconnected events occurring over many years. Whether they are one radical change in direction or a series of incremental adjustments, Evolutionary Moments put us on destiny's track.

Strangely, an Evolutionary Moment often occurs unnoticed. Only later, if at all, do we recognize its significance. Even though our dreams, expectations, abilities, personalities, histories, and futures all collide in these unusual experiences, it may be a long time before we admit it "was all meant to be." Most often we're so busy with attending to all the details of flying our lives that we can't take time out to look back. When the moment occurred, we may have had a vague sense that something of importance was happening, but we were too occupied to stop and make sense of it. That's why once we've reached a certain destination point, usually around middle age, we often decide to take out the map and examine both where we've been and where we'd like to go next.

Admittedly, some eminent achievers fail to recognize that these were the particular events that shaped their calling. Yet the majority of self-actualizers who closely examine their lives underscore certain moments as the crucial turning points that made all the difference in their world, and ultimately in ours. Call them serendipitous. Call them a part of our fate or our destiny, but in hindsight, each of us can point to experiences that now, seen in full context, are recognized as having given our life its current shape and definition. Ideally, if we take advantage of the moment to relax and enjoy the view, we can properly assess whether or not we are moving in the direction we were meant to go. Then we can plot the next stage(s) of our course accordingly.

Most Everyday Geniuses don't sit down when they are youngsters and say, "I'm going to design the electric car"—or organize a citizen's action lobby, or write the biography of a future president of the United States. Even when we announce what we are going to be when we grow up, we're usually mistaken. If that weren't so, lots of our friends would now be race car drivers, ballerinas, and astronauts. Instead, it is through a series of Evolutionary Moment turnabout events and awakenings that exemplars of liberated Everyday Genius follow a deeper and sometimes inexplicable impulse that magnetizes them toward their true destiny. In real-world time the process may appear as a single moment. In actuality, it is a series of seemingly unrelated events over years that don't coalesce until the purpose becomes plain. This is the point at which Everyday Geniuses have enough dots to connect to see a meaningful picture of their life's work.

THE CATALYZING
EVOLUTIONARY MOMENT

When I was a young woman, I received a chemistry set as a gift. I loved it. There were lots of test tubes, graduated cylinders and beakers, and even a balance for weighing out the chemicals. The experiment that I loved most and which probably best serves to illustrate my point about Evolutionary Moments involved adding, drop by drop, a substance into a beaker of water. Those drops represent the many experiences we have as our lives unfold. As each drop combines with the molecules of the water, the concentration of the molecules changes and thus the chemical composition of the water is altered. Eventually the concentration reaches a level such that one additional drop catalyzes a reaction that crystallizes the water in the beaker and changes it from a liquid to a solid. In much the same way, the accumulation of our experiences—the accretion of our Evolutionary Moments—changes our composition. Most often the ways in which we are changing are not immediately visible or obvious, but we may experience one catalyzing Evolutionary Moment that alters our state of reality.

Suddenly it is as though we have been handed some new information that allows us to honor ourselves and embrace our true mission. We no longer feel as though we have to dilute our gifts or our unique traits; rather, we can use them full strength in service of the greater good. The reason so many of our previous Evolutionary Moments have gone unnoticed is that memory is selective—in fact, research into brain chemistry and memory supports this. We tend to remember either the highs or the lows because they produce more potent chemical reactions in the brain. Consequently, for many people, the true catalyzing Evolutionary Moment occurs when we experience either trauma or ecstasy. However, without those previous "drops" of experience, the reaction would not be as strong, the results not as far-reaching.

The lack of clarity at the time when the initial Evolutionary Moment happens helps explain why being an early prodigy is not predictive of eventual eminence or even success. What appear to be the most apparent signs of later high achievement often don't bear fruit. The pathway upon which our destiny will take us into the future rests in the realm of intuition. Personal evolution is a process, not a singular incident. For most of our lives we cannot create it or force it to happen, though eventually wisdom offers us the opportunity to help facilitate it.

Even when people tell me it was a single monumental event that changed the direction of their lives, I have a hard time believing it. Even when we don't remember these subtler awakenings, we can rest assured that they have occurred. Never let the revisionist-history tactics of friends, family, or coworkers convince you otherwise. A common human response to an Everyday Genius' seemingly inevitable success usually sounds something like Uncle Pete presiding over the family reunion: "There was never a doubt in my mind that Harold would become a Wall Street wizard. I knew it all along."

Evolutionary Moments are critical to Advanced Development for two primary reasons: they break high potential open and force it to move beyond mere hard work and expertise, and they have the power to turn us around and set us back on our true course. Fortunately, we do have a hand in shaping our lives, because most often we can't see where we're going until we arrive. Incrementally, each Evolutionary Moment identifies the piece of the personal-destiny puzzle that we will later add to the

others. Well before we realize it, such events shape our lives and rein-
force our goals and keep us on course with our quest. To identify our Evolutionary Moments, we must possess enough life experience to examine
them with the wisdom of hindsight.

As suggested, these moments that cause our abilities and drives to
jell are frequently catalyzed by discontent or dire necessity. At other
times the Evolutionary Moment appears as a dare when others plant their
feet and effectively defy us to do what they have determined we cannot.
Sometimes they involve contact with a mentor or a brush with mastery
at just the right time to shed a guiding light on what was previously
a darkened pathway. Sometimes we are revitalized when an external
event demands our attention, and we suddenly realize, "This is where I
belong!"

TRUE-LIFE EVOLUTIONARY MOMENTS

Eminent individuals frequently help us unveil the essence of the Evolutionary Moment when they describe it in retrospect. They are usually
staggered by the resulting strength of the Self that emerges and are
shocked by the ensuing clarification of their goals. Most find the transfor-
mative experience surprising, expecting such epiphanies to be either
more dramatic or less ambiguous. Perhaps the journey doesn't work that
way—clear-cut blueprints of our individual destinies are not to be had
for the asking.

In 1934 Admiral Richard Byrd "found himself" during his solo vigil
at a weather base in Antarctica. Later he realized the momentous nature
of the event:

> Aside from the meteorological and auroral work, I had no important
> purposes. There was nothing of that sort. Nothing whatever, except one
> man's desire to know that kind of experience to the full, to be by him-
> self for a while and to taste peace and quiet and solitude long enough to
> find out how good they really are.[1]

Of course, the Evolutionary Moments are different for each of us,
often being a cascade of realizations that fit our uniqueness and individual purpose. Unlike Admiral Byrd, most of us will not travel to the
South Pole to find ourselves or to figure out our life's work. The true Self
is not bound to a particular locale or encumbered by calendars, academic

degrees, age, or gender. The maturation of our philosophy of life, our skills, influence, and calling, contain a good bit of mystery that stems from an enigmatic core directive that has escaped our conscious detection for many years.

Let's take a look at the Evolutionary Moments of eight eminent Everyday Geniuses.

Alexander Graham Bell, inventor of the telephone, was born in Scotland in 1847. Accounts of his life's work point to three primary Evolutionary Moments. The first occurred when Bell's grandfather, concerned that the fifteen-year-old boy was withdrawn and sullen, decided to invite him for a visit to London. This yearlong stay proved pivotal in the would-be inventor's evolutionary growth:

> Away from his demanding father, Alexander felt freer. Instead of constantly having to prove himself, he at last could act however he wished. At home his parents discouraged him from reading books for fun. But his grandfather loved to read novels and plays. Together, he and Alec read through the plays of Shakespeare, many of which Alec learned to recite word for word.

When his father came to take Alec home, "he could barely recognize him. Alec had an air of confidence that made him seem like a different person."[2]

Like his father, Alexander Graham Bell taught the deaf to speak. As a professor of oratory in Boston, he fell in love in 1873 with a deaf woman whose parents denied him her hand in marriage until he could prove himself. It was this challenge from his bride's parents that sparked his lifelong obsession with invention. He turned his attention to experimenting with machine-made sound, declaring: "If I can make a deaf-mute talk, I can make metal talk."

The last of these key Evolutionary Moments in Bell's life occurred as he was forced to defend his sole right to the newly invented telephone in court. His legal victory won him fame and fortune; the fortune was what financed *Science* magazine, established the National Geographic Society, and funded a school for the deaf where Anne Sullivan's work with Helen Keller was later conducted. Bell's greatest hope was to be remembered for his service to the deaf.

Akira Kurosawa, the legendary Japanese director, is considered to be one of the greatest filmmakers of the twentieth century. As a youngster, he loved movies, although many in his community disapproved of his interest. His father's acceptance of his son's obsession with the cinema was an early Evolutionary Moment in Kurosawa's life. With the exception of courses in writing and art, Kurosawa was a poor student who generally kept to himself. Eventually he took up painting as a career, but was forced to give it up during the Great Depression. This served as a second Evolutionary Moment, which soon triggered another one. When desperate for work he answered on impulse an ad for an assistant film director. Years later, as an Academy Award–winning master of the cinema, Kurosawa acknowledged this "whim" as the vital turning point in his life.

Dian Fossey, the famed zoologist, had loved animals since her childhood days in San Francisco. Her parents did not share her affinity for animals and did not allow her any pets other than a goldfish. Later in her life, Fossey would recall the death of her pet goldfish—an early Evolutionary Moment—as the most painful event of her childhood. In her college years, Fossey aspired to become a veterinarian, but changed her mind because she felt a strong internal conflict about her choice. She knew she was close to her destined vocation, but not close enough. This discontent was yet another in a series of Evolutionary Moments that reached its apex when she realized her lifelong dream of going to Africa. It was a dream that had haunted her for years, which she acknowledged as an inner call to encounter the wildlife there. In 1938 she confessed: "I had this great urge. . . . I had it the day I was born. Some may call it destiny. My parents and friends called it dismaying."[3] Ultimately Fossey's work with gorillas, her "gentle giants," brought her fame and notoriety. Her unflagging, pioneering research and devotion to animals raised the consciousness of millions worldwide to continue her fight to preserve gorillas and other endangered species after her death in 1985.

Billy Klüver, an electrical engineer with a gift for improvisation, learned to blend his technological expertise with his passion for art. He was born in Monaco in 1927, and shortly thereafter he and his parents moved to Sweden. Early on he was seriously involved in the study of science, tossing off his fascination with art as "just another form of intellectual activity." At the time, Klüver could not have interpreted this seemingly strange pair of interests as a true Evolutionary Moment. In college he built his first recognizable bridge between technology and art when he joined the Stockholm University Film Society—an unheard-of choice for an engineering student. He would later become the president of that same organization. Another Evolutionary Moment occurred when his graduate school advisor, Nobel prize winner for physics Hannes Alfvén, gave him permission to produce an animated film about the motion of electrons. Following his education, he worked with famed oceanographer Jacques Cousteau on his ship, *Calypso,* helping to develop one of the first underwater cameras. At age twenty-six another Evolutionary Moment occurred when he acknowledged his lifelong desire to emigrate to the United States: "I always knew I wanted to come here. I saw the movies and wanted to see for myself." Though he expected to find suitable work in a laboratory or in radio, his relocation coincided with the McCarthy hearings. As a foreigner, he thought it wise to avoid being questioned, as so many researchers were, so he took time out to pursue his Ph.D. at the University of California, Berkeley.

Although his path was unique, like several of his colleagues he went on to became a veteran at Bell Laboratories. Yet Klüver still felt the calling of his deep-rooted love of art, which pressed him to seek out new ways to blend the visual arts with technology. An unforgettable Evolutionary Moment occurred in Klüver's life when Swiss kinetic sculptor Jean Tinguely asked him to help find some old bicycle wheels for one of Tinguely's projects. This unusual tie changed his life forever because in that partnership he learned two vital lessons: how to listen to an artist, and when enough must be enough: "I knew I could solve the problems, if I took a day, but the curtain had to go up. Artists still complain that engineers never learn that the curtain must go up."

Although during the early 1960s Klüver was tagged by *Life* magazine as "The Mr. Fix-It of kinetic art," he was later relabeled by the *New York Times* as the "artist's scientist." He took his coalition-building style into the theater arts by cofounding "Nine Evenings: Theater and Engineering," which integrated the creative talents of ten artists with thirty scientists. This was but one of many Evolutionary Moments in Klüver's fascinating Renaissance-man career.

Many consider this daring move as the beginning of Klüver's efforts to reshape the face of technological art in the twentieth century. His collaboration with artists such as Andy Warhol, Robert Rauschenberg, and Jasper Johns required him to innovate all the time. His behind-the-scenes influence was instrumental in the founding of Experiments in Art and Technology, the first organization created to bring artists and engineers together. Although the engineers often found the artwork "ridiculous," it was ultimately the process of collaboration that was most valuable: "The one-to-one collaboration between two people from different fields always holds the possibility of producing something new and different that neither of them could have done alone."[4]

In the 1930s in the midst of the world's enormous problems, few were aware of the underlying anguish that the forceful-appearing Franklin Delano Roosevelt was suffering. FDR covered over his physical impairment—even going so far as to deny its existence to himself—but he paid dearly for it. FDR biographer Hugh Gregory Gallagher, himself a polio victim, went to Warm Springs for rehabilitation, as Roosevelt did. Gallagher considers the onset of polio and incurable paralysis to be the primary event that shaped Roosevelt's life. Gallagher's writing underscores the importance of the full range of Evolutionary Moments—public and private, thrilling and traumatic—that shaped the life of FDR, whose Evolutionary Intelligence required him to reinvent himself as a paraplegic with a Mandated Mission, integrating Humanistic Vision and initiating the Revolutionary Action that made him a true shaper of our world. As Gallagher writes: "Failure to appreciate this is to risk misunderstanding the man and his achievement."

Just beneath the hardened exterior of one of history's all-time paragons of vision and fortitude resided the private FDR, the one we never knew, who fought so hard to overcome his feelings of isolation. And like most evolutionaries on whose shoulders progress leaps forward, Roosevelt probably had little awareness of the sweeping ripple effects caused by his bold acts and his personal travails. For instance, he felt such kinship with other polio victims that he pushed for Warm Springs to be more than a treatment center—he wanted it to be a springboard for a cure. He enlisted the help of his friend George Allen, a businessman, to raise money (later through the March of Dimes) to fight for a cure for polio. Another ripple effect of FDR's vision funded the work of Jonas Salk and Albert Sabin, the heroes whose efforts have nearly wiped the disease from the face of the earth.

Like most evolutionaries, FDR had some enemies, but his public expression of his natural optimism and his radical New Deal programs won the confidence and hearts of the majority of Americans. Through the insightful lens of retrospection the turning points that stand out as the major dots in FDR's destiny picture become obvious, though we will never know exactly how or when he himself discovered the picture within the puzzle. Yet history makes it clear to us that the Evolutionary Moments in his life coalesced to make Roosevelt someone altogether different at the very time in the country's evolution when something altogether different was exactly what was needed.

THE REWARDS OF GENIUS

Since 1981, the MacArthur Foundation Fellowship—the so-called genius award—has been bestowed upon an array of Everyday Geniuses in fields that range from carpentry and anthropology to the cinema and poetry.

Denise Shekerjian became fascinated with the life stories of the MacArthur Fellows and investigated the individual recipients in search of answers to her questions about what creativity really is and how "through creative achievement we find a new measure of human dignity."[5] In *Uncommon Genius: How Great Ideas Are Born*, she retraces the circuitous path of the award winners' creative development and delves into the real-world process that results in exceptional achievement. Within these stories we can see the turning points in these individuals' lives that provided the momentum for the Evolutionary Moments process.

Shekerjian's interviews offer fascinating insights into the creative process and identify the turning points that parallel the Evolutionary Moments process. Andy McGuire is a MacArthur Fellow whose life exemplifies the seemingly random course of Evolutionary Moments and how fate intervenes in unexpected and timely ways to sculpt our identities and aim us toward our entrusted life purpose. The twists and turns in his life that liberated his Everyday Genius and allowed his special abilities to find their niche were not the kind most people would consciously choose. McGuire was raised in a blue-collar neighborhood by "plain folks" parents:

> "My father was a factory worker, the kind of guy who sees things very simply. Something is either black or it's white, right or wrong. No middle ground. No special words with which to duel. No frills. I grew up with the idea that problems should be viewed in very basic terms."
>
> Growing up wasn't easy. He [McGuire] spent a lot of years on an assembly line. College was a struggle both academically and financially. When he finally made it out, he traveled east to apprentice himself to a harpsichord maker in Waltham, Massachusetts. As an illustration of his naïveté, he mentions that he didn't think to write or

call the man to say he was coming. He just showed up one day on the doorstep, ready to go to work. Naturally, the master craftsman couldn't use him but promised to consider him in eight or nine months when the next opening came up. In the meantime, McGuire took a job as a machinist in a manufacturing shop.

At this stage of his life, McGuire had already experienced several Evolutionary Moments, like the vocational about-face in Massachusetts. However, soon after, he was handed an article in the *Boston Globe* that instantly transported him back in time to the morning of his seventh birthday when an Evolutionary Moment occurred that, now nearly twenty years later, would once again transform his life:

> "The article hit something pretty deep. When I was seven I was severely burned. My bathrobe caught fire on the kitchen stove. It was early in the morning, the morning of my seventh birthday actually, and somebody must have left the stove on all night. My sister was the one who found me. . . . In all, I spent three and a half months in the hospital and had four different skin grafts. Later, much later in my life, I recreated the scene together with my sister. . . . It's incredible how much of it I could recall—the contortion of my limbs, the changing of dressings, the mental games I devised to cope with the pain."

The article McGuire read helped him to see the link between his childhood tragedy and his life direction. He learned of the formation of a political action group to lobby for laws requiring flame-resistant sleepwear for children. McGuire went to every meeting of the group from that day forward. His plans to manufacture harpsichords went by the wayside in favor of his Mandated Mission to advocate for public health and safety.

> It was the start of his lifelong involvement with issues of public health and safety. From there he tackled the ominously powerful tobacco industry and won the fight for fire-safe self-extinguishing cigarettes. At the same time, he expanded his concern to include mandatory seatbelt laws, handgun laws, and the rights of the disabled. . . . Step-by-step, person-by-person, McGuire forms armies of concerned citizens—one hundred, eight hundred, thousands strong. He steps aside and lets them shine in the spotlight of press conferences and public hearings. . . . In this way, he builds a groundswell and fans out the power base . . .

Unimpeded by the fact that he had no experience with filmmaking, McGuire went on to make documentary films to advance his causes, one an "artistic, medically accurate, socially sensitive film" about burn injuries, another for the Shriners' Burn Institute that amazed him by winning an Emmy. Shekerjian asked him what issue of social importance was left for him to tackle. Pondering the question, he replied, "War, I guess. It's the ultimate injury."[6]

Ellen Stewart, another MacArthur fellowship winner, undertook an exceptional journey that was one of Shekerjian's favorites because "it's about love. . . . If the creative impulse were better understood physiologically, it wouldn't come as a surprise to me to learn that it is the heart and not the mind that controls the sparks and directs the inventiveness." The Evolutionary Moments in Stewart's life can be easily traced. In 1950 when she left her Louisiana home to go to Chicago she envisioned herself as a fashion designer. She eventually made her way to New York with the dream of entering a fashion design school that allowed entry to young women of color. But the friend who had agreed to room with her never showed up at Grand Central Station. She prayed for a job and got one that same day—at Saks Fifth Avenue sweeping floors and picking loose threads off the clothes. As Shekerjian tells it:

> For years Ellen worked at Saks Fifth Avenue, exploring the city on her off time, which is how she met a little Rumanian immigrant named Papa Abe Diamond in the Jewish neighborhood down on Delancey Street. He became her good friend who supplied her with odd bits of cloth; she became his adopted daughter, the future fashion designer.
>
> One day, the story continues, disaster struck in a dressing room at the store. One of the rich white ladies was in a frenzy over some mishap with a ball gown. It was lunchtime and no one was around to fix it. Ellen stepped in and earned a promotion to the design department in the process. The best part of the promotion, she tells me, was that she got to take off the blue smock all the colored girls had to wear in those days. In itself, that was an achievement, but the real coup was that her dress creations, sewn up from Papa Diamond's remnant fabrics, were finally noticed. One thing led to another and Ellen's ball gowns were put in Saks' windows carrying price tags of fifteen hundred dollars.

If Stewart's story of genius stopped here, it would still be a wonderful example of Intensity, Complexity, and Drive woven into excellence. Yet there is far more to tell. As with all who are compelled to liberate their

Everyday Genius, Stewart's First Nature traits—her inescapable heightened receptivity and the urge to perfect—could never be silenced. More Evolutionary Moments were on the way that would disrupt her life and reshape her focus of attention:

> She worked as a designer at Saks, but increasingly she felt resentment from blacks and whites alike. Eventually she got so sick that she thought she was dying, quit, and went off to Morocco to recuperate. There, in a vision, the late Papa Diamond appeared to her. He repeated a story he had often told her, which ended with the moral: Get a pushcart, daughter, and push it for other people. If you do that, it will always take you where you want to go.

In typical Evolutionary Moment style, this was about the same time Stewart's foster brother was struggling to produce a play he had written. The play quickly closed, leaving him penniless. It was suddenly clear to Stewart that here was her pushcart. She was determined to create a theater for people down on their luck like her brother—the nearly starving stage artists who needed her support to express their talents. She also decided that no one would be denied an opportunity.

Stewart told Shekerjian how the little theater began in a shabby old store that had to double as a coffee shop to meet New York's license requirements. Ironically, she financed her new project by designing high-society dresses for the most exclusive stores in New York, for Dior in Paris, and for guests at Queen Elizabeth II's coronation. The people in the neighborhood were confused by her well-dressed garment-business visitors calling on her on these somewhat mean streets. They decided that she must be running a prostitution ring. Her door was pelted with garbage and she was spat upon on the street. They called the police. But clearly fate had more in mind for Ellen Stewart. The policeman who responded to the call was a former performer. Inspired by her story, he gave her much-needed advice to help her comply with all of New York's regulations and laws.

Stewart persevered as the founder and artistic director of La MaMa, an experimental theater that is internationally renowned for its global vision and cultural harmony.

> Located on the lower east side where it has become a vital and stabilizing component of its neighborhood, La MaMa has grown from its early basement theatre with nine tables and chairs to a multi-purpose art

complex encompassing four buildings, housing two theatres, a cabaret, seven floors of free rehearsal space, and an archive extensively documenting the beginnings of off-off Broadway theatre. . . . La MaMa E.T.C., long a laboratory for artists, dancers, writers, musicians, actors, and directors to gather, investigate and create, has come to symbolize the very nature of innovative risk taking.[7]

Eventually Stewart began to receive queries from aspiring playwrights. She was committed to telling people's life stories. She took Lanford Wilson and Sam Shepard under her wing for years. Both went on to win Pulitzer prizes. The list of now-famous artists who have graced her career-forming stage is formidable, including Bette Midler, Nick Nolte, Danny DeVito, and Billy Crystal.

Her theater was so off-off-Broadway that at the time her productions were considered illegitimate art. Rather than fight popular opinion, Stewart packed her bags and headed for Paris, forming an American theater company that was a smash hit. She was then invited to return to New York as a true artist. None of these things has deterred Stewart from her mission of caring, handing out lunch money to street people, and nourishing the budding artist who is in need: "Without these people what would I be? Zee-rrr-ooo, and I'm the first to know it."[8]

Over its nearly four decades of operation, La MaMa's works have been recognized worldwide and have been honored with hundreds of drama awards. Yet none of the renown has changed the organization's original commitment to nurture the artist's creative development, not merely produce plays.

Remember, for some Everyday Geniuses the path of advanced development is clearly marked by a single event that stands out as the primary turning point—something so powerful that nothing again is ever the same. For these individuals life as they knew it instantly evaporates into thin air—they instantly become foreigners in their own lives. For others, Evolutionary Moments are a string of events that are just as timely and commanding though more subtle. Often they are spread out over time and far less obvious in their influence. Nonetheless, as we have seen, later on in life hindsight reveals a road map of these seemingly unconnected events that give rise to new insights and a sense of relief that underneath life's haphazard veneer there is an invisible game plan. With a sigh and a knowing smile, we can finally say: "Oh, now I see it—that makes sense after all."

Franklin Roosevelt's Evolutionary Moment experience was shocking and monumental, the loss of his ability to walk due to polio. Eleanor Roosevelt's path of liberated Everyday Genius represents the second type of Evolutionary Moment process, a string of less dramatic events that shaped her extraordinary Mandated Mission and reinvigorated her seemingly indefatigable dedication to a lifelong series of Revolutionary Acts.

Eleanor Roosevelt's life story is particularly relevant to the Everyday Genius for two reasons. First, she is one of a handful of exceptional human beings who wrote openly and extensively about her inner experience. Second, she is a perfect example of the development process of the gifted individual: she felt compelled to evolve herself; she retained her humility; she was an Everyday Genius driven to integrate her remarkable abilities, her First Nature traits, and her Intensity, Complexity, and Drive in the form of service.

Eleanor Roosevelt has been one of the very few clearly gifted women who has shared enough of her inner life with others to serve as model of developed and integrated Everyday Genius. In many respects she is the consummate evolutionary. Her life has been the focus of countless biographies, and has served also as a case study for the exploration of adult giftedness and Advanced Development. Michael Piechowski has examined Eleanor Roosevelt's life from this perspective and written a biography that reveals the discipline and directedness of her inner life. She was indeed a woman with a deep and abiding sense of her Mandated Mission.

Eleanor Roosevelt's reputation as a humanitarian was the result of numerous Evolutionary Moments—some external, many internal. Piechowski tells us that whenever she felt unprepared or uninformed, she suffered feelings of great shame that propelled her to learn and broaden her mind:

> On her honeymoon in England, she was stumped by a question about the difference between state and federal courts in the United States. She felt ashamed of her ignorance and vowed to herself to learn how government works. Although she grew up with prejudice against Negroes and Jews, Jews later were among her closest friends. She also had close friends among blacks and became an effective champion of their rights. She was ignorant about raising children, cooking, running a household. Yet, she became an active child advocate as well as a writer and counselor à la "Dear Abby" on raising children and understanding their growth. . . . She became a manager and supervisor

of large numbers of personnel at the governor's mansion and the White House. Through her work in the Democratic Party, she became a public figure—and through her remarkable work at the United Nations, an international one. She became a political campaigner and functioned, though not officially, in the capacity of Franklin Roosevelt's vice president.[9]

Eleanor Roosevelt's life illustrates the process of self-actualization and moral development that comprises the journey toward the fulfillment of special abilities and their manifestation in the world via Evolutionary Intelligence. As a child, Eleanor was very aware that she was exceptionally sensitive, particularly struck by feelings of empathy for the poor little newsboys who lived in shanties or on the streets. She was highly receptive to the suffering of others, relentlessly curious, tuned in to all around her, and wildly imaginative. Everything about her young life was intense. Underneath her shyness was a robustness of spirit and powerful resolve. Though she didn't have the answers, at the age of fourteen she wrote: "I am always questioning because I cannot understand and never succeed in doing what I meant to do, never, never. . . . I can feel it in me sometimes that I can do much more [than] I am doing and I mean to try till I succeed."[10]

Throughout her life, Roosevelt held to ideal images for herself and the well-being of others. In many ways it was her sensitivity that made her heroic. She would indeed need to develop outstanding self-mastery skills to forge ahead with her Mandated Mission as a world leader and humanitarian lest she lose ground and herself along the way. In fact, like the swan in the duck yard, Eleanor also became lost as she grew into womanhood. In her twenties her amazing powers of self-reflection led her to discover that she had developed a false self: "I was simply absorbing the personalities of those around me and letting their tastes and interests dominate me."[11] She needed an experience that would cause her to relocate her true self. She found exactly what she needed when she worked for the Red Cross for two years. There she was exposed to an enormous variety of people in all kinds of situations. This was the point at which she really learned to see people for who they are, to suspend judgment, and to be truly accepting: "I learned then that practically no one in the world is entirely bad or entirely good, and that motives are often more important than actions."[12] Roosevelt began to cement her own values and principles for living, taking a giant step toward self-trust.

Her persistent investigation of the outer world and her inner land-scape illustrates her tremendous drive, sense of Mandated Mission, and devotion to that mission even before it had become clear to her. She knew that the process of becoming oneself was lifelong. She also knew that even within a lifetime the period for self-discovery is short; the inner sense of urgency never dies away entirely, but only is calmed. She was conscious of the need to reinvent herself, without ever going back to the false self, as opportunities presented themselves; change was the only constant. Always, above all else, her spirituality tugged at her, urging her to discover and stay her true course in the service of the betterment of the world. This is what she ultimately advocated as the key to living life to its fullest: "Somewhere along the line of development we discover what we really are and then make our real decision for which we are responsible. Make that decision primarily for yourself because you can never really live anyone else's life, not even your child's. The influence you exert is through your own life and what you become yourself."[13]

As is true of many Everyday Geniuses, Eleanor often struggled with relationship issues. In line with her Everyday Genius commitment to Advanced Development, she was determined to succeed in this domain as well. She found love to be paradoxical, a balancing act of close attachment and letting go, autonomy paralleled with attachment. She endeavored to grow to a point where her form of love was not needy or demanding, but respectful and liberating: "The hard part of loving is that one has to learn so often to let go of those we love, so they can do things, so they can grow, so they can return to us with an even richer, deeper love."[14]

Piechowski describes the importance in Roosevelt's integrative process of learning to cope with emotional pain and inner conflict. He tells us that she dealt with these things by transcending them.

After her brother's and Franklin's deaths, Eleanor found refuge in meaningful work in the service of others. She recalled sometimes working so hard at the Office of Civilian Defense that she was on the verge of collapse. She believed that sorrow and regret were hard enough to manage, so she could not afford to feel bitter. Throughout all of this, Eleanor knew the true source of her strength. She was a deeply prayerful person who consistently petitioned God for peace, to provide for the welfare of children and friends, and to grant her the wisdom to counsel others well. She did not simply utter her prayers, but manifested them in her Mandated Mission.

DECLARING A PERSONAL MISSION

In the lobby of the headquarters of most large corporations and institutions we find a plaque inscribed with the company's mission statement. It defines in a few sentences the organization's purpose and overall goals. The words are placed there so customers, visitors, and employees can readily determine what the company is aiming at, its direction, its criteria for success, and its values and purpose.

Unfortunately, like many less-than-successful enterprises, we individuals often fail to follow our own guidelines, or, worse yet, have no personal mission statement at all. A meaningful mission statement evolves from insight and the recursive processes of change, both of which surface when we become serious about increasing our knowledge of our Self. The closer we are to our true mission, the more intense is our energy and enthusiasm—though, strangely, many of us are brought to insight by "accidents" of experience that compel us to go in a direction our thinking mind initially finds repugnant. Over time, we learn that what initially repelled us now compels us.

In *The Seven Habits of Highly Effective People*, Stephen Covey writes, "The most effective way I know to begin with the end in mind is to develop a *personal mission statement* or philosophy or creed. It focuses on what you want to be (character) and to do (contributions and achievements) and on the values or principles upon which being and doing are based."[15] Without knowing who we want to be and what we want to do, we will flounder when storms arise, or we will reach a goal with faulty expectations of permanent glory, eventually becoming lost in dark disillusionment and surrendering our hope.

Agnes de Mille observed, "No trumpets sound when the important decisions of our life are made. Destiny is made known silently." Goals matter. They are what keep us from staying (and stagnating) close to home and hearth, huddled under a lap robe. Remain cognizant of the fact that every achievement is the result of many minutes, hours, and even years of labors, all of which have value and enrich your life. Assess your accomplishments more accurately from a transcendent point of view in which every "win" of significance does not get entered into a public record book. Unsung heroes are often the ones who make the differences that matter.

Don't allow yourself to get stuck in a pose, looking the part instead of doing something to make your reimagined role real. It is far too easy to think of a revised life than to enact it. Simply wearing the guise of a truly independent seeker who supports his or her own actualization efforts is a monumental waste of the soul's time.

Whether we accept it or not, in order to create and advance toward the realization of our true Self each of us must grapple with demons, question again and again, wander about aimlessly for a while, spend time in the wilderness, and agonize in exile during times of turmoil and pain. Wrestle we must, but perhaps with less trepidation in knowing that gifted people are equipped to face down adversity, which is fitting since we are naturally inclined to push the limits anyway.

Connecting with a power greater than our own is the fundamental work of the liberated Everyday Genius. Advanced Development begins by pushing away obstacles that delay personal growth: fear, criticism, overcontrol, and limitation of experience. As our integration proceeds, previously vexing dichotomies blend, and what formerly seemed like an either/or situation turns into a both/and opportunity.

BEYOND I-NESS

Being distracted by our own wants and satisfaction takes precedence over much of our lives—for many of us it is our primary agenda until we are well into midlife. Though we may not admit it, much of our thinking, reacting, and planning is in the service of "I." Indeed, *I* is the word that occurs with the greatest frequency in most of our conversations. Yet at some point, either slowly over the years or immediately in the face of a life-changing calamity, we realize that too much ego and self-focus can stifle and eventually suffocate the best of human nature.

One way or another it becomes obvious that we have overemphasized our "I-ness." And in doing so we have become separated from the world. This realization is yet another paradox of Advanced Development: *More* for *me* turns out to be *less* substantial. Sustained I-centered living is ultimately an affront to the Divine purpose for which we were created, and at the very least it trivializes our exceptional gifts as showpieces of ordinary hedonism. This is the basis of genuine philanthropy—the reason why so many highly successful individuals strive so hard to attain wealth, power, and influence, only to find it unfulfilling, which leads them to seek charitable causes to move beyond their "I-ness" and give much of it away.

The ultimate goal of Advanced Development is to shift our visionary gaze to look at the world through more universal eyes. Apparent in the most eminent contributors to humanity is a synthesis of "I" and "we." Abraham Maslow describes this adopted perspective of the collective good as a "fusion between the person and his world which has so often been reported as an observable fact in creativeness, and which we may now reasonably consider the *sine qua non.*"

As the individual self advances, the personality and soul become integrated, and a complementary motivation emerges—the urge to apply abilities in ways that make a difference for others. Service is a natural activity of the highly evolved person. It is more than an urge to contribute to the progress or well-being of another out of a sense of "should" or to eradicate feelings of guilt; rather, it is a service response—an increasing awareness that we have a need to give. This need to give confirms how and why we have been redirected in Evolutionary Moments. We realize that we have been preparing our best resources not simply for ourselves, but for the betterment of the world.

Gift-oriented service is what truly completes the evolutionary circle. In *Dimensions of Growth*, authors John Firman and James Vargiu explain the relationship between Advanced Development and service:

> We see the essential divinity underlying the whole of the world's process of growth, and the fundamental rightness of helping that immense work forward as best we can in the time we have. . . . The dichotomy between self and others, between responding to others' needs and taking care of one's own disappears, as one acquires the practical wisdom to see the intrinsic legitimacy of both and the relative priority of each.[16]

Contrary to so many people's fears, our destined life of service to the greater good enhances rather than destroys individuality. In a very real sense, benevolence is the fait accompli of our exceptional gifts. It also implies that personal fulfillment must join forces with meaning on a larger scale.

I have never felt comfortable with the sanctimonious notion that to be genuine, altruism must be purely sacrificial, mostly miserable, or permeated with endless suffering. Wouldn't it make more sense that fulfilling our purpose, realizing our talents and freely using our given abilities, would be the peak of experience? If service allows us to achieve both honor and glory, no matter how difficult the journey, what could be more satisfying or more exhilarating than that?

When we honor our traits as gifts given not merely for our own use, we choose to honor our destiny and those whose lives we affect through our acts of omission and commission. To whom the glory shall go is a very personal matter. The overriding question may instead be: Can there be glory at all when one's efforts are unilaterally constructive—when "good for me" means "bad for you"? If we are to agree that our potentialities are directly connected to the whole of a Divine plan for evolution, then failure to participate in ways that honor all is a failure of self-realization. The union of self-attainment and attending to others offers us a true sense of perfection.

Sounds good. Sounds like a reasonable plan: solve the identity puzzle, develop and grow, reach out, do something that matters, leave the world better than we found it. Yet, as always, there's a catch. If our gifts are not given for free, then it is also true that our characters are not given at all—they must be earned, and often the hard way. All of the great works of religion and philosophy are replete with wilderness stories. The hero's journey is predicated on suffering, enduring confusion and despair, facing deep-seated fears of being alone, and ultimately finding the way back home. We meet ourselves and the representation of the Divine in those difficult times and in those rugged places. In, out, and through renewal is the cycle of life itself. It has always been the evolutionary way.

Now at the center of the Self is the integrated "I," whose eyes see as never before, who can utter "I am" with absolute certainty. Although it is hard to grasp in its entirety, the integrated "I" contains an absolute core of reality that is: (1) constant, (2) consistent over time, (3) pure, whole, and undamaged, (4) unrestricted by human wisdom, and (5) carries the essence of the Divine. This is the transcendent Self.

TEN SIGNS OF ADVANCED DEVELOPMENT

Everyday Geniuses live, breathe, and survive on hope and advancement. For this reason, and because the path to liberated Everyday Genius can be long and hard, self-reassurance is critical. Whenever you find yourself in the throes of self-doubt, review the Ten Signs of Advanced Development. They will remind you that your exceptional gifts are indeed solidifying and that you are entering the realm of Evolutionary Intelligence.

TEN SIGNS OF ADVANCED DEVELOPMENT

1. A conscious awareness of life as process
2. Increased respect for self and others, and a strong preference for diversity
3. Greater vitality and satisfaction in your endeavors
4. Acceptance of setbacks and pressure as catalysts that crystallize talents
5. Becoming comfortable with necessary risks
6. Willingness to be more authentic across situations
7. Growing intolerance for being out of balance
8. Powerful compulsion to use special abilities to contribute to society
9. Heightened trust in intuitive powers and transcendent experience
10. A growing sense of cooperating with a universal plan for the greater good

RECONCILING THE NINE DILEMMAS

The underlying principles upon which a fulfilling evolutionary life are founded—a life that is rationally passionate, serenely active, creatively mature, energetically patient, and a genuine gift to all—hinges on reconciling the Nine Dilemmas of the Everyday Genius:

1. *Either* define, accept, and develop your gifts, *or* deny your gifts by fulfilling the wishes of others.
2. *Either* honor your need for independence *and* find some true peers, *or* tolerate isolation, misunderstanding, or loneliness.
3. *Either* take reasonable risks and avoid those that endanger your mission, *or* play it safe on the sidelines, risking a life full of regrets.
4. *Either* manage the boundaries in interpersonal relationships to be wisely discriminating, *or* pass up intimacy altogether.
5. *Either* listen to inner guidance and activate your soul's intention, *or* refuse to hear and bury your creative spirit in a one-dimensional reality.
6. *Either* use your exceptional gifts to benefit humankind, *or* indulge yourself in spirit-devouring self-gratification.
7. *Either* value the different traits and abilities of others, *or* remain

immaturely intolerant of others, chronically impatient and perennially disappointed.

8. *Either* turn frustration and rejection into creative energy, *or* cling to resentment and surrender your dreams.

9. *Either* initiate a balance plan of Self-maintenance strategies, *or* wait for external sources to dictate and control your life.

TRUE GENIUS

In order for our Multiple Intelligences and Gifted Traits to come to fruition as completely as possible, we must repeatedly shape and polish the Five Facets of Freedom. First, to accurately identify and interpret who we are and are not, garnering the courage to get to know ourselves all over again. Second, it is essential to reexamine our traits in the light of the gifted personality and debunk outdated notions about intelligence. The Evolutionary Intelligence Profile can be used to help us redefine ourselves and see our traits as diamonds in the rough.

Next, the third facet can be fashioned to reveal and heal ourselves. It is important that we reunite with the true Self to find the courage to uncover the false self, heal old wounds, and defy the Ten Criticisms that have restricted us. This third facet was one of clarification also, one that required us to come face-to-face with the shadow side of giftedness and be very honest with ourselves about our habits and motives and the effect we have on others when our Intensity, Complexity, and Drive are poorly managed. These three facets restore our strength and hope, so that we can look closely at our gifted traits again to see how they can turn against us in exaggerated and collapsed forms. The fourth facet—self-mastery—allows our Everyday Genius characteristics to operate as the true assets they are intended to be. This work involves a new commitment to balance plans that will keep us on our true course. Relationships are key to the brilliance of our lives, so they require us to create a plan to balance attachment and love with autonomy and respect.

The fifth facet of freedom—self-liberation—is the conscious recognition of the importance of Evolutionary Moments in our lives. It allows us to interpret setbacks and opportunities within the context of the Everyday Genius liberation process. It is no longer unreasonable to embrace our Humanistic Vision, trust our Mandated Mission, and dare Revolutionary Action. We learn to cooperate with our soul's intended purpose and to lead ourselves in accordance with the mandates of our personal mission.

There is much to be done. We all know that the destructive individuals of the world have a way of finding each other, organizing, and building a forceful assembly that at times has had the power to destroy us all. The similar but opposite opportunity has been handed to us as Everyday Geniuses. Despite our need for autonomy and our preference to work alone, we are faced with the urgent need to gather our constructive forces together. The inner sense of responsibility that comes with giftedness urges each of us to create the Next Network—an alliance of Everyday Geniuses who have liberated their gifts from the ego to become the community of world servers.

We have no choice but to build a future that will be more than just a faster, more technical, and more dangerous version of today. And because we hear the evolutionary call, we must answer, make our way toward each other, and together give progress a forward and humanistic push with all of our collective might.

ACKNOWLEDGMENTS

It has become increasingly obvious to me that in order to break the mold, one must never underestimate the vital role of collaboration. I am especially struck by the creative breakthroughs that occur when individuals undertake the enormous effort to blend their unique personalities, viewpoints, life experiences, and approaches for the greater good. Although it is my name that appears on the cover of this book, it has not been a solo effort. My deepest gratitude goes to my brilliant editor, Cheryl Woodruff, my devoted guide and traveling companion, for envisioning this book within the original manuscript and staying the course until its potential was made real; to Judith Curr, for believing in my work in its infancy; and to Robert Fleming and Gary Brozek, who made inestimable contributions to the final manuscript. And a very special thank-you to my outstanding agent and friend, Stephanie Tade, to Tami Hoag for sending me her way, and to everyone at the Jane Rotrosen Agency for their enthusiasm and warm professionalism.

I am endlessly thankful to my three gifted children, Todd, Christen, and Ross, who inspire me and grow exponentially more wonderful with each passing year, and to Rick, who has been an unsinkable buoy during times of doubt and frustration, encouraging me to use my own voice to say what I know is important. And a heartfelt note of appreciation to my dear friends and fellow seekers, Betina Krahn, Linda and Jim Hoskins, Connie and Jim Knight, and Martha and Harry Mueller, who practice the art of friendship with gifts of extraordinary love. Hats off to my loyal brother, Doug Reuteler, a brilliant wit with a big heart who shared in the exceptional love, painful strains, and early loss of our parents. I am also grateful to Terry Meihofer, my die-hard laughing partner, who has offered me unwavering acceptance and support. Thanks also to my lifelong friend Katy Boone, to Susan Vass, an outstanding comedian and wise observer of life, and to Joye Bennett, my gifted confidante, who sees the universe through the same lens as I. My deepest thanks to Chuck Smith, Ph.D., my teacher and guide, whose wise words and canny gifts of soul have been unprecedented in my life. I am proud to be a part of the psychology faculty at the University of St. Thomas, which is a model of progressive education that continues to enhance my endeavors. I am thankful to the participants in my *I Am Indeed!* workshops and retreats, who have repeatedly confirmed my belief in the future of humanity. And to my noble clients, I am honored to accompany you as you search for your true Self, endeavor to answer the call of destiny, and deliver your exceptional gifts to the world.

Although I realize that progress leaps forward on the backs of extraordinary individuals, I am humbled by and indebted to all those before me whose hard work and sacrifices can never be fully accredited. I offer gratitude especially to the thirty-three Masters who assist us all in the process of human evolution and the expansion of consciousness.

NOTES

CHAPTER TWO

1. Tolan, Stephanie. (1994) "Discovering the Gifted Ex-Child." *Roeper Review, 17,* no. 2, p. 134.

CHAPTER THREE

1. Andersen, Hans Christian. (1966) "The Ugly Duckling." Adapted from *Andersen's Fairy Tales,* translated by Pat Shaw Iversen. New York: Penguin Books/ Signet Classics, pp. 136–147.
2. *Library of Congress Knowledge Cards.* (1997) Rohnert Park, CA: Pomegranate Publications.
3. Carroll, Andrew (ed.). (1997) *Letters of a Nation.* New York: Kodansha America, pp. 281–282.

CHAPTER FOUR

1. Andrews, Denison. (1975) "Stupid." *Harvard Magazine, 78,* pp. 6–8.
2. Kaufman, Alan S. (1990) *Assessing Adolescent and Adult Intelligence.* Needham, MA: Allyn and Bacon, pp. 26–29.
3. Adapted from *The Gifted and Talented Child.* (1999) Silver Spring, MD: Maryland Council for Gifted and Talented Children, Inc.
4. Azar, Beth. (1995) " 'Gifted' Label Stretches, It's More Than IQ." *The APA Monitor,* January, p. 25.
5. Azar, Beth. (1995) "Searching for Intelligence Beyond *g*." *The APA Monitor,* January, p. 1.

CHAPTER FIVE

1. Michalko, Michael. (1998) "The Art of Genius." *Utne Reader,* July/August, pp. 75–76.
2. Michalko, Michael. (1998) "Thinking Like a Genius." *The Futurist, 32,* no. 4, p. 25.

3. Schick, Elizabeth (ed.). (1997) *Current Biography Yearbook.* New York: The H. W. Wilson Company, p. 465.

4. Ibid, p. 642.

5. Michalko, "The Art of Genius," p. 73

6. Alverado, Nancy. (1989) "Adjustment of Gifted Adults." *Advanced Development, 1,* pp. 78–79.

7. Rose, Phyllis (ed.). (1993) *The Norton Book of Women's Lives.* New York: W. W. Norton, p. 12.

8. Beckett, Samuel. (1959) *The Unnamable,* in Calder and Boyars (eds.), *Molloy: Malone Dies: The Unnamable.* London.

9. Maslow, Abraham. (1971) *The Farther Reaches of Human Nature.* New York: Penguin/ Arkana, p. 305.

CHAPTER SIX

1. Gardner, Howard. (1993) *Multiple Intelligences.* New York: Basic Books, p. 114.

2. Nicholson-Nelson, Kristen. (1997) *Developing Students' Multiple Intelligence.* New York: Scholastic Professional Books.

3. Csikszentmihalyi, Mihaly. (1994) "How to Shape Ourselves." *Psychology Today, 27,* no. 1, p. 38.

CHAPTER SEVEN

1. Isaacson, Walter. (1997) "In Search of the Real Bill Gates." *Time,* January 13, p. 44.

CHAPTER EIGHT

1. Estés, Clarissa Pinkola. (1991) *The Creative Fire.* Boulder, CO: Sounds True Recordings.

2. Bucky, Peter A. (1992) *The Private Albert Einstein.* Kansas City: Andrews and McMeel/Universal Press Syndicate, p. 110.

3. Ibid., p. 29.

4. Ibid., p. 142.

5. Lewis, C. Day. *O Dreams, O Destinations.* In *The Golden Treasury,* selected and arranged by Francis T. Palgrave. New York: Oxford University Press, 1996 (sixth edition).

6. Kopp, S. (1977) *This Side of Tragedy: Psychotherapy as Theater.* Palo Alto: Behavioral Science Press, p. 4.

7. Silverman, Linda Kreger. (1993) "Counseling Needs and Programs for the Gifted." In K. Heller, F. Mönks, and H. Passow (eds.). *International Handbook of Research and Development of Giftedness and Talent.* New York: Pergamon, p. 644.

CHAPTER NINE

1. Roeper, Annemarie. (1991) "Gifted Adults: Their Characteristics and Emotions." *Advanced Development, 3,* pp. 85–98.

2. Lovecky, Dierdre. (1986) "Can You Hear the Flowers Singing? Issues for Gifted Adults." *Journal of Counseling and Development, 64,* pp. 572–575.

3. Hoffman, Edward. (1988) *The Right to Be Human: A Biography of Abraham Maslow.* Los Angeles: Jeremy Tarcher, Inc., p. 187.

4. Maslow, Abraham. (1987) *Motivation and Personality.* New York: Harper & Row, pp. 160–161 (third edition).

5. Roeper, "Gifted Adults."

6. Wertheimer, Max. (1959) *Productive Thinking.* Published posthumously and edited by Michael Wertheimer. New York: Harper & Bros., pp. 218–219.

CHAPTER TEN

1. Shnayerson, Michael. (1994) "A Star is Reborn." *Vanity Fair,* November, pp. 153, 194.

2. Hoffman, Edward. (1988) *The Right to Be Human: A Biography of Abraham Maslow.* Los Angeles: Jeremy Tarcher, p. 32.

3. von Greiffenberg, Catharina Regina. (1978) "On the Ineffable Inspiration of the Holy Spirit." In C. Cosmar, J. Keefe, and K. Weaver (eds.), *The Penguin Book of Women Poets,* New York: Viking, p. 140.

4. Madigan, C., and A. Elwood. (1998) *When They Were Kids.* New York: Random House, p.8.

5. Barron, F., A. Montuori, and A. Barron. (1997) *Creators on Creating: Awakening and Cultivating the Imaginative Mind.* New York: Jeremy Tarcher/Putnam, pp. 80–81.

6. Sutton, Caroline. (1984) *How Did They Do That?* New York: William Morrow, pp. 69–75.

7. Schick, Elizabeth (ed.). (1997) *Current Biography Yearbook.* New York: The H. W. Wilson Company, p. 509.

8. Ferrucci, Piero. (1982) *What We May Be.* New York: Putnam and Sons, pp. 61–67.

9. Barron, Montouri, and Barron, *Creators on Creating*, pp. 189–92.

CHAPTER ELEVEN

1. Rocamora, Mary. (1992) "Counseling Issues with Recognized and Unrecognized Gifted Adults." *Advanced Development, 4,* pp. 75–89.

2. Ellis, Robert, and Robert Harper. (1975) *A New Guide to Rational Living.* Englewood Cliffs, NJ: Wilshire Book Company, p. 207.

3. Bell, Lee Anne. (1990) "The Gifted Woman as Imposter." *Advanced Development, 2,* pp. 61–62.

4. Mother Teresa. (1983) *Life in the Spirit: Reflections, Meditations, Prayers,* Kathryn Spink (ed.). San Francisco: Harper & Row, pp. 31, 45.

CHAPTER TWELVE

1. Miller, Alice. (1997) *The Drama of the Gifted Child: The Search for the True Self,* revised edition. New York: Basic Books.

2. Pacht, A. R. (1984) "Reflections on Perfection." *American Psychologist, 39,* no. 4, pp. 386–390.

CHAPTER THIRTEEN

1. Benbow, Camilla. (1986) "Physiological Correlates of Extreme Intellectual Precocity." *Neuropsychologia, 24,* pp. 714–725.
2. Piechowski, Michael. (1992) "Giftedness for All Seasons: Inner Peace in a Time of War." In N. Colangelo, S. Assouline, and D. Ambroson (eds.), *Talent Development: Proceedings of the Henry B. and Jocelyn Wallace National Research Symposium on Talent Development.* Unionville, NY: Trillium Press, pp. 180–203.
3. Eysenck, H. J., and P. T. Barrett. (1993) "Brain Research Related to Giftedness." In K. Heller, F. Mönks, and A. Passow (eds.), *The International Handbook of Research and Development of Giftedness and Talent.* New York: Pergamon, p. 116.
4. Ibid.
5. Shore, Bruce, and Lannie Kanevsky. (1993) "Thinking Processes: Being and Becoming Gifted." In K. Heller, F. Mönks, and A. Passow (eds.), *The International Handbook of Research and Development of Giftedness and Talent.* New York: Pergamon, pp. 137–139.
6. Eysenck and Barrett, "Brain Research Related to Giftedness," p. 126.
7. Galton, Francis. (1875) *English Men of Science: Their Nature and Nurture.* New York: D. Appleton and Co., p. 175.

CHAPTER FOURTEEN

1. Safire, William, and Lawrence Safir (eds.). (1990) *Leadership.* New York: Simon and Schuster, p. 22.
2. Goleman, Daniel. (1995) *Emotional Intelligence.* New York: Bantam Books, pp. 80–81.
3. Seligman, Martin. (1998) *Learned Optimism: How to Change Your Mind and Your Life.* New York: Pocket Books, pp. 48–50.
4. Rutledge, Joel. (1993) "The Uncommon Path to Success." *Executive Excellence,* January, pp. 15–16.
5. Peters, Thomas J., and Robert H. Waterman, Jr. (1982) *In Search of Excellence.* New York: Warner Books, p. 13.

CHAPTER FIFTEEN

1. Miller, Alice. (1997) *The Drama of the Gifted Child: The Search for the True Self,* revised edition. New York: Basic Books, pp. 34–36.
2. Scarf, Maggie. (1987) *Intimate Partners.* New York: Ballantine Books, pp. 241–242.
3. Lederer, William, and Don Jackson (1968) *The Mirages of Marriage.* New York: W. W. Norton, pp. 272–273.
4. Gottman, John, Cliff Notarius, Jonni Gonso, and Howard Markman. (1979) *A Couple's Guide to Communication.* Champaign, IL: Research Press, p. 144.
5. Gottman, John. (1994) *Why Marriages Succeed or Fail.* New York: Fireside, p. 57.
6. Kanarek, Lisa. (1994) "The Perils of Perfectionism." *Executive Excellence,* January, p. 12.

CHAPTER SIXTEEN

1. Byrd, Richard E. (1938) *Alone.* New York: G.P. Putnam's Sons, pp. 3–4.
2. Soman, Kathryn K. (ed.). (1997) *Concise Dictionary of Great Twentieth Century Biographies.* Avenel, NJ: Gramercy Books, pp. 50–52.
3. Ibid., pp. 304–306.
4. Ibid., pp. 180–182.
5. Miller, Paul. (1998) "The Engineer as Catalyst." *IEEE Spectrum, 35,* no. 7, pp. 20–29.
6. Shekerjian, Denise. (1990) *Uncommon Genius: How Great Ideas are Born.* New York: Penguin Books.
7. Ibid., pp. 11–15.
8. Ibid., pp. 213–214.
9. La MaMa E.T.C. (1998) La MaMa E.T.C. Home Page. http://www.nytheatrewire.com/LMhome.htm.
10. Shekerjian, *Uncommon Genius,* p. 221.
11. Piechowski, Michael. (1990) "Inner Growth and Transformation in the Life of Eleanor Roosevelt." *Advanced Development, 2,* pp. 35–36.
12. Lash, Joseph P. (1971) *Eleanor and Franklin.* New York: Norton, p. 112.
13. Roosevelt, Eleanor. (1937) *This Is My Story.* New York: Harper, p. 162.
14. Ibid., pp. 259–260.
15. Lash, *Eleanor and Franklin,* p. 325.
16. Lash, Joseph P. (1982) *Love, Eleanor.* New York: Doubleday, p. 499.
17. Covey, Stephen R. (1989) *The Seven Habits of Highly Effective People: Restoring the Character Ethic.* New York: Simon and Schuster, p. 106.
18. Firman, John, and James Vargin. (1975) "Dimensions of Growth." In *Synthesis 2: The Realization of the Self.* Redwood City, CA: The Synthesis Press, pp. 117–118.

RECOMMENDED READING

Armstrong, Thomas (1993) *7 Kinds of Smart: Identifying and Developing Your Many Intelligences.* New York: Plume.

Covey, Stephen. (1989) *The Seven Habits of Highly Effective People: Restoring the Character Ethic.* New York: Fireside/Simon and Schuster.

Csikszentmihalyi, Mihaly. (1990) *Flow: The Psychology of Optimal Experience.* New York: Harper and Row.

————. (1993) *The Evolving Self: A Psychology for the Third Millennium.* New York: HarperCollins.

Ferrucci, Piero. (1982) *What We May Be.* New York: G. P. Putnam's Sons.

Gardner, Howard. (1993) *Multiple Intelligences: The Theory in Practice.* New York: Basic Books.

————. (1993) *Creating Minds.* New York: Basic Books.

Gill, Brendan. (1996) *Late Bloomers.* New York: Artisan.

Goleman, Daniel. (1995) *Emotional Intelligence.* New York: Bantam Books.

Madigan, Carol, and Ann Elwood. (1998) *When They Were Kids.* New York: Random House.

Maslow, Abraham. (1971) *The Farther Reaches of Human Nature.* New York: Penguin/Arkana.

Miller, Alice. (1997) *The Drama of the Gifted Child: The Search for the True Self,* revised edition. New York: Basic Books.

Pipher, Mary. (1994) *Reviving Ophelia.* New York: Ballantine Books.

Seligman, Martin. (1991) *Learned Optimism.* New York: Random House.

Shekerjian, Denise. (1990) *Uncommon Genius: Tracing the Creative Impulse with Forty Winners of the MacArthur Award.* New York: Penguin Books.

Sternberg, Robert. (1996) *Successful Intelligence.* New York: Simon and Schuster.

Storr, Anthony. (1988) *Solitude: A Return to the Self.* New York: Ballantine Books.

Winner, Ellen. (1996) *Gifted Children: Myths and Realities.* New York: Basic Books.

RESOURCES

OmegaPoint Resources for Advanced Human Development
Mary-Elaine Jacobsen, Psy.D., Director
4640 Slater Road, Suite 114
St. Paul, MN 55122
Phone: 651-882-0866
Voice mail/Fax: 651-686-9344
Web site: http://www.everydaygenius.com

Institute for the Study of Advanced Development
and the Gifted Development Center
Linda Kreger Silverman, Ph.D., Director
1452 Marion Street
Denver, CO 80218
Web site: http://www.gifteddevelopment.com

The Council for Exceptional Children
ERIC Clearinghouse on Disabilities and Gifted Education
1920 Association Drive
Reston, VA 20191
Phone: 800-328-0272
Web site: http://www.cec.sped.org/ericec

National Research Center on the Gifted and Talented (Javits Center)
Joseph Renzulli, Director
The University of Connecticut
362 Fairfield Road, U-7
Storrs, CT 06269-2007
Phone: 860-486-2900

National Association for Gifted Children
1701 L Street, NW, Suite 550
Washington, DC 20036
Phone: 202-785-4268
Web site: http://www.nagc.org

INDEX